Psychology for Christian Ministry

Psychology for Christian Ministry is a comprehensive and unique introduction to psychology as it is relevant to those training for and working in the clergy. Proceeding from the understanding that psychology is the discipline that illuminates those processes of personal change and growth central to religion, the volume ranges over many aspects of the subject, covering social, developmental, educational, occupational and counselling psychology, as well as the psychology of religion. Material is structured according to four major themes:

- orientation
- personal aspects of religion
- psychology of the church
- psychology of pastoral practice

This professional handbook, the definitive textbook in its field, is tailored to meet the specific needs of Christian ministers as they encounter psychology in their training and their everyday work.

The authors are all members of the Psychology and Religion Research Programme at the Centre for Advanced Religious and Theological Studies, University of Cambridge. **Fraser Watts** is also Starbridge Lecturer in Theology and Natural Science in the University of Cambridge, a Past President of the British Psychological Society, and the author of several books on psychology and religion. **Rebecca Nye** is an authority on children's spirituality. **Sara Savage**, a social psychologist, is a lecturer in psychology in the Cambridge Federation of Theological Colleges.

Psychology for Christian Ministry

Fraser Watts, Rebecca Nye and Sara Savage

With cartoons by Séan

London and New York

First published 2002
by Routledge
11 New Fetter Lane, London EC4P 4EE

Simultaneously published in the USA and Canada
by Routledge
29 West 35th Street, New York, NY 10001

Routledge is an imprint of the Taylor & Francis Group

Typeset in Ehrhardt by Bookcraft Limited, Stroud, Gloucestershire
Printed and bound in Great Britain by MPG Books Ltd, Bodmin

British Library Cataloguing in Publication Data
A catalogue record for this book is available from the British Library

Library of Congress Cataloging in Publication Data
Watts, Fraser N.
  Psychology for Christian ministry / Fraser Watts, Rebecca Nye, and
Sara B. Savage.
     p. cm.
  Includes bibliographical references and index.
  1. Pastoral psychology. I. Nye, Rebecca. II. Savage, Sara B., 1953–
III. Title.
  BV4012 .W34 2001
  253.5'2—dc21   2001034798

ISBN 0–415–24036–0 (hbk)
ISBN 0–415–24037–9 (pbk)

For John Marks

Contents

Boxes

Figures

Tables

Preface

The church works with people, and there is a human aspect to everything the church does. Psychology can help to clarify those human aspects, and make Christian ministers more aware of the personal impact of their work. It is also good to remember that Christianity is, among other things, about changing people, and psychology is the discipline that can help us to understand how people change. In this book we have tried to present what psychology has to contribute to an understanding of the church's work.

Nevertheless, we are aware that there is sometimes suspicion of psychology in the church. This stems partly from the fear that psychology is always trying to explain things away, reducing them to a mere matter of psychology. This anxiety is misplaced. Our approach here does not imply that Christian ministry is 'just' a matter of psychology. It is clearly much more than that, but it always has a psychological aspect.

Another concern is that the Christian gospel is always about communities and society, not just about individuals. Of course we agree that the communal aspect of Christian life is important, though individual aspects are important too and should not be neglected. However, it would be a misconception to imagine that psychology is exclusively about individuals. It includes social psychology, which is relevant to the communal aspects of the Christian life.

But perhaps a basic source of resistance to psychology is simply conservatism. Over years, the range of academic disciplines on which Christian thinking has drawn has broadened significantly, and history and philosophy have a well-established place. Other newer disciplines like sociology and psychology have taken a long time to become established. The fact that there are relatively few people in the church who are competent in them tends to lead to their being kept at arm's length.

In applying psychology to Christian ministry, we have taken a broad view of the discipline. Generally, we have paid most attention to those areas of psychology that are grounded in empirical research, and approached the subject as it is currently taught in Universities. However, we have also drawn occasionally on the approaches to psychology stemming from Freud and Jung. However insightful their approaches might be, they sit rather uneasily with the discipline as a whole because of their lack of a research basis.

Psychology includes a variety of sub-disciplines. In the first part of the book we have drawn mainly on the psychology of personality and of religion. In Part 2, we have drawn mainly on developmental and educational psychology. In Part 3, the focus is on abnormal and clinical psychology. In Part 4, we turn to social, organisational and occupational psychology. Then, in the final chapters, we draw on a variety of theoretical approaches to personality. There are a number of different approaches within the discipline of psychology, and it is wise for the church to draw on them in an eclectic way. Different aspects of psychology can illuminate different aspects of the church's work. Suggested introductory textbooks to these various aspects of psychology are listed at the end of the preface.

We have also taken a broad view of Christian ministry. The breadth of our approach is what makes this book distinctive. For example, there are many books applying counselling psychology to Christian pastoral care, but that is only one of many applications of psychology considered here. We know of no other book that has taken such a broad view of the church's work, nor of one that has applied psychology to so many different aspects of that work. In the course of this book we look, for example, at prayer and church services, the religious life of children, at the church as an organisation, and at clergy.

In writing the book we have had in mind primarily those who are studying psychology as part of their training for ordained ministry. However, we hope it will be useful to those already in ministry as well as to those in training, and to lay ministers as well as to ordained. It may also serve the needs of students who want a text on the psychology of religion, and who warm to the applied approach we have taken here. As far as we know, this book is unique in taking such an applied approach to the psychology of religion.

The three of us who have written this book have worked together closely over the last few years. We have expertise in slightly different areas of psychology, but we have arrived at a common approach to Christian ministry. Most chapters are the primary responsibility of one of us, as follows: 1 – FW; 2 – SS/FW; 3 – RN; 4 – SS; 5 – RN; 6 – RN; 7 – RN; 8 – RN/SS; 9 – FW: 10 – FW; 11 – SS; 12 – SS; 13 – FW; 14 – FW; 15 – FW. However, we have discussed all the chapters together. Moreover, we are enormously indebted to Dr Thomas Dixon who, as the project's Research Assistant, has worked over all our chapters, raising the standards of the book, and helping to integrate the different chapters into a unified whole.

This book arises from the Psychology and Christianity project in the Centre for Advanced Religious and Theological Studies in the University of Cambridge. That project itself flows from the initiative and enthusiasm of John Marks, and we are more grateful to him than we can properly express. He has been the ideal patron and encourager. We are also most grateful to the Mulberry Trust for its financial support.

Fraser Watts
Rebecca Nye
Sara Savage

Suggested psychology background reading

General

Atkinson, R. L. *et al.* (2000) *Hilgard's Introduction to Psychology*, 13th ed., London: Harcourt.
Gleitman, H. (1995) *Psychology*, 4th ed., London: Norton.
Gross, R. D. (1996) *Psychology: The Science of Mind and Behaviour*, 3rd ed., London: Hodder & Stoughton.

Personality psychology

Pervin, L. and John, O. P. (1996) *Personality: Theory and Research*, 7th ed., Chichester: Wiley.

Psychology of religion

Wulff, D. M. (1997) *Psychology of Religion: Classic and Contemporary*, 2nd ed., Chichester: Wiley.

Developmental psychology

Clarke-Stewart, A., Perlmutter, M. and Friedman, S. (1988) *Lifelong Human Development*, Chichester: Wiley.

Abnormal psychology

Davison, G. C. and Neale, J. M. (1998) *Abnormal Psycholoy*, 7th ed., Chichester: Wiley.
Rosenhan, D. L. and Seligman, M. E. P. (1995) *Abnormal Psychology*, 3rd ed., London: Norton.

Social psychology

Hewstone, M., Stroebe, W. and Stephenson, G. M. (eds) (1996) *Introduction to Social Psychology: A European Perspective*, 2nd ed., Oxford: Blackwell.
Sabini, J. (1995) *Social Psychology*, 2nd ed., London: Norton.

Organisational psychology

Greenberg, J. and Baron, R. A. (1997) *Behavior in Organizations: Understanding and Managing the Human Side of Work*, 6th ed., London: Prentice-Hall International.

Psychoanalytic

Erdelyi, M. E. (1985) *Psychoanalysis: Freud's Cognitive Psychology*, Oxford: W. H. Freeman.

Part 1

Personality and religion

1 Spirituality

QUESTIONS FOR MINISTRY

- Do you have to be a 'spiritual giant' to have a spiritual experience?
- How common are spiritual or mystical experiences?
- What is their meaning in people's lives?
- Why don't more people talk to the clergy about their religious experiences?
- What happens to me when I pray?
- Is it selfish to pray for myself?
- Is authentic spirituality necessarily emotional?
- What are the key elements of 'spiritual direction'?

'Spirituality' is currently one of the most popular aspects of religion, and religious people often attach a great deal of importance to the inner, spiritual life. Furthermore, non-religious people are often sympathetic to broadly spiritual values and practices, even when they have little room for orthodox religious beliefs or the institutional church. In this chapter, we will approach the psychological aspects of spirituality from three perspectives, looking first at the concept of spiritual experience, then at the psychology of prayer, and lastly at psychological aspects of the spiritual path.

Spiritual experience

Though the concept of 'spirituality' is attractive to many people, it is also controversial. In its modern sense, it has developed only over the last two hundred years, and it reflects a growing divorce between the private and the public, and between the religious and the secular. Spirituality is the non-secular, non-public aspect of religion. What some object to in the concept of spirituality is the way it focuses on the private aspects of religious life to the exclusion of other aspects of collective and cultural life. Though there is a long and varied history of writing on Christian spirituality (see Jones *et al.* 1986), some would argue that we tend to misread this historic tradition from the vantage point of a more recent preoccupation with private religious experience (e.g. Turner 1995).

One of the most important influences on contemporary conceptions of spirituality has been William James, whose Gifford lectures in 1901–2 on *The Varieties of Religious Experience* caught the mood of his time and have exerted a continuing influence. James' position is seen clearly in his emphasis on 'the feelings, acts, and experiences of individual men in their solitude, so far as they apprehend themselves to stand in relation to whatever they may consider the divine'. This formulation reflects his emphasis on feelings and experience, with nothing about beliefs and knowledge. He also emphasises the individual person, and sees collective religious life as very secondary. Note also his attempt to avoid any explicit assumption about the existence of God by invoking the formula 'whatever they may consider the divine'. It is an approach which implies a very broad concept of religious experience. However, James is cautious about following through the implications of his definitions and finds it 'convenient' to settle for what people conventionally mean by religion.

Despite the influence that James has exerted, his views have been criticised from the outset, for example by von Hugel, for their neglect of the role of corporate Christian life. Criticisms have continued to be advanced from both philosophical (Proudfoot 1985) and theological (Lash 1988) points of view. Proudfoot's approach can be illustrated from his comments on the four hallmarks of mystical experience that James enumerates. James' four hallmarks are that such an experience is:

- Ineffable (i.e. cannot adequately be described in words)
- Noetic (i.e. imparts knowledge)
- Transient (i.e. a brief, passing experience, not a continuous state)
- Passive (i.e. an overwhelming experience that happens *to* the subject)

Proudfoot sees these so-called characteristics of mystical experience as 'social constructions' rather than reliable reports of what the experience is actually like. For Proudfoot, the fact that people describe mystical experiences in these ways is largely due to their having been trained to do so while preparing themselves for mystical experience. Rather than taking their descriptions at face value, he asks why people invoke them. For example, he suggests that people call mystical experience 'ineffable', not because they can't describe it but because they think that one should not try to do so.

This raises general issues about the nature of 'social constructionism'. There is no doubt that terms like 'ineffable' and 'noetic', like all words, are in a sense products of our collective attempt to understand and talk about the world. However, it is a big step beyond that to suggest that they are *mere* social constructions and that they do not actually describe mystical experience.

Lash has been particularly critical of the idea of 'pure' or 'direct' religious experience. Many accounts of religious experience suggest, in some way or other, that those concerned are penetrating the veil that normally shields us from ultimate spiritual realities, and seeing things as they really are. Lash wants to emphasise, in contrast, that all experience is shaped by language and culture, and this must be true of mystical experience as well. The idea that such experience is 'direct' is thus exposed as an illusion.

Another point of dispute concerns whether religious experience is essentially the same in different faith traditions, as James and other 'perennialists' would suggest, or whether it is significantly different from one faith tradition to another, reflecting the impact of different sets of beliefs on the nature of mystical experience.

There has been a vigorous response to critics of the Jamesian view by Forman (1990). Forman wishes to take seriously the idea that in mystical experience there is a core of absolutely pure experience that is the common core of various mystical traditions. However, it is perfectly compatible with this position to accept that, when describing such experience, people inevitably interpret it in ways that reflect their cultural background and faith tradition.

As so often happens, debate here tends to become rather polarised, and it is worth stating an intermediate position that has some plausibility. Let us accept that all experience is to some extent shaped by its cultural context, and that it is impossible to escape that context absolutely. However, let us also accept that there is something unusual in mystical experience in that it goes further towards escaping cultural context than normal experience.

It would be helpful for the debate to generalise less sweepingly about mystical experience. For example, there is probably an important difference between apparently spontaneous mystical experience, and experience arising from meditation or other practices. The social constructionist critique fits induced much better than spontaneous experience.

Though this is essentially a theoretical debate about psychological processes, it is also regrettable that it generally proceeds without any reference to empirical psychological research. However, there are a number of research findings which, if not decisive, are relevant to the debate. David Hay, in a survey conducted at the Religious Experience Research Unit in Oxford, asked people: 'Have you ever been aware of, or influenced by, a presence or power, whether you called it God or not, which is different from your everyday self?' As with similar surveys in the USA, he found that about a third of the population reported such experiences (see Hay 1990).

One of the most interesting aspects of the survey concerns how such experiences relate to religious orthodoxy. He found that 24 per cent of atheists/agnostics reported such an experience, a proportion slightly less than that found for the general population, but not massively so. More relevant than the orthodoxy of people's religious beliefs, or whether or not they went to church, was how important they thought 'the spiritual side of life' was. Of those who regarded it as very important 74 per cent reported religious experiences, compared to only 11 per cent among those who thought the spiritual side of life was not important.

Such findings are not easy to interpret. At first glance, the fact that a substantial proportion of atheists and agnostics have mystical experiences seems to suggest that enculturation is not particularly important. However, it might be argued that in our culture virtually everyone, even atheists and agnostics, have imbibed a certain amount of cultural predisposition to such experiences. Another interpretative problem with such data is that it is hard to know what is cause and what effect. Religious belief might influence the likelihood of people having a religious experience. On the other hand, it is possible that religious experiences incline people towards religious belief. Without monitoring a substantial group of people both before and after such experiences, it is difficult to be quite sure in which direction the main causal influence lies.

Other relevant research is that of Ralph Hood (see Hood *et al.* 1996, Chapter 7), who examined mystical experiences using questionnaire methods. Particularly interesting in the present context is his finding that the terms people use to describe mystical experience tended to group into two main clusters. One seems to be concerned with basic aspects of the experience such as timelessness, spacelessness, unity, and ineffability. The other group is more obviously interpretative, describing their experiences as involving such things as a sense of holiness or the presence of God. This empirical demonstration that descriptions of mystical experience cluster into two groups is at least consistent with a two-component view of the experience, that is, the view that there is a relatively pure core of experience, but that this is surrounded by culturally mediated interpretations that vary from one faith tradition to another.

Similar issues arise in connection with the role of the brain in religious experience. Though research on this is at a fairly early stage of development, it promises to be an increasingly lively research area in the future. One of the best-known current theories about the role of the brain is that put forward by Michael Persinger (1987), to the effect that there is a similarity between religious experience and the experiences of people suffering from temporal-lobe epilepsy, and that the same part of the brain is involved in both cases. However, the research support for this idea is not good. Though it has often been suggested that people with temporal-lobe epilepsy are particularly likely to be religious, careful research does not support that. Also, there are important dissimilarities. For example, epileptic experiences are generally unsettling, whereas religious experiences tend to occur at a time of distress and to induce a state of deep peace or happiness (as Hay among others has found). The claim of similarity between the two kinds of experiences seems to derive from poorly designed research (see Jeeves 1997).

However, other more promising ideas about the relationship of the brain to religious experience are developing, for example in the work of d'Aquili and Newberg (1998). One attractive feature of their approach is that they distinguish between different facets of religious experience, and look for the different brain mechanisms that underpin them. Specifically, they have suggested that there is a 'holistic operator' that underpins the sense of unity in religious experience, and a 'causal operator' that underpins the sense of divine action in the world. Though this is a speculative theory, it is a pointer towards the kind of neuro-psychological theory of mystical experience which is likely to be developed in the coming years.

The main point at issue here concerns the implications of such research for the nature of spiritual experience. Persinger's most recent research (e.g. Cook and Persinger 1997), involving the induction of a 'sensed mystical presence' by stimulation with magnetic fields, has led some to conclude that religious experiences can be explained away by such findings. The logic here does not follow – the perception of green light, say, can be induced in similar fashion, but this does not mean that green light is not real. Some might want to claim that spiritual experience was independent of the physical brain, and would see research on brain processes in religion as incompatible with the value they placed on religious experience. Others, less sympathetic to religious experience, might argue that the involvement of the brain implies that spiritual experience is 'nothing but' a spin-off of brain activity. In fact, the involvement of the brain seems to be neutral as far as the nature and validity of religious experience is concerned. It would be equally consistent with such research for (a) the experience to arise wholly from the brain, or (b) for it to arise from communion with God but to be mediated through the physical brain. From a theological point of view, the brain is part of God's creation, and there is no reason why it should be bypassed.

There are thus many controversies and ambiguities surrounding mystical experience, including terminological confusions about whether the same or different things should be meant by terms such as 'mystical', 'religious', 'transcendent', 'spiritual' experience, etc. It may help to set out a list of five issues about religious experience.

1   *Phenomenology*
    The first question is how far such experience has a distinct phenomenological quality. For example, sensations may have an unusual brightness and immediacy, and there may be an unusual sense of all things being united together, and a sense of unity between the perceiver and the perceived. Such special phenomenological qualities are probably an essential requirement of experiences properly termed 'mystical', but not necessarily of 'religious' experiences.

2   *The object of experience*

The next question is whether or not the experience is presumed to be of some special world or being, such as an experience of God or of the spiritual world. Certainly, this is sometimes assumed to be the case. However, it is also possible to regard religious experiences as a special way of seeing the ordinary world, rather than as an experience of a special world. There is a fundamental disagreement here between those who regard the presumption of a distinct spiritual world as essential to a proper understanding of mystical experience, and those who regard it as a confusion arising from a philosophically objectionable form of dualism.

3   *Causation*

Various accounts can be offered of causal factors that contribute to mystical experiences, such as background cultural conditioning and context, the state of mind of the person at the time and what they are doing, their brain processes, etc. At the extremes, some would regard these as the whole causal story, others would regard them as causally irrelevant. An alternative position is that they are relevant causal factors, but do not exclude the possibility of the experience having a different kind of source in God or the spiritual world. However, where this is claimed, it is important to be clear that we are talking about different kinds of causes (natural and divine), not alternative causes of the same kind.

4   *Directness*

For some people, the key hallmark of mystical experience is that it is direct or unmediated. This may mean that there is direct experience of the material world, bypassing the normal constructive processes of perception. Alternatively, it may mean that there is unmediated experience of God or the spiritual world. We have suggested above that religious experience cannot be completely direct or wholly unmediated. However, it remains a plausible position that is has a greater degree of directness than most other experience.

5   *Interpretative framework*

For some, the most important characteristic of religious experience is that it is experience to which a religious interpretative framework is applied. Indeed, some people would regard this as the only distinctive characteristic of religious experience. Certainly, it is a remarkable feature of many spiritual traditions that very ordinary activities can be interpreted in a religious way, and an example is in the prayers of the Celtic tradition about lighting fires, milking cows, and so on. Children are also often good at seeing spiritual or religious significance in the everyday world (see Chapter 5). My suggestion would be that the interpretative framework is an important, though not the sole, characteristic of religious experience. There may have been an evolutionary change in the way such interpretative processes arise, from a primitive animistic experience in which a religious interpretative framework is applied in an automatic and involuntary way to the more recent state of affairs where it seems that a religious interpretative framework has to be voluntarily and deliberately adopted. Increasingly, it seems that a religious interpretative framework needs to be applied deliberately, or it doesn't arise at all.

SUMMARY OF KEY THEMES

- William James' view of mystical experiences: ineffable, noetic, transient, and passive.
- The social construction of spiritual experiences.
- The idea of 'pure' religious experiences.
- The frequency of mystical experiences among atheists and agnostics, and among those who value the 'spiritual side of life'.
- The role of the brain.
- Five different perspectives: phenomenology, object of experience, causation, directness, interpretation.

QUESTIONS TO CONSIDER

- How many people in your congregation have (or have had) spiritual or mystical experiences?
- Have they talked to you about them?
- What causes such experiences?
- What value do they have? Do they contribute helpfully to religious development?
- Are they reliable sources of religious knowledge and understanding?
- Should you encourage the attainment of such experiences as part of a full religious life?

Prayer

Next in this chapter we will consider the psychological processes that arise in prayer. This immediately raises issues about causation, such as those indicated above. The assumption is that prayer is in part a psychological activity, and that psychology can illuminate, from one point of view, what is going on in prayer. However, this does not imply that there is nothing more to prayer than psychology. To talk about the psychology of prayer is not to deny that prayer can be a communion with God, that it can have a special phenomenological quality, and so on. There can be a psychology of prayer without assuming that prayer is 'nothing but' psychology.

Some aspects of prayer involve reflection on experience, especially confession and thanksgiving. Such experience is valuable psychologically, especially where there are stressful or unfamiliar experiences, and prayer provides one opportunity for the necessary 'working through'. The part of prayer that is a reflection on experience can thus be seen essentially as an interpretative activity, learning to apply a religious interpretative framework to recent events.

Thanksgiving and attributions

Thanksgiving can be approached in terms of the psychological study of attributional processes. It seems to be natural for people to make 'causal attributions' of why events in their lives have occurred. Moreover, there is abundant psychological evidence that the psychological impact of events is considerably affected by how things are attributed. One key distinction has been between 'internal' and 'external' attributions. Generally, if successes or failures are attributed internally, they have more emotional impact than if they are attributed externally. On the other hand, if too many things are attributed externally, that can induce an unpleasant feeling of helplessness.

Thanksgiving involves bringing God into this framework of causal attributions for recent events. If people thank God for what has happened to them, that presupposes that he is in some way responsible for it. However, from a theological point of view, it is important to be clear that God is not the same kind of cause of events as other natural causes. Furthermore, God is not an alternative to natural causes but a supplementary cause of a different kind. The nature of God's presumed influence on events has not been adequately appreciated in some recent psychological work on causal attributions made to God (e.g. Hood *et al.* 1996).

The next interesting issue that arises about attributions to God is whether they should be seen as internal or external attributions. Some people tend to attribute negative events internally, putting them down to their own failings, and to discount positive events as caused by external factors over which they have no control. Other, more self-confident, people tend to do the opposite, taking pride in their own successes, and discounting failures and losses as down to chance external factors. For Christians, however, there will be attributions to God, alongside normal internal and external attributions. The interesting thing here is that God is neither an internal nor an external attribution in the normal sense. In one sense, as the transcendent source of all being, He is external; in another sense, as an indwelling presence, He is internal. In fact, it may be one of the interesting features of attributions to God that they are a hybrid between internal and external. Internal attributions, which put everything down to one's own personal influence on events, can be egocentric, whereas external attributions, which put everything down to chance or the outside world, can be alienating; attributions to God may help avoid both these unattractive extremes (Watts and Williams 1988).

Finally, there is the interesting issue of exactly which events Christians do, or should, attribute to God. In ordinary life, people say thank you for 'good' things. However, as D. Z. Phillips (1965) has pointed out, there is a kind of naturalistic fallacy involved in applying this to thanksgiving to God. He is properly thanked for everything, not just selectively for the nice things. Christians are pulled in competing directions here. On the one hand, we feel that everything that happens is within the providence of God and could not happen without him. On the other hand, we feel that some things are particularly inspired by God and in accordance with his will; other things not. This can be handled, theologically, in terms of the distinction sometimes made between general and specific providence. There is a sense in which Christians see everything within the general providence of God, but some particular things can be seen as specific acts of his providence. There will be different qualities of thanksgiving in the two cases.

So how do Christians identify the particular things that they wish to attribute to

God in a special way? This has not yet been investigated in a rigorous way, but it does lend itself to empirical research. The basic issue is whether we divide events into welcome and unwelcome ones, or into what St Ignatius called 'consolation' and 'desolation' (that is, experiences that draw the person closer to, or further away from God). It is perhaps an important part of the spiritual transformation from immature to mature thanksgiving that it should be offered particularly for consolations rather than just for agreeable events. Surveying experience for consolations brings into play a specifically religious interpretative framework, and it is perhaps part of the human value of thanksgiving that it trains people in doing that.

Confession and guilt

Confession also involves attributional reflections that are in some ways the mirror image of those involved in thanksgiving, though it is a matter of attributing blame to oneself rather than goodness to God. Fraser Watts and Mark Williams (1988) have argued for the importance of a distinction between causal and moral aspects of such attributions. It is one thing to try to discern more clearly what has gone wrong and the contribution one has made to it, it is quite another to blame oneself in a moralistic way.

Christian language about sin sounds oppressive to many people. However, there is a distinction to be made between the general 'original' sinfulness of humanity, and the specific sins of particular individuals. This parallels, in many ways, the distinction between general and specific providence that arises in relation to thanksgiving. The Christian assumption is that individual people are caught up in a web of sinfulness that goes far beyond them and for which they are not personally to blame. With this in mind, it is possible to recognise where one's actions have been affected by this sinfulness, without feeling unduly weighed down by it. The key requirement for Christians is that they should recognise sinfulness and try to resist it rather than that they should blame themselves excessively. This psychologically important distinction is reflected in the story of Jesus and the woman caught in adultery (John 8). Jesus does not condemn the woman but simply tells her not to sin again.

Confession raises issues about guilt, a subject that has often seemed to be the focus of dispute between psychologists and Christians. To handle this, a discriminating approach to guilt is needed. The essential distinction is between realistic and neurotic guilt. There are undoubtedly circumstances, in which wrongdoing has actually occurred, where guilt is appropriate. This is particularly so where the wrongdoing is not trivial, but serious. Also, guilt is particularly appropriate where the wrongdoing was deliberate (not just inadvertent) and where circumstances made it perfectly possible to have acted otherwise. Neurotic guilt is a very different matter. Realistic guilt is selective in the sense that it only arises in appropriate circumstances, whereas neurotic guilt is unselective in that it arises all the time, regardless of whether it is appropriate or not. Whereas realistic guilt only occurs after serious wrongdoing, neurotic guilt is equally likely to arise after trivial wrongdoing.

The psychological tradition is actually more mixed than might at first appear. Though therapists and counsellors have been much concerned with the ravages

flowing from excessive guilt, there has been a marked tendency in recent psychological theories of the emotions to emphasise their value. The assumption is that we
would not have emotions at all if they did not serve an important function for us.
Even negative emotions such as guilt can be 'rational' in the sense of conveying
information about the real world and helping people to adapt to it appropriately.
The function of guilt is then to facilitate a necessary and appropriate change of
direction. Though guilt can serve this valuable function, the sad fact is that it does
not always do so. It is all too easy to get stuck in repetitive guilt without making the
reforms in our behaviour that should properly flow from it. Guilt can be 'cheap', and
less costly than to change how one lives one's life. It then becomes a chronic state
that serves no useful purpose.

There is a similar need for a discriminating approach to shame, an emotion that is
rather similar to guilt but also subtly different from it. Guilt focuses itself on our
behaviour and on specific actions we have carried out, shame on who and what we
are. Another contrast is that guilt is a rather thought-laden emotion in the sense that
it leads to much rumination and reflection. In contrast, shame is more immediate
and physical. When people are ashamed, they want to shrink back and be swallowed
up; they blush with embarrassment and can't bear to be looked at. There is no doubt
that excessive shame is a very destructive emotion, and can lead to various forms of
self-abuse. It can also isolate people from others because, for the person prone to
shame, every close relationship is a potentially shaming one.

However, some shame is appropriate. It is perhaps before God that it is particularly appropriate for people to feel shame. In comparison with Him, we can only be
deeply aware of our limited, fallible and perverse nature. It is more doubtful whether
shame is appropriate before another human being. It is also worth noting that the
most intense feelings of shame arise when other people deliberately embarrass and
humiliate us. God does not do that; we may feel ashamed in comparison with Him,
but we are not shamed by Him. When we feel ashamed in front of other people, it is
often because we sense that they can see through us and there are no defences left
against their critical gaze. Though God can see through us, and there are no more
places to hide from Him, His gaze is a benevolent one. The critical gaze of God thus
has a different effect.

Petition

Petitionary prayer also raises very interesting psychological issues, and one fruitful
approach to take initially is the developmental one. We know something about factors that influence whether or not children pray, such as their church attendance,
their parents' church attendance, and their denominational identity (Francis and
Brown 1991). However, the most fruitful issues arise in connection with how
children pray. An early classic study that examined prayer, among many other
aspects of the development of children's intellectual understanding of religion,
was that of Goldman (1965). He describes a developmental sequence from seeing
prayer as a magical way of achieving material results (ages 7–9); seeing prayer more
in terms of inner experience, though expecting things to happen as a result of

prayer (ages 9–12); to a stronger emphasis on altruistic and compassionate prayers, and an emphasis on the benefits of prayers to the person who prays (ages 13+). (Further issues in religious development will be addressed in Chapters 5 and 6.)

There are also changes in how children make sense of prayer *not* working, from their having been naughty, to their asking for the wrong things, and finally to their not having enough faith. Subsequent research has come to somewhat similar conclusions (Brown 1994, Chapter 11). One of the things that emerges from such research is the changing nature of what children pray for. For adults too, there is something of a dilemma about the maturity of the wishes and desires that are framed in prayer. The most 'immature' extreme is to simply pray for whatever one most wants. Children may begin by praying in that way but, for the most part, move beyond it. This presumably results from a growing sense that what one prays for is constrained by the purposes of God, not just one's own wishes. However, there are problems at the other end of the spectrum, and prayer that simply articulates what people feel they *ought* to be praying for can be sterile.

It is helpful to see prayer as providing an opportunity for the refinement of desires. One of the key assumptions here is that people can easily be misled about the nature of their desires (May 1982). What people think they want can be strangely unfulfilling if what they desire actually occurs. This reaches its most extreme form in the phenomenon of addiction, where people develop intense cravings for things that give them little pleasure, beyond temporary release from the craving. Prayer provides us with an opportunity to explore our desires and to probe beneath the surface. As Watts and Williams (1988) suggest, it is rather like the 'chasing down' that is used in cognitive therapy. For example, a depressed patient might cite something that they are upset by, and the therapist would then probe to find why they were upset by it. In a similar kind of way, it can be helpful for people to take a desire, and examine why they want what they want, leading to a deeper understanding of fundamental desires. Petition can be seen as an exercise in the exploration of desire in the presence of God. As Ann and Barry Ulanov (1982) put it: 'Prayer is the place where we sort out our desires and where we are ourselves sorted out by the desires we choose to follow' (p. 20).

It may be helpful to formulate this process of the exploration and transformation of desires within the Freudian framework (Lee 1955). One can see untransformed desires as arising like primitive impulses from the id. On the other hand, many such desires will be censored by the super-ego as reprehensible and unsuitable for prayer. There is then a conflict between id and super-ego as to what to pray for. The most psychologically healthy solution to this problem is one of integration and the strengthening of the ego. That is what takes place when desires are transformed.

To move from prayer for oneself to prayer for others represents another important stage in the transformation of desires. Intercessory prayer can be seen as requiring a reasonably well-developed ego, with a capacity to engage with external reality in the way that is required for love and work. Intercessory prayer involves the use of a number of ego functions, such as a capacity for perspective-taking, that is, seeing things from the point of view of another person. It also involves an empathic sensitivity to the feelings of other people, and concern for them. Intercessory prayer thus challenges people to strengthen their ego functions, and itself contributes to that strengthening.

Another important developmental aspect of prayer, as Goldman's research made clear, is a change in understanding of how prayer can be effective. Initially, people may make anthropomorphic assumptions about God, to the effect that, unless they pray, He may not know what they want, or be disposed to give it. Such assumptions are hardly credible, and are inappropriate theologically. Donald Capps (1982) has suggested that prayer can be seen rather as a process of 'co-orientation' in which there is an alignment of desires and purposes. He reaches this formulation from the perspective of communication theory, and likens the co-orientation involved to that which takes place within the family. His position is similar to that of John Polkinghorne (in press) who talks of a 'resonance' being established between God and the person who prays, which becomes part of the channel by which prayer is efficacious.

No, I won't come down the pub for a 'quickie' — I'll pray for the souls of all imbibers instead.!!

Huh! That's a spiritual cop-out.!!

SUMMARY OF KEY THEMES

- Prayer as both a psychological activity and communion with God.
- Attributing positive or negative life events to self, chance, or God.
- Discriminating between appropriate and inappropriate guilt and shame.
- Petitionary prayer as an opportunity to refine and transform one's desires.
- How prayer can change oneself and change the lives of others.
- Resonance between one's desires and the will of God.

QUESTIONS TO CONSIDER

- What are the psychological functions of prayer?
- What happens to you when you pray? Do you see yourself, other people, and your own desires in a new light?
- For what kind of events in our lives is it appropriate to thank God?
- Do you know people who are prone to excessive guilt, and is it 'cheap' guilt that stands in the way of personal change?
- Which of our desires is it appropriate to bring to God in prayer?
- Do you find praying for others hard work? What areas for growth might this suggest?

The spiritual path

Spiritual development

We will turn now to psychological aspects of the spiritual path, and spiritual direction. The concept of progress or development in the spiritual life is one that lends itself to interpretation within the framework of developmental psychology. This is a theme that is addressed in more detail in Chapters 5 and 6. However, it is important to note at the outset that there is no straightforward way in which concepts of progress or development can be applied to the religious life. Individuals are not sufficiently predictable for there to be one orderly and standard model of religious development; nor is a later stage of development always 'higher' or 'better'. In fact, there are good theological reasons for seeing value in childlike spirituality as well as in psychological maturity. Talk of spiritual progress gives inadequate regard to how God can encounter people praying or meditating in different ways. He is not restricted to people who have reached a supposedly 'advanced' stage of spiritual development.

Spiritual guidance

Nevertheless, the fact is that many people encounter problems from time to time in their spiritual life, and seek help in overcoming them. The practice of giving such help used to be called 'spiritual direction'. However, there has been a movement to talk in more egalitarian terms of 'guidance', or simply having a 'soul friend' (Leech 1994). The nature of spiritual guidance has changed markedly in recent years and has become much more sophisticated psychologically (Schneiders 1986). Whereas spiritual directors used to see a clear distinction between their role and that of psychological counselling, it is now increasingly recognised that there is a close interplay between the two (see Chapter 10).

The problems that arise in the spiritual life are in some ways rather similar to those that arise in counselling for personal problems, and Robert May (1982, Chapter 5) has given a good account of them. He suggests that most of the standard psychological defences described by Freud can arise in response to a religious experience. People can deny or repress it, engage in some form of intellectualisation to discount it, isolate the cognitive content from all emotional connotations, and so on. There is also a similar set of resistances to spiritual practices, such as avoiding prayer because of anxieties about what might surface in the quiet time, or there can be a rebellion against the discipline required for steady prayer, or an excessive diligence in prayer without any real spiritual engagement, and so on.

There are also psychological maladjustments that arise in the spiritual path. May suggests that the two most common are spiritual 'cop-out' in which the person uses their spiritual practice as an excuse for escaping the responsibilities and relationships with which they should be engaging, and spiritual narcissism, in which the person's spiritual life is used to bolster their sense of self-importance.

Self and spirituality

Attitudes to the self and their relationship to spirituality have been particularly problematic. It is a central part of the Christian tradition that the spiritual life involves, in some sense, turning away from 'self'. However, this is open to alternative interpretations. Psychologically-minded guides to the spiritual life have become increasingly aware that too sweeping a renunciation of the self can involve the suppression of personal problems that need to be dealt with, and make any real spiritual development impossible.

It is helpful here to make a distinction between true and false selves, such as would be made, for example, by Thomas Merton. From a theological point of view there is a true self that is made in the image of God, and which it is people's vocation to realise more fully. The true self is thus an integral part of the spiritual life, rather than an impediment to it. On the other hand, there is a false self that arises out of unresolved personal problems and needs, and which is antagonistic to spiritual development. Under the impact of twentieth-century psychology, there has been a discernible shift of emphasis in Christian spirituality, from repression of a false self towards realisation of the true self.

Similar issues are raised by James Hillman in his paper 'Peaks and Vales', in terms of the classic distinction between soul and spirit (Hillman 1976). These terms have been used in a fluctuating way within the Christian tradition. Hillman's charge is that Christianity has too often promoted a flight into spirit, when what was needed was 'soul-making'. The path that Hillman is advocating is an explicitly psychological, rather than a Christian one, though there is perhaps no other contemporary psychologist who has written more richly and sensitively about the life of the soul.

Emotional engagement

It is increasingly recognised that people need to be emotionally engaged in psychotherapy or counselling if these are to be effective (see also Chapter 10). It seems that spirituality, to be an effective agent of personal change, also needs to involve the whole person. One of the key issues here is the degree of emotional engagement in spirituality. This has been the subject of a good deal of controversy among Christians over the centuries. Some, especially revivalists, have regarded evident emotionality as a key requirement of authentic spirituality. Others, have seen emotionality as at best incidental, and at worst dangerous, distracting people from a calm focus upon God.

It is relevant here that there has been a substantial shift in psychological views about the nature and value of emotions in recent years. There has long been a sense of an opposition between reason and emotion. However, recent theories of emotion have emphasised the close intertwining of cognition and emotion, that emotion can be an integral part of human understanding, rather than an impediment to it. The phrase 'emotional intelligence' captures well this new view of emotion.

Emotions are highly informative. For example, when danger arises, the fear that sweeps over us instantly makes us aware of it, before we have had time consciously to work out what the threat is. Psychotherapists use their own feelings about a client as a vital clue to what the client may be feeling themselves. In everyday life too, we learn much about other people by noticing how we respond to them. Perhaps most important of all, we learn about ourselves by noticing what emotions we feel, and what rouses them. Spiritual practice in which people cut themselves off from their emotions would be 'flying blind' without a crucial source of information.

For these reasons it is of great importance to be in touch with and engaged with one's emotions in the spiritual life; it is not desirable to repress or ignore them. However, it is equally dangerous to live by nothing but one's emotions. A spiritual life given up to nothing but emotionality would be an undiscerning and disorderly one. Reflection on one's emotions, and some degree of control over them and their expression, are important aspects of emotional engagement.

Understandings of God

Spiritual guidance also needs to have sensitivity to how concepts of God often arise from, and can be distorted by, a person's psychological background and problems. Freud's (1927) view of this, in *The Future of an Illusion*, was essentially that ideas about God serve a compensatory function, so people who are oppressed with a sense of helplessness may deal with that by invoking the idea of a good and powerful God. However, it is equally possible that people's ideas about God are consistent with their personal problems rather than a compensation for them. Thus, someone who felt helpless might be tempted to overemphasise the arbitrariness of God's judgement, and someone who felt excessively guilty might overemphasise the severity of God's commands.

This is a key issue in the psychology of religion that would repay more careful investigation. There seems little doubt, however, that images of God often arise from, and are distorted by, key personal relationships. There have been a number of questionnaire studies investigating the relationship between concepts of God and concepts of parents, and the results are consistent with the idea that God is often seen as a kind of ideal parent. However, the connections found in such studies are relatively weak, and they certainly do not prove a causal connection, that is, that concepts of God arise from concepts of parents. In some ways more compelling are clinical studies such as that of Rizzuto who has demonstrated, in detailed case studies, an incredibly close similarity between how people conceptualise God and their parents (Rizzuto 1979). Though the nature of the causal relationship remains ambiguous, it is difficult to dismiss the similarity as mere coincidence.

Discernment of God's revelation of himself is a subtle matter, and one that is potentially open to psychological understanding. It was noted above that William James and others have often described mystical experiences as being 'ineffable'. One could put this psychologically by saying that they often occur as what Gendlin has called 'self meanings', understandings that cannot readily be articulated. Alternatively, and more formally, they can be seen as meanings that arise within the 'implicational' subsystem rather than the 'propositional' subsystem of the Interacting Cognitive Subsystems model of mind (Watts 1999). What begins as a felt meaning then needs to be re-coded in a form in which it can be articulated.

Such psychological formulations are fully consistent with the traditional theological insight that God is, in some sense, beyond full human comprehension. Sometimes, felt meanings gather around some particular powerful symbol, phrase, scriptural text, or whatever. Even when this happens, the full significance of the symbol or text usually remains a felt meaning, and the task of articulating its significance remains.

SUMMARY OF KEY THEMES

- No single model of development to which everyone should conform in their religious life.
- Problems on the spiritual path and spiritual direction.
- Turning away from false selves towards the true self.
- Engaging with emotions but not being ruled by them.
- The relationship between psychological make-up and concepts of God.

QUESTIONS TO CONSIDER

- Are you aware of the different stages along the spiritual path that members of your congregation have reached?
- Have you ever received the help of a spiritual counsellor or 'soul friend'? What was most helpful about their approach?
- How do you respond to people with an 'immature' spirituality (for example, one that is narcissistic or escapist)?
- How should people understand and respond to the Christian call to die to the old self? How is such language related to psychological ideas of true and false selves?
- Who do you know who is closed off to their emotions or, conversely, uncritically ruled by them?
- In your experience, is it true that a person's image of God is often conditioned by their individual psychological make-up, and their views of their parents in particular?
- If so, should they be encouraged to develop a different understanding of God, or not?

Further reading

Spiritual experience

Beit-Hallahmi, B. and Argyle, M. (1997) *The Psychology of Religious Behaviour, Belief and Experience*, London: Routledge, Chapter 5.
d'Aquili, E. and Newberg, A. B. (1999) *The Mystical Mind*, Minneapolis: Fortress Press.
Forman, R. (1990) *The Problem of Pure Consciousness*, New York: Oxford University Press.
Hay, D. (1982) *Exploring Inner Space*, Harmondsworth: Penguin.
Proudfoot, W. (1986) *Religious Experience*, Berkeley: University of California Press.

Prayer

Brown, L. B. (1994) *The Human Side of Prayer*, Birmingham Alabama: Religious Education Press.
Godin, A. (ed.) (1968) *From Cry to Word: Contributions Towards a Psychology of Prayer*, Birmingham Alabama: Religious Education Press.
Phillips, D. Z. (1965) *The Concept of Prayer*, London: Routledge & Kegan Paul.
Ulanov, A. and Ulanov, B. (1985) *Primary Speech: A Psychology of Prayer*, London: SCM Press.
Watts, F. (ed.) (2001) *Perspectives on Prayer*, London: SPCK.

The spiritual path

Benner, D. G. (1988) *Psychotherapy and the Spiritual Quest*, London: Hodder and Stoughton.
May, G. G. (1982) *Will and Spirit: A Contemplative Psychology*, New York: HarperCollins.
May, G. G. (1982) *Care of Mind, Care of Spirit: A Psychiatrist Explores Spiritual Direction*, New York: HarperCollins.

2   The psychology of church services

Ritual and worship

Human beings are active collaborators in their religious faith, not just passive recipients. We bring to worship all that we are. Ritual, worship, and healing, in both traditional and charismatic church contexts, engage us on all levels: physical, emotional, volitional, intellectual, spiritual, and social. This chapter looks at these religious practices from a psychological perspective, asking how they can help or hinder personal and spiritual growth. As in other chapters, this perspective is complementary to (rather than an alternative to) religious accounts of worship, ritual, and healing, which focus on their transcendent dimensions. We take a broad view of ritual, considering it to apply equally well to the unspoken but fixed format of many charismatic traditions as to more formalised liturgy.

The psychology of ritual

In order to understand how people engage with church rituals, it is important to have a broad concept of ritual and its place in society. One prominent psychologist who has understood this is Erik Erikson (1977). Another is Bani Shorter (1996), who has written from a Jungian point of view about how people develop rituals in a variety of contexts in everyday life. In the United Kingdom, the death of Princess Diana was a particularly interesting occasion that seemed to cry out for ritualisation. An astonishingly large proportion of the population lit candles, gave flowers, or performed some other tribute. Intriguingly, little of this was organised from above; it welled up spontaneously because of a heart-felt need to find rituals that caught the moment.

To be worthwhile and effective, rituals need both to connect with psychological needs and also to offer an effective way of meeting and transforming them. There are thus two ways in which rituals can fail. When rituals fail to connect with anything that matters to people, they can degenerate into empty formalities, what Erikson calls 'ritual excess'. On the other hand, if rituals fail to meet psychological needs effectively, they are not adequate to their task. Looked at from this perspective, there seems much more danger of church rituals falling into the first trap than the second. Too often, they become empty and detached from real human experiences and concerns. This raises the question of continuity and change in ritual. It is in the nature of ritual that it should be predictable and to some extent formal. Only so can it transcend ordinary unritualised activities. However, if it becomes too inflexible, it fails to adapt to meet people's ritual needs.

Erikson has suggested that religious rituals are particularly related to the earliest infant phase of life development (see Erikson 1977; also Capps and Browning (eds) 1983). In his view, the rituals that develop in infancy naturally connect with the numinous, and religious rituals are a continuation of this form of ritualisation. One important feature is looking and being looked at, which harks back to the mother and baby gazing at one another. Various aspects of church ritual, such as the priest giving a blessing, or the sacred use of icons seem to reflect the importance of looking in numinous rituals.

Eugene d'Aquili and Andrew Newberg (1999) have approached ritual from a rather different, neuropsychological, point of view, suggesting that a key function of ritual is to modulate the levels of arousal that people experience. Looking at rituals across a variety of traditions and cultures, they argue for the importance of the distinction between rapid and slow rituals. Rapid rituals, perhaps involving ecstatic dance, produce a state of arousal and hyper-excitement. Slow rituals, on the other hand, can produce a quiescent state. Looked at from this point of view, the majority of church services in the West seem likely to induce relatively low levels of arousal, but do not do so in an extreme way. Innovations in church ritual seem often designed to make the ceremony more effective at inducing high or low states of arousal. Some recent charismatic practices, discussed later in this chapter, are clearly likely to raise arousal levels. In contrast, meditation and other contemplative practices, when introduced into church services, will induce low levels of arousal.

Though the contrast between hyper-arousal and quiescence seems clear, d'Aquili and Newberg claim that 'spill-over' phenomena can occur. Thus, when one system is induced very strongly, a spill-over effect can occur whereby the other system is also activated, producing a particularly powerful experience in which arousal and quiescence are combined.

Rites of passage

Like all religions, the Judeo-Christian tradition marks important points of transition in the life cycle – birth, 'coming of age', marriage, death – with their own specific rituals. Roger Grainger describes these rites of passage as 'essential tools for living' (Grainger 1988a: 45).

Developing the ideas of Arnold van Gennep (1909/1977), Grainger describes the ways that baptisms, marriages and funerals follow three discernible ritual stages:

1   *Separation*
    Before the transition to the new stage of life can be made, a separation from the old life must be effected. For example, the bride and groom separate from their birth families; they 'leave' in order to 'cleave'; the baptismal candidate is separated from the previous state of 'natural', sinful life by repentance.

2   *Transition*
    A period of great change, a return to chaos and formlessness in which the person is dissolved in order to be reformed. For example, the baptismal candidate is submerged under the water, the bride and groom are joined via the symbol of a wedding ring.

3   *Reincorporation*
    Re-entering the communal structures at a different level, as a new person. For example, in death entering the community of heaven and the communion of saints; in bereavement, re-entering social structures as a person with a new identity.

As well as being a celebration of a significant moment in the life cycle, rites of passage have a performative power: they actually bring about the social changes to which the ritual points. The adolescent is now seen as, and (ideally) treated as, an adult in society; the couple are now seen as, and treated as, married; the baby is now seen as, and treated as, a member of the church or social group. It is no accident that these rituals rely strongly on non-verbal symbols. Non-verbal symbols, such as the placing of hands on the one to be ordained, the drenching with water of the baptismal candidate, the exchange of wedding rings, the anointing with oil in healing rituals, the putting on new clothes for the religious taking vows, symbolise *and* bring about the change in status, not only for the individual in question, but for the whole social group. The use of non-verbal symbols allows for multiple levels of interpretation; such symbols can point to the numinous more easily than words. In a Jungian sense, the symbols allow for the person to integrate the profound (and sometimes threatening) realities represented by the ritual at a depth and rate that the participant can handle without being overwhelmed by the unknown and mysterious. A sense of awe, holiness, and profound unity can accompany such rituals, enabling these threatening realities to be held in a safe, controlled atmosphere. Radical life changes can be negotiated without either the individual or the social group being overwhelmed.

The public recognition and involvement in these momentous transitions serve the purpose of creating a new social equilibrium for the group. Not only is the individual communicant or baptismal candidate embarking on a new stage in life, so too is the group in relation to that person. The wisdom of such religious practices is now recognised also in psychological contexts such as family counselling: if one person in a family is to change their behaviour, there are knock-on effects for the whole family that the whole family needs actively to accommodate. To facilitate individual change, the group needs to embrace the new identity and behaviour of the changing individual.

Funerals are among the most significant of religious ceremonies marking rites of passage. They are important times not only to honour the memory of the deceased, and to offer comfort to the bereaved, but for the social group itself to re-affirm the ongoingness of life, even in the face of death. The symbols used in funerals provide clear, usable images that help structure the changed world for the bereaved, helping them eventually to re-emerge from mental and emotional chaos. The sense of being part of something greater than oneself, something that survives the onslaught of disruptive change, is, according to Durkheim, the very essence of religion. Those in the Christian faith take this implicit psychological and sociological aim of the funeral ritual even further by actively identifying themselves as a faith community with the One who went into death, and after three days, showed himself to be the resurrection and the life. The funeral rite signifies this final journey towards the divine source of being.

Although there are secular 'rites of passage' now on offer (civil ceremony marriages, eighteenth birthday celebrations, even a proposed government-approved secular celebration for a newborn), many people (including those with no explicit Christian faith) still look to the church for rites of passage such as baptism for their children. Can this be understood as an inarticulate groping towards a religious view of life? Or is a religious ritual, such as baptism, emptied of its meaning when used as a social rite of passage rather than a specifically religious rite? In the long-term, the spiritual meaning of the ritual (and the church which performs the ritual) may suffer when used merely as a social marker by people who do not espouse faith. On the other hand, what are the immediate (and perhaps long-term) psychological effects of turning someone away because they haven't 'measured up' to the expectations of the faith community? Far-reaching damage can occur on either side of this tightrope. Where church doctrine does not constrain such decisions, ministers have to wrestle out their own position concerning requests for church ceremonies marking rites of passage by those outside the faith community. Although the risk of real faith being short-circuited always exists, even a seemingly shallow request for a rite of passage might provide an opportunity for someone to connect with the springs of his or her own religious impulse.

Holy Communion

The service of Holy Communion, or Eucharist, is the most powerful ritual of the church, and its human side can be elucidated at a psychological level (see Jung 1958; Lee 1955; Murphy 1979) without in any way suggesting that it is just a matter of psychology. Part of the richness of the Communion lies in the fact it has so many aspects, and can be approached in many different ways. How the service is conducted affects which of these aspects is to the forefront. For example, when the priest faces the people, it emphasises the 'fellowship' meal aspect of the Communion; when priest and people all face the altar, it emphasises that they are approaching God together.

The Communion can have a powerful psychological resonance. However, it fails to fulfil its potential if it becomes just a time for cheerful but superficial worship, or mainly for intellectual reflection on the faith; and it is certainly not just a spectacle. If it is to 'work', it needs to be conducted in a way that invites deep psychological engagement, and that engagement also needs to be effectively contained. In this it is like a funeral service when the grief is intense; the service needs both to connect with that grief, but also – by containing it in the ritual of the funeral – to help to transform it. Something similar should happen in the Communion service, though the balance is not easy to hold. The ritual can become either so sterile and formalised, or so mundane and unevocative, that it no longer makes contact with any real human experience, and so nothing transacts.

Perhaps the central strand of meaning in the Communion service concerns the relationship between God and humanity. It is about their drawing close to one another, and achieving a kind of union when the consecrated bread and wine are received. Different parts of the service prepare for that in different ways. There may be a formal start to the service when the priest and his assistants draw close to the altar, representing a drawing close to the transcendent God. Confession helps people to recall their unworthiness, while worship (e.g. 'Lift up your hearts') encourages people to raise their sights to this God.

While all this is going on, people are engaging with the discrepancy between their real self and their ideal self (or, in Jungian terminology, between the ego and the Self). Worship helps people to aspire to the ideal self, while penitence makes them aware of the inadequacy of the real self. Offering or sacrifice prepare for a mystical union between Christ and the congregation; both the offering of Christ that is recalled, and the offering by the people of themselves. It is through this mutual offering that there can be the drawing close which culminates in the act of Communion, that helps to heal the gulf between real and ideal self.

Different meanings are fused here. There is an historical meaning that arises from what Christ did at the Last Supper and on the Cross, a meaning in which God and humanity are relating to one another in the present, and another meaning where the Communion is experienced as a foretaste of the kingdom of heaven. Equally, there is a meaning in the Communion that is symbolic, where the bread and wine represent the body and blood of Christ, but another meaning that transcends the symbolic in a real and actual mutual indwelling, of the congregation with one another, and of all with Christ. If the Communion is to 'work' at the level of human experience, it is essential that these different meanings are held together, and are not collapsed. As R. G. Lee (1955: 106) comments, 'this union of the historical and the symbolic is of great importance psychologically viewed'. Only then is the Communion a powerful integrative and transforming experience.

How different people respond to the Communion, or indeed whether it affects them at all, will depend to some extent on their psychological style and capacities. It

requires them to engage both emotionally and intellectually, and to hold those two
aspects of their response together. It requires them to draw deeply from their own
experience, to relate to those around them, and to reach out to God, and again to
hold all of these together. Above all, it requires people to overcome the dry literalism
that has been a feature of much thinking since the Enlightenment, and to recover a
new kind of more holistic or participatory cognition that is somewhat similar to the
primitive, animistic thinking that has now largely died out (Barfield 1957). All that is
a tall order, and helps to explain why many Communion services fall so far short of
the powerful human experience they can be. A psychological perspective can help to
clarify what is required if the Communion is to be celebrated in a way that transforms people.

Music, liturgy, and movement

Worship is more than a ritual activity; it is relational in intent and content. The collective dimension of worship can provide a sense of being related to others, joined in
a corporate relationship to God. It is an occasion for worshippers, individually and
collectively, to enter into a relationship of love, trust and thanksgiving that over-
flows into creative expressions of praise. From earliest history, humans have
expressed their deepest emotions through music and dance. The Christian church
has its own rich repository of hymns, songs, and liturgical gestures to express the
phases of the human heart.

Music is a carrier of the emotional flow of worship services. Listening to music,
or singing hymns or choruses in a service, engages worshippers via their bodily
senses, emotions, intuitions, and intellects. A well-planned liturgy is sensitive to
the emotional trajectory of a service, and provides a variety of ways for the wor-
shipper to engage in a transformative religious experience that takes people from a
starting place to a goal. This journey of transformation is aided by various devices:
standing to sing, gesturing to signify important liturgical moments, moving to the
altar rail to receive Communion, kneeling in prayer, sitting to listen to readings or
sermons, or lifting hands and arms in worship, are all movements that enable a
person to enter into the experience more fully. The emphases of Christian services
may vary greatly: they may be primarily intellectual and word-centred, or dominated by sacrament or aesthetics, or they may seek ecstatic emotional experiences.
Whatever the emphasis, a successful liturgy will follow a trajectory that is faithful
to the 'narrative' flow of human emotions. You can't push a person from deep
despair into joyous praise, whatever forms of worship are used. A human being
needs to move through stages of emotional transformation gradually and
authentically.

Good liturgies are like helpful psychological aids to growing in a spiritual relationship with God. In designing a liturgy it is possible to err on either side of a fine
boundary: either the worship service is emotionally manipulative or it is remote and
disengaged. Many would argue that large parts of the traditional church don't do
enough to engage the whole person in worship; services are felt to be boring, irrelevant, or incomprehensible. Religious practices that may have been meaningful in

one era have become foreign currency to many in the new generation. Churches can be emptied by this factor alone.

Over time, the way in which social and psychological needs and desires are expressed changes. Traditionally, Western Christianity has tended to espouse the Neoplatonic elevation of the intellect over the physical and emotional aspects of our being. This has led not only to an over-intellectualising of the faith, but for many, has contributed to a deep divide in their own person, relegating emotions, physicality and sexuality to a garbage bin left outside church walls. Forms of worship that engage the body and the emotions, such as symbolic movement, pilgrimage, dance and drama, are potent vehicles for healing this split between mind and body. These ancient forms of worship (but forms which are relatively new to parts of Western Christianity) resonate with our contemporary culture. The average person today is bombarded with fast-paced visual and auditory stimulation. In this social context, traditional church services can appear flat and lifeless. It is no wonder that new styles of worship are reflecting contemporary cultural norms and psychological needs. How far this should be taken is a sensitive question. The need for Christianity to be relevant to our culture, and to involve the whole person, needs to be balanced with guarding against sheer sensation-seeking.

SUMMARY OF KEY THEMES

- The need for rituals that connect with psychic energy, and contain and transform it.
- Different levels of arousal induced by different rituals.
- The symbols and psychological importance of rites of passage.
- Historical, symbolic, intellectual, and emotional aspects of Holy Communion.
- The roles of body, movement, and music in Christian rituals.

QUESTIONS TO CONSIDER

- Does the worship style of your church seek states of hyper-arousal or of calm quiescence?
- What kind of match is there between this and your own personal preferences?
- How do you feel after your 'average' church service? Bored? Transformed? Calm? Excited?
- Which elements of church services do you find most effective yourself?

  1   Music and singing?
  2   Liturgical rituals (such as Communion and rites of passage)?
  3   Symbolic movements (crossing oneself, kneeling, lifting hands in worship)?
  4   Practice of charismatic gifts?
  5   Bible readings and preaching?
  6   Prayer (intercessory or in ministry)?

- Which aspects of your being do these different elements engage (e.g. body, emotions, intellect, unconscious, will, spirit)?

Confession and forgiveness

Confession of sin is central to Christian ritual and worship; it is a sacrament in its own right and a central part of the Communion service. It therefore provides an interesting case study in the psychological processes involved in, and the psychological issues raised by, Christian liturgy and ritual.

Confession focuses our attention on the crucified and risen Christ, through whom flows the forgiveness for which we long. Even outside religious circles, any therapist worth her salt knows that the confession of wrongdoing (or even wrong attitudes) is a turning point in personal growth. This vital practice, which forms a key part of most Christian worship services, can be an agent of astounding liberation. The relief and joy of being forgiven is a fount of spiritual renewal, and a place from which real change can occur. However, ritual confession can sometimes be ineffective in dealing with stubborn problems of guilt and habitual sinful patterns. Why does confession sometimes 'work', and sometimes not?

First, non-specific confession of sin which rehearses a general sense of 'I am bad' will not tend to provide real liberation. In fact, vague confession of sin can be used by some as a tactic to avoid a more precise confession rooted in an active awareness of specific wrongs (intentional or unintentional). Confession that pinpoints actual wrongs, and is infused with a realisation of sin's impact on others, self and God, can lead to a surgical contrition, which is active in its desire to be rid of sin, and to make amends wherever possible. It is well known in counselling circles, as well as in the confessional, what extreme lengths we will go to in order to avoid this kind of precise reckoning. Christian teaching prompts us to ask the Holy Spirit to bring about the grace of real contrition in the face of our (sometimes unconscious) efforts to avoid it. On the other hand, we are not personally responsible for everything that is wrong in life. The realistic or right taking of responsibility for sin entails a realistic attribution of self-blame within a wider network of causality; our own sinful responses may comprise only one aspect of a complex interweaving of social and interpersonal wrongs. Realistic attribution of sinfulness takes into account that for which we are responsible, and distinguishes it from sins that lie at someone else's door. Fraser Watts and Mark Williams (1988) point out that it is crucial for this realistic attribution to occur in the 'felt presence of God' which reframes our acknowledgement of sin in the context of being (already) forgiven by God. After precise, realistic confession has occurred, liberation is made complete when forgiveness is *received*, which also needs to happen at a 'felt' level.

Some people have developed frameworks of understanding sin, guilt and forgiveness based on a faulty, overly negative sense of self. Our sense of self is developed in the context of relationship. This happens in a profound way in infancy and childhood, and continues throughout life. What is mirrored back to us in the reactions of others becomes a part of our 'looking glass' self. For a child, the responses of their 'god-like' parents (or other powerful others) form a potent source of information about the self. Because the security parents provide for children is so vital, clinicians have noted how children often construe their parents as being 'all-good' and their pronouncements as 'all truth'. The child, in his dependent state, needs to rely on a carer who is seen as good, powerful and right. Further, children do not have the cognitive development to query or critique the behaviour of their parents. In a situation where the child is being unfairly criticised, punished, abused, or neglected, the child is likely to construe this sad state of affairs as 'my good parent is meting out to me the punishment I deserve' (Rowe 1987). Repeated abuse (verbal, emotional, physical or sexual) drums in a message that the child is inherently bad, and deserving of punishment. Cognitively, negative events tend to carry more psychological weight than positive events, exacerbating an already negative sense of self. What can result is a profound subjective sense of guilt which is based upon rejection, not upon actual wrongs. Confession of sin may provide little relief from this subjective sense of guilt as long as the psychological roots remain unexamined. It is possible for such individuals to feel guilty for every mishap in the universe. Feelings of guilt can be hidden by an overblown self-righteousness, or a tendency to project one's own faults onto others. Meanwhile, objective wrongs may be mounting up. A person can act out their sense of being despicable as if fulfilling, through destructive acts, some prophetic pronouncement. These real transgressions further embroil the person in an intolerable burden of guilt.

A person may also suffer from a subjective sense of guilt because they require of themselves an unrealistic degree of perfection. Confession of sin can fail here as well; the harsh inner taskmaster (or super-ego in Freudian terms) has not been assuaged.

Howard Gordon (1997) points to the need to understand that a sense of guilt can result from three different sources:

1   Transgression guilt: real, objective guilt resulting from moral wrongdoing.
2   Rejection guilt: subjective guilt feelings resulting from rejection, abuse or neglect.
3   Perfection guilt: subjective guilt based on the self's own harsh demands of perfection.

Many people who come to confession bring a complex mixture of all three types of guilt. A token waving of 'Jesus died for your sins' may not lift feelings of unacceptability, especially if the sources of guilt are other than objective transgression. Gordon (1997) found that the people he interviewed on this topic reported that their feelings of objective and subjective guilt, which are often conflated, found alleviation from four sources:

1   A balanced Christianity whose creedal convictions and community life emphasised grace as well as law, and which advocated openness to people with all their faults, limitations and hurts.
2   Caring professionals who were good listeners, understanding, non-judgemental and encouraging.
3   Supportive relatives and friends who exhibited the same characteristics.
4   An individual who, through special skill or insight, was able to make a precisely relevant – and therefore liberating – pronouncement.

Ministers in all denominations will pastor people who need to talk, formally or informally, about their struggle to receive forgiveness and release from guilt, subjective and objective. If properly handled, confession to a human intermediary, and receiving of absolving statements (to the effect that God has forgiven the wrongdoing), can help a person appropriate forgiveness in the context of a real relationship. Forgiveness is not some abstract entity that merely requires intellectual assent; forgiveness is participation in a loving, accepting relationship. As most of our wounds in life have been delivered through (faulty) relationships, it is not surprising that our healing, and our ability to receive forgiveness, also develops in the context of relationship. It is here that a relationship with a priest, minister or caring professional can help a person build the necessary scaffolding for a relationship with God through Christ, which extends to others.

Forgiving others

Our (in)ability to receive forgiveness can also be tied to our (in)ability to forgive others. Jesus himself suggested that the two are intimately linked: 'Forgive us our sins, as we forgive those who sin against us.' It may be helpful to understand that forgiving others, especially those who have deeply damaged us, is a long process that should not be forced or glossed over with a 'surface' offer of forgiveness. Robert Enright and the Human Development Group (Enright *et al.* 1998) propose four phases, which themselves have several sub-stages:

1   *Uncovering phase*
    An injured party examines his own defences, and confronts anger, in order to release it. Any shame, or cognitive rehearsal of the offence, is acknowledged. Awareness that one may be permanently changed by the offence, along with one's previous conception of a 'just world'.

2   *Decision phase*
    The injured party decides that the old strategies are not working and that forgiveness is an option. A commitment is made to forgive the offender.

3   *Work phase*
    Reframing, through role-taking, who the wrongdoer is by viewing him or her in context, developing empathy towards the offender. An acceptance and absorption of the pain.

4   *Deepening phase*
    Finding meaning for self and others in the suffering. Realisation that self has needed forgiveness in the past, insight that one is not alone in suffering. Realisation that the self may have new purpose because of the injury; negative affect decreases. Emotional release.

A number of other psychological models of forgiveness also focus on the importance of reframing (phase 3). Reframing involves the reworking of attributions of blame in view of the complex interplay of situational and other factors that contribute to wrongdoing. Our attributions of blame commonly suffer from a number of cognitive distortions (for example, overemphasising personal rather than situational aspects of causation), so the outcome of reframing is to bring about a more realistic view, enabling understanding of, but not condoning, the offence. At the same time we must be wary of merely excusing someone's offence ('he couldn't help it') rather than truly forgiving someone ('she could have done something different, but I forgive her anyway').

Reframing means that the hurtful behaviour is not the defining feature of that person in our eyes: 'The story is not usually about an innocent lamb and a bad wolf. Most of us have to do our forgiving while we are being forgiven' (Smedes 1988: 7). Understanding our enemy (even if only partially) brings back down to size the wrongdoer who has appeared in our imagination as 'twice as large, twice as powerful, and twice as evil' (Smedes 1988: 99).

However, reframing cannot explain freely chosen evil, and, in fact, examination may reveal its full horror and incomprehensibility even further. In the face of enormous acts of brutality, it is reasonable to ask whether it is always morally correct to forgive. Does not an easy 'forgiveness' add further outrage to the victim, while minimising the crime? Is it even humanly possible always to forgive? Can a child who has been tortured by parents find the resources within to forgive them? Can survivors of the Holocaust, or ethnic cleansing, whose lives have been devastated, find the strength to forgive their tormentors? Stephen Burns (1996) argues that in pastoral care it is not helpful to present total forgiveness as yet another burden survivors *must* embrace.

Forgiveness is not to be confused with a martyrish passivity. Forgiveness may only be possible after the victim's outrage has spurred action to ensure there are structural impediments against future abuse. Burns also points out that we must realistically consider the level of forgiveness to which a deeply scarred person can aspire. Survivors of profound trauma may be so wounded that they need to be accepted in their limited 'ungenerous' state; to require impossible feats of forgiveness from them may only cause further damage. However, to aim for some level of forgiveness is helpful; at the very least, forgiveness seems to release us from those who have hurt us, while resentment and vengeance binds us to those whom we cannot forgive. While there may be realistic human limitations to the degree of forgiveness of which we are capable, it is helpful to realise that God is not limited in either his concern for justice or his ability to forgive, whose forgiveness alone can release us from the inevitable cycle of sin begetting sin. This sort of reframing takes place within a divine context; our own limited ability to forgive can be placed within the context of God's unlimited capacity both to forgive and to suffer with those who suffer.

Studies have further shown that reframing alone may not be as successful in promoting forgiveness as reframing along with strategies to encourage empathy with the offender. Imagining the distress, or neediness, of an offender, and realising our own need for forgiveness, may initiate feelings of compassion. An apology can promote empathy as it makes it possible for the injured party to see the offender's distress over the wrongdoing. However, apologies are not always forthcoming; and it is sometimes impossible to feel compassion for the wrongdoer. Here, we must turn to the possibility that God's compassion is not limited, relieving the injured party from having to shoulder the task of forgiveness alone.

A third strategy, 'role-taking', imagines what it would be like in the future if one was fully able to forgive. By acting out the chosen role of forgiver, a person can gradually 'grow into' the experience of being able to forgive. Indeed, employing an array of strategies (reframing the past, developing empathy in the present, and growing into a future role as forgiver) may, in combination, help a wounded person take realistically sized steps in the arduous journey of forgiving others (Gulliford 1999).

SUMMARY OF KEY THEMES

- Using confession to discern the extent to which we are responsible for bad events in our lives and the lives of others.
- Different kinds of guilt: transgression, rejection, and perfection guilt.
- Choosing to forgive others, through cognitive reframing and empathy.

QUESTIONS TO CONSIDER

- What is your own experience of weekly confession in church services? Are you able to deal with concrete, specific sins? Does weekly confession sometimes merely confirm a sense of being 'bad'?
- Are you able to forgive yourself for your sins and shortcomings, or do you feel you don't 'deserve' to be forgiven?
- Think of the person(s) in your life that have caused you the most hurt. If you visualise yourself on a long journey that leads towards forgiveness, how far have you travelled so far?
- What might help you on this journey?

Charismatic worship and spiritual gifts

Although it is widely acknowledged that Western society is increasingly secular, and that traditional forms of Christianity seem to be waning, recent decades have seen a world-wide explosion of Pentecostal and charismatic forms of Christianity. In the UK, the fastest growing churches are new, independent charismatic churches (Brierley 1999). This contrasts with the gradual, seemingly inexorable decline in attendance in most mainstream denominational churches. Worldwide, this century has welcomed 400 million new Pentecostal or charismatic Christians, the largest spurt of growth in Christian history. We do well not to ignore this vibrant group of Christians.

Two very different accounts of this sort of worship are available. The discourse of Pentecostal and charismatic insiders is full of references to the power and presence of God, and all but eliminates human agency from the picture. Psychologists and sociologists, by contrast, draw attention to social norms, conformity, use of language, emotional manipulation, hysteria, and other human factors. A third approach, and the one taken in this chapter, suggests that the human–divine relationship is one of active collaboration. Spiritual seekers are human beings who, through active collaboration with God, receive spiritual gifts. This model accepts that religious experience, however real, will be shaped to some degree by the teaching and social rules of the faith community, as well as by the psychological propensities of the person involved. Misunderstandings of the Pentecostal and charismatic movements are prone to arise when either an exclusively theological or an exclusively reductionist approach is taken. In this section, two spiritual gifts in particular are examined from this dual perspective: speaking in tongues and healing.

Speaking in tongues

Controversy has long attended the practice of the charismatic gifts (speaking in tongues, the interpretation of tongues, healing, miracles, the discerning of spirits, prophecy; see 1 Cor. 12). There are those who are vehemently for the practices and defend them on biblical and doctrinal grounds. Then there are those who are against them, also for biblical and doctrinal reasons (for example, those who adopt a 'dispensational' interpretation of the biblical narrative, according to which the miraculous gifts of the Spirit belong to an earlier 'dispensation' – the Age of the Apostles – which is now over). Others dislike the practice of the gifts of the Spirit simply on social and emotional grounds; to them these practices seem wacky and embarrassing. For some, the practicalities present a stumbling block: 'Won't church services get out of control?'

   The scientific community has tended to take a sceptical view of the mysterious gift of speaking in tongues, also called 'glossolalia'. Early studies tended to confirm prejudices: glossolalia was considered the 'loose jargon of a maniac' (e.g. Le Baron; cited in Malony and Lovekin 1985: 293). Later studies soon demonstrated, however, that the kind of nonsensical jumble of words found in the private languages of schizophrenics (termed 'word salads') bore no relationship to speaking in tongues. Linguistically, tongues cannot be considered the language of the mad. But is it a language?

Linguists and psychologists in the early part of the twentieth century were fascinated with the question of whether, as many Pentecostal tongues speakers insisted, tongues was an actual language (variously described as God's own language, a heavenly language, or some real, but unknown, earthly language). Opinions on either side seemed to assume that if this could be demonstrated one way or the other, then the debate regarding the appropriateness of speaking in tongues to Christian experience would be settled. As it turned out, linguists studying numerous examples of glossolalia have concluded that tongues is not a 'real' language (Malony and Lovekin 1985). Tongues does not have the syntactic structure of a real language; the sounds generated often bear striking resemblance to the typical phonemes of the speaker's own mother tongue; and the variety of phonemes is quite restricted. Characteristics such as echoing a key sound are common, for example: 'she miya, ne kiya, sonoriya e-kiya'.

However, this finding does not settle the question regarding the appropriateness of speaking in tongues in Christian experience one way or the other. Indeed, why should we assume that God would merely duplicate the uses and functions of a learned language with another 'tongue' similar in kind to the one we already have? It may be more useful to think that something else is afoot, and that perhaps speaking in tongues achieves other purposes.

Further, speaking in tongues is not simply gibberish. Linguistic studies show that it is speech-like in its rhythm, cadence and intonation (if not in its syntax). Nor can it be readily faked. Pretend speaking in tongues is easily distinguished from the real thing by both linguists and by tongues speakers. Speaking in tongues appears to be expressive; the emotions and the mood of the utterance are clearly discernible to listeners and those speaking. However a one-to-one word correspondence is generally not feasible. A useful analogy may be that tongues speaking is like an improvised song or dance. An improvised dance is, at one level, a flow of expressive movement whose meaning cannot be put into exact words, but it is not thereby meaningless. Similarly, tongues is an expression that is beyond words, yet one that may bear a narrative structure.

Another, rarer, form of glossolalia is reported to involve speaking a real foreign language that is completely unknown to the tongues speaker. Ever since the account in Acts 2, there have been numerous anecdotal accounts of tongues speakers speaking in a language that is understood by the hearers, but not the speaker. The utterance is understood by the hearers to be a message to them directly from God, delivered in this surprising way. This is termed 'xenoglossolalia', and appears to be similar to the experience of the disciples on the first day of Pentecost. Early Pentecostals believed that such experiences would become normative, enabling them to share the gospel in foreign lands without having to bother with the lengthy process of learning a foreign language. Despite recurring stories that such events do occasionally happen, researchers have had little luck in actually observing

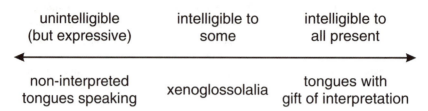

Figure 2.1 Degrees of intelligibility in glossolalia

xenoglossolalia in process; hence it receives little empirical support in the literature. More commonly, a message in tongues is interpreted within the context of a Christian gathering. In such instances, another person receives the 'gift of interpretation', and gives an interpretation (not a direct one-to-one 'translation') of the original tongues utterance. Figure 2.1 shows that these three kinds of tongues speaking can be located along a dimension of intelligibility.

Quite apart from doctrinal differences, there have been arguments concerning whether or not speaking in tongues is psychologically healthy. As speaking in tongues appears linguistically to be a regression to earlier, more primitive forms of speech, it seemed possible that such activity could induce an unhealthy psychological regression as well. However, a host of studies over several decades showed that there was no evidence for mental illness or pathological regression among tongues speakers in comparison with the general population. Some theorists, such as Jung, have taken a more benevolent view. Jung is well known for his view that the religious quest is central to healthy individuation and, along with others, has suggested that glossolalia may connect a person to this deep religious impulse within the collective unconscious of the human personality at a pre-verbal level. The temporary loosening of thought from its normal verbal anchor may be a healthy way of integrating other layers of the personality. Ego psychologists have suggested that speaking in tongues is indeed regressive, but that some speaking in tongues could be regressive 'in the service of the ego' (e.g. helping the ego to do its organising, integrating work in the personality). In contrast, other researchers have concluded that the regression involved in speaking in tongues can be indicative of deep inner conflict. E. Mansell Pattison (1968) observed that some speaking in tongues was 'playful' and conflict-free; this could indeed be healthy and positive for the personality; other forms of speaking in tongues seemed more conflictual; Pattison wondered whether perhaps this form could have negative functions in the psyche. From research so far, it seems plausible that the ability to speak in tongues is dormant in all humans, and may reflect an earlier developmental speech stage.

There has also been debate concerning whether speaking in tongues is the result of an involuntary, trance-like state. Charismatics today generally eschew the idea of 'out-of control' states of mind. Dennis Bennet, one of the charismatic leaders of the 1970s stated: 'Christian speaking in tongues is done as objectively as any other speaking, while the person is in full possession and control of his wits and volition, and is in no strange state of mind whatever' (quoted in Malony and Lovekin 1985:

105). This recent emphasis on 'normalcy' accords with the observation that the charismatic movement is a more middle-class, socially acceptable and inclusivist movement than its Pentecostal forbears (who were more working class and separatist). Far from being 'out of control', there is recent evidence that speaking in tongues has a learned component: people become better and more fluent with practice. Not surprisingly, people often receive the gift with the help of other tongues speakers praying for them, and even coaching them to take the first steps towards utterance. Speaking in tongues happens today, as it did historically, most frequently where it is expected and hoped for. It is to be expected that the social context shapes people's expectations about tongues, and influences the way in which the gift is sought, and then described afterwards. This does not mean that speaking in tongues is mere fabrication; as we have said, pretend speaking in tongues is easily recognised as such. Further, not all those who seek the gift receive it (which may be in part due to psychological factors, such as being over-controlled, that militate against relaxing into speaking in tongues).

Whether speaking in tongues ultimately comes from God, or puts one in direct touch with God, is beyond the scope of empirical psychology to determine. However, a strong tradition in qualitative research asserts that psychologists should listen to what tongues speakers themselves say about the experience, and should respect the religious framework in which it is understood. Tongues speakers today describe the experience variously as 'a prayer language', 'a way of speaking to God when I don't know what to say', something that 'helps me to feel God's presence', or as the writer of Romans puts it: 'the Spirit himself intercedes for us with groans that words cannot express' (Romans 8. 26). Repeated speaking in tongues can be thought of as a personal ritual that allows the person to 'pass out of a world determined entirely by pragmatic, rational, structured parameters and to pass into a new world of meaning where freedom, spontaneity and feeling dominate' (Malony and Lovekin 1985: 138).

Psychology can, of course, ask such questions as 'what are its effects?' For this question, it seems that what ultimately determines whether speaking in tongues has healthy outcomes psychologically has more to do with the framework of teaching within which it occurs. A framework of Christian teaching (and its attendant social context) which is imbalanced may contort the experience of tongues, over-inflating its importance. Early Pentecostals used to insist on the presence of the gift of tongues to identify a 'true' Christian, twice blessed. Pentecostals and charismatics are rarely so hardline nowadays. The tendency to consider speaking in tongues to be mandatory, or evidence of spiritual 'superiority', is now diminishing, if not disappearing altogether. It is equally possible that a balanced framework of Christian teaching may enable a person to grow in the use of the gift of tongues, and in all aspects of the Christian life, in a healthy, life-giving direction.

Social psychology helps us to understand that publicly uttered glossolalia occurs within a social milieu, whose explicit and implicit rules guide the practice of speaking in tongues. Although tongues do sometimes occur spontaneously in a social setting, observation of charismatic meetings indicates that a kind of implicit 'charismatic liturgy' frequently guides its practice. Often, a charismatic service begins with singing energetic songs of praise in which worshippers can turn their attention towards God, and expel unhelpful tension or lassitude. A series of quieter, more meditative songs often follows. After this, and especially if the musicians keep strumming, a time of unstructured worship is signalled, during which some, or many, will begin to sing or speak in tongues. This commonly followed chain of events does not so much contrive glossolalia as provide a process through which people are able to move from the hectic pace of their ordinary lives into a more relaxed, meditative state of mind which is conducive to speaking in tongues. Far from being out of control, a key factor here is that an implicitly understood signal has been given through this chain of events: 'It is now okay, even desirable, to speak in tongues publicly.'

Of course, not all services run smoothly along such implicitly understood lines. At times, a person may stand up in a meeting and deliver, unexpectedly, an utterance in tongues. An awkward silence may follow. Whether such an event turns out to be helpful to the meeting will largely depend on how the leaders deal with it. Perhaps the worship leader will ask those present to be receptive to giving an interpretation of the utterance, which will then be discerned by those present for its integrity as a spiritually inspired utterance. Most churches develop guidelines for good practice, where maverick and unhelpful occurrences can be identified and gently disciplined. As in private glossolalia, the helpfulness, or not, of public glossolalia largely depends upon the presence of understood social rules and balanced Christian teaching that together ensure a flexible, discernible order.

Healing

More empirical research has been carried out on speaking in tongues than on any other charismatic gift, although some of the findings mentioned above may also be applied to the gift of healing. As with tongues, there is an unavoidable human dimension to this spiritual gift. It is as multifaceted beings that we collaborate with God in seeking healing from sources both natural and divine. A multi-causal understanding of healing is increasingly recognised in medical circles. Social and psychological factors (such as stress) are known to influence the prevalence of various medical conditions, the functioning of the immune system, and rates of recovery (see also Chapter 8). Healing from physical and psychological ailments necessarily involves all aspects of our humanity: intellectual, emotional, volitional, physical, and social. A model of healing that reckons with humans as active agents, rather than passive recipients, may more adequately capture the complexity of healing, and the variety of ways in which healing can occur.

The use of the gift of healing in Christian practice, like tongues, has both its adherents and its detractors. Physical healings are an important part of the 'full gospel' of classical Pentecostalism and the charismatic movements. These understand the gift of healing as flowing from the atoning death of Christ, and his resurrection, which has wrought for Christians release not only from sin, but from mental and physical affliction as well. Throughout Christian history, from the gospels onwards, there have been numerous accounts of healings, although it seems that since the recent resurgence of Pentecostalism, healing has become more of a focus of Christian religion than ever before.

Empirical researchers have not, however, found much hard evidence to support the many claims made about miraculous healings. This does not mean that these claims are false, but rather that healing is a complex phenomenon, and rarely fits into the kind of clear-cut 'before and after' template which testimonies of healing can suggest. The Roman Catholic church has very strict criteria by which miraculous healings are measured; few of the healings commonly reported would conform to such strictly 'miraculous' contours, where all possible medical or natural causes of healing are ruled out by medical experts. More commonly, reported 'healings' occur through the body's natural healing processes, through the aid of medicine, through an improved social context, through the lifting of psychological stress, or as a result of strong expectations of healing which alter perceptions of the current state (the 'placebo' effect). Healing may also be influenced by God, and by prayer, through any of these channels, or in some other more direct way. Given the complexity of healing, approaches that acknowledge the interplay of social and psychological factors without ruling out the divine are preferable to approaches that rely on mono-causal explanations (whether in medical or in faith-healing circles).

The few empirical studies on the gift of healing indicate that is almost impossible to separate social and psychological factors from experiences of healing. Pattison *et al.* (1973) carried out a study of forty-three Pentecostal individuals, who had in sum reported a total of seventy-one healings. Pattison found that these individuals participated in faith-healing rituals not primarily for the relief of their symptoms, but mainly as a way of re-affirming their belief system and lifestyle. These subjects were not primarily asking themselves 'Have I been healed?', but 'Am I living in the right way?' Attending healing services answered the second question, and that was enough. Although those who claimed to have received healing could give no evidence of changes in symptoms, all did report that their certainty in the belief in God and in their religious conviction had markedly increased (Pattison *et al.* 1973: 401). Another study (Ness and Wintrob 1980) found that people sought out faith-healing more for emotional reasons than for physical ones. People report feeling better, even if there is no alleviation of symptoms at the time.

Studying faith-healing empirically is therefore not a straightforward venture. A research design which poses a simple yes or no question – 'did it work?' – is bound to represent many prayers for healing as having failed. The argument here is that a much broader research design is required, and answers to prayer must be sought for on a much more subtle, complex, and long-term canvas of life experience, but one that does not, however, foreclose the possibility of divinely aided healing.

While some claims of healing have been shown to be exaggerated, a simple observation does seem to hold true: healings do increase when we pray for them (Parker 1993; Parker and Lawrence 1996). Nevertheless, it is remarkably difficult to find any way to predict when healing might occur. Some who have been recipients of faith-healing report having great faith for their healing, others report little faith, and some report having no faith. Some report being healed from terminal conditions, others from minor, even trivial ailments. The gospel accounts of healing also show tremendous variety; the only regular pattern is the prevalence of Christ's miraculous healing occurring among the social outcasts, the poor, the marginalised and the despised

(Percy 1998). The meaning of Christ's healings is seen not only in the restoration of physical bodies, but also in the meeting of spiritual and social needs. Therefore the critical feature of healing ministries today needs to be whether suffering people are re-woven into relationship with God and the community. This must not be dependent upon the reversal of physical symptoms, lest we make God's acceptance through Christ appear to be conditional upon being 'well'.

While accepting that healings do sometimes occur in various ways, it is clear that healings can also fail to occur, at least in the way hoped and prayed for. How this mystery is handled is the crux upon which helpful or unhelpful outcomes from the practice of Christian healing turns. Recent publications have described 'failed healings' where those suffering are blamed for their lack of healing ('you didn't have enough faith'; 'there must be sin in your life'). People who are not healed publicly at the hands of a faith healer pose a threat to a narrowly conceived healing ministry which has to prove itself with regular concrete successes. Charismatic healers, feeling this pressure to 'succeed', can succumb to the familiar tendency to blame victims for their suffering. By blaming victims, we uphold a view of a 'just world' where people get what they deserve (good or bad). This cheap solution only does further damage to those already suffering.

These lessons are for traditional as well as charismatic churches. Far from being marginal to church life, the ministry of healing is becoming a normal feature in many churches. A recent Church of England (2000) report, *A Time to Heal*, describes a large number of recommendations (including guidelines for good practice) designed to enable every parish church to become a safe place where people can come to receive prayer for healing. It is normal for people who are sick to feel guilty about being sick: 'What did I do to deserve this? Am I being punished?' Helpful healing ministries address this directly, and through balanced teaching enable people to take responsibility for seeking healing through every possible means, medical, spiritual, social, and psychological, while removing from them the burden of blame and failure.

A wider view of healing – that both uncovers the roots of our illnesses and psychological pain in our condition of alienation from God and from our fellow human beings, and seeks for healing in all facets of our being – allows for both the grace of physical and psychological healing, *and* the ongoing reality of suffering. The gospels juxtapose these realities: the multitudes are healed, but the Son of God is tortured. The first disciples had the gift of healing others, but many of them faced early, violent deaths. A ministry of healing that cares for the sick, praying for their healing, while remaining alongside those who continue to suffer, is a realistic way forward when living in a world that is on its way to being healed, but is not there yet.

SUMMARY OF KEY THEMES

- Reductionist and non-reductionist accounts of charismatic religion.
- Attitudes to the Bible and spiritual gifts.
- Speaking in tongues as meaningful but non-syntactical.
- Different sorts of glossolalia.
- Healing as a holistic process.

- Miraculous healings and alternative explanations.
- Psychological and physical dimensions of being 'healed'.

QUESTIONS TO CONSIDER

- What do you think about speaking in, and interpreting, tongues?
- Could there be a place for it in your church? If not, why not?
- In what ways does the Holy Spirit work through your liturgy and worship?
- What can you learn from the success of Pentecostal and charismatic forms of Christianity? Why are they psychologically attractive?
- How are charismatic practices such as tongues and healing open to abuse?
- In what ways does your ministry bring healing to people?

Further reading

Worship and ritual

Beit-Hallahmi, B. and Argyle, M. (1997) *The Psychology of Religious Behaviour, Belief and Experience*, London: Routledge, pp. 49–62.
Capps, D. and Browning, D. (eds) (1983) *Life Cycle Theory and Pastoral Care*, Philadelphia: Fortress Press.
Grainger, R. (1988) *The Message of the Rite: The Significance of Christian Rites of Passage*, Cambridge: Lutterworth Press.
Grainger, R. (1994) *The Ritual Image: The Phenomenology of Liturgical Experience*, London: Avon Books.
Lee, R. S. (1955) *Psychology and Worship*, London: SCM Press.
Shorter, B. (1996) *Susceptible to the Sacred: The Psychological Experience of Ritual*, London: Routledge.
van Gennep, A. (1977) *The Rites of Passage*, London: Routledge.

Confession and forgiveness

Enright, R. D. and North, J. (eds) (1988) *Exploring Forgiveness*, Madison WI: University of Wisconsin Press.
Parker, R. (1993) *Forgiveness is Healing*, London: Daybreak.
Smedes, L. (1988) *Forgive and Forget: Healing the Hurts We Don't Deserve*, London: Triangle.
Watts, F. and Williams, M. (1988) *The Psychology of Religious Knowing*, Cambridge: Cambridge University Press.

Charismatic worship and spiritual gifts

Elliot, C. (1995) *Memory and Salvation*, London: Darton, Longman and Todd.
Malony, H. N. and Lovekin, A. A. (1985) *Glossolalia: Behavioural Sciences Perspectives on Speaking in Tongues*, Oxford: Oxford University Press.
Martin, D. and Mullen, P. (1984) *Strange Gifts? A Guide to Charismatic Renewal*, Oxford: Blackwell.
Middlemiss, D. (1996) *Interpreting Charismatic Experience*, London: SCM Press.
Smail, T., Walker, A. and Wright, N. (1995) *Charismatic Renewal*, London: SCM Press.

3   Diversity among Christians

QUESTIONS FOR MINISTRY

- Why can't Christians get along with each other?
- Why do so many disagree about what is the best form of religious belief, liturgy, or practice?
- What motivates people to go to church? What do they hope to get out of it?
- Are some sorts of religious belief better than others?
- How useful are personality tests like the Myers-Briggs indicator?

Think shape not size: different dimensions of being religious

For anyone with experience of Christian ministry, it is obvious that there can be considerable variety in the ways people engage with religion. One way this is seen is in the diverse approaches to worship, theology and church among Christians of different denominations. However, the differences in religious approach between people within the same denomination, even the same church, may be just as significant. In contrast to the distinguishing marks of variety between denominations, these individual differences can be harder to put words to. For this task, the language of psychology, especially its ways of understanding personality, can be helpful.

Faith is conceived as something we share, a common feature that marks our likemindedness with each other. In many ways church practices echo this: creeds, corporate prayer, and public rituals imply we enjoy a united, uniform perspective. This can create the illusion that conformity in a more general sense is a desirable and necessary quality for faith. There is a temptation for Christians to behave as if personal differences do not, or should not, exist. How can authentic, personal faith flourish under these standardised conditions? Nurturing a person's spiritual life may depend on connecting the shared faith tradition with the distinctiveness of his or her

Box 3.1 Five dimensions of being religious

1 **Intellectual**
what a person *knows about* religion (information and understanding).
2 **Experiential**
whether a person *has religious experiences* of some kind (e.g. a 'born again' experience, or a mystical experience).
3 **Ideological**
what kind of *beliefs* a person has (e.g. conservative/liberal).
4 **Ritualistic**
what religious *practices* the person observes.
5 **Consequences**
how religion seems to guide a person's actual *behaviour*.

personal character. To ignore this diversity and individuality may be to fail to nourish the spiritual well-being of those in our care.

Poorly understood differences between people often become a source of conflict. Conflict and intolerance within the church can be especially difficult to manage. The pastoral responsibility to handle conflict between church members (including those in leadership) may be eased if differences are seen in terms of the psychological variety that occurs in any group of people. Many unnecessary conflicts might be avoided by accepting that people see and do things differently (including the way they practise their faith) as a function of their personality profile.

What kind of relationship should personality and faith have? The way personal differences can seem to shape our religious perceptions can work for us and our faith, or against us. In some cases, when religious style is able to accommodate the contours of individual character, this can be a positive foundation for an authentic personal spirituality. In other cases however there is a danger that a person's approach to faith can be imprisoned by faults in their personality. For example, unrecognised psychological needs or anxieties may in effect dictate the way faith *has* to be pursued for that person. Every pastoral encounter demands some attention to this personality–faith relationship, and a discerning response to it. Psychological frameworks can improve our ability to notice ways in which personal characteristics add to faith, and other ways in which they can disable it.

Differences between Christians are often attributed to crude quantitative variations – 'she's more religious than he is'. However there are different dimensions of being religious, such that faith for each person has its own kind of shape rather than merely an overall 'size'. Instead of asking 'How religious is she?', we should be asking 'How is she religious?'. Charles Glock and Rodney Stark (1965) suggested that there were five important dimensions to consider (see Box 3.1). These provide a first step in characterising the variety that is common among any group of Christians. There is clearly much on which we can differ from one another.

These dimensions of being religious help to point out the complexity of the whole picture – every single person has a different profile of light and darker shading on each dimension. To understand ourselves, and others, it may be helpful to reflect on how faith features in each dimension. Certainly, it is not helpful to restrict the character of our faith to any one of these dimensions alone. However, our personal characteristics may lead to an emphasis being placed on one criterion more than the others and can lead to self-justification that this is the definitive sign of faith. It can be helpful to check our intolerances against this list of dimensions. Redescribing what offends us about another's way of being religious in more psychological categories (intellectual, emotional, attitudinal, or behavioural differences) can help us to be more rational and tolerant, and as we compare ourselves across all five dimensions we may discover we have more in common than we realised.

SUMMARY OF KEY THEMES

- How a shared faith can mask personal diversity.
- The importance of personal differences in faith for spiritual authenticity.
- Avoiding intolerance by conceptualising variety in terms of 'personality' rather than 'religious' differences.
- Five dimensions of how people are religious: intellectual, experiential, ideological, ritualistic, consequences.

QUESTIONS TO CONSIDER

- Should differences be encouraged within the church?
- How can sharing a common tradition allow personal faith to flourish?
- Why do some Christians seem so different from me? Are they 'true' Christians?
- Can personality factors shed light on conflict and tolerance within my church?

Religious styles and motivations

Different personal motivations are reflected in the ways people are religious. People want and get different things from religious commitments, but pursuing different priorities can easily bring us into conflict with one another. Some kinds of motivation seem better than others for supporting the spiritual life and Christian behaviour. Pastoral practice can use information about differing religious motivations in various ways: to inform conflict resolution and tolerance, to offer faith in ways that appeal to a range of personal motivations, and to guide efforts to challenge and change people's motivations when appropriate.

The 'psychological motivation' approach to understanding religious diversity is supported by a strong body of empirical research, initiated by the work of G. W. Allport (1950). His model of personality identified three core attributes of the 'mature' personality:

Table 3.1 Characteristics of extrinsic and intrinsic religious motivations

Extrinsics	*Intrinsics*
More prejudiced attitudes (e.g. racist)	Less prejudiced attitudes
Authoritarian tendencies (e.g. abuse of power)	Non-authoritarian
Poorer than average mental health	Better than average mental health
Deviant or criminal behaviour similar to secular	More likely to obey moral code
Interest in charity similar to secular	Report more charitable acts

1   Interest in ideals and values beyond immediate physical needs.
2   Ability to objectify oneself, to see self from other's perspective and laugh at oneself.
3   Possession of some unifying philosophy of life, though it need not be religious, articulated in words, or entirely complete.

These core attributes have a marked resonance with the perspective generally associated with being 'religious'. Yet it is clear that many who profess to be religious have far from ideal or mature personalities. Indeed, research comparing church-goers and non-believers found certain undesirable personality features, such as racism, were especially prevalent among religious people. There was a need to distinguish between different ways of being religious – the ways that perhaps did contribute to personality integration, and the ways that did not.

Extrinsic and intrinsic motivations

Further research identified the key difference. Allport and Ross (1967) measured the differing contributions of extrinsic and intrinsic motivations to a person's religious commitment. Extrinsic motivations included the appeal of the external, social opportunities church-going offers, such as the chance to make friends or to acquire some status in the community. In contrast, intrinsic motivations included the appeal of religious truths in their own right and the meaning this lent to the person's sense of purpose in life. There might not be any outward differences between extrinsics and intrinsics; for example both might be regularly involved in church activities. However, identifying this simple underlying difference – motivational emphasis – helps to make sense of anomalies and conflicts within religious groups.

Allport and Ross's key finding was that, when compared to non-religious people, church-goers with mainly extrinsic motivations did have personality traits at odds with psychological and spiritual well-being. However, those of an intrinsic bent enjoyed the better-than-average personal integration Allport had initially expected to find, as can be seen in Table 3.1.

Looking at these personal attributes from a Christian perspective, it is clear that being mainly intrinsically motivated is the preferable way for people to be religious. Yet research suggests relatively few people enjoy a deep faith they can live by and live for. In fact, at least 60 per cent of most congregations are mainly extrinsically oriented. This suggests that many Christians are religious in ways that are both psychologically and spiritually undesirable.

Pastoral practice can make constructive use of this intrinsic/extrinsic distinction however. It encourages us to consider the balance of psychological motivations each person brings to their faith, and to identify those with a predominately extrinsic style. This sector of the congregation represent those with a basic level of need in terms of sensitive pastoral guidance and targeted Christian nurture. People whose faith tends to be motivated by extrinsic factors need to have that channelled appropriately and need to be encouraged to complement this with a measure of intrinsic motivation too.

The extrinsic/intrinsic motivation approach to religious variety helps to pinpoint the negative personality features that can cluster together in certain kinds of religious people. Authoritarian and prejudiced attitudes and behaviours cannot be accommodated in the light of the Gospel, and yet the church may unwittingly serve as a haven for people (both laity and leaders) with these tendencies. To remedy this, ministry needs to amplify the Christian position on issues of prejudice and social responsibility. As this is likely to prompt some people to recognise a need to turn away from their previous convictions and habits as 'unchristian', ministry will need to provide good ongoing support for this process of personal change. It may also be wise to avoid a situation where extrinsically loaded features come to define the character of church life. One might consider auditing the extent to which the social programme (church trips, lunches, concerts, committee meetings, and so on) overshadows the programme for worship, prayer and study for spiritual growth.

I DON'T KNOW WHETHER YOUNG SMITHSON IS EXTRINSICALLY MOTIVATED OR JUST LETTING HIS HAIR DOWN!!

Quest motivation

Recent research has proposed a third dimension of motivation: 'quest' motivation (Batson *et al.* 1993), though not everyone agrees on the usefulness of this extra dimension. Quest refers to being driven by a desire to search, to discover more (whereas intrinsic motivation sees faith as an end in itself, and extrinsic sees it as a means to a self-serving end). Proposing a third kind of motivation tries to differentiate more precisely the kind of psychological profile associated with an authentic and enriching way of being religious. It challenges the view that intrinsic motivation is the benchmark of a genuinely religious psychological profile.

Closer study of intrinsically motivated religious people suggested that in many cases their admirable attitudes (compared with the extrinsically religious) were not necessarily lived out in their behaviour. Had the simple self-reporting intrinsic–extrinsic measure misconstrued these people as genuinely religious when in fact they were self-deceiving hypocrites? Batson *et al.* (1993) identified quest motivation as an alternative way of being religious in which high standards of compassion were met in both attitudes *and* behaviour. This pattern was associated with other distinguishing features too. For example, predominately quest-motivated people are more likely to treat religious material in a creative, open way. Their religious style is more cognitively complex, and as the quest classification suggests, this way of being religious sees faith as an ongoing process of searching for meaning at ever greater depths. In contrast, intrinsics are faithful to orthodoxy, preferring a simpler conservative style – motivated to reach closure. They live by the truth they have found, while 'questers' are motivated by the endless search that faith represents to them. This further differentiation of how people approach being 'religious' captures a difference that many in ministry can easily recognise in members of their congregation.

Religious styles and religious development are closely intertwined. For example, it might sometimes be more accurate to regard quest (and all the features that cluster around it) as a stage or phase in religious development rather than as a fixed 'style'. (The possibility of regarding extrinsic motivation as a developmental stage from which a person might progress has also been suggested.) It might sometimes also be useful to consider how the developmental experiences of childhood have led an individual to a particular religious style. For example, a lack of security in childhood might be reflected in an intrinsic style in which authority and tradition are faithfully upheld.

Pastoral implications

Motivational style and pastoral needs go hand in hand. Using the E/I/Q distinctions Batson *et al.* (1993) suggest ways that people can be imprisoned or liberated depending on their particular religious approach, as can be seen in Table 3.2.

This classification of religious psychological profiles develops the idea that there are better and worse ways a person might be religious – both in terms of initial motivations and social consequences. But still this does not offer a clear recipe for the

Table 3.2 Imprisoning and liberating features of E, I and Q motivations (adapted from Batson *et al.* 1993)

	Imprisoning features	*Liberating features*
Extrinsics	Shallow grasp of religious ideas means they are trapped by belief set, they use it but are not inspired by it.	Faith is closely linked to personal needs (though some may be dubious).
Intrinsics	Intense dependence on beliefs/tradition may obstruct ability to depend on God. Trapped by inflexibility, change is frightening.	Strong faith to live by confers a kind of personal freedom: freed from anxieties about death, doubt, angst. Also from self destructive behaviours (e.g. drug abuse).
Questers	Can be trapped by existential doubt and angst, endlessly unsatisfied and uncertain. Faith is never a safe space.	Faith is free to explore and develop.

psychology of an ideal Christian type. The relative merits of I/Q seem to involve some trade-off between faithful orthodoxy and good works. Although it may be difficult to judge which way is really 'best', these distinctions at least help to identify some of the key features it may be prudent to monitor in planning the nurture of different people in any Christian group.

These ways of differentiating three key religious styles should be treated as a helpful, but rather rough-and-ready kind of tool. Beyond describing the cluster of features each style has, it is not always clear what these distinctions may be tapping into. The Christian minister should be aware that other situational influences may make an important contribution. For example, extrinsic religious motivation is particularly associated with lower levels of education and class. Ministry may need to judge when it is called to tackle these inequalities as a first step, rather than urging people simply to rethink their motivations.

In every church, diversity exists beneath the veneer of surface uniformity. The quest dimension especially seems to make a case for allowing a personal way of being religious, that may to some extent jar with the shared tradition. The fact that many different sets of motivations bring people to church helps to clarify why effective ministry to all often seems such an impossible goal. One way of meeting this challenge might be to ensure the church offers a balanced package of different features attractive to different motivational mind-sets – a blend of social rewards (extrinsics), opportunities that indulge the need to preserve the central significance of the faith tradition (intrinsics), and contexts in which searching and questioning are valued too (questers).

Balance is important across the congregation (not only within the individual's motivational orientation). Each of the profiles (E/I/Q) can be viewed as having its own particular strengths and weaknesses as a way of being religious (thus avoiding being too judgemental about which way is 'the best'). In this sense each style offers the group something the other styles lack. Extrinsics will often make important contributions to the fabric of church life. Intrinsics can be relied on to maintain the tradition and draw attention to its authority. The questers may offer a voice of critical challenge. While there are particular features (especially of extrinsics) that have little place in a Christian setting, a general balance between styles within the body of the church seems desirable. Aiming for this balance as a way of ministering to the diversity of entrenched styles in the adult congregation is also a good model for Christian formation among the young or new enquirers. Deliberately holding such a balance might help to develop a more rounded religious style, and to reduce the probability of conflicts between people with opposing religious motivations.

SUMMARY OF KEY THEMES

- How different ways of being religious can result from different motivations.
- Extrinsic, Intrinsic, and Quest motivations.
- The strengths and weaknesses of each of these profiles.

QUESTIONS TO CONSIDER

- Which style, E, I or Q, do you most identify with?
- What steps might you take to tackle the 'problem' of the extrinsic majority in a congregation?
- How far do the E/I/Q distinctions illuminate nuances of particular Christians you have encountered?
- How much do they caricature differences?

Personality profiling and faith

Psychologists still have more questions than answers about personality. There are many different theories, numerous conceptual problems, and yet also a range of apparently definitive tests (such as the Myers-Briggs Type Indicator discussed below). These tools can be helpful ways to make sense of the incredible variability between the people we relate to. However, the different theories and tests do not share equivalent status among professional psychologists. Ministers need to bear the following things in mind as they choose ways to think psychologically about diversity among Christians.

There are at least five approaches to personality, each with a host of attendant theories and tests. For example, some argue that personality is a question of distinct 'types', others say it is made up of common 'traits' that differ in how intensely these are expressed in different people. Whatever short cut we use, it helps to remember that it will illuminate only one view of the bigger picture. Recognising the limitations of any one approach can be important for psychological and theological reasons. Some approaches imply that personality is more of a fixed set of features than others. As personal transformation is at the heart of the Christian process, it would be strange to become too closely tied into an approach that took this view. Psychologists also differ on how far personality is integral to the person or socially constructed through our experiences. Christians who are tempted to buy into theories and tests that disregard social influences could inadvertently use this to shield themselves from realising when personality patterns are in fact connected to social injustices such as racial or sexual inequalities.

Personality profiles help to describe features that cluster together – introversion, extraversion, and so on. This can tell us things to expect in the relationship between personality and behaviour, but it is hard to say much about the rules that govern the relationship – the direction of cause and effect. Does my behaviour shape my personality, or vice versa? As people explore ways in which their faith relates to their personality, it is important to make clear that this relationship does not unyieldingly dictate how their faith has to be.

Some psychologists question whether we have 'a' personality at all. We often have different roles that bring out different personalities. At one moment we may be the calm, authoritative leader of our flock, and the next an emotional, clueless parent unable to handle a rebellious teenager. Bruce Reed (1978) makes the point that, as people enter worship, their everyday pattern of relating often changes, as control and independence are replaced by a kind of regression to dependence and naivety (see also the section on dependence in Chapter 4). So, when Christians look to personality theories and tests, who are they discovering? Can tests fathom a 'real self' among our many roles? The question of what constitutes my authentic self may be best dealt with using Christian discourse rather than this or that personality test; my real self being the person God has created me to become. Psychological help to understand the idiosyncrasies of personality and faith needs to be seen against the bigger theological picture too.

In choosing a personality test to demonstrate the variety among supposedly like-minded Christians, it is important to realise that the theoretical basis of many tests has a different emphasis from a Christian understanding of a person. Several popular tests, such as Hans Eysenck's Personality Inventory (the EPI or EPQ), have been developed using hospitalised samples on the basis of deviant or pathological forms of personality. The EPQ is a popular choice in psychology of religion research, and is a well-supported psychometric measure of personality, lending itself to comparisons with other psychometrically measured variables (e.g. IQ, mental health). A Christian understanding of the person, however, focuses on a movement in personality to become more like Jesus, rather than toward a non-pathological statistical norm. Furthermore, although the EPQ is a useful tool for research, key personality dimensions within it, such as Psychoticism, do not lend themselves to easy interpretation by the layman.

Other tests, such as the Enneagram, state things in a way that readily amplifies the more interpretative, quasi-religious, style of reading between the lines for meaning. However, users of this should be aware that its way of picturing personality lacks any psychological support for its reliability as a scientific measure – it has not been tested against other measures or validated by any external tests (see Innes 1996).

The Myers-Briggs Personality Indicator (discussed below) is far from perfect, yet it manages to combine a non-pathological basis with a reasonable amount of evidence for its validity and an ability to speak in a language that is user-friendly for many

Christians. As a result, the practical applications of this tool to Christian ministry are already well developed. Also important, because of its popularity in British churches especially, there is already a body of criticism to inform ministry about its misuse too.

SUMMARY OF KEY THEMES

- The danger of being satisifed with just one approach to personality.
- The different concerns for Christians raised by different approaches.
- Striking a balance between tools that are scientifically robust and those that are 'interpretative' and popular.

QUESTIONS TO CONSIDER

- Have you been aware of someone whose personality seemed to change because of their faith?
- What have you learned about yourself from psychological tests? In what ways was this useful to your Christian life?
- When you pray, what part of your personality is most engaged? Your 'ideal self'? Your 'real self'?

Myers-Briggs personality types and spiritual styles

The importance of integrating different strands of our personality lies at the heart of Jungian psychology. This is known as the 'individuation' process. Integrating personality and spirituality is a key part of this process, which enables both personal and spiritual life to flourish and mature.

Greater self-awareness is a key to individuation, since this makes possible a creative integration of both conscious and unconscious personal characteristics, and of the acceptable public 'persona' and the darker 'shadow' side of ourselves. Without this recognition and integration of who we really are as individuals, our personality is potentially unstable and our development remains unfinished. The way a person is religious should be consonant with their personal authenticity realised so far in personality development. Indeed, a spirituality that does not attend to (or perhaps emerge from) the contours of individual personality will itself be in danger of being inauthentic and dissonant. Individual religious variety is depicted in Jungian psychology as the door to spiritual maturity.

So, for Jung there should be as many ways of being religious as there are people. However, as he studied the human psyche, and the interplay of personal and spiritual matters, Jung observed a set of familiar patterns: different personality types identified by their characteristic ways of functioning (e.g. extrovertedly or introvertedly). This provides a heuristic short cut for recognising the strands of individual differences in ourselves and other people. The Myers-Briggs Type Indicator is a selective application and interpretation of Jung's basic personality typology and his understanding of how the functions operate.

The MBTI personality model

The Myers-Briggs Type Indicator (MBTI) is based on a selective application and interpretation of Jung's basic personality typology and his understanding of how the functions operate. The MBTI has become a popular tool for recognising and responding to individual diversity in the workplace, education and in interpersonal relationships. In church contexts too, it has been useful both as a means of promoting individual self-awareness and as a tool that can shed light on diversity within a specific group of people, such as in a team ministry context.

The basic features of the different aspects that contribute to a person's type (outlined below) make clear the distinctive strengths or preferences we can have in the way we live our lives, process information, and make decisions. These personal nuances also suggest characteristic shapes for our religious lives – the way we pray or worship or express love for our neighbours.

MBTI: basic features

Each person's type is made up of four preferred aspects of personality. As can be seen in Table 3.3, each aspect is made up of two possible functions, and these functions can be combined in sixteen different ways, making sixteen possible personality patterns or types in all. Type is assessed through forced-choice questionnaire responses that ask people to identify their habitual or preferred mode of operating in various everyday circumstances. These questions have been designed to address each of the four aspects of personality. For example, some questions will address the aspect of orientation to determine whether the person is habitually more introvert or extrovert. Type is referred to by a four-letter pattern such as ESTJ (Extrovert, Sensing, Thinking, Judgement) or INFP (Introvert, iNtuition, Feeling, Perception). Two of the four aspects of personality are processes, one aspect describes the person's orientation and one describes his or her attitude. So, for example, a person who is an ENFP has Intuition as her preferred perception process, Feeling as her preferred judging process, an Extrovert orientation, and a general attitude of Perception.

Dominant function, auxiliary function and inferior function

The interplay between functions (as proposed by Jungian theory) can reveal as much about our differences from one another as the preferred functions themselves.

Each of the four process options (Sensing, Intuition, Thinking and Feeling) is appropriate to a different sort of situation: sometimes Sensing is called for, in other moments Intuition will be invaluable. However, we each develop a 'dominant function', and this is the mode in which we function especially well. Only processes can be dominant functions; in our example, a person who is ENFP will have a dominant function of either Intuition or Feeling depending on which score was highest on the test.

Our preferred orientation modulates how and where the dominant function is used. If someone is generally Extrovert, her dominant process will be used for

Table 3.3 Summary of characteristics for MBTI functions (adapted from Briggs Myers 1976)

---

*preferred **PERCEPTION** process (habitual way of gathering and processing information)*

Sensing	iNtuition
facts, multi sensory	abstract, symbol
real, proved, known	inspiration, hunch, possibilities
'eyes tell mind'	'mind tells eyes'

---

*preferred **JUDGING** process (habitual way of making decisions)*

Thinking	Feeling
logical analysis	personal consequences
issues rather than feelings	principles may be overlooked
justice, what's fair	emphasis on sympathy
others' feelings may get hurt	

---

*preferred **ORIENTATION** (habitual reference point for preferred processes, as above)*

Extrovert	Introvert
outer world, public, social	inner world, privacy
groups are energising	solitude is refreshing

---

*preferred **ATTITUDE** (habitual general attitude to tasks in external world)*

Judgment	Perception
ordered, planned	open, flexible,
like closure, lists welcomed	further information, other possibilities
favours coming to clear decisions	final decisions postponed

---

situations in the outer, real world. Howeve,r someone who is more Introvert will use their dominant function in dealings with their more highly-prized inner life.

To compensate for this diversion of the dominant function to either the real world (if Extrovert) or the inner life (if Introvert), there is a distinctive patterning of habitual responses in the less preferred location (inner life/public world). The individual's 'auxiliary function' fulfils this compensatory role. This arrangement means that people employ merely their 'second best' (auxiliary) process to operate in the orientation that appeals less to them. If our ENFP example has Intuition as her dominant function, then her auxiliary function is Feeling.

This means that Introverts use merely their 'second best' process (auxiliary function) when dealing with the outer, social world, putting them at an inevitable disadvantage in such dealings. On the other hand, Extroverts will use their 'second best' process (auxiliary function) for their inner life, setting them at a disadvantage in that realm. This differential allocation of dominant and auxiliary functions among Introverts and Extroverts can have interesting interpersonal implications. The Extrovert can play her strongest suit in the social world, so she can find Introvert people a bit slow on the uptake, withdrawn and difficult to get to know. But Introverts can find Extroverts equally bewildering because they seem, in comparison to their own strengths, 'all on the outside', shallow – limited in their approach to deep and inward matters. This distinctive use of respective strengths offers a way of transcending the temptation to be judgemental about others' weaknesses, not least as these differences appear as divergent approaches to religious life.

The 'inferior function' is the process that is especially weak and underdeveloped. This will be the exact opposite of the dominant function, so in our example, if the ENFP's dominant function is Intuition, then her inferior function must be Sensing. Being aware of the inferior function can be vital; it operates like an Achilles' heel and so is the area in which we are more likely to mess things up. Especially under stress people may find themselves locked into trying to operate using their primitive inferior function, and cut off from their developed dominant function. Ministers will be familiar with crisis situations where the person seems to be compounding their problems by approaching them in a chaotic way. Pastoral care can help them to relocate whatever their 'strong suit' (dominant function) might be – normally the very opposite of the approach they have been hopelessly pursuing!

Religious style and the personality functions

The Jungian basis of the MBTI offers scope for interpreting personality differences in terms of their implications for diversity of religious styles. Indeed, this seems a good use of the tool given Jung's insistence that individuation depended on an authentic integration of personal and spiritual material.

Robert Repicky (1988) provides an analysis of the different religious styles that might be logically associated with each of the four possible dominant functions: Intuition, Sensation, Thinking, and Feeling. Additionally, he outlines further nuances of religious variation within each of these types, depending on whether the dominant function is accompanied by an extroverted or introverted orientation.

Repicky (see Table 3.4) sets out how spiritual gifts are often differently distributed among different personality types. By the same token, knowing our personality type can alert us to our susceptibility to particular spiritual weaknesses or difficulties. This can be either because the religious life has become gripped by processes characteristic of our inferior function, or because inflation of the dominant function has occurred. (Inflation refers to an unchecked confidence in the use of the dominant function, at the expense of other processes needed to balance its effects.) The integration of the whole picture of personality functioning (dominant, auxiliary and inferior) is the ultimate key to a fulfilling religious life.

Table 3.4 Religious styles of different personality types (adapted from Repicky 1988)

Dominant INTUITION   *Gift of 'wisdom'*

INTUITION WITH INTROVERSION

- Attracted to anything that fosters a sense of the presence of God, such as contemplative prayer. May have strong prophetic qualities.
- Inferior function = extroverted sensation: this may lead to a struggle to integrate demands of real situations in their spiritual perspective. For example, a tendency to overlook practical details of current reality, or find such details overwhelm and disable 'spiritual gifts'.

INTUITION WITH EXTROVERSION

- Inclined towards outward prayer, service to others, meditation that seeks to illuminate course of future action or direction; wisdom with a practical emphasis.
- Inflated dominant function can tempt construing one's own gifts and role in God-like terms.
- Inferior function = introverted sensation: so, predisposed to a neurotic obsession with activity/detail leading to exhaustion.

Dominant SENSATION   *Gifted in simplicity of life and life-style*

SENSATION WITH INTROVERSION

- Prayer with icons or images, sensitivity to others and their specific situations. A strong sense of carefulness or prudence in all things.
- Inferior function = extrovert intuition: this can distort this spiritual quality into prudishness and rigid attachment to the 'simple way'.

SENSATION WITH EXTROVERSION

- Sensual experience, for example, through beauty of nature or access to God found in participation in sacrament and liturgy.
- Inflated dominant function can predispose towards superstitious practice.

Dominant THINKING   *Gifted in reason and knowledge*

THINKING WITH INTROVERSION

- Meditation on mysteries of faith, engaged by the intellectual complexity of faith; preference for theological routes to religious knowing.
- Inferior function = feeling: this means irrational emotions can usurp thinking under stress; tendency to be hemmed in by a simplistic emotional reaction or view.

THINKING WITH EXTROVERSION

- Engaged by religious teaching, traditional and vocal prayer; gifted in organisation of community life. Faith revolves round social justice, ethics and moral behaviour.
- Inflated dominant function can create rigid compulsion, for example to 'say the office'. Anything (especially disorganisation or unplanned situation) which prevents this can arouse inferior feeling function, leading to primitive expressions of emotion (e.g. irrational anger, guilt).

---

continued on next page

Table 3.4 Religious styles of different personality types (cont.)

Dominant FEELING   *Gifted in relations with others*

FEELING WITH INTROVERSION

• Nurturing an intimate relationship with God. A mystic style, need for personal spiritual solitude. Yet, has a gift of seeming unusually 'present' with other people.

• Inferior function = thinking: therefore susceptible to being naive. Mystical, joyous experience can be at the expense of a more balanced engagement with the complexities and difficulties of faith.

FEELING WITH EXTROVERSION

• Intercessory prayer. attuned to discernment, naturally given to perceiving the core and value of others' situations.

• Inferior function = thinking: use of discernment can be distorted into manipulative treatment of others.

Cautions about the MBTI

The MBTI offers a user-friendly way of pinpointing personal differences, and lends itself to interesting explanations of differences in religious styles. It enjoys a widespread popularity in churches and many seminaries, especially in the UK. This enthusiasm needs careful monitoring since its insights represent such a small part of psychology's overall contribution: knowing what type you are cannot explain everything! To ensure good practice, church leaders can observe the following guidelines:

• *Beware of over-simplification*
  MBTI is a secular tool that simplifies Jung's much richer original theory concerning the complex process of individuation as different aspects of personality are integrated. Jung viewed this process as necessarily spiritual, the crucible for personal and religious interplay. It is important to guard against all this being reduced to an exercise in assigning 'letter strings' to people (he's ESTJ, I'm INFP, and so on), and exploit its potential as a starting point for combined personal and spiritual insight. Even more simplified and ready-to-use versions of Myers Briggs/Jungian typology are also available (e.g. Keirsey and Bates 1978).

• *Don't let your MBTI be an excuse not to change*
  The 'letter string' mentality tends to operate as a licence: 'that's just how I am'. It is important to respect one another's differences, and having a way to recognise these can help. However, the heart of both Jungian and Christian thought points to personal transformation. Rather than a licence, our personality types suggest our personal curriculum for growth by setting out the mixed skills and tools we have and by implication the work to be done to balance out our personality portfolio. Good pastoral practice means viewing the MBTI as a basis for spiritual guidance and growth.

• *Be sensitive to similarities as well as differences*
  The MBTI uses benign language, but may too easily 'pigeonhole' people

nonetheless. Sorting people by 'type' can be divisive, and detracts from ways in which people may be similar (e.g. the mildly extroverted and the mildly introverted). There is often enough division in our churches; we should be cautious about promoting more.

- *Distinguish between 'everyday' and 'spiritual' selves*
  Which 'self' is being assessed by the MBTI? Questions in the MBTI refer to everyday, often public, scenarios which may not best represent the layer of self we reserve for the intimate spiritual relationship with God. Trying to make sense of our spiritual needs or habits on the basis of a relatively ordinary version of ourselves may be misguided. Caution is needed in view of the test's ordinariness and rather crude measurements.
- *The MBTI cannot deliver scientific truths*
  The MBTI and Jungian theory in general lie on the fringes of mainstream psychology. Their claims are not easily substantiated. People should be discouraged from assuming their type is an objective scientific truth.
- *Complement the MBTI with a broader theology*
  The MBTI should be set against the broader horizon of Christian theology in which personal transformation is always possible. Sometimes differences between people may have important ethical messages for Christian action (e.g. the question of whether personality type is influenced by education, sex, class or race).

The value of the MBTI

To end on a positive note, there are a variety of ways in which this personality type approach can genuinely help ministry grapple with the challenge of diversity among Christians.

- *A useful short cut for spiritual and organisational church life*
  Personality types make it easier to recognise patterns in ourselves and others. This can also illuminate differences in religious approaches and preferences, strengths and weaknesses. Typology can free us from casting the different ways we prefer to picture God, pray or preach as inevitably theological or ecclesiological disagreements. It can also help in understanding diversity in other forms of church social life – personal styles of learning, making decisions or communicating. Many a church conflict (e.g. in team ministry, or the church council) may be less a matter of religious rights or wrongs and more a matter of clashing personality styles.
- *Sin and inferior function*
  People are not uniform victims of the circumstances life throws up; it is important to recognise the contribution our personality styles make to overcoming or succumbing to impoverished standards of behaviour. Asking how someone's inferior function played a part in their human failings can help to identify broader patterns of weakness in need of redemption, and where grace is especially needed to resist temptation.

- *Reconciliation*

  The inferior function is characterised as having both destructive and healing (balancing, integrating) potential, depending on the use to which it is put. This can be a helpful way of responding to sinful patterns of behaviour, in seeking, for example, ways of channelling strongly negative tendencies (e.g. irrational anger) in a more constructive, self-controlled manner (e.g. righteous indignation in the service of a just cause).

- *Christian group dynamics*

  A balance of different types will help to ensure the healthy, balanced functioning of any group – individual weaknesses can be compensated for by others' individual strengths. However, groups often attract just one kind of type, unwittingly excluding others. Being the odd one out can be an important, but difficult role in a group. This person can find herself representing the group's inferior function – the things it collectively finds challenging, unpleasant or of less value. Not only can this 'scapegoat' suffer, the group may cease to operate effectively as its collective energy is diverted through its least developed channels. But a 'different other' can be a good thing for a group that is perhaps more aware of its typology dynamics. Personifying the inferior function, he or she can act as a channel to what is normally unconscious – the group's route to a source of creativity and transformation. (See Chapters 11 and 12 for further discussion of group dynamics.)

- *Nurturing a personal faith*

  Identifying type can help to flag up how spiritual life may stagnate or implode. The dominant function can destabilise the balance of the spiritual life if it becomes too influential – leading to inflation. Problems of spiritual disillusionment or fixation might be traced to aspects of personal style taken to an extreme. With reference to what is uncharacteristic for that person's type according to the theory, a direction can be suggested for experimenting with an obviously 'opposite' style of worship, prayer or religious instruction. In cases where the pastoral problem is a feeling of spiritual stagnation, individually tailoring this experimentation might be an effective release and source of new growth (employing the opposite, inferior function as a channel of creativity). Of course, it would be important to establish first of all that the person *has* been pursuing a spiritual style consistent with their type up till now, otherwise this mismatch may be the source of their frustration.

- *Leading collective worship – mission impossible?*

  With at least sixteen varieties of type – each with different personal and spiritual preferences, strengths and weaknesses, and at different stages of awareness of any of this – the task of providing common, yet effective, worship is a tall order. Sharing ministry between different people can help counteract a one-track approach based on the minister's own personality style (which might really appeal only to the one-sixteenth of the congregation who share his style). To encourage people to furnish their faith in an authentically personal way, specially suited nourishment is required at least some of the time. Auditing the range of styles represented in a church service may prove worthwhile. One might ask, for example, whether the images in sermons or hymns, or the approach to teaching, provides something appealing for thinking, feeling, intuitive and sensation types at different points.

'...THE MINISTER'S OWN PERSONALITY STYLE MIGHT REALLY APPEAL ONLY TO THE ONE-SIXTEENTH OF THE CONGREGATION WHO SHARE HIS STYLE'

SUMMARY OF KEY THEMES

- The sixteen different basic MBTI types, which can affect work, leisure, and faith styles.
- The interplay of dominant and auxiliary functions.
- How MBTI profiles can illuminate likely spiritual strengths and weaknesses.
- Reasons to be cautious of MBTI.

QUESTIONS TO CONSIDER

- Which tasks in your ministry appeal to your dominant function?
- Which tasks require that you operate with your inferior function?
- How might you constructively manage the different levels of fulfilment/stress these tasks present you with?
- Do you recognise your own 'spiritual giftedness' in Repicky's analysis of religious style and personality type?
- To what extent does this fit what you consider your personality type to be?

Conclusion

Psychological evidence supports the casual observation that there are many ways of being religious. The three kinds of approach covered in this chapter offer ways of characterising and categorising the confusing array of these differences, not so much as religious differences, but in terms of personality variation.

Psychological insights do not lead to the conclusion that any one way of being religious is inevitably better or healthier than the rest. However, each of the approaches clarifies some of the ways in which a religious approach may be a weak or even destructive basis for genuine faith. In all cases, there seems to be a good case for attending to personality characteristics in any attempt to discern the shape and quality of a person's religious style.

The difficult question of how far personal characteristics should dictate people's religious styles remains. Doubts have been raised about the quality of a faith that is cut off from personal nuances. Equally, it is evident that a person's character can swamp and distort what Christian faith is meant to be about, and prevent faith from having a transforming influence on that person. Tools and heuristics that maximise an awareness of individual differences can make an important contribution to recognising the particular kind of relationship that exists between personality and faith in different cases.

Further reading

Different dimensions of being religious

Batson, C. D., Schoenrade, P. and Ventis, W. L. (1993) *Religion and the Individual: A Social-Psychological Perspective*, Oxford: Oxford University Press.
Malony, H. N. (1995) *The Psychology of Religion for Ministry*, New York: Paulist Press.

Personality profiling

Briggs Myers, I. (1976) *Introduction to Type*, Oxford: Psychologists Press.
Kline, P. (1993) *Personality: The Psychometric View*, London: Routledge.
Leech, K. (ed.) (1996) *Myers-Briggs*, Croydon: The Jubilee Group.

Myers-Briggs personality types and spiritual styles

Innes, R. (1996) *Personality Indicators and the Spiritual Life*, Cambridge: Grove.
Repicky, R. A. (1988) 'Jungian Typology and Christian Spirituality', in R. L. Moore (ed.) *Carl Jung and Christian Spirituality*, New York: Paulist Press, pp. 188–205.

4 Unhealthy religion

QUESTIONS FOR MINISTRY

- Why do some people become religious 'nutters'?
- How can you tell the difference between a healthy faith and a religious 'crutch' that feeds a neurosis?
- What is it about the church and Christianity that is sometimes oppressive to women?
- How can you distinguish between a dangerous Christian cult and a deeply committed, but healthy, Christian group?
- What enables some religious leaders to abuse their followers?
- Why do fundamentalists think in the way they do?

Introduction

The bad fruit of 'unhealthy' religion can be all too apparent: broken lives, financial or sexual scandals, abuse of power. A number of publications in recent years have detailed various kinds of unhealthy religion: the disasters of Jonestown and Waco, the alleged brainwashing tactics of cults, the cognitive control of fundamentalist sects, sexual abuse in the 'alternative' Nine O'Clock service and in mainline denominations, 'heavy shepherding' practices in charismatic house churches. The long-term damage of those affected is hard to estimate. Sometimes it is irreversible. Trust, at its very core, has been shattered.

Instances of harm and abuse in religious contexts do not, of course, demonstrate that religion as a whole is harmful or abusive. They do demonstrate, however, that religion is potentially destructive and that ministers need to be cautious and self-aware in order to ensure that their ministry avoids such dangers. Even in our most 'ordinary' churches, the bad jostles side by side with the good – as a charismatic church leader replied in response to criticism: 'Where there is life, there are mistakes.'

This chapter first addresses the broad question raised in last century by Freud: can religion (and Christianity in particular) be conceived as an unhealthy psychological crutch, or even a collective neurotic obsession? We then assess whether Christianity is unhealthy for women, before asking how good religion can turn bad. Finally, we examine the psychological processes that can contribute to unhealthy religion.

Is Christianity bad for your mental health?

Care must be taken in interpreting studies or reports of unhealthy religion for a number of reasons. These concern the multivariate nature of religion (see Glock 1962), the culture-dependent nature of markers of good mental health, bias in those of us who carry out research (many scholars or reporters who undertake research in this area have a strong prior commitment to religious or to atheistic views), and bias in those of us who read the research (readers feel strongly about this topic as well). We need to beware of clinching our own arguments too readily. An overview that weighs all the evidence, both positive and negative, from a range of studies seems to be the best way forward as we pick our way through the minefield of unhealthy religion.

Is Christianity, as argued by Freud and others, bad for your mental health? Freud developed his theory of personality as a result of many years of clinical work psycho-analysing patients who came to him with personal problems. He proposed that their troubles could be understood in terms of deep-seated, unconscious factors that had taken hold at a much earlier stage in their development. A person's character was a reflection of how key moments and issues in the formative years of their early child-hood had been coped with, particularly how the different 'parts' of the personality system (the ego, the id, and the super-ego) had reacted to the stresses and dynamics of childhood. In Freud's view, many of these had a sexual – or at least sensual – nature, underlining the unavoidably primitive, biological basis of human personal-ity. So, for example, problems in adult personalities could be explained in terms of how satisfactorily individuals had resolved their loving, sexual feelings for their opposite-sex parent, the so-called 'Oedipal crisis' (or in the case of girls, the 'Electra' crisis). These highly charged early emotional situations could develop into various neuroses, which Freud considered were ways of converting the raw pain of the unre-solved crises into, for example, melancholy (depression) or anxiety.

Freud observed how religion, in a number of his clinical cases, seemed to be sup-porting and maintaining neuroses. It seemed that people suffering with obsessive behaviours and feelings were particularly drawn to religious ritual. Freud argued that religious rituals provided such people with a vehicle for exercising their need to repeat the same action again and again, investing it with overwhelming significance in an attempt to assuage endless feelings of anxiety or guilt. Just as Freud viewed neurosis as a deflection away from intolerably painful emotions, he also considered that religion involved a similar, collectively shared defence against mental pain (Loewenthal 1995).

Freud also observed that the different ways people envisaged their God resulted from a transference of the feelings and experiences of their human father onto their image of God. This might take a compensatory form: for instance, God could be the perfect parent who, unlike their human father, would never abandon them. It seems intuitively correct that for children the thought of losing the love and care of a parent is terrifying. So, according to Freudian theory, it is normal for children to internalise the parent to defend against the fear of losing the parent's love and protective presence. This way, the child can always carry around within her the internalised parent. Religion, in Freud's view, was an illusion to defend against the harshness of reality, deflecting awareness from authentic sources of pain such as abandonment or rejection. As religion involves social organisation and consensus, so religion becomes humanity's *collective* defence against intolerable feelings, which need to be faced in their own right, if the personality is going to blossom fully. In brief, Freud believed that religion as a collectively shared neurosis 'spares the individual the task of forming his own neurosis' to defend against the pain of life (Loewenthal 1995: 34).

Decades later, Freud's claim that all religion is a collective neurosis is now widely viewed as overstated. Nevertheless, a germ of truth remains. Christianity *can* be used in the service of neurosis. An unhealthy use of religion *can* deflect a troubled individual away from the authentic source of their distress into a whirlwind of 'religiosity' that defends and reinforces the pathology. Freud, living in a much more patriarchal age, paid primary attention to the projection of the internalised father as the basis for the God-image, whereas more recent studies point to the importance of the mother. There is, however, little doubt that a child's experience of parental care does indeed have an impact on perceptions of God, although these perceptions tend to reinforce, rather than compensate for, early experience.

Detecting whether a person's Christian faith is unhelpfully intertwined with unmet psychological needs requires sensitive pastoral skills. It is only by getting to know a person quite deeply that we can begin to understand the meaning, and perhaps any hidden purpose, of religious behaviours and beliefs. Subtle, but systematic distortions in aspects of a person's religious/theological understanding sometimes flag up areas worth exploring. However, simply to confront a person with their over-reliance (or perhaps neurotic reliance) on religion can be alienating. It may be more fruitful to begin with the assumption that believers have the germ of healthy religion within them; Christian faith can be self-correcting under the right conditions. It is also helpful for us, as ministers or church members, to become aware of the ways in which we have, at times, relied on our own faith in unhealthy ways. Over time, we may have outgrown this, and this process of development may provide a model for others. The role of spiritual direction is, at least in part, to enable the healthy, truth-oriented aspects of a person's faith gradually to take ascendancy over any defensive purposes lurking behind religious faith.

The focus on personality problems disguised as religious faith obscured for Freud the possibility of 'real' faith, and its role in mature personality function. Other psychologists, for example G. Allport and C. G. Jung, believed that some form of religious outlook was essential for optimal personality development (Jung's views are discussed further in Chapters 3 and 15). Empirical research points now, by and large, to the healthy effects of religious faith. A review by Dan Batson and his colleagues (1993) of 197 empirical studies on the relationship between religiosity and mental health showed that, on the whole, having a religious faith correlates positively with mental health. Religious individuals report less anxiety (especially death anxiety), less guilt, less depression and a greater sense of happiness. However, it is important to take into consideration just how religiosity and mental health are being defined; different ways of being religious (for example, extrinsic, intrinsic and quest styles of religiosity, discussed in Chapter 3) do show different mental health outcomes.

Batson *et al.* (1993) found that the Freudian claim that religion is a mark of an immature and neurotic personality was found to be true only with the extrinsically religious, those who use their religion for self-serving ends. In contrast, they found that both Quest and Intrinsic showed positive mental health outcomes, but in different ways. Intrinsic believers, who have deeply internalised their faith, and are firmly committed to it, showed freedom from guilt, freedom from existential anxieties and freedom from the fear of death. Persons high on Quest showed a greater sense of self-acceptance and self-actualisation, and more self-reliance in comparison with Intrinsic (who showed higher reliance on God). It is hard to say which orientation, Quest or Intrinsic, had the healthier outcome; it depends upon one's prior definition of mental health. Questers may suffer more existential anxiety than Intrinsics, and their propensity to doubt may indicate the early, seeking stages of faith. On the other hand, argue Batson *et al.*, it is possible that the freedom from guilt and worry gained by Intrinsics is won at the price of bondage to belief, a commitment to a rigid belief system which cannot be questioned. Inflexible belief systems will be addressed later in this chapter.

SUMMARY OF KEY THEMES

- The possibility that religious faith may be used to bolster and defend against unresolved personality problems (Freud).
- The need for discernment and spiritual direction within the church to disentangle these problems.
- Relationships between childhood experiences and adult faith; between parental images and God-images.
- Correlations between different forms of religious belief and different aspects of mental health.

QUESTIONS TO CONSIDER

- Have you (or anyone you know) ever used an aspect of your Christian faith to defend yourself from facing some painful reality?
- What were the factors that helped you (or the person you know) move beyond that position (e.g. prayer, bible reading, support from others, spiritual direction, counselling, an inner realisation concerning what needed to be faced)?
- How would you help someone that you think may be stuck in an unhealthy use of their religion?
- Would you confront them with the limitations of their position? What in their faith commitment might be salvaged and transformed?

Is Christianity bad for women?

Both historically and in the present, religions in a variety of cultures have often been used to legitimate rather than to challenge the existing social order. Christianity is no exception. In this sense at least, some share of the blame for patriarchy's subordination of women throughout the centuries in Western culture rests upon the Christian church. It can further be argued that patriarchy has extended itself through the church's hierarchy, its religious practices and use of language, all of which traditionally have excluded and marginalised women. The church's teaching on morality and sexuality has prescribed for women subsidiary, dependent roles. Its teaching has sometimes conflated sin with sexual temptation, and has penalised women as 'temptresses'. Women have felt silenced by a male definition of life and the world.

   Yet, statistically, women are more likely to attend church than men and more likely to have a religious experience. And, as some feminist theologians have been keen to point out, Christianity did not invent patriarchy, nor did it necessarily increase it. Such theologians point out that the Jesus of the gospels defends the intrinsic value of women, has close associations with several women, and that his teaching bears the seeds of emancipation. There is, then, no simple, clear-cut answer to our question 'Is Christianity bad for women?' In this section, some psychological evidence will be examined to try, at least, to shed some light on it.

   As well as being over-represented in church congregations, women use one-and-a-half times more medical and psychological resources than men. Are women the sicker, as well as the more religious, sex? Or is there something in the way the female role is structured that is unhealthy for women? Evidence shows that women tend to suffer from different psychological conditions from men. The rate of depression is twice as high among women than among men. Anxiety disorders, paranoias, and anorexia are largely suffered by women. While men tend to be more destructive of others and more cut off from reality when they suffer from mental illness, women's mental illnesses are often 'destructive of self' (Szasz 1961). A connection may be made with the 'Christian' virtues that women are socialised to exhibit: submission, dependence, self-effacement, helplessness, emotionality. These patterns can develop into styles of coping that are similar to depressive states.

   This tendency has been reinforced by some Christian teaching that has advised women to accept the violent behaviour of their husbands in a 'submissive' manner. Brown and Harris (1978) suggested that women who live out traditional roles as wives and mothers with no outside employment are more prone to depression than those who work outside the home. To put Mary the mother of Jesus forward as the Christian ideal of the feminine can be a source of frustration (as well as comfort) for women: who can aspire to being both a virgin and a mother? The church's offerings to women have clearly been mixed.

   Other studies suggest that women's poorer mental health is by no means universal, and may be a feature of late Western modernity (Cochrane 1983). In traditional societies, the differences between the male and female rates of depression and anxiety are slight. The marked sex difference in mental health has occurred quite recently, and correlates with non-traditional societies in eras of increasing opportunities for women. Loewenthal (1995) explains this in terms of expectations. At times and in places where women's aspirations are confined to the kitchen sink (and women are valued for their traditional roles), depression rates for women are even with men. Loewenthal suggests that when there are greater opportunities for women, the disparity between what is possible but not actual in women's lives can lead to increased rates of depression.

We are forced to conclude that any connection between women's poorer psychological health and Christianity is mediated by a number of factors, especially the prevailing social conditions, and how much support they provide for women. Also, the greater use that women make of medical and psychological services may suggest that women are in fact healthier than men in that they seek out help for their problems more readily, and through getting some help, carry on with their lives. The prevalence of women in the church can also be interpreted as a sign of women's greater readiness to confront their own personal (and spiritual) problems, and to do something about them. The relationship between Christianity and women's mental health is not simple.

Christian women vary in their experience of the church. For some women, Christianity has done them great harm, for others it has been a source of enormous good. For most, perhaps, it has been a mixed experience. Contemporary Christian women are probably somewhat torn between feminist and traditionalist influences, as both are present in society and the church. Women are not helped in making their choices if the church is overly prescriptive either way. With the ordination of women in many denominations, and most women in employment, women now do have a choice about how they live out their Christian lives. It takes courage for a woman to work out the exact balance for herself. This balance will depend on a number of factors present in a woman's own personal circumstances. Helpful religion provides women with a safe place to discover the outworkings of God's call without being overly prescriptive about sex roles.

SUMMARY OF KEY THEMES

- Ways that the church can be harmful to women.
- The greater frequency of psychological problems, such as depression, among women.
- Women's coping strategies.
- A time of transition in women's roles in the church.

QUESTIONS TO CONSIDER

- How would you describe the ideal Christian man?
- How would you describe the ideal Christian woman?
- How would you describe the ideal Christian (sex unspecified)?
- Does your description of the ideal Christian (sex unspecified) come closer to your description of an ideal Christian man, or an ideal Christian woman? What are the implications of this?

- What does your church teach concerning the role of women in the church, in the family, in society? Does what it teaches relate to what it models in practice?
- What effect does your church's teaching, and modelling, have on you?

How does (good) religion go bad?

In recent years, there has been an increasing number of reports of religious abuse. Faithful Christians have suffered sexual abuse by ministers under the guise of 'healing'; believers' decision-making abilities have been usurped by overly-dominant leaders; money has been embezzled or extorted by corrupt ministries; Christians have reported feeling that their thinking was controlled by overly-rigid, dogmatic Christian teaching, and that their inner selves were violated with repeated exorcism sessions. It is important to be aware of, and try to understand, religious abuse; it can take many different forms, some of which are considered here.

Cults and sects

In recent decades, there has been a great deal of concern about religious sects and cults (the latter are also referred to as New Religious Movements, NRMs). Churches, sects and cults are often differentiated by the degree of their separation (in ascending order) from wider culture. (See Hood *et al.* 1996: 301–333, for a discussion of the complexities of this classification).

Cults are, by definition, novel religions unassociated with existing religious groups, whereas sects usually arise from within an existing religion, and later move toward a new religious form or expression. Cults maintain the most distance from the host culture through espousing radically alternative belief systems and practices, as well as requiring a high degree of social (and sometimes geographical) separation. Opposition between the cult and mainstream culture can become mutually reinforcing, sometimes producing catastrophic consequences (such as the mass suicides of Jonestown and of the Californian Heaven's Gate cult). Among some cults, there is evidence for the use of manipulative techniques ('flirty fishing', sleep deprivation, enforced fasting and chanting, required renunciation of former ties), which can rapidly erode a person's normal mental state. These are, however, in the minority. Eileen Barker's seminal research on NRMs (1989) found that most people who join cults (usually healthy, middle-class young people with good employment prospects) 'convert' themselves to the cult, and find the experience to have some positive benefit (discovering a purpose in life, the fellowship of a like-minded community, taking a corporate stand against the perceived evils of the host culture, and enjoying accelerated promotions to positions of leadership within their own community).

Even without the presence of coercive or manipulative practices, cults can bind people increasingly to their chosen belief system and hence to their involvement with the group supporting that belief system. Daniel Batson and his colleagues (1993) describe three normal social psychological processes that contribute towards bondage to a belief system. First, the increased sense of self-esteem generated by being among those who have 'seen the light' would have to be sacrificed if the cult member were to renounce their beliefs. Second, the public commitment the new adherent makes to the cult would have to be disclaimed publicly; an aversive experience for most. Third, it is normal to depend on those who give us the social support required to uphold our beliefs against a disbelieving majority; this becomes even more intense as the cult member becomes isolated from former friends and family. Even when a belief system is subject to empirical disconfirmation, these normal processes are enough to foster belief-intensification strategies. For example, if a member of the Physical Immortals, a cult that believes in their own physical immortality, should fall ill and die, a typical response might be: 'She must not have *really* been one of the elect; we all must strive to make sure that we are!' Intensification of belief under such circumstances reveals the normal tendency in all people to maintain cognitive consistency: certainly we as rational people have chosen a 'rational' belief system; hence that belief system must be protected at all costs.

The interaction of these normal social processes can enslave a person in maintaining their commitment to their cult. The dangers are not to be underestimated. However, the experience of being kidnapped at the behest of anguished family members and forcibly de-programmed is experienced by some former cult members as even more damaging than the worst practices of their NRM. On either side of this tight-rope, a person's freedom to think for themselves has been violated.

Research on sectarian churches and Christian groups pinpoints the way commitment is handled, and how sometimes similar influences can come into play. Conversion can be the first step on a required pathway of escalating commitment, unforeseen by the new convert. The more social isolation that a Christian group imposes on its members, and the more commitment and involvement is required, the more its religious discourse is felt to define reality. The situation can become ripe for religious abuse.

The ingredients of religious abuse in churches and Christian groups

Religious abuse is essentially an abuse of power (Osborn and Walker 1997). It can happen when a Christian leader has too much power and influence over their flock, or when leaders seek to fulfil their own needs by 'helping' others. Intense involvement and commitment on the part of followers/church members can provide a ready arena for abuse; especially if there is inadequate accountability and supervision for ministers. Another key ingredient in religious abuse is vulnerability or dependence on the part of the follower. We will see that it is the misuse and interaction of these ingredients, rather than their mere presence, that sets the wheels of religious abuse in motion.

Dependence

In our individualist culture, we tend to pathologise dependence. Yet Reed (1978) describes a normal 'regression to dependence' that is part and parcel of any act of worship. Worship services are times when the individual can lay down their burdens and responsibilities and rest in a caring God. This sort of regression to dependence happens at various periods throughout our lives (especially in childhood) and even in the course of an ordinary day! Normal regression to dependence provides the needed sustenance for healthy living. It does mean, however, that a state of dependence is easy to promote in religious circles.

Beyond this healthy dependence, many individuals come to church with long-standing problems. There are individuals whose normal psychological development has been stunted through ineffective parenting or outright abuse. Some may exhibit a full-blown dependent personality disorder, or simply seek to lean on others, especially religious leaders, who are often identified with God, the ultimate parent. This more serious dependency is further complicated by Christian norms and teachings that value characteristics like submission, gentleness, selfless giving and obedience more highly than autonomy and the ability to disagree. A virtual powder keg of dependence is present in some churches or Christian groups, which could explode, with potentially disastrous consequences, should a leader ever be motivated, or allowed, to strike the match.

Over the centuries, many churches and denominations have developed helpful organisational structures that check pastoral power and thereby prevent some forms of religious abuse. Newer, more experimental churches may not yet have this built-in protection. At the same time, new churches are less hampered by bureaucracy and traditionalism, and may be more likely to step out and offer help to hurting individuals, thereby running greater risks. While the more outrageous forms of religious abuse tend to happen in the newer, charismatic or fundamentalist churches, these churches do not have a monopoly (evidenced by child and adult sexual abuse cases in the Roman Catholic and Anglican churches). To be fair, newer churches are often pressing into areas of members' need more than traditional churches; at the same time they tend to engender (and sometimes require) more commitment. Dependence, intense personal involvement, and lack of structural accountability set the stage for religious abuse.

A psychological model of the 'nuts and bolts' of religious abuse

The purpose of this section is to propose a psychological model of how religious abuse happens, once the ingredients listed above are present. The model is based on two psychological theories: social exchange and dual role relations. This model of religious abuse has not been tested empirically (it would hardly be ethical to set up such an experiment!), but the model does appear to fit the descriptions of religious abuse in circulation. For the sake of clarity, religious abuse is represented here as a simplified dyad, an interaction between leader and follower. (Undoubtedly, the dyad takes place within a larger church or group context, which also exerts influence. To add another dimension to this simplified model, the social processes discussed in Chapter 11 should also be taken into consideration.)

Social Exchange theory

Social Exchange theory posits that any interaction between two people will depend on the perceived rewards and costs. Rewards and costs can be material (money, tithes, practical help) or non-material (counselling, friendship, teaching, spiritual blessing). A simple exchange model says that people are 'rationally' hedonistic; they will seek out relationships that do them more good than harm, and that people expect to gain from a relationship in accordance with what they have put in (Homans 1950, 1974). A more complex model of social exchange says that both participants in a relationship not only weigh up the costs and benefits of any interaction, they compare these to the costs and benefits of hypothesised alternative interactions with others (Thibaut and Kelley 1959, Kelley and Thibaut 1978). This model has been seen to predict quite accurately what happens in relationships and how they develop over time. It can usefully be applied to a religious setting; for example, Percy (1996) has described how the Toronto Blessing can be understood in terms of professional, middle-class adults surrendering pride, control, and rationality (the costs) to those who administer the spiritual experience of the 'blessing' itself (the reward).

In religious abuse, the second part of Kelley and Thibaut's model gets short-circuited: the comparison of costs and benefits with those of other possible interactions. As stated in the theory, people normally not only weigh up the costs and benefits of the present interaction, but they continually compare over time the changing ratio of the present costs and benefits to the costs and benefits of other possible interactions ('things are getting bad with X, I might be better off with Y'). In the religious setting, the initial costs and benefits might look like this: the follower exchanges a degree of submission and involvement with the leader for spiritual help and a sense of belonging. The leader exchanges time and energy in ministering to the individual for loyalty to the leader's calling and the satisfaction of personal aims through helping others. At this point, this is a potentially positive exchange, rewarding to both. A crucial ingredient of religious abuse creeps in when the explicit teaching (or the implicit world view) of the religious group prevents the follower from being able to compare rationally the costs and benefits of the present interaction to the costs and benefits of possible other interactions. For example, a group's implicit or explicit teaching may tell a follower: 'you will only get healed through this ministry', 'we are the only ones who are able to help you', 'salvation is only possible through this church or denomination', 'you will forfeit God's blessing if you leave this group/church'. Physical and/or social separation of religious groups or churches has the same effect of limiting the universe of possible other interactions. The follower is compelled to see the present interaction in a positive light because the cost of leaving is perceived as too high, and, importantly, there appear to be no other interactions available that might confer the desired benefit.

At this point in describing a psychological model of religious abuse, it is important to recognise that the interaction between leader and follower is not only psychological/social; there often is a genuinely spiritual element: the God of grace responds to the faith of both in the interaction, and the relationship is strengthened through this.

As in the parable of the wheat and the tares, both good and bad elements grow up over time in the interaction. Religious abuse often starts imperceptibly, and may be masked by the original and even ongoing spiritual blessings of the exchange. The follower gets 'stuck' in the interaction: there is too much to lose by leaving; there are no other alternatives. At this point in the process of religious abuse, followers often report feeling confused. This confusion may reflect the way the normal cost-benefit analysis is being short-circuited. Followers are experiencing the growing costs of the interaction, but without the ability to make a realistic assessment in comparison to other possible interactions. To reduce a growing dissonance, followers may recon-figure the cost-benefit ratio in their own mind, producing an inner sense of confu-sion. The follower is having to deny to herself how it really is. The ability to trust one's own decisions and to act falters as a result.

Dual-role relations theory

So far, we have explored how the follower gets gradually drawn in to an abusive rela-tionship. What happens to the leader? For this, we turn to dual-role relations theory (this is also discussed in Chapter 13). One of the facts that dual-role relations theory seeks to explain is the large proportion (37 per cent) of surveyed ministers reported having inappropriate sexual relations with persons within the sphere of their minis-try (Blackmon, cited by Malony and Hunt 1991: 35f). This rate of sexual impropri-ety is four times higher than in other helping professions, where the helping professional also is intimately involved with a client. H. Newton Malony and Rich-ard Hunt (1991) try to make sense of this data by suggesting that it may result from what he terms 'dual-role relations'. In other caring professions, the professional will have only one role towards the client. Meetings take place only in the doctor's sur-gery, or the solicitor's office. Social interaction outside this is normally absent. Ministers, in contrast, have more than one role towards their church members. As well as worship services and other church meetings, they meet for coffee after church, they may be involved in bereavements, family problems, celebrations, counselling. The multiple roles the minister may have in a person's life can lead to the minister becoming very important in the minds of both. As ministers are human beings with needs like the rest of humanity, it can be very appealing to become 'all in all' to others, to be the 'saviour'. This kind of grandiosity is inviting for anyone with unmet emotional or ego needs. Grandiosity can lead to poor judgement, and a mis-reading of the follower's signals; emotional vulnerability may be misperceived as a sexual invitation. Imbalanced theology or Christian teaching can provide ministers with a self-justification: 'this person needs to completely submit to God through my direction'.

Although dual-role relations theory specifically seeks to explain the unusually high incidence of sexual impropriety among clergy, a similar process of grandiosity followed by poor judgement may occur in other kinds of religious abuse. Ministers can make increasing demands on a follower's obedience, finances, time, commit-ment, thinking and participation in counselling or exorcism sessions. And of course, this is more likely to happen in the absence of sufficient ministerial accountability.

So, the follower is confused by the growing costs of the interaction, but wants to be 'good', wants God's blessing, and strives to maintain the relationship despite increasing inner conflict. Eventually, the balance shifts to the extreme, the relationship becomes insupportable and breaks. The believer leaves feeling violated, betrayed, confused, and full of self-hate for tolerating the abuse. A legacy of mistrust ensues that can make continued faith in God or involvement in church impossible, and can lead to mental and marital breakdown.

Dual-role relations helps us understand (but not excuse) abusers' claims of 'innocence'. Leaders accused of abuse often feel unjustly accused; they can not understand what went wrong. Their original good intentions can be used to deny the way self-serving motives took over. Sometimes leaders need to have the 'good' of their original intentions recognised before they can bear to face the way those intentions decayed, and the harm that resulted. Some come through to full repentance and take responsibility for what they have done. Others do not. It is possible, although costly, for the damage done by religious abuse to be healed. Religious organisations, as well as abusive individuals, need to take responsibility for how the structures failed to protect the vulnerable. The wounded need help to express and work through their legitimate anger and pain, and over time, come to forgive. 'Felt' forgiveness should not be forced or recommended prematurely. An understanding of the gradual slide into an abusive relationship would probably help both abused and abusers.

The above model does not account for all forms of religious abuse. There are cases of intentional, criminal abuse, for example, the sexual abuse of children, where the religious leader methodically prepares his prey with a religious pretext. In recent years, the full extent of sexual abuse within the church (and church-related organisations) on a worldwide scale is coming to light. It is now recognised that religious organisations can provide paedophiles (in guise of 'children's workers') with a perfect environment in which to 'groom' their victims: 'good' children make 'good' compliant victims. Legally-required safeguards are now in place in many churches, but the effects of generations of abuse are not so easily reversed. Extortion of funds on false grounds also falls into a criminal category. Tragically, some cases of the 'gradual' abuse described above end with criminal consequences, for example, the death of victims of mishandled exorcism ministries, where mental illness was mistaken for demon possession with fatal consequences (abuse that can happen in a context of healing is further addressed in Chapter 2).

SUMMARY OF KEY THEMES

- Religious abuse as an abuse of power.
- Other ingredients: intense personal involvement, commitment, separation, dependence and lack of outside supervision.
- The danger of a gradual slide into religious abuse.
- How social, psychological or geographical isolation can prevent followers from being able to make rational decisions and assessments.
- Taking steps to prevent paedophilia and other abuses within the church in future.

QUESTIONS TO CONSIDER

- What are the ways your church or group seeks to keep religious abuse from happening?
- Is there an over-reliance on the good intentions of the minister to keep such things from happening?
- Have you, or anyone you have known, experienced religious abuse? What was the experience like? Does the proposed model seem an adequate description of the psychological 'nuts and bolts'?
- Did this experience of religious abuse indicate some unfinished business (e.g. a need to deal with anger and pain, to confront the abuser with help from church eldership or superiors, or to work with your church to promote structures and practices that could prevent abuse in the future)?

Cognitive processes that can contribute to unhealthy religion

Fundamentalism

The way Christians think can also contribute to unhealthy religion. Fundamentalists Anonymous, an organisation formed to help those who exit fundamentalist Christian groups or churches in the US, report that many 'leavers' describe the way of thinking as rigid, dogmatic and maladaptive. Fundamentalism has received a particularly bad press in the past decade: it seems to stand for everything that is contrary to a liberal, rational, open society. As a result, psychologists researching Christian fundamentalism often start out with a hypothesis that there must be something wrong with fundamentalists: they must be mad, bad, or stupid. Within these limitations, studies that have examined how Christian fundamentalists think have been more fruitful than studies that posit some kind of personality aberration within fundamentalists as individuals (see Savage (in press) for a review of psychological studies of fundamentalism).

A broad definition of fundamentalism (for example, used by Percy (1996)) places fundamentalists, conservative evangelicals, charismatics and Pentecostals into one overarching category of 'fundamentalism', denoting an enthusiastic, revivalist, and traditionalist approach to faith. A narrow definition of fundamentalism focuses on the way creedal Christian beliefs are organised around an authority belief – the inerrancy of scripture. (Traditionally, 'word-based' forms of religious authority eschew other sources of authority, such as subjective experience or the charismatic gifts. Therefore, self-identifying Christian fundamentalists and conservative evangelicals who adhere to a literal, inerrant view of scripture would be included within this narrow definition of Christian fundamentalism).

Fundamentalism can also be described as an over-confidence in a single conceptual system. It goes beyond believing that the profound realities to which it points are true. It optimistically believes that this system (and only this system) exactly corresponds to these realities. This is accompanied by a concern that we will lose our grip on these truths if this particular conceptual system is dented. At times, a fundamentalist belief system can inspire more devotion to itself than it does towards the realities to which it points. So great is the human desire for order and understanding that vast amounts of energy can be devoted to maintaining the conceptual system itself.

This potential underside to intrinsically held beliefs has also been identified by Batson *et al.* (1993). Instrinsically motivated believers, among whom fundamentalists number, enjoy the real benefits of freedom from existential anxieties and guilt by virtue of their deep religious commitment, but the price they pay may be a certain 'bondage to belief'. Their belief system can become inflexible in the ways outlined earlier in this chapter in the discussion on cults, and it is reasonable to question how much the benefits, over time, outweigh the costs.

Whether one takes a narrow or a broad definition of fundamentalism, it is important to underline that it is not the beliefs themselves that create unhealthy religion, but rather the way the beliefs are organised (see Rokeach 1960). In fact, any belief system can be 'fundamentalist' in its cognitive organisation. One can be a 'Catholic fundamentalist', or a 'liberal fundamentalist', or a Marxist or feminist fundamentalist if one's central authority belief or beliefs are granted an inviolable status, and are used to uphold peripheral beliefs in an inflexible and unquestioning way.

It is the unintended way this form of 'closed' central organisation of the fundamentalist belief system interacts with other cognitive and social factors, such as separatism, and an oppositional stance towards outsiders, that can lead to unhealthy religion. Because of the way all the beliefs in fundamentalism are connected to each other through the central authority belief, if one part of the system is threatened, the whole belief structure is in danger of collapsing. As the collapse of a belief system is a frightening prospect, it is normal to try to avoid it. A closed-belief system therefore exacerbates a normal tendency to avoid the uncomfortable state of cognitive dissonance (the awareness that certain beliefs conflict either with our own behaviour or with other beliefs or information). To reduce cognitive dissonance, fundamentalist believers adopt various strategies. These include selective exposure, seeking out belief-consistent information, and avoiding belief-disconfirming information (e.g. only going to more fundamentalist meetings, avoiding 'liberal' sources of information, and so on; see Festinger 1957).

There are both advantages and disadvantages to a centrally organised belief system. A centrally organised belief system structures a chaotic world and helps a believer to make clear-cut decisions. However, as it tends to be stored in memory in easy-to-recall 'sound-bites', the fundamentalist belief system can easily become over-simplified in people's minds. Hence a simplified version of fundamentalism tends to be used by adherents when confronting complicated moral problems (Savage 1998).

Cognitive complexity

As well as having a centrally organised belief system, fundamentalists also appear to use black and white categories in their thinking. Beliefs are either right or wrong, people are either good or bad, saved or not. This tendency to low levels of cognitive complexity has been remarked upon by fundamentalists themselves (Dobson 1986). Cognitive complexity is a measure of how a person combines and classifies information. A simple, undifferentiated way of classifying information chops up reality into one or two clearly defined categories (like right and wrong). A more differentiated approach recognises that options can have many, sometimes contradictory, effects that cannot be easily categorised on a simple right–wrong dimension. In some research, fundamentalists have shown a lower level of cognitive complexity concerning religious material in particular (Hunsberger *et al.* 1996).

We are all cognitive misers, and prefer to do as little mental work as possible. Gestalt psychologists have observed that with ambiguous images such as Figure 4.1, a person will organise the image in one way, for example, as a vase. With effort, the viewer may be able to 'see' the image also as two faces, but both views are not possible at the same time.

A tendency similar to this preference for one 'gestalt' (view) was seen among both Christian fundamentalists and non-fundamentalists when they were asked to solve complex moral dilemmas (Savage 1998). Fundamentalists tended to represent the moral problem focusing on the person, or issue, in and of itself, apart from the social context. This is similar to the way we focus on the 'figure' of a picture, ignoring the background. Non-fundamentalists tended to view the moral problem in terms of its social context. This way of 'seeing' can be described as focusing on the 'ground' or background of a picture. Both figure and ground perspectives are important components of thorough moral reasoning, and *together* provide a more complete view of moral dilemmas than just one view on its own. However, a single 'gestalt' or view of the problem was preferred by

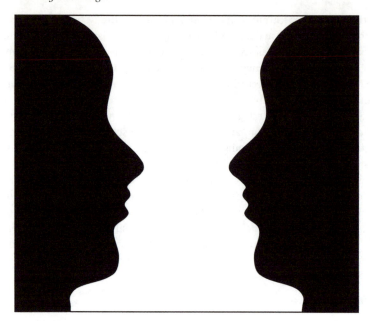

Figure 4.1 Vase and two faces image.

most subjects in both fundamentalist and non-fundamentalist groups. Subjects who solved the moral problem from a consistent figure or ground perspective spontaneously expressed emphatic *certainty* about their moral solutions. In contrast, one third of both fundamentalist and non-fundamentalist subjects solved the moral problem using both figure and ground perspectives at the same time. While the moral reasoning transcripts of these subjects were more 'expert' in terms of comprehensiveness, subjects expressed more *uncertainty* over their solution: the world was no longer simple or clear-cut. In sum, a complex moral problem may be like an ambiguous image: there is a tendency to choose a perspective which then determines which problem facets are noted and which problem facets are ignored. Not surprisingly, subjects tended to choose the view that accorded with the beliefs about the world that they already held, and this was exhibited in a feeling of certainty about their moral solution.

The inability on the part of both fundamentalists and non-fundamentalists to see the other's point of view creates the social climate of mutual opposition in which fundamentalism is sustained. The ability to see the other group's point of view comes only at the cost of sacrificing the certainty that single 'gestalt' brings. Fundamentalists and non-fundamentalists share this desire for order and under-standing, and both devote energy to maintaining their own conceptual system. It would seem that some of the 'unhealthy' ways of thinking supposed by many to be features of 'fundamentalism' result from the tendency of both fundamentalists and non-fundamentalists alike to try to avoid cognitive dissonance and cognitive complexity.

SUMMARY OF KEY THEMES

- The cognitive organisation of fundamentalist belief systems: how this can lead to maladaptive ways of thinking.
- The tendency to avoid cognitive dissonance.
- Reduced cognitive complexity.
- Social separatism.
- How a single 'gestalt' or world view can reinforce group closure, and mutual opposition and incomprehension.

QUESTIONS TO CONSIDER

- Does the teaching of your church/denomination encourage the exploration of doubt and of opposite viewpoints?
- Do you feel more comfortable making a black and white judgement on, for instance, a moral issue?
- Have you ever experienced being aware of seeing a problem in two, seemingly contradictory ways? What did it feel like? Could this tension become a resource?
- For example, what would happen if a non-fundamentalist was prepared to see some valid points in a fundamentalist's moral reasoning and vice versa?
- Given the choice, would you prefer to read something that supports and confirms your religious viewpoint or something that challenges your viewpoint?

Further reading

Is Christianity bad for your mental health?

Hood, R., Spilka, B., Hunsberger, B. and Gorsuch, R. (1996) *The Psychology of Religion: An Empirical Approach*, 2nd ed., London: Guilford Press, Chapter 12.
Loewenthal, K. (1995) *Mental Health and Religion*, London: Chapman and Hall.
Meissner, W. (1984) *Psychoanalysis and Religious Experience*, New Haven: Yale University Press, esp. Chapters 3, 4, 6, and 7.
Palmer, M. (1997) *Freud and Jung on Religion*, London: Routledge.
Schumaker, J. F. (ed.) (1992) *Religion and Mental Health*, New York: Oxford University Press.
Wulff, D. (1997) *The Psychology of Religion: Classic and Contemporary*, 2nd ed., New York: Wiley, esp. Chapters 6, 7, and 9.

Is Christianity bad for women?

Bons-Storm, R. (1996) *The Incredible Woman: Listening to Women's Silences in Pastoral Care and Counselling*, Nashville, TN: Abingdon Press.
Carr, A. (1990) *Transforming Grace: Christian Tradition and Women's Experience*, London: Harper Row.
Graham, E. and Halsey, M. (1993) *Life-Cycles: Women and Pastoral Care*, London: SPCK.
Storkey, E. (1985) *What's Right With Feminism*, London: SPCK.

How does (good) religion go bad?

Barker, E. (1989) *New Religious Movements: A Practical Introduction*, London: HMSO.

Howard, R. (1996) *The Rise and Fall of the Nine O'Clock Service: A Cult Within the Church?*, London: Mowbray.

Osborn, L. and Walker, A. (1997) *Harmful Religion: An Exploration of Religious Abuse*, London: SPCK.

Wallis, R. (1984) *The Elementary Forms of the New Religious Life*, London: Routledge and Kegan Paul.

Cognitive processes that can contribute to unhealthy religion

Barr, J. (1981) *Fundamentalism*, 2nd ed., London: SCM Press.

Boone, K. (1990) *The Bible Tells Them So: The Discourse of Protestant Fundamentalism*, London: SCM Press.

Festinger, L., Riecken, L. and Schachter, S. (1956) *When Prophecy Fails*, Minneapolis: Minneapolis University Press.

Percy, M. (1996) *Words, Wonders, and Powers: Understanding Contemporary Christian Fundamentalism and Revivalism*, London: SPCK.

Part 2

Development and teaching

5 Childhood and adolescence

QUESTIONS FOR MINISTRY

- Who are the children and young people in your life? What sense do you have of their spiritual qualities?
- What are their spiritual strengths and how can we build on these?
- How can we teach the faith to young people in a way that doesn't produce a naive or literalist faith, which will only be jettisoned as they grow up?
- What are the 'accident black spots' of children's and teenagers' religious development, how can we protect against the development of religious misinterpretation?

Ministry with children and young people presents special opportunities, responsibilities and challenges. For many of us these special needs make working with the young a daunting prospect. There is much about Christianity and the church that seems so adult. It can seem impossible to know how to pitch this in a way that is engaging or meaningful for younger people. A working knowledge of their psychological and religious capacities is therefore essential.

Scripture is clear that childhood deserves our full attention. Jesus' treatment of and comments about children remain a challenge to our typical assumptions about religious authority and the adult-centredness of religion. The idea that children are not only to be 'set in the midst', but to present a significant spiritual example to us is perhaps the clearest challenge for ministry today. What kind of ministry, based on what kind of understanding of the child's strengths and limitations, can do justice to Jesus' perceptions and warnings in Matthew 18?

This chapter will first look at the psychology of the child. The church is called to work with children and their families in many contexts (e.g. infant baptism and thanksgiving, admission to Communion, all-age worship, confirmation, Sunday schools, church schools, and in all manner of community projects). Effective ministry benefits from being aware of the range of psychological problems that can disrupt childhood. The most extreme problems reflect the complicated challenges all children encounter in growing up and remind us of their vulnerabilities and their strengths. Understanding the normal course of development provides a number of helpful indicators for how children may respond to faith. Many studies of the nature of childhood religion have important implications for more sensitive approaches to religious nurture.

Teenagers also require special understanding (set out in the second part of this chapter). Adolescence can be a difficult period of transition, with its own set of potential psychological problems. Research studies offer a way of empirically testing some of the popular myths about adolescence. Appreciating some of the contours of adolescent psychology, on the basis of the intellectual, emotional and social developments of this stage of life, suggests many ways in which spirituality and faith may be negotiated.

Readers will find it helpful to refer to Chapter 6 on religious development and Chapter 7 on education as these provide additional angles to many of the ideas discussed below. Chapters dealing with the psychological understanding of religious diversity, illness and bereavement, depression, counselling, group processes, worship and ritual are also relevant for work with children and young people.

Children's psychology

Common problems

All parents worry about their child's psychological well-being at some stage, if not most of the time. In childhood we face some of the most revolutionary changes of our lives, in our thinking, in our physical capacities, in our ability to communicate, in our social groupings and so on. Some measure of disturbance, some of the time, is a normal reaction to this.

Individual differences and the pace of change during childhood can make it hard to assess whether a child has a serious problem or not. Most psychological problems in childhood consist of perfectly normal childlike qualities manifested in an abnormal quantity – for example, an excess of timidity or insufficient self-restraint. Guidelines about developmental norms can help to suggest what it is reasonable to expect children at different ages to be like. For example, temper tantrums are normal in toddlers, but a more worrying sign in an 8-year-old when self-control and other means of expressing strong emotions should have developed.

Clarifying what is really wrong

Children experience problems in three main areas – in behaviour (e.g. anti-social or violent behaviour), in emotion (e.g. anxiety or depression) and learning (e.g. dyslexia). Often problems multiply, and what seemed at first to be the obvious problem turns out in fact to have been the by-product of a deeper, previously unidentified issue. Martin Herbert (1988) suggests that academic underachievement and social 'friendlessness' are best understood as consequences of other underlying psychological difficulties, which are likely to create new problems too. For example, poor school performance may indicate specific neurological damage affecting reading and writing (dyslexia), but not IQ. Being misperceived as 'stupid' is likely to trigger negative emotional and behavioural responses – damaged self-esteem and disobedience perhaps. Having friends is an important factor for learning (from peers), for emotional well-being (self-esteem, self-awareness) and for behaviour (accommodating to others needs, making one's own needs heard in appropriate ways). However, friendlessness often arises because the child has inadequate psychological skills in the first place – lacking sensitivity to others, confidence, the ability to resolve personal disputes or negotiate joint actions. Identifying the component parts of these kinds of general problem can help to break into the negative cycle, working remedially on specific issues or skills.

The role of the family

Ministers are usually in close contact with the child's most effective problem-solvers: the parents. However, once problems arise parents can feel de-skilled and inadequate, and so both for their sake and their child's they need encouraging support in meeting their child's special needs. Tackling the sense of confusion and powerlessness over their child's situation can be helped by adopting clarification strategies such as keeping a journal recording the ABCs of the problem: the Antecedents, to learn what triggers problem episodes; the Behaviour itself; and the Consequences that this led to.

Some child problems are better understood as family problems – help is needed to stabilise the whole family system of which the child's problems are just one symptom. For example, a child may provoke a recurring psychosomatic illness in the knowledge that this temporarily stops her parents' arguments. Parenting difficulties (the inability to cope, a lack of emotional engagement, or even abuse) may only come to light in the form of child problems too. Child abuse can be physical, sexual or emotional. Suspicions should *always* be referred to professionals, never investigated by ministers.

Whether part of the solution, or part of the problem (often both), parents should not be overlooked when our attention is drawn to the plight of the child.

Divorce

One of the most significant ways that parents can influence the development of their child is if their relationship breaks down. Losing a parent through divorce, especially when contact is lost, can have a more negative impact on a child's well-being than the death of a parent. The longer-term consequences are hard to determine, since marital disharmony, poverty and/or single parenting themselves all contribute to delinquency and other problems. Table 5.1 summarises the immediate effects on children at different ages.

Table 5.1 Common difficulties as children deal with recently divorced parents

Pre-school	Sad, frightened, clinging, demanding, vivid fantasies about abandonment by or death of parent(s). Aggression towards other children.
5–8 years	Hurt as above, more anger, often towards remaining parent (mum typically) who is blamed for situation. Absent parent is idealised.
8–12 years	Displays less hurt, hard to encourage to talk, seeks distractions.
Teenage	Depression, opts out of family life, creates alternative 'family' of friends.

Spotting the signs

Children express and deal with psychological distress in less obvious ways than adults. For example, a depressed child may not explicitly say that they feel desperate prolonged sadness. To identify and to respond to children's problems, it helps to listen to 'languages' in which they may be more fluent: their behaviour, their fantasy, their play and storytelling. Children only gradually acquire the intellectual sophistication to reflect on their own mental states, but easily project their feelings onto fictional characters with whom they can identify. They might even appropriate characters from Biblical stories to do this.

Ego defence mechanisms help us to understand a variety of problems. In childhood, the emerging sense of self tends to be naturally fragile. Parental anxiety can lead to a temptation to overprotect the child, especially when wider support (e.g. from parents, teachers, or peer group) for self-esteem and self-worth seems lacking.

'To identify and respond to children's problems, it helps to listen to 'languages' in which they may be more fluent'

Table 5.2 Children's problems: when self-protection (ego defence) backfires

Ego defence mechanism	Example of child's problem
Emotional insulation	
Cutting off links to anything involving feelings	Becoming mute after witnessing something traumatic, refusing to be cuddled
Displacement	
Removing the source of anxiety to another context	Aggressive towards peers as reaction to domestic conflict
Projection	
Locating distressing feelings about oneself in others	Bullying as a way of dealing with being bullied by others, including parents/siblings
Fantasy	
Unrealistic ideas and self beliefs	Conjecture that 'I am adopted' to explain parent's insufficient love; or hopeless wishful thinking that divorced parents will get back together
Reaction formation	
Going to the opposite extreme	Adopting a 'don't care' stance, such as anti-social conduct or indifference to others' feelings when in fact the 'ego' craves care and empathy
Escapism	
Denial of reality in form of non-co-operation or withdrawal	Dyslexic says 'I can read, I just don't want to'

Thinking about the child's problem as the consequences of ego defence can help us to trace some problems back to less apparent root insecurities and needs. Table 5.2 gives some examples.

Just a phase?

It is reassuring to know that many childhood problems resolve themselves as the child grows older – though they may be disabling and distressing at the time. Problems with toileting, speech, fears (e.g. of strange places, the dark, leaving mum) usually improve with each year of life. Lying and insufficient appetite peak in early childhood, but are less common thereafter. Sleep problems, bad dreams, timidity, irritability, attention seeking, overdependence, and jealousy peak as children start school, and again when they transfer to secondary school (Herbert 1988). Serious conduct disorders, seen in excessive aggression, uncontrolled temper and overactivity are grown out of much more slowly, especially in boys. While most children with problems will develop into normal functioning adults, conduct problems need extra attention to break the habits that can lead to an anti-social adolescence and a criminal adult life.

SUMMARY OF KEY THEMES

- Childhood difficulties as exaggerated versions of 'normal' traits.
- The importance of the family context.
- Tracing problems back to their root causes.
- How children can be helped to grow out of their problems.

QUESTIONS TO CONSIDER

- What is your experience, if any, of ministering to families whose children have emotional, behavioural, or educational problems?
- In what ways might the parents be part of the cause of the problems?
- In what ways can the parents help solve the problems?
- Which problems can you help to deal with as a minister and which are outside your capabilities?

The development of religious understanding in children

Jean Piaget's model of general intellectual development

St. Paul noted there was an important disjunction between child and adult thinking: 'When I was a child, I talked like a child, I thought like a child, I reasoned like a child. When I became a man, I put childish ways behind me' (1 Cor. 13. 11). The gap between children's and adults' thinking and reasoning abilities is not simply how much each can do and how much each knows. There are important qualitative differences affecting the *kind* of thinking children are able to do. Jean Piaget's groundbreaking studies of children's thinking on a variety of matters maps the psychological landmarks that distinguish the intellectual style of the infant, the pre-schooler, and the school-age child until the emergence of a recognisably adult style in adolescence.

EXERCISE

- What happens at a service of worship at your church that might speak to a child's way of thinking at 18 months, at 4 years, and at 8 years?
- If the children withdraw for part (or all) of some services, to what extent do the 'children's groups' they go to offer fair substitutes of how the main worship service conveyed religious thought in physical movement, imaginative representation, and in the exploitation of immediate context?
- What is the relative importance for you to express your faith in physical, imaginative, concrete and abstract ways?

Piaget's analysis suggests children need opportunities to think in ways that engage them on their own terms – talking down to them in simplified versions of adult thinking (e.g. about ideas, principles, analogies) is an inadequate response. Children think effectively initially through their bodies (sensorimotor 0–2), then also through their

Box 5.1 Piaget's phases of intellectual development

'Sensorimotor' thinking (age 0–2)

Thinking is in terms of the child's own bodily experience. Exploring through the 5 senses how things feel, look, sound, taste, smell; differentiating between light and dark, banging bricks together, chewing rattles. Expanding perception of the world through physical development: grasping, holding, rolling, sitting up, tasting, crawling, pointing, standing, listening.

'Pre-operational' thinking (age 2–7)

Thought is imaginative and fluid rather than logical or reasoned: pretending, magic and make-believe. As language develops, the ability to refer to things and mentally represent them revolutionises children's thinking capacities; thought becomes more than just the processing of physical encounters. But the 'operation' of thinking skills is chaotic. Children at this stage think in terms of how things feel and appear to them; their 'thinking' seems dominated by their feelings and impulsive guesswork.

'Concrete operational' thinking (age 7–11)

Thinking at this stage depends heavily on the actual context; there is an emphasis and reliance on strict rules and on literal interpretations. Development of some control over the operation of thought processing begins. Children now begin to appreciate logical explanations and connections between things, they are sensitive about whether things 'make sense'. Children at this stage can make rational judgements and be objective only in terms of what appear to them as the literal, 'concrete' features under consideration.

'Formal operational' thinking (age 12+)

Thinking includes playing with and making connections between ideas, and being able to reflect on principles behind rules. In this stage the legitimately childish qualities of thinking are overcome. Abstract ideas can be entertained. Issues and hypotheses, rather than actual situations, can enter mental currency.

(Piaget 1926, 1953)

---

feelings and imagination (pre-operational 2–7) and later through basic, literal reasoning with 'hands on' ways to sort out their understanding (concrete 7–11). Engaging children's minds means offering different things at different ages.

Ronald Goldman's three stages of children's religious thinking

In many ways religious thought is abstract and conceptual and so would seem to become possible only in Piaget's final stage of thinking – the 'formal operational' – which normally only develops during the teenage years. However, research shows

Table 5.3 Goldman's three stages of religious thinking in children

Stage 1	*Intuitive religious thinking*
Scripture	Magical explanations, e.g. of miracles; images rather than narrative sequences are recalled.
God image	Magical potentate.
Prayer	Wishful, magical activity.
Morality	Good happens if you are good; fear authority.
Religious identity	Automatic, unquestioned, like my name.
Stage 2	*Literal and concrete religious thinking*
Scripture	Engrossed by narrative but can't extract meaning; metaphors are superfluous.
God image	Anthropomorphic: man with beard, sandals, sits on cloud.
Prayer	Instrumental; bargaining to get things I'd like.
Morality	Rules to obey; appease authority and earn favour.
Religious identity	Literal logic: I'm Christian because my family is, so our cat is too!
Stage 3	*Abstract and conceptual religious thinking*
Scripture	Uses symbolic, metaphorical levels of meaning to make sense. Can identify conceptual representations (e.g. of salvation, of sacrifice).
God image	Abstract, multifaceted, e.g. love, creative force, Trinity, judge.
Prayer	Exploration of oneself before God; communicative.
Morality	Refer to 'rights', 'principles', 'duty', breaking rules to achieve greater good.
Religious identity	Outcome of personal choice.

that during the earlier stages of their development, children are able to engage in a variety of different sorts of religious thinking. For example, the British psychologist Ronald Goldman (1964) investigated how children's approaches to thinking affected their understanding of religious material. Two hundred children were asked about their interpretations of three Bible stories (the burning bush, the crossing of the Red Sea, and the story of Jesus' time in the Wilderness). The youngest (pre-operational) children gave magical explanations, those somewhat older (concrete operational) remained close to 'the facts' even when these were peripheral to the heart of the story, and only the oldest (aged 12 or older; formal operational) seemed able to think about the stories' symbolic meanings. Goldman concluded that children's religious thinking is shaped by the same developmental processes that Piaget had identified more generally; manifesting themselves in three stages of religious thinking.

These three stages can be illustrated in interpretations of the Red Sea story. At the first stage, children would think that God supernaturally separated the waves, at the next stage they would think that he did it by some physical means, and at the final stage might seek other explanations such as that God put it into the minds of the Israelites to make use of naturally occurring conditions.

Children's religious thinking tends to lag behind the stage of thinking they employ in other areas (e.g. even when they start to reason in a literal way about things in the real world, they may still opt for an intuitive approach for religion). Moving from literal to abstract can be the slowest shift of all, up to six years from first signs of transition (Peatling 1973). Many never make the shift, but simply reject their underdeveloped religious understandings as their other cognitive capacities develop. Goldman termed this phenomenon '11-year-old atheism'. His findings led him to question the wisdom of introducing children to religious ideas before they have the skills to deal with abstraction, symbols, and so on. He worried about the consequences of allowing children's 'distorted' explanations to develop, since it seemed so hard for children to move beyond a literal style in many cases, confused as they were about how they could give up cherished understandings without seeming to turn their back on faith. Other children never moved on because their literal understanding of religion seemed primitive, crude, or irrational in comparison with their ability to think rationally in other areas (from about age 11), so they discarded religion as childish.

This is a difficult transitional stage for children to negotiate, especially if 'understanding' has been too closely identified with having 'faith'. Support for change can make a difference: Abraham (1981) found that encouraging children aged 12 to face up to the 'cognitive conflict' produced by a literalist understanding of religious teachings helped them to move forward, but made no difference to younger children. Without this prompting to engage their new mental skills, 12- year-olds' literalism became even more entrenched.

Alternative perspectives on Goldman's research

As with all generalised 'stage' models, Goldman's scheme should be handled with care. His methods have been criticised for not giving children the best chance to show their understanding. By improving the context of investigation, the language of the stories and the questions, other studies have shown children are not as limited as Goldman first thought (e.g. Murphy 1978). Being sensitive to the success or failure of our communication with children is vital to drawing any conclusions from what they say.

In addition, children may often have more 'tacit' knowledge and implicit understanding than is revealed by what they can explicitly articulate. For example, young children show considerable implicit understanding of how people's thoughts and feelings can influence their actions before they can explain this in words. Implicit religious understanding might mean children appreciate the frisson of a metaphor (the light of the world), or the counterpoint offered by analogy (he is the shepherd, we are the sheep) without the ability to comment explicitly on this. Petrovich (1988) found young children readily offered abstract images for God in spontaneous discussion, but when asked directly 'what is God like' they reverted to stage-limited magical or anthropomorphic images. How we create opportunities for children to share their understanding, as well as our response to this, can make the difference between glimpsing personal insights and simply seeing their cognitive machinery at work.

A further caution about Goldman's findings is that the stage-like development of logical, conceptual reasoning skills may not be so central to religious processing. Other, non-rational kinds of knowing (e.g. Donaldson (1992) writes about the development of a 'value-sensing' mode; Watts and Williams (1988) refer to empathic insight) may be more relevant and not put children at an automatic disadvantage – in fact their childish ways of thinking may assist these more intuitive modes of understanding. It is sensible to make allowances for the ways children's thinking limits their religious understanding, but emotional and attitudinal factors may offer the real keys to developing children's religious sensitivities.

Finally, criticism has been levelled at Goldman for the effect of his liberal theological stance upon his conclusions about religious development. Goldman viewed a non-literal understanding of events such as the crossing of the Red Sea to be superior to and to preclude a literal understanding, rather than considering the possibility of holding both a literal and a more complex symbolic interpretation alongside each other.

SUMMARY OF KEY THEMES

- Piaget's four stages of intellectual development: sensorimotor, pre-operational, concrete operational, and formal operational.
- Goldman's three stages of religious thinking: intuitive, literal and concrete, abstract and conceptual.
- The problem of '11-year-old atheism'.
- How younger children's tacit and emotional knowing may outstrip their intellectual and explicit knowing.
- Other perspectives on Goldman's research.

QUESTIONS TO CONSIDER

- How might the child's stage of religious thinking affect his understanding of receiving Communion?
- What is 'Christian' parenting? What are its goals?
- Do mothering and fathering develop distinctive spiritual qualities?
- How is pastoring *not* like parenting?

Children's spirituality

Rather than just being aware of psychological weaknesses that can compromise an intellectual basis for belief, ministry can look for strengths that support a spiritual basis for faith in children of different ages.

Spiritual life and infant psychology

It is now recognised by psychologists that infants are far more sophisticated and sensitive to their experiences and environment than was once thought (see e.g. Bower 1989). Psychodynamic theories (especially the object relations school) draw attention to the foundational basis for a sense of 'self' that is laid down in infancy. There can be parallels between patterns of self-other relations set down during infancy and subsequent adult experiences of relationship with God (St. Clair 1994; Kirkpatrick and Shaver 1990). Many, even Freud, have observed the resonance between mystical perception and the infant's embodied, undifferentiated, unitary consciousness prior to the development of a separate ego–consciousness. In addition to this, the psychosocial context of infancy focuses intently on a range of issues that will be vital ingredients of faith at later stages of development, such as intimacy, dependence, personhood, and trust.

These various characteristics of infancy all point to the value of relating well to children from the start, not only out of concern for their general well-being, but also because of what these earliest experiences may mean for their spiritual well-being. Carol Newberger's (1980) 'levels of parental awareness', as shown in Table 5.4, offer a useful guide for helping adults (parents, ministers, or teachers) to recognise and improve on their attitudes in relating to children from birth onwards.

Different qualities of relationship, depending on the adult's awareness of the child, are likely to have different consequences for the child's spiritual welfare, and the adult's in return. Increasing awareness depends chiefly on recognising the infant's complex psychological, and potentially spiritual, capacities.

Spiritual life and pre-schoolers' psychology

The psychological life of a child aged 2–6 is far from shallow. Dealing with power and powerlessness, autonomy and self-doubt, taking initiative, and experiences of guilt and failure give the child plenty to work out in everyday experiences. Limited verbal and conceptual skills (still at a pre-operational and intuitive level) give added intensity to emotional experience. There are many strengths to the child's non-rational approach, and developing these may help to protect childhood religion from the hard-to-recover-from diversions that early rational (literal) approaches are likely to cause (see the discussion of 11-year-old atheism above).

Pre-schoolers' perception is holistic rather than analytic. They enjoy 'knowing' but are unconcerned about 'how I know'. Being unsystematic means there is little sense of religion being compartmentalised as distinct from everyday life; God is as natural as breakfast. Children of this age are curious and open to knowledge and to relationships, including God. They are also familiar with an experience of being overwhelmed by the intensity of emotions, and through this can be aware of a sense of power that is mysteriously personal and transcendent. In a limited way they can consciously note these feelings, and need a simple way to contain or mark this: names ('God'?), images, and gestures (e.g. kneeling, silence, dancing, singing) can provide helpful ways to channel and develop these feelings. James Fowler's (1981) empirical study of faith structures at this stage give a special place to the power of images. Children easily project their feelings onto images, creating an external symbol of meaning from the ambiguous stuff of emotion.

Religious images have a great power for evoking and expressing human emotions, and so often appeal to children. The feelings and meanings children invest in these images may be unconventional at this stage. To avoid the pitfalls of entrenched literalism later on, exploring a few contrasting images prevents too narrow an identification of feelings and meaning. For example, Sofia Cavalletti (1983) offers both 'Good Shepherd' and 'Light of the World' as images through which children explore their own feelings about Jesus.

There will be better emotional engagement with certain aspects of an image if it can speak to the child's psychosocial concerns. For example, Cavalletti's research found that pre-schoolers engaged with the 'Good Shepherd' as a maternal, nurturing, 'name knowing' figure. They did not respond in the same way to the shepherd's care for the lost sheep, which speaks more to a moral issue about forgiveness – a concern of middle childhood. Nor did the image of the Good Shepherd as guide and self-sacrificial figure resonate as deeply, since these features speak more to adolescent issues of searching for identity and role-models, and of painful losses and gains.

The pre-school child's limited vocabulary, understanding, attention and knowledge make it harder to recognise spiritual insights at first glance. Research evidence offers some guidance about how to see through this unpromising surface psychology to verbal and non-verbal responses (Cavalletti 1983; Nye 1998; Taylor 1989; Coles 1992). Verbal responses at this age will be spontaneous, fleeting, and often very quietly spoken comments – the child thinking aloud rather than attempting to converse. Their language often has a physical, emotional or intuitive accent: for example, saying 'my body is so happy' (commenting on their reaction to becoming absorbed in religious play), 'God is walking here' (commenting on a breathtaking view), 'I can feel God better in the dark' (after a long silence sitting in a garden at dusk). Non-verbal clues include a period of calm absorption culminating in joy, clearly distinguishable from the frenetic happiness of ordinary childhood pleasure (Cavalletti 1983). Clues can also be uncovered through careful observation of children's play (see Berryman 1991) in which their most serious 'work' can be seen to take place (Axline 1947). Observing play for this purpose invites questions about the deeper meanings of simple activities, the attitude of Level 4 parental awareness described above.

An application: prayer

The various spiritual capacities arising in pre-schoolers' psychology pose many challenges for ministry. In what ways might prayer be an appropriate activity for this age group? Psychological theory and empirical observations provide some guidelines here (Cavalletti *et al.* 1994). Praise and thanksgiving are religious responses to which the child feels naturally drawn; prayer should capitalise on what is natural and easier. The child may have wide, undifferentiated prayer concerns (e.g. 'Thank you God for Jesus, my Barbie and our cupboards') reflecting their holistic perception of

Table 5.4 Newberger's levels of parental awareness

Level 1 Me first	The adult's own needs eclipse any thought for the child's and the way the world might be for him or her. When asked about the child's needs, parents actually describe their own. Egocentric and oblivious of the child's spiritual potential, possessive about their own.
Level 2 Follow the rules	Fixed rules dictate what makes a good parent and a good child. Standards determine interactions with the child, their needs have been decided centrally. This conveys little confidence in the spiritual: rules are bigger than people, worshipping the letter of the law not the spirit of the law.
Level 3 We are individuals	The child is recognised as having her own unique needs and gifts, as does the adult. An aware way of relating to the child draws less on preconceived rules and more on a respect for the child's own 'special' needs and personality. Lends itself to a spirituality of individual respect and tolerance.
Level 4 Living and growing together	The child's individuality is not only admitted but treated as meaningful. The parent is motivated by a desire to understand rather than control the child. The search for meaning conveys the sense of deeper truths to be discovered in all manner of relationships. The child can sense inclusion in this web of value and meaning, establishing the spirituality of her own life as piece of a much larger puzzle.

NEWBERGER'S LEVEL 1: EGOCENTRIC 'ME FIRST' APPROACH TO PARENTING

Box 5.2 Qualities of children's spiritual experiences

- Elicit a strong sense of relation – a sense of wider connections, a feeling that there is more than 'just me'
- Expressed in various 'languages': themes including religious, science fiction, natural world, birth and death
- Eager for 'terminology' that can deal with the ambiguity and power of these experiences – 'mystery', 'invisible force', 'out of body', 'holy'
- Show desire to craft these into a spiritual world view – to use their organising and reasoning skills
- Children look out for explanations for these experiences – Conscience? God? A trick of the mind? – but tend to adopt the first on offer

(Hay and Nye 1998)

---

religion as continuous with everyday life. The integrity of a personal prayer is more valuable than its orthodoxy – the latter is alien to the child's mind.

Petitionary and penitential responses are uncommon responses to religious feeling at this age. Prayer in these forms will be harder and the child will be more dependent on copying others' formulae. Misconceptions of the purpose of prayer are more likely here (magic charm, wishful thinking) promoting neurotic, superstitious and ultimately unconvincing prayer experiences. Prayer is an unusual use of language and pre-schoolers are novice language users: it is vital to keep things very simple. One or two word prayers can work well, drawing on other ways of communicating (gesture, silence) to extend the prayer time. (For a discussion of the role of prayer in adults' spirituality, see Chapter 1.)

Spiritual life and schoolchildren's 'concrete' psychology

As children reach the ages of four and five they discover a new ability and desire to organise and sort information. They become capable of reasoning about their own and others' beliefs and behaviours; they are now less dependent on intuition, and more conscious that inner life has its own kind of reality and rules. These developments coincide with the beginning of formal education and the widening social horizon of school life.

This also marks the stage at which children's spirituality can be more directly observed. Despite their limited religious understanding, they report having spiritual experiences and feelings (whether or not they practise any faith). In a large scale survey Tamminen (1991) found 80 per cent of 7-year-olds and 60 per cent of 11-year-olds reported special experiences of God's closeness. This compares with just 30 per cent in adults. Qualitative research confirms this high incidence of religious experience among schoolchildren, and provides important information about the features of these experiences and the child's responses to them (Coles 1992; Hay and Nye 1998; see Box 5.2).

Possibilities for religious development created by a
'concrete' mindset

School children can more systematically identify and ask questions, but are still curious enough not to censor 'awkward' questions. This open and searching approach is an ideal quality to encourage for faith. However, being able to organise their thinking more clearly can compromise their earlier non-compartmentalised attitude to religion. They may want to put it in a box and see it restricted to 'church' or 'Sunday'. This can be offset when a place for religion is made apparent in other contexts, for example, at home. The child's perception of his mother's religiosity is the single biggest influence on his own religiosity (Hunsberger and Brown 1984). Children can use their concrete images and understanding in the service of their own kind of theological reasoning. They pile up literal images and weave them into a story-like form to produce coherence. Literal thoughts are qualified, extended, reasoned about: they feel driven to make meaning (Hull 1990).

Application: telling Bible stories

Goldman's (1964) research alerts us to problems school children often have with explaining Bible stories. However, stories are ideally suited to their minds in other ways. Children's capacity and need to organise without recourse to argument or abstract generalisations is attracted to the story form's ability to place feelings and images carefully into patterns and sequences to create meaning (Fowler 1981).

Children are much better than adults at projecting themselves wholeheartedly into stories. They relish the chance to visit a 'transitional space', loosening their grip on 'real' time, and on their ego, to allow inner reality and outer reality to meet and dialogue in a safe way. Bible stories, especially parables, have the ingredients to work in exactly this way. They are neither just fairy tales nor are they just moral codes or propositional statements of religious fact. They are a rich distillation of both life and ideas, of lived experience and intellectual meaning.

This natural capacity of the story to communicate to the child means it is often unnecessary and unhelpful to attempt to explain stories to them by using them as a platform for a teaching point (something the teacher tells them). This might even disconnect them from the primary experience of being carried into the meaning of story as it is told. In hearing and telling stories, schoolchildren use their distinctive psychological capacities to discover layers of meaning for themselves (Bettelheim 1978; Wolff Pritchard 1992).

SUMMARY OF KEY THEMES

- The power of religious images and stories in working with children.
- Levels of parental awareness.
- The pitfalls of encouraging literalism in childhood spirituality.
- Reading between the lines for fleeting verbal and non-verbal spiritual responses.
- The prevalence and characteristics of children's religious experiences.

QUESTIONS TO CONSIDER

- Could 'levels of parental awareness' (and their spiritual implications) also help to describe levels of 'pastoral awareness' in the way ministers variously respond to an individual's spirituality at any age?
- What in your childhood felt 'sacred' to you? Who did you share this with?
- Girls report more religious experience than boys. Why might this be, and how might ministry support boys especially in this area? What is there about a boy's psychology that could offer a few guidelines for your practice?
- What kinds of liturgy might appeal to children's psychology?
- Are you aware of approaches to children's ministry that might inadvertently damage or undermine their spirituality?

Adolescents, teenagers, and young adults

One of the most important things to recognise about teenagers, as about all general-ised groupings of people of a certain age, is that they are not all the same. One of the keys to a successful ministry with children and adolescents is avoiding the trap of treating them all the same way, as 'kids' or 'adolescents'.

Youth ministry is often seen as a need to respond to a crisis in our churches. Indeed, many do give up on faith and church in their youth (although the greater proportion of leavers are, in fact, adults). Young people have to deal with problems associated with sex, drugs, vandalism, and theft: these occur just as much among Christian young people as among their secular peers (Roehlkepartain 1998; Schuller (ed.) 1993). However, the adult reaction to this – to protect or distract young people from this reality – can be driven too much by adult psychological anxieties and pay too little attention to the young person's own psychological needs and strengths.

Psychological issues in adolescence: identity, sex, independence

Opportunities to meet a wider range of people (new school, clubs, choosing one's own friends) and increasing powers of reflective thinking mean that young people are primed to give more attention to their own identity. A new kind of self-discovery becomes possible and interesting. But this sense of individuality has to contend with increasing awareness of others, which can urge conformity to the peer group in which the individual self can find camouflage.

The widely held opinion that adolescents experience an 'identity crisis' is not supported by the research evidence, which shows that most young people have fairly stable and positive self-images. Anxiety and distress can occur if too large a gap develops between self-concept (how I see myself) and idealised self (how I would like to be), with girls most at risk, perhaps because they are more likely to include media images of women in their wider range of social reference.

The onset of puberty is an important feature of the transitional quality of adoles-cence. Losing child status, but not yet having full adult status arouses ambivalent

Box 5.3 The youth of today are *not* all the same

Adolescents, teenagers, and young adults are most definitely **not** a homogenous group. The differences in psychology and experience of 12-year-olds and 20-year-olds are enormous, not to mention the many differences within each age group. J. Nelson suggests at least three (empirically based) stages within this 'youth' period, each with its own particular emphases.

Joining and drifting
Age 12–15   Being uniquely oneself and / or belonging to a tradition.
The joining and drifting issues of early adolescence suggest the key image for ministry might be 'Jesus as a Way of Life', someone to model, someone with whom to develop allegiance.

Drifting and searching
Age 15–18   Exploring what is true for oneself and / or accepting what is received from someone else.
The drifting and searching of the mid-teens suggests the key image for ministry here might be 'Jesus the Friend', when the interpersonal is in ascendancy in their lives and closest relationships are highly valued as the place where 'truth' may be found.

Searching and owning
Age 18–21   Possessing one's own meaning system and / or being confused about purpose and occupation in one's life.
The searching and owning of young adulthood suggest the image of 'Jesus: The Goal and Meaning of Life'. This image can provide identity and coherence to life in a way that is more settled and reflective.

(Nelson 1997)

feelings. It can be liberating to no longer look or feel like a child, but frustrating that emerging adult characteristics (particularly sexuality) are not enough to complete the transition to adulthood. If puberty occurs earlier or much later than the rest of the peer group these problems can be compounded by social anxieties.

In adolescence a new kind of intellectual independence can develop. Not only are teenagers physically and socially less dependent on their primary carers, but they discover new mental skills that allow them to identify their own values, direction, feelings, and plans more explicitly than before. They can organise these into a 'system' in which logic and argument are prized, seemingly infallible, tools. Learning about these skills and tools requires freedom to practise and the support of a safety net if things go wrong. Families and churches can help (or hinder) this development of conceptual independence, allowing for the likelihood that aspects of faith may be re-evaluated by the young person too.

Popular perceptions of adolescence characterise it as problem-filled and angst-ridden. Serious psychological problems are slightly more common in this period than in childhood, but for the majority the teenage years are not an emotional war zone. Some psychological problems that *are* particularly associated with adolescence include the onset of schizophrenia, anorexia, and bulimia. General moodiness, bouts of misery, worry and self-criticism, fears about school, achievements and social acceptance are fairly common though in surprisingly few cases result in clinical depression or serious emotional disturbance.

Implications for ministry

Adolescence is not inevitably or excessively problematic, but the expectation that it is tends to pathologise youth and may sometimes act as a self-fulfilling prophecy. Churches need to be especially careful about the effects their negative assumptions about this period can have on young people's vulnerable self-images. Too easily, perhaps through an overemphasis on the theology of sin and salvation, young Christians can be made to feel unduly 'bad' in contrast with the church and faith, which are characterised as the opposing 'good', their only hope of refuge from themselves. Approaches that focus more on the emerging psychological strengths that young people bring to this challenging time in their lives can be more productive. Negative assumptions about young people (e.g. exaggerated fears about anti-social, anti-authoritarian tendencies) can result in practices that isolate them, as if they were diseased, perhaps to their own club or their own service. Adults need to be honest about their own sources of motivation for this. They may be resisting adolescent characteristics in themselves or the church (e.g. questioning authority, exploring different relationships, uncertainty about identity, ambivalence about dependency).

An overly protective approach to young people (e.g. hiding the social realities of sex, drugs or conflicting world views from them by enclosing them in churchy activities) can be psychologically misjudged too. Treating them like innocent children fails to help them with their current life tasks: survival skills in decision-making, exploring independence and responsibility.

Viewed as a problematic period, churches may have low expectations for young people. This can manifest itself in a policy of entertaining young people and soft peddling Christianity in an easy-to-swallow or completely disguised form (for example, as merely a club with no explicitly Christian title or purpose), and waiting until the storms blow over. However, head-on, deep engagement with Christianity has much to recommend it when adolescent psychology is seen in terms of its riches. This can speak to teenagers' and young adults' search for identity, their clear sense of existential struggle and of the complexity of moral choices, and their doubts and their desire for truth beyond this.

Orphans of independence

The new psychosocial need for independence can obscure the significance of dependable relationships with adults in teenage years. As capacities for self-awareness increase, fuelling identity issues, there is a greater need for a wide range of sources for comparison. Greater self-awareness also means young people can be more sensitive to messages about their self-worth – how others see them and support them. Well-intentioned separate youth programmes may cut young people off from a mainstream relationship with their church and suggest abandonment to – rather than support for – their emerging independence.

Peer relationships do not always offer a reliable basis for religious nurture. Research shows teenagers typically grossly underestimate their peers' religious beliefs – one study (Gibson 1994) of 900 British young people found that, while 49 per cent said they believed in God, only 22 per cent thought their friends did. Explanations of this include general lack of discussion about religion with peer group, the cultural prominence of secular views, and the possibility that atheist viewpoints are more voiced while religious belief is deemed conservative, or 'goody goody', and therefore something to keep quiet about. Relationships with adults prepared to discuss matters of belief may help to reduce the misperception that 'no one else is religious'.

Adolescent confirmation psychology

Thinking about confirmation (or similar rites that mark an autonomous decision in faith) can ignite the tension between the need for relationship and individual freedom of identity. On the one hand confirmation is a statement about conforming to the community's faith tradition. On the other it is the opportunity for a young person to realise their own voice in faith (following what others may have previously said on their behalf, for example, in infant baptism or dedication). Opposite ends of this inherent tension can be taken to extremes in the young person's mind. The conforming aspect may appeal to some for unhealthy reasons; it may signify a regressive avoidance of developing conceptual independence. Or it may put them off altogether. For others the independence aspect can be off-putting; it may seem too onerous a decision to take alone, too 'adult'.

Young people can be helped to recognise and resolve this tension. For example, against the background of a shared conformist faith they may have opportunities to develop a new kind of religious identity and autonomy through opportunities to speak for themselves and take on responsibilities in church.

Faith structure – the master story

James Fowler's (1981) research on faith development (see Chapter 6) observes there is often a shift in adolescence from the 'story mode' to a 'master story mode'. This entails a desire to search for, and discover, a master narrative that can pull earlier stories and experiences into one meaningful whole: a unifying ideology or worldview.

The appeal of ideology, which may be religious faith, a particular form of churchmanship or perhaps a political, environmental or ethical cause, reflects adolescents' new intellectual skills. They also become better at reflecting on their own cognitive processes, observing how knowledge is acquired and evaluating the validity of its sources. They are proactive in seeking the best fit for their various views and experiences. Whether or not the resulting world view (Fetz and Reich 1989) is overtly religious, it will be an attempt to incorporate their religious stance in some form. Increased awareness of their own mental processes also helps them to realise the limits of knowing, and suggest an exciting category of things that it is logically impossible to know, which can be important for faith too.

Cultural change may have subtle but not fundamental effects on adolescent psychology. Among post-modern youth, a layering of many philosophies and world views should not be mistaken for the absence of 'master-story'. Together these can have the same function, in a sense a post-modern attitude of 'everything goes' (not the same as 'anything goes') is its own kind of master-story or 'faith' in such cases.

Self-awareness and vulnerability

Developments in self-awareness in adolescence (who I am, how others see me, how I feel about who I feel and think I am, and so on) can give rise to a different sensitivity to vulnerability. As young people's sense of themselves increases, they recognise the ways in which they are not at the centre of things (though in their weaker moments they can be defiant about trying to make this the case after all!). They become aware of being 'at the edge' in terms of knowledge, power, adulthood, and of physical and sexual maturity. This can have implications for their faith, their spirituality, and their perception of the church.

Faith may provide a source of support for some young people: when faced with the reality of their marginality they may nevertheless be comforted by the idea that they have a place at the centre of God's concern. For many others this message is unconvincing in the face of so many other messages about their marginal, vulnerable, incomplete status. Between the ages of 11 and 16, many young people develop increasingly negative attitudes towards religion, and move from loving to punitive images of God (Francis 1992; Gibson 1994).

Compared with religion, 'spirituality' may be more resonant with adolescent psychology. Many construe spirituality as less concerned with power, facts, belief claims and explanations, and more open, unfinished, questioning, and explorative (Nye and Hay 1996; Hammond *et al.* 1990; Wulff 1997). With their heightened sense of vulnerability, 'religion' can seem too self-assured and self-important to the young person, whereas spirituality offers languages and practices that are appealingly ambiguous and uncertain about the sacred.

Often the church is perceived by disaffected young people as a barrier to spirituality, concerned with controlling thoughts and impeding free thinking. This too easily plays into a rebellious need to cast the 'organisation' as the enemy against which they must struggle as 'individuals'. The church's strength of identity forged over many years, its power and status, and the confidence of purpose it projects can deeply irritate their completely opposite feelings about themselves. They should not be shielded from opportunities to see that churches (and clergy) have their own areas of vulnerability and self-doubt. Equally, accepting some of these adolescent projections can be an important check on ways in which the church can lose sight of its own limitations and sense of humility.

SUMMARY OF KEY THEMES

- Variety among adolescents, teenagers, and young adults.
- Avoiding 'problematising' adolescence unnecessarily.
- Psychological challenges: identity, sex, independence.
- The danger of ghettoising teenagers in their own clubs and services.
- The appeal of the 'master narrative'.

QUESTIONS TO CONSIDER

- Listen to the lyrics of a song currently in the charts. Why might this resonate with youth psychology? Does it reveal something about their spirituality too?
- What sorts of responses to you have towards adolescents? Interest? Annoyance? Do you feel threatened or uneasy in their presence?
- What is 'adolescent' about your church? (Remember to think about this in positive as well as negative terms!)
- What is 'adolescent' about you? What influence does this have on your faith?

Further reading

Children's psychology

Herbert, M. (1988) *Working With Children and Their Families*, London: British Psychological Society and Routledge.

The development of religious understanding in children

Batson, C. D., Schoenrade, P. and Ventis, W. L. (1993) *Religion and the Individual: A Social-Psychological Perspective*, Oxford: Oxford University Press.
Francis, L., Kay, W. and Campbell, W. (1996) *Research in Religious Education*, Leominster: Gracewing.
Hull, J. (1990) *God-Talk With Young Children: Notes for Parents and Teachers*, Birmingham: University of Birmingham; Derby: Christian Education Movement.

Children's spirituality

Hay, D. and Nye, R. (1998) *The Spirit of the Child*, London: Fount.
Kimes Myers, B. (1997) *Young Children and Spirituality*, London: Routledge.

Adolescents, teenagers, and young adults

Robins, L. N. and Rutter, M. (1990) *Straight and Deviant Pathways from Childhood to Adulthood*, Cambridge: Cambridge University Press.
Various (1997) 'The spirituality of young people', *The Way Supplement* whole issue.

6   Religious development

QUESTIONS FOR MINISTRY

- How can I grow as a Christian?
- Is there a normal pattern of stages of spiritual growth to which most people conform?
- Can recognising people's different stages of religious development help to provide more sensitive pastoral support?
- What are the crises and stumbling blocks that can attend religious development?
- How can I recognise when people are caught up in abnormal developmental situations – when faith seems immature, stagnant, or off the wall?
- What is the spiritual journey a journey towards? What is it a journey away from?

Introduction

Change and growth affect us in every area of our lives. An understanding of psychological development is a basic necessity in the Christian ministry toolbox. We can only be sensitive to people's needs and gifts when we appreciate their developmental context – their previous history, current issues and future potential.

Religious development is a central issue for Christian ministry, but its meaning can be difficult to pin down. On the one hand it stands for something at the heart of the Christian understanding of a religious life – a growing relationship with God involving significant and ongoing personal transformation. Pastoral support for religious development in this sense is the *raison d'être* of Christian ministry. On the other hand, talk of religious development can suggest that spiritual growth is a quantifiable psychological variable like any other. Injudicious application of psychology's perspective can distort Christian understandings of development, for example by implying that religious growth is constrained wholly by our psychological timetabling, or that religious maturity or immaturity are simply and objectively measurable. This chapter contains psychological ideas that may make it easier to recognise typical patterns in development, and suggests how, when handled with due caution, these can assist approaches to ministry.

Many different kinds of metaphors have been used to characterise religious development: images of inner revolution, a journey, horticultural growth, changing nutritional needs, rebirth and death. Different metaphors illustrate the various characteristics involved in religious growth – God's grace, our effort and accumulating experiences, the timeliness of change as a natural unfolding and, conversely, the dramatic subversion of life's ordinary timetables, for example in the image of rebirth.

This rich mixture can be confusing – how do the metaphors translate into real lives? Lay understanding of what 'religious development' means reveals a degree of ambivalence. Many people experience a yearning to develop, driven by what Paul Tillich (1957) called 'the urge to self transcendence', a dim sense of our personal incompleteness. Yet too many regard the dynamic change inherent in 'development' as a threat to 'solid' faith, ironically resisting religious growth on religious grounds. Kenneth Stokes (1989) reports that 39 per cent of church members questioned in a USA study on Faith Development in the Adult Life Cycle said they believed a person's faith should *not* change throughout life.

In this chapter we shall explore the landmarks in normal patterns of human development, and the ways these can shape different aspects of religious growth. Addressing landmarks of intellectual, personal, social, emotional and faith development we need to consider: is there such a thing as a predictable pattern to Christian religious development? What might be the benefits and hazards of trying to anticipate the course of faith?

'RELIGIOUS DEVELOPMENT CAN SUGGEST A VARIABLE WE CAN ASSESS IN TERMS OF PROGRESS AND SPEED'

Patterns of development

Some of the most dramatic personal change occurs in the earliest years of our lives. The special care that is required for children's ministry is dealt with in Chapter 5. The material in this chapter focuses primarily on *adult* development. It is important, however, to check the tendency to think of religious development as an exclusively adult pursuit. Childhood can be a very significant period for religious change. Jesus himself drew our attention to the subtlety of this issue in his instruction that a developmental goal might be to become like little children; we should not restrict our attention solely to adult versions of maturity. Also, an appreciation of childhood's patterns is essential to understanding our adult nature: we can see better where we might be going, if we know where we have come from.

There is subtlety within adult development also. An awareness of this is especially important since a greater proportion of people come to faith these days as adults. In the UK, only a small minority (less than 15 per cent) have contact with a Christian denomination in childhood, and adolescence is no longer the primary period for conversions or confirmations (see Finney 1992). Ministry with adults is therefore more complicated than ever before: older adults may have a young faith, other adults with less life experience may have many years in the faith. It is difficult to know what to expect from such interactions of general development and religious development. Two kinds of tool seem necessary for this job: a working knowledge of some general patterns in psychological development, and a sense of the natural history of religious growth in particular. Since religious commitment engages us on so many levels – intellectual, emotional, social – the developmental psychology of each of these facets of mental life offers a distinctive and valuable set of resources that can be applied to people's specifically religious development.

Putting childish thought away?

Developmental psychology identifies the hallmarks of the adult intellect as an ability to think in abstract terms, drawing on concepts and principles, and employing powers of logic and reason to most topics. Piaget's analysis of intellectual development (see Chapter 5) is clear that adult thinking is distinguished by these qualities regardless of the differences in the quantity of knowledge a person has. Developing these general characteristics of 'adult thinking' would appear appropriate for thinking about religion also. After all, religious thought involves understanding abstract meanings, extracting principles for living, and wrestling with complex ideas.

With the benefit of secondary education, most people develop a general aptitude for logical thinking in readiness for adulthood. However, religious thinking does not always follow suit. For some people (or perhaps for all people, some of the time), more elementary ways of thinking about religious matters may continue to be cherished. Despite having an ability to think in more 'abstract' terms, it may seem safer to stay within the parameters of literal, or even more impressionistically emotional or sensory, kinds of thinking (see Chapter 5, especially boxes 5.1 and 5.2). It seems plausible that, for an adult, such an approach may have its own kind of primitive potency. However, when there is a mismatch between an adult's everyday approach to thinking and their approach to religious thinking, that person may be suppressing opportunities for their own spiritual development. Sensitive pastoral support and permission for religious thinking to 'grow up' may help such people to face this challenge successfully.

The transition from thinking about religion in concrete, literal terms to a form more suited to the qualities of the adult mind can be a particularly awkward moment in religious development. Many adults seem frozen in a state of what Ronald Goldman called '11-year-old atheism', ever since the emergence of adult rational logic made a literal interpretation of the religious tradition untenable (see Goldman 1964; see also Chapter 5). In such cases, recognising the form of the objection (an insult to adult 'intelligence') may help to frame approaches to adult evangelism, for example by presenting faith as a means of engaging with exceptionally difficult life questions, rather than as a set of simple, reassuring certainties. The awkward experience of recognising that an earlier perspective on religion needs to be discarded and replaced with something quite different, can be a spiritually instructive and refreshing experience in itself.

'Too many regard 'development' as a threat to 'solid' faith, resisting religious growth on religious grounds'

When religious thinking *has* acquired the qualities associated with an adult intellect, there are two ways in which adults can feel uncomfortable about this development. Some adults may recall the literalistic religion of their childhood as relatively stronger and more 'real'. They may feel guilty about having developed doubt, questions and alternative world views. Appreciating that these developments are appropriate features of applying their adult intellectual abilities can assuage that guilt. The shift away from the passion of emotionally governed 'thought' (pre-operational stage thinking) or literal certainties (concrete stage thinking) does not need to be interpreted as a withering of faith when seen in the context of the normal process of intellectual development.

For other adults, the revolution in religious understanding since their childhood may lead them to think that they did *not* have 'real' faith as children. For example, people may feel uncertain about the validity of religious commitments they made to a God they understood in simple, literal terms, when subsequent understanding has fuelled an apparently much more complex, deeply informed sense of God. Accepting that it is normal for our approach to thinking to change in these ways can help people feel more comfortable with the full course of their religious development and to identify the significance of their own (and others') religious feelings regardless of intellectual understanding.

SUMMARY OF KEY THEMES

- Benefits and hazards of thinking about religious 'development'.
- Different metaphors for religious growth: gradual or revolutionary.
- Legacies of childhood religious development.
- How the development of religious thinking can lag behind more general intellectual development.
- Accepting the need for development in religious thinking.

QUESTIONS TO CONSIDER

- Which metaphor (inner revolution, journey, organic growth, death and rebirth) do you favour as a way of thinking about your own religious growth? Why?
- What suggests to you that your faith is still developing?
- What has been the most constant feature of your faith; what has been the most changeable?
- Do you welcome change in your own spiritual and religious life? If so, why? If not, why not?

Religion through the lifespan

Despite the obvious changes that occur in the ways people think about religion during the course of their lives, religious development is perhaps more often about changes of heart than changes of mind. Psychological theories of emotional or personality development are helpful here because they look at psychological patterns and processes in a way that resonates with traditional Christian ideas about spiritual growth and personal transformation. Such theories suggest distinctive 'seasons' of personal growth, outlining a possible pattern of natural stages in religious development too.

Jungian 'individuation'

C. G. Jung observed a special relationship between religious and personality development, especially in mid- to late adulthood. In the first half of life, the normal orientation of the psyche is extroverted as the ego works to establish a firm sense of 'I' in the material world. This achieved, in the second half of life a new kind of developmental process becomes possible – the 'individuation' process. Jungian individuation relies on the realisation that ego is not the whole self: there are deeper unconscious aspects to selfhood. The Jungian account of how adult personality development can proceed – once the ego begins to realise this is not a 'one man show' – emphasises the importance of integrating psychological opposites. Examples include reconciling 'outer world' and 'inner world' orientations, and recognising the personal 'shadow' (the unattractive, darker aspects of ourselves), the anima (feminine side of male psyche), and the animus (masculine side of female psyche). By integrating these features, and finding a new balance in which the ego no longer rules in isolation but recognises its place in a much larger 'whole', the person can experience a radically different sense of completeness. (For more on Jungian individuation, see Chapter 15; and see Chapter 3 for a fuller explanation of Jungian personality types and orientations.)

This rich account of personality development offers various insights applicable to ministry. It suggests, for example, that ministry should consider the special potential for religious development that may be primed in mid- to late adulthood, since this 'season' of personality development may be specially ripe for a re-orientation towards the spiritual. It specifies the kind of spiritual activity someone at this point in life is likely to find necessary and rewarding, namely a re-orientation towards the significance of inner experience, and the desire to explore and integrate the neglected regions of personality.

While supporting this, another pastoral task might be to keep in check the temptation to become lost in inner exploration at the expense of more outward and 'worldly' religious activities such as mission or fellowship. Equally, the more inward spiritual orientation of older adults might be a useful frame for the typically more outwardly oriented younger adults, demonstrating the range of ways that religious energies can be invested and developed. Mismanaged, this kind of diversity of religious interests between people at different points in development might become a source of tension.

Freud and religious development

Freudian psychology has also been applied to religious development in at least two different ways. Sometimes it provides a developmental *explanation* of people's attachment to religion (Rizzuto 1979). For example, religion can be seen as arising from unresolved issues between infants and their parents. So, if people have had problematic relationships with their own fathers, those problems may be transferred to their relationship with God and constrain their religious development.

The Freudian approach can also be used to provide a *map* of how people develop religiously, making use of the scheme of oral, anal and Oedipal (or genital) stages, though these are usually interpreted as rather loose metaphors (Faber 1976). At the first stage there is an emphasis on felt unity with God, at the next stage an emphasis on religious legalism, and at the third stage a movement towards a freer sense of relationship to God. Erik Erikson's approach to personality development provides greater attention to detail.

Erik Erikson's eight stages of development

While Jung recognised a religious dimension in personality development in later life, Erik Erikson's model of eight stages of development offers a different kind of attention to detail. He categorises the lifespan in terms of the social conditions people typically face at different stages of their lives. This offers a simple reminder of some of the important life events we might expect people to have faced, be facing or have yet to face (e.g. marriage, becoming a parent, retirement). Such 'critical life events' are very often crucibles for (initial) religious questioning and growth, especially when a number of important events coincide (Stokes 1989, Chapter 6). This underlines the fact that religious development is more often stimulated by features of our personal context, rather than the entreaties of a church-led agenda. Grasping such golden opportunities for religious development will depend on reaching out to meet people in these life experiences; consequently, having a way of making reasonable guesses about what and when these might be – having a degree of 'developmental savvy'– is vital.

Erikson observes important changes in our social context at various stages of the life cycle. We begin, in infancy, in a state of vulnerable dependence on other people. Then we pass through periods of tentative self-control and independence in childhood. In adolescence we begin a new kind of referential engagement with our social context, working out 'who' this independent person is in relation to a growing circle of significant others (e.g. peer groups, heroes, and role models). Early adulthood is typically a period when having new kinds of exclusive friendships (dating, marriage) are the primary currency of the social context. In middle adulthood the social situation may revolve around providing for others, as parent, mentor, or in the form of greater responsibility for others in the workplace. Old age involves a degree of detachment from the familiar social world (facing loss in various forms: physical abilities, bereavements, retirement), and a final evaluation of personal integration.

Erikson's main message concerns the sequence of emotional conflicts that are primed at each social period. Our development depends on how these conflicts are resolved – positively or negatively (see Table 6.1). Positive resolution strengthens the personality for the ongoing journey through life, since the outcome furnishes the personality with a new virtue at each stage (hope, will, purpose, and so on). Unfavourable resolutions scar the personality and destabilise future development, and

Table 6.1 Erikson's eight stages of development

Stage	Psycho-social conflict	Outcomes
Infancy	Basic trust versus mistrust I'm dependent on others – can I trust in this system?	Hope or withdrawal
Toddler	Autonomy versus shame and doubt I can seize control in some areas, sometimes – is this independence met with encouragement, even when my efforts miss the mark?	Will or compulsion
Pre-school	Initiative versus guilt I can more freely exercise my will, physically and emotionally – is taking such initiatives rewarding or too likely to end in tears?	Purpose or inhibition
School age	Industry versus inferiority I am aware of my peer group and our differing abilities – am I basically competent or inferior?	Competence or inertia
Adolescence	Identity versus identity crisis I become properly self-conscious; who am I? with whom and what should I identify?	Fidelity or role repudiation
Early adulthood	Intimacy versus isolation I am ready to share my identity with special others – how far can I give of myself in intimate relation? Should this risk be avoided altogether?	Love or exclusivity
Middle adulthood	Generativity versus stagnation I have distinctive experience to pass on – how far can I extend a creative influence on others? Should I keep all my energies for myself?	Care or rejectivity
Old age	Integrity versus despair I take stock of my life as a whole, past, present and limited future – does this 'end game' add up to a worthwhile synthesis and overall meaningfulness? Or has there been no point at all, and no time left to change this?	Wisdom or disdain

the outcome is characterised as a kind of pathology (withdrawal, compulsion, inhibition, and so on).

As a pastoral tool, this model offers a way into the likely contours of people's emotional lives from cradle to grave. In the emotional conflicts, and in the emergent virtues or pathologies, it is possible to discern a religious quality to development at almost every turn. This offers a way of making reasonable guesses about the particular spiritual concerns a person is likely to be open to working on, depending on their stage in life. For example, the early adulthood conflict

---

Box 6.1 Erikson exercise

For each stage in social development (e.g. infancy, toddler, and so on), identify someone you know, perhaps from your congregation.

- How has the psychosocial conflict associated with their current stage in life been apparent in your ministry with each of these people?
- Reflect on the 'outcomes' they are each working on.
- How can the positive outcome option (e.g. hope, will, and so on) be encouraged as a timely gift they bring to church life?

'intimacy versus isolation' is vital not only for developing human relationships, but also for developing intimacy in relationship with God. This may be a critical period of readiness in which to develop openness in prayer, for example, such that hopes and fears are honestly divulged before God, and also the time to recognise God's intimacy towards us.

A crucial feature of this tool as a reference for ministry is the provision it makes for seeing a person's current religious life as a product of their emotional history. In some cases, poorly resolved conflicts may have prejudiced religious development, resulting in a kind of twisted growth. There may be some personal work to do, facing up to the legacies of long-forgotten periods of life, so that religious and personal development can proceed in synchrony. Occasionally it may be possible that religious commitment itself can compensate for any missing or underdeveloped aspects of personal development. Imagine, for example, the plight of someone who had failed to develop a core sense of fidelity at the end of adolescence. Through positive forms of church fellowship, and perhaps a particular connection made with someone serving as a significant, reliable role-model, fidelity might be restored.

Erikson's theory of development has been employed by Meissner (1987) to formulate the human side of how people grow in grace. He sees grace as providing an additional resource that enables people to move on from one stage of psychological development to another when their own ego resources are insufficient. One attraction of this object relations framework is that the focus is clearly on the development of relationships rather than intellectual development. If faith is primarily a matter of relationship with God rather than of cognition, that makes it a more appropriate approach than the Piagetian one used by Goldman. Another attraction of Meissner's approach is that he keeps the theology and psychology more distinct than some other developmental theorists, such as Fowler (see next section).

Though Erikson's eight stages of development have become widely known, some may find his scheme over-complex. Michael Jacobs (1993), in *Living Illusions*, has offered a simplified model of just four stages, relating them more explicitly to religion, and also to the developmental schemes of Freud (and of James Fowler, whose work is discussed in the next section).

Jacobs' first stage is Trust and Dependency. These are the dominant concerns for infants in their relationship with parents, and provide the basis for adults' sense of relationship to God. Jacobs' next stage is concerned with Authority and Autonomy. This is an important issue in the development of all children, and in religious development as well. There is a tendency to take pleasure in an absolute acceptance of authority, and a zealous performance of religious requirements, though alongside this issues of autonomy are beginning to surface. Next, for Jacobs, is the stage concerned with Co-operation and Competition where people are increasingly concerned with the authenticity of their religious experience and with finding their own identity. This raises the question of how to find appropriate co-operation with the religious community from such a stance. Jacobs' final stage, concerned with Complexity and Simplicity, is something of an idealisation, as is often the case in stage models of religious development. It is concerned with finding the simple essence of religious faith through all the complexities of tradition and belief. Jacobs' first three stages are seen as basically corresponding to the Freudian oral, anal and Oedipal stages mentioned above (for a fuller exposition, see Jacobs 1993).

SUMMARY OF KEY THEMES

- Seasons of personal transformation in 'lifespan' psychology.
- Carl Jung's idea of 'individuation': the process of personality integration.
- Being aware when people are ready for a period of transformation and growth.
- The emotional and spiritual challenges that attend each season of life.

QUESTIONS TO CONSIDER

- Is your church a refuge for people who want to 'find themselves'? Should it be?
- What does the Christian tradition have to offer to those on this quest?
- What would be unique to younger adults on this quest? Older adults?
- Have you encountered someone with passionate spiritual concerns that are very different from your own?
- How might this difference have been explained by your different stages in the life-cycle?
- Erikson describes development as moving from one emotional crisis to the next! How far does the church provide a ministry to those experiencing the particular kinds of crisis outlined here?
- Might there be special issues concerning the anima for male clergy? And the animus for female clergy?

James Fowler's *Stages of Faith*

In this chapter we have seen how understanding general psychological development provides important clues about issues that can arise in the course of religious development. James Fowler's (1981) *Stages of Faith* takes this a step further by identifying a developmental pattern for faith itself. He listened to people talk about their faith and

Table 6.2 Fowler's stages of faith

	Type of faith	Characteristics	Pastoral needs
0	Undifferentiated	Faith emerges as a pre-language of trust.	Positive early relationships of infancy to create the sense of 'being in relation', leading to a general attitude of trust about one's place in the world.
1	Intuitive–Projective	Faith is led by imagination and feelings, mystery and curiosity. Thoughtful coherence is lacking, but there is an intuitive attraction to strong images onto which overwhelming feelings of power or powerlessness, safety or danger can be projected and 'held'. Emotion and curiosity can spill over into an unwitting fascination with darker material and images.	Sensitive channelling and boundary setting will allow imaginative flow and offer an appropriate range of images in which to invest. These vessels for faith need not always be religious images and stories – fairy-tales may be effective too.
2	Mythic–Literal	Faith becomes a kind of simple thinking. Narrative and stories provide the mental structure to a sequences of ideas, feelings or values. Meaning and reflection outside the story form have little to offer, all attention is focussed on the powerful clarity of the surface meaning.	Opportunities to work within a narrative mode as a way of connecting feeling and thought. It is important not to let the religious life become limited to what can be thought about, but keep a deeper engagement process open through what can be experienced 'in' story. Otherwise faith will become a mental straitjacket – inflexible or untenable.
3	Synthetic–Conventional	Faith becomes a form of loyalty. It is influenced by self-awareness and awareness of others. There is a growing sense of meaning to be found beyond the concrete – for example, in parable, in drawing ideas together. Faith is expressed in personal relationships with the like-minded, and affirmed in feeling connected to the consensus though conventional religious commitments. God and the church are viewed in idealistic interpersonal terms, a new form of family.	The coherence provided by relationships needs to keep a check on reality. Being too idealistic about the value of community and harmony can shield important questions and admissions of diversity. Relationship breakdown (e.g. feeling let down by a faith role model) can destabilise faith itself. There can be too much dependence on thinking like the crowd rather than for oneself – this may flatter leadership egos.

continued on next page

Table 6.2 Fowler's stages of faith (cont.)

Type of faith	Characteristics	Pastoral needs
4 Individuative–Reflective	Faith becomes a style of self-directed examination and exploration of ideas, away from the 'people centred' faith of relationships and roles. Coherence comes in intellectual pursuit of clearer understanding and de-mystification. Emotion and experience can be sidelined as analysis of meaning increases.	There is a need to feel released from patronising or authoritarian styles of church. Fellowship can seem unappealing, but totally independent exploration can become overwhelmingly lonely or proud. Worship or prayer may provide important moments to let go of a self-managed objectivity.
5 Conjunctive	Faith becomes a symbolic space where emotion and reason, tradition and the personal, and numerous other apparent paradoxes are held together. Coherence is found in the creative, conscious tensions of opposites viewed as balancing elements in the whole picture. With the insights of stage 4 reasoning, there can be a nostalgic return to the value of symbol, story and relationship.	There is a valuable willingness to dialogue with very different others, such as people of other faiths. The renewed sense of God as a mystery that reason alone can't contain may inadvertently tip the balance towards God's 'otherness'. Guard against the sense of alienation and aloneness that may ensue, or a retreat into a private world of spirituality.
6 Universalising	Faith is finally transformed into a selfless state of relationship with God and everything in His creation. Faith of this kind is very rare. Expression is often found in a consuming commitment to higher, universal causes – justice, love	Protection from self-sacrifice and exploitation.

Box 6.2 Fowler exercise

- What do you recognise of your own journey in Fowler's stages of faith?
- Make a list of salient features and events in your personal life (in 5- or 10-yearly blocks).
- Include significant relationships, achievements and interests.
- Then try to recall the quality of your faith in each of these periods – your concept of God, of the church, of personal spirituality.
- How have these two areas (personal history and religious growth) been related for you?

life stories, and observed six types of faith-perspective among people ranging from four to eighty years of age. These different forms of faith shared a number of characteristics with staged development in other areas – thinking, morality, emotion, ego development and social conditions. This suggested a developmental sequence for the six types of faith – providing an interesting attempt to describe the typical life-cycle of faith.

The 'stages of faith' idea has proved powerful and popular in Christian ministry, although Fowler does not insist this sequence is specific to Christian faith development, but rather sees it as a pattern of growth and modification that characterises any kind of faith. Fowler has not only worked on the theoretical aspects of religious development's relation to stages of faith. He has also explored what these stages mean for more sensitive pastoral support of Christian growth. Table 6.2 summarises the key features of each stage of faith, and the pastoral support on which these depend according to Fowler.

Fowler's 'stages of faith' offers ministry a tool that can make short work of the many challenges of engaging with people's religious development. We will discuss briefly the reasons to be cautious when using this tool, then look at the ways it can helpfully be applied within the context of ministry.

Cautions and limitations

It is unwise to have exact and rigid expectations about the age at which people will reach particular stages in their faith. Being older does not automatically mean having a 'higher' stage of faith. Most adults have stage 3 or 4 faith styles, some stage 5 and very few stage 6. An earnest form of adult faith can sometimes still demonstrate characteristics of stage 2 – which reflects more of a childlike psychology in terms of thinking, moral simplicity and so on. Age and lived experience provide foundations that are often necessary, but not sufficient, for key aspects of faith development.

We also need to be cautious about the tool's ability to predict the future course of a person's faith journey. People are more likely to respond to the power of these stages to make sense of changes retrospectively, recognising a similar sequence to their faith history. More longitudinal research is needed to show whether people necessarily pass from one stage to the next in this sequence. So at best it suggests what growth could be like, but not what it should be.

This tool is not meant to be used judgementally. Be wary of the temptation to equate higher numbered stages with a higher order of faith. Fowler is adamant that every stage has gifts for the church. Faith development is not about being 'better' than others, but adaptation in pursuit of what is personally best and authentic. This tool is designed to promote sensitivity, not to create conflict and condescension.

Finally, be tentative about how valuable the stage characterisations are for individuals seeking insights about their own journey. It seems easier to recognise generalisations about other people's religious development in these categories, but less easy to find a stage corresponding with the subtlety of one's own faith. The sharp demarcation of separate stages does not always fit with people's experience of development in adulthood; there is often a stronger sense of continuity and gradual unfolding.

Pastoral applications of the 'Stages of Faith' model

Bearing all these caveats in mind, the 'stages of faith' model can be applied successfully and constructively in pastoral ministry in a variety of ways. The content may be
best reserved as a heuristic for ministers, but sharing the *methods* more widely may
be valuable for individual growth. There is virtue in encouraging people to talk (or
write) about their faith in a way that listens out for the ways that changes in it are
connected to other aspects of their lives. Framing faith and life as a unique 'story'
can be a revelation. The story format of different chapters can encourage people to
look out for themselves for an appropriate way for the 'story so far' to be followed
up. Hearing other people's faith stories is also an important way of appreciating the
developmental quality of faith, and an ideal way to kindle fresh development.

Identifying the nature of each stage may also be helpful in detecting ways in which
people need to develop within that stage. The suggestions about the different ways
in which coherence for faith is sought (stage 1: in emotion-laden images, 2: in narratives, 3: in the interpersonal, 4: in argument, 5: in paradox) point to the most likely
means of contributing to development for each form of faith. For example, growth at
stage 3 will not come through inspiring theological argument. Rather, faith is likely
here to be sustained through opportunities to build up strong bonds of fellowship.
Stage 3 faith will also feel supported by open leadership and a clear, uncomplicated
approach to theology. However, extra effort may be required to avoid undue neglect
of faith's 'difficult corners', and to make clear the value for the spiritual life of being
honest to oneself rather than unfailingly loyal to the perceived consensus.

The potential for a strength of a particular stage (often the 'coherence' giving feature)
to become a handicap if taken to extremes is worth taking into account in pastoral
support for religious development; feeding a 'dependency habit' will imprison faith
rather than help it grow. There may be a limit to how far one can go on developing
within one kind of faith. This makes clearer what it might mean to be 'stuck' in terms
of faith development, why it can be hard to get out of this rut, since it means giving
up investment in the thing that has been of most importance. For example, people
may find it particularly difficult to move beyond a cycle of critical analysis in stage 4
into a more experiential, joyful engagement in faith because they have become
hooked on the significance of 'ideas'.

This analysis also explains why religious development can sometimes feel
unnervingly like a loss of faith, hopefully for only a short period, until a new form of
coherence can be discovered. In ministering to people in this kind of unsettling transitional situation, it might be reasonable to offer the kind of material indicated as
fundamental to the next stage of faith in Fowler's model. For example, it might be
productive to meet despondency in someone (at stage 2) who feels let down by the
unreasonable expectations of a literal approach to faith, with (stage 3) opportunities
to feel part of the social structures of the church, and with relational images of God,
for example, in the Trinity, and the family qualities of faith: God as Father, being
brothers and sisters in Christ.

Social processes and conflict situations in a church can benefit from a 'stages of
faith' perspective. Often church congregations manifest a modal stage – church A

has mainly people with stage 3 faith, church B is more stage 4, and so on. This raises questions about the experience of outliers. Through a kind of conformity process that imposes the developmental values of the majority, anyone in the minority may feel unduly hurried to catch up with the rest or feel ostracised. Another scenario might be where someone has a higher stage of faith than the majority and feels pressure to regress to a former style to fit in. The individual may be more vulnerable to these group pressures just when he or she is ripe for personal growth. As mentioned above, being in transition can feel uncomfortably like losing faith. People (including clergy) may be troubled if they become aware of this happening to someone – feeling they are growing away from the group. There may be a strong urge to undermine this necessary 'death' (leading to new life) process by insisting on resuscitating the old familiar approach to faith. Fowler refers to this as the messiness of people in transition, and the desire this brings out in others to 'tidy' them up, or sweep them out. In some cases experiencing developmental 'difference' might lead some people to give up on a particular church, and perhaps faith, altogether. (For a further discussion of conformity within churches, see Chapter 11.)

Is development different for women?

Having a framework of common patterns should also make it easier to recognise idiosyncratic features of faith and development and so to respond more sensitively to the complexity of individuals. Reference to the stages of faith framework has helped to show that women's religious development may diverge from what initially seemed to be the norm (Slee 1996).

In Fowler's model, a move from interpersonal dependence (stage 3) to a self-styled autonomy (stage 4) is proposed as a key step in typical faith development. The self is at first defined through its roles and relationships. Fowler draws on the ego development account of Robert Kegan (1982) here, suggesting that this stage gives way to a need to recognise a 'self in my own right' perspective. The move to disengage from others (and its correlate in faith perspective) may not be typical of a female way of developing. Women's lives are often rather differently characterised by their greater investment in relationship roles and the interpersonal domain. For example, the roles and responsibilities of being a wife, mother, or adult daughter have a different quality to their male equivalents, husband, father, or adult son. Consequently, a period of interpersonal development may be elongated and more complex for women.

Sharon Parks' (1990) research suggests women's faith passes through extra substages of deepening development within the interpersonal stage 3 period. Finding themselves embedded for longer in a world of relationships and loyalties, women can pass through a phase of 'probing commitment'. This allows them to explore divided feelings about commitment while remaining loyal overall. Later a 'tested commitment' phase may emerge which seems to reflect greater self-awareness, centred in living out the chosen commitment rather than driven to separate from it, as seems to be the case for men.

In another study of women's distinctive faith patterning, Shirley Mader (1986) observed that an autonomy-seeking 'separation' period (like stage 4) occurs much later in women's lives, after many seemed to have enjoyed a period of stage 5-style faith. A more common sequence of stages for women (although it would, of course, be much too much of a generalisation to imagine just one sequence for all women) might then be 1, 2, 3, 3a, 3b, 5, 4. It is important to note here that the life patterns for women are rapidly diversifying. There are different expectations for women about careers, remaining single, choosing not to have children or to have them much later. The delay in seeking a more autonomous perspective out of loyalty to 'home and family' commitments before one's own needs may become less representative of women's psychological development in the future, though perhaps more so in men's lives. If authentic religious development is a dialogue with a person's life then it seem wise to assume that all kinds of variations in the basic pattern may affect it. Others have noted that life patterns may differ across different social classes or as a function of education.

SUMMARY OF KEY THEMES

- Fowler's six stages of faith development.
- Dangers associated with this approach: for example, being too prescriptive or judgemental, or over-generalising.
- The value of telling the story of one's own religious journey.
- Using the stages of faith model to highlight spiritual and pastoral needs.
- How sex affects religious development: why women's experience may be different.

QUESTIONS TO CONSIDER

- Who (or what) determines the modal stage of faith of a congregation? The minister? Church tradition? The congregation? The elders?
- Should a congregation seek a minister with the same stage of faith as the majority of their membership? List the advantages and disadvantages concerning your decision.
- How might religious development be a source of division between a husband and wife? How could marriage preparation (and support thereafter) help people to engage with their religious development?
- In your church are men, women and children given equal opportunities to tell their faith stories?
- Might some groups need positive discrimination to encourage this valuable activity?
- What steps could you take to protect outliers, especially those in transition, from social pressures to adopt the same kind of faith as the majority?

Religious maturity

Is there an ideal end point or goal for religious development? How can religious maturity be most helpfully characterised? In the first place it is clear that maturity itself is an organic, dynamic feature, as opposed to an all-or-nothing property. Asking about maturity is helpful here because it highlights a number of biases or omissions in the psychology of religious development explored in this chapter. The psychological perspectives drawn to our attention in this chapter do not (with the possible exception of Fowler's stage 6) really provide images of extraordinary or exceptional faith. It is not clear how psychological theories help to map out developmental processes that produce saints, mystics or prophets. Neglect of an ultimate kind of religious development perhaps reflects psychology's emphasis on natural and passive aspects of development as opposed to development that is deliberately sought. In psychology questions about deliberate actions to nurture development, of one kind or another, are normally dealt with in the different, but related frame of educational psychology (see Chapter 5). However, for Christians, development has often been thought of as something deliberately sought after, sometimes through following the specific disciplines of a spiritual tradition. A pastoral view of maturity has to take into account both psychology's insights about the more natural and passive qualities of development, and the image of development as something Christians consciously strive for.

Psychological studies may implicitly suggest that people are passively being led through their religious life by universal and inevitable processes of human psychological development. Much religious literature, however, places more emphasis on the role of the will, self-discipline, and active co-operation in the process of transformation. Maturity may depend on a discovering a balanced way of combining passive and active processes of change and growth, in which case, an understanding of religious maturity has to draw on psychological *and* theological interpretations of development. While both are relevant, finding a viable way of combining psychological and theological perspectives is hazardous and should be done cautiously. A popular criticism of Fowler's stages of faith model is its unacknowledged trespassing into a particular theological vision of mature development, reflecting Fowler's own denomination's way of interpreting faith (liberal Episcopalian). The focus in this chapter on the psychological means that the reader should be aware that only half the work has been done. In terms of practice, the point here is that while encouraging a sensitivity to the dynamic of religious change found in what is psychological and 'natural', it is important to guard against this becoming the only measure of development.

It is also worth being wary of a psychological bias towards development of individuals. Religious maturity may not be best characterised as having a basically self-serving or self-qualifying goal. A Christian perspective might attend more to evidence of maturity as something with a relational outworking and goal. Erikson's mode of generativity touches on this, since it acknowledges a kind of maturity in the desire to share the fruits of personal development. Again it is important to be aware of the potential divergence between the psychological and Christian perspectives. Psychology's more descriptive accounts of normative patterns of development do not necessarily chart change for the better; there is room here also for reflection about what might be religiously prescribed.

Authenticity and the desire for change

Despite these limitations, the psychological accounts explored in this chapter do provide some clues to themes in religious maturity. One is attention to the value of authenticity (discussed at length by Lonergan 1958). In many stage accounts, personal transformation arises from an accumulation of developments in different areas of our lives. Religious maturity may depend, at any stage, on the degree to which the most current of all of a person's abilities (e.g. thinking, ego development, social skills, emotional conflicts, moral and faith development) are employed in their religious life. Applying personal 'bests' in each of these domains ensures that religious growth is more likely to be holistic and authentically personal. It is not easy to be as comprehensive as this all of the time, so this kind of vision of maturity is something we are always working on. It may be helpful consciously to audit this goal, to identify areas that need work to catch up with the rest. Pruyser and Malony's 'religious status inventory' and 'religious status interview' (in Malony 1995) provide ready-made tools to explore this. They can detect, for example, areas in which there may be disjunctions between maturity in belief and the outworking of this in practice – in other words, whether life and faith are deeply connected.

Another theme of religious maturity is a positive attitude to or desire for change. Neither complacency nor a sense of closure can exist alongside maturity. In the different accounts of development discussed above, we have seen a common movement of investment, detachment and reattachment. Maturity is conveyed in this as a layering process of perspectives in which the same thing is allowed, even encouraged, to be re-evaluated, re-connected, but kept fresh. Being committed to this process of revision is perhaps much more important for deepening faith than commitment to one particular, potentially stale, version of faith's content (see the distinction between quest and intrinsic orientations discussed in Chapter 3). Fowler's image of faith (and Piaget's image of mental style) as a kind of structure that develops as it is built, and rebuilt when faults in the old construction become apparent, tells us something important here. A mature perspective is one always ready to embrace starting again, giving up mastery, and temporarily adopting the position of a novice. Maturity emerges in most stage accounts of development as an ability to make the widest connections; a highly sophisticated kind of perspective-taking that is able to hold the many different aspects of faith together. In Christian teaching, it is made clear that this process is not completed this side of physical death.

Finally, an important hallmark of maturity that a psychological perspective highlights is a capacity for failure. It may be that that too many Christians assume religious development and maturity consists of positive achievements, abilities and understanding. The slippery notion of 'sanctification' prevalent in some religious approaches to development conjures up images of a concentration of all that is good. This is probably neither helpful nor adequate. Maturity is also about being able to deal with failure and frustrations. In this sense it suggests that, at a psychological level, maturity is a quality of tolerance of the good and bad as realistic features of one's life. Jung's account of personality integration, especially in terms of the personal shadow, illustrated this clearly. In Christian ministry, this may be the significance for maturity of a realistic awareness of sin, both personal and collective and, as it was noted above that optimal development consists of consistency across all levels, maturity is not only about a confessional self-awareness but something that evokes a need to respond, to change. It's not just knowing about shortcomings, it's about doing (and knowing how to do) something about them.

SUMMARY OF KEY THEMES

- Thinking about what the goal of religious development might be.
- Combining developmental psychology with Christian ideals.
- Looking for an authentic and holistic development of all a person's faculties.
- The desire for change itself as a sign of maturity.
- Being prepared to fail and falter on the religious journey.

QUESTIONS TO CONSIDER

- Whose maturity (religious or otherwise) have you been most impressed by? What were their signs of maturity?
- Should we be spiritually mature in the same way that others are?
- What are the most important goals of spiritual maturity for you?
- As a Christian, what do you think about the apparent destinations of development suggested in Jungian, Eriksonian and Fowlerian theory?
- When you are called on to be a guide to others, what will you do about differences between what psychology describes and what you believe a Christian perspective prescribes?

Conversion

This chapter has been largely concerned with gradual changes in religion over the lifespan. However, there are also more dramatic changes, of which 'conversion' is the most conspicuous and extensively researched. Various definitions of conversion have been proposed. However, the criteria suggested by George Coe (1916) would still be quite widely accepted, that conversion is (a) a transformation of self that (b) comes about through some definite process, that is, not just maturation, (c) has radical consequences, (d) leads in a higher direction, and (e) occurs in a social context.

Though sudden conversions are the most conspicuous, some conversions can be gradual, as has been recognised from the earliest studies. There seem to be quite broad-ranging distinctions between sudden and gradual conversion. Sudden conversions tend to come earlier in life, to be more emotional, to be linked to a conservative theology, to have a strong emphasis on the release from sin and guilt, to arise from a sense of deprivation, and to be relatively passive. The differences between sudden and gradual conversions are not confined to religious matters, as those who undergo sudden conversions are more conservative politically as well.

Though these broad-ranging differences between sudden and gradual conversions substantiate the validity of the distinction, 'sudden' conversions may not in fact be as sudden as they appear. There often seem to be precursors in the form of a period of religious searching and re-evaluation. However, in the nature of things, the build-up to apparently sudden conversions is difficult to investigate in a systematic empirical way.

It is widely assumed that conversions represent a change from non-belief to belief. However, this is seldom the case. The majority of people who undergo a 'conversion' are lapsed believers returning to their faith, rather than people who have never had one. This has practical implications. There seems to be a historical trend for there to be an increasing number of people who have never had a religious faith and, if they experience conversion at all, it may well be of a different kind from that which obtains when lapsed believers return.

Another misconception about conversion is that it represents a permanent change. In fact, many so-called conversions are relatively short-lived, and indeed some people experience a whole series of conversions. If so, conversion should be seen as one phase of an oscillation in and out of religious commitment rather than a permanent change.

One of the problems in studying conversion is that it is probably a very heterogeneous phenomenon. The distinction between sudden and gradual conversions, though useful, fails to provide an adequate classification. Various other more elaborate classifications have been proposed, such as that of John Lofland and Norman Skonovd (1979), who distinguish among intellectual, mystical, experiential, affectional, revivalistic, and coercive types of conversion. That kind of more elaborate classification may well be needed, but it has not yet proved its worth nor been widely accepted. The result is that most general ideas that have been advanced about conversion are probably true of some conversions but not all. That is probably true, for example, of the ideas that conversion arises out of social deprivation, that it resolves a sense of personal crisis, and that it is a regression into a more passive form of religion. These are no doubt true of some conversions but almost certainly not all of them.

The tendency for people to experience conversion as a kind of exhilarating resolution to mental, and perhaps spiritual, distress can create special pastoral needs. Ministry with converts needs to be alert to longer-term personal problems being temporarily masked, or assumed to be solved by the conversion, and to be ready to help the convert work through these and their possible disillusionment once the honeymoon feelings of exhilaration subside.

One of the intriguing aspects of conversion, in the context of general theories of religious development such as that of Fowler, is that it often seems to be more a regression than an advance. Quite often, in conversion, there is a return to a more literal mode of belief, and a greater acceptance of religious authority. However, that does not necessarily cast doubt on the value of religious conversion. It can equally well be taken as pointing to the limitations of current concepts of religious development.

Christian ministry deals with people at all stages in life. It also endeavours to support people wherever they are on their journey to faith. A basic understanding of both child and adult developmental psychology can ease this daunting responsibility. This chapter has looked at models that offer tools for supporting adult development, both in terms of a general sensitivity to different phases of adult psychology and in terms of specific support for patterns of religious growth. These are not the only psychological accounts of religious development (others are referred to in the further reading list). What the models discussed here offer are a ready supply of tips and insights to guide the tasks of ministry. We cannot assume to affect directly the course of the Holy Spirit's transformational power in anyone's life, not even our own. We can however attend to the conditions that promote or inhibit growth, and learn to recognise seasonal patterns through which religious life can pass.

Further reading

General

Cupitt, D. (1986) *Life Lines*, London: SCM Press.
Faber, H. (1976) *Psychology of Religion*, London: SCM Press.
Tillich, P. (1957) *Dynamics of Faith*, New York: Harper.

Religion through the lifespan

Capps, D. and Browning, D. (eds) (1983) *Life Cycle Theory and Pastoral Care*, Philadelphia: Fortress Press.
Erikson, E. (1965) *Childhood and Society*, London: Penguin.
Jacobs, M. (1993) *Living Illusions: A Psychology of Belief*, London: SPCK.
Stokes, K. (1989) *Faith is a Verb: Dynamics of Adult Faith Development*, Mystic, CT: Twenty-Third Publications.

James Fowler's Stages of Faith

Fowler, J. (1981) *Stages of Faith: The Psychology of Human Development and the Quest for Meaning*, San Francisco: Harper and Row.
Fowler, J., Nipkow, K., and Schweitzer, F. (eds) (1992) *Stages of Faith and Religious Development: Implications for Church, Education, and Society*, London: SCM Press.
Parks, S. and Dykstra, C. (eds) (1986) *Faith Development and Fowler*, Birmingham, Alabama: Religious Education Press.
Slee, N. (1996) 'Further on from Fowler: Post-Fowler Faith Development Research', in L. Francis, W. Kay and W. Campbell, *Research in Religious Education*, Leominster: Gracewing.

Conversion

Beit-Hallahmi, B. and Argyle, M. (1997) *The Psychology of Religious Behaviour, Belief and Experience*, London: Routledge, pp. 114–123.
Gillespie, V. B. (1991) *The Dynamics of Religious Conversion*, Birmingham Alabama: Religious Education Press.
Hood, R., Spilka, B., Hunsberger, B. and Gorsuch, R. (1996) *The Psychology of Religion: An Empirical Approach*, 2nd ed., London: Guilford Press, Chapter 8.

7 Teaching and preaching

QUESTIONS FOR MINISTRY

- Do sermons have to be boring?
- How does meaningful learning happen?
- How can my teaching and preaching support this?
- What are the emotional factors in Christian learning?
- Does everyone learn in the same way?
- Should a good sermon make people change?

Christian teaching: the basic challenge

Christian ministry involves teaching people of all ages and all abilities in a wide variety of contexts: in the pulpit, in small study groups, in the Sunday school and in the training of new ministers. There can be high expectations of minister's expertise as a teacher, though few have had formal training as educators. Clergy mostly learn how to teach as they go along, picking up what works or doesn't work through trial and error. Although some teaching duties may be delegated to others (e.g. Sunday school, leading a home group or Bible study), ministers may implicitly provide a role-model for these too.

There are many 'new teaching methods', with attendant controversies and suspicions about how far these are just fashionable or offer real potential for more effective learning. The traditional 'teacher at the front of the class' approach has to compete with 'hands on' learning experiences, buzz groups, peer tutoring and interactive learning supported by information technology. Often ministers' own experiences of teaching and learning have been in the more conservative academic setting of the seminary. Ministers may be tempted to default to more familiar approaches, but suspect this may be limiting the potential of their teaching ministry. Or they may find they are pressured to use new methods without really understanding *why* they should do so. By appreciating the psychology behind these, and some of the bad psychology behind the old methods, ministers may be able to overcome their reluctance to step even further outside their zone of expertise and become better teachers (and learners!) in the process.

These days, people are more educated in general, but have often learned less about the Christian faith than have previous generations. The church faces the challenge presented by the widespread disappearance of routine Christian religious education that used to occur through school and society. However, these days people are likely to know more about a variety of faith traditions, and are often better equipped than previous generations to construct agnostic and atheistic world views on the basis of their general education. Given that the school system no longer provides a basic Christian education, there is an unprecedented need for Christian ministers to understand more about the underlying processes of teaching and learning; in other words, to have a sense of what is sound educational psychology. In this way, psychological analysis has much to offer the church's educational ministry.

Religious experiences and feelings can be difficult to articulate and to understand. The ideas and doctrines of the Christian tradition (such as the Trinity, salvation, sin, or grace) are attempts to do this. Yet these ideas themselves can be frustratingly opaque, presenting both teachers and learners with added difficulties rather than straightforward classifications. Our minds have to cope with the fact that religious ideas are a peculiar class of concepts in many respects. Many have no visible referent, but exist as inferences. We think of these referents (e.g. God the Father, the Holy Spirit) as having agency in a special kind of way, and as intangible but profoundly 'real' at the same time. Religious ideas are often made up of multiple representations held together at once, and frequently make a point of combining contradictory features to achieve the power of paradox. Furthermore, religious ideas are usually built up from other religious ideas, rather than from more accessible kinds of concepts. The first thing Christian educators have to allow for, therefore, is the heavy mental burden, what psychologists call 'cognitive complexity', of religious ideas for most people.

Interestingly, emerging research (Levine 1999) suggests that children have a degree of *natural* psychological ability to take on religious ideas despite their complexity, but that children's experience of education in general may actually suppress this. This is encouraging on the one hand, since it makes the task of putting across religious ideas seem less like an unrelenting uphill struggle, and more like something our minds are naturally set up for. On the other hand, it is both a depressing and important point for Christian ministers to be aware of, that their efforts to educate, especially children and youth, may unintentionally contribute to the suppression of this natural facility for religious thinking.

The effect cognitive complexity has on learners' minds is to make them slow down or reach saturation point with relatively little input. Even simple ideas are likely to seem complex when we first encounter them; their sheer novelty can take up all our capacity to think. So ministers need to take into account not only the advantage their own familiarity with religious ideas gives them over novice learners, but also the added load imposed on those learners by the complex nature of religious ideas.

The sensible way of tackling this is the same as for any kind of complexity, namely to break the ideas down into smaller component parts and to allow extra time. The natural sequence in which our responses to religion develop can offer some clues here (see also Chapter 5). Understanding things purely as ideas is in fact the last stage in the developmental sequence. A sense of an idea through *experience*, through *image* and through *story* leads up to this point. Helping adults to take in and work with complicated religious ideas, such as salvation, can benefit from chances to meet (or revisit) the idea in these different component forms.

Teaching religious ideas presents another kind of challenge too. The mind's grasp of religious ideas is endlessly changing. This change is both *inevitable* as our minds develop new ways of processing information (see Chapter 5), and also *desirable* as a symptom of dynamic engagement with faith (see Chapter 6). Not only can our psychological development alter how we take in religious ideas, but getting to grips with these ideas can also change us. As well as teaching content, Christian education has to equip people to cope with all this discontinuity.

SUMMARY OF KEY THEMES

- Challenges for ministers – many new teaching approaches.
- Teaching people with less knowledge of Christian faith but more educated generally than earlier generations.
- Complexity of religious ideas for novices.
- Facilitating this learning: slow, following developmental sequence, establishing expectation that comprehension will be fluid.

QUESTIONS TO CONSIDER

- Who has been your best teacher? Why?
- Who has been your best Christian teacher? Why?
- In what sense can teaching the laity be termed a 'subversive' activity?
- As ministers, what psychological 'hang-ups' in us may prevent the laity from being empowered through learning?

Active learning

It is essential that Christian ministers have an understanding of what Christian education is, and what it is not. The proper need to develop an orthodoxy of Christian thought can all too easily give rise to an overly dogmatic view of Christian education as simply a tool for imprinting the 'right' answers to pre-set religious questions. However, creative, personal and sometimes unconventional approaches to teaching and learning can often have more transforming and lasting results.

In Deuteronomy (6. 20–25) teaching is characterised as natural opportunities provoked by a child's question. The Psalmist declares that religious learning has given him more 'insight than all my teachers ... more understanding than the elders' (Ps. 119. 99–100). Important aspects of Jesus' own learning (as a child) included listening and asking questions in the temple. He subsequently taught in numerous ways: through explanation, story-telling, imagery, living examples, his life, questioning, showing, letting others make their own mistakes, and so on – an early master of a mixed teaching approach!

It is a salutary fact that much of what is taught is not actually learned. Psychologists estimate that three hours after hearing something people can hope to retain about 70 per cent of that information, but that after three days only 10 per cent, and after three weeks only 5 per cent is likely to be recalled. In addition what *is* learned may not accurately reflect what the teacher thought she taught. A key task for the church's approach to education is to identify kinds of learning that can compensate for the wastage and change religious ideas are subject to.

But what can be taught that could have enduring or continuous value for faith? The answer, it turns out, may lie in switching focus from concern about what is taught and learned, to thinking about how Christian learning can transform people's lives.

Active learning principle

Learning improves when people actively participate in the learning process. When learners are predominately passive recipients of the teacher's knowledge, less is learned and even that learning tends to be superficial. Deeper learning is promoted when learners are directly involved and are encouraged to work themselves with the ideas being taught (Kolb and Frey 1975). It goes almost without saying that learning that offers deeper and more personal engagement must be the preferred option for religious education.

One way of encouraging more active engagement is to hear from the learners themselves, by listening to their reflections and questions. Talking about their own experience (an area of expertise) can be a basis for connecting teaching with things that are real and personal, rather than abstract and theoretical. However, even trained teachers are likely to monopolise about 70 per cent of classroom discourse, and the contributions from learners are generally determined by the teacher's agenda. It is easy to give the impression of learner involvement, without really giving opportunities for people to take hold of ideas for themselves enough to derive the benefits of active learning. Identifying some active learning building blocks is an important way of checking the provision we offer in ministry.

Schemata

As people try to learn anything they look for ways to organise their thoughts. They form a 'schema'; a mental map of a particular area or set of issues. Schemas allow new ideas to be fitted into what is already understood. They offer the framework and ready reference points of an existing kind of understanding, rather than the overwhelming experience of trying to set down new ideas on a completely blank mental page (for a discussion of religious schemata in a different context, see Chapter 4). Piaget described how the learning process depends on the construction of these schemata, which become more robust the more new ideas and experiences are incorporated into them. A schema furnished with a good number of examples produces a sense of mastery about the learning it represents. This feeling of mastery, in turn, gives people the confidence to use and build on the learning represented in their mental schemata.

However, from time to time a schema can become restricting. Its frame of reference can exclude new information that doesn't easily fit the old pattern. For the learner this might mean that a new idea simply washes over them. Or the new idea might be distorted to force it to fit into the existing mindset, and so be misunderstood. A breakthrough can be made when someone realises that this new information (often a mounting backlog of instances) needs a whole new schema. This 'back to the drawing board' phase liberates the mind into a more creative mode, but also robs the sense of mastery that a robust schema had provided. In Christian learning, this need for a dramatic reconstruction of schemata may be experienced with central concepts such as 'God', 'Christ', 'Spirit', 'grace', or 'sin'; there may come a time when new images, ideas, and experiences have ceased to fit with our old religious schemata. Such an experience can be both disorienting and revitalising. It is important for Christian ministers to be aware of the work being done by their own and others' mental schemata.

Play and cognitive conflict

Child psychology has led the way to recognising how a playful kind of engagement is a valuable way of building up and knocking down our schemata (Piaget 1951; Garvey 1977). In play we give ourselves the licence to move ideas about and to try things out. We can take risks about what could go together with what, like the child who plays being 'Daddy' and sets their current sense of themselves alongside their perceptions of an adult world without having to assume any of its real responsibilities. In religious thinking, this might be playing a 'what if' game with ourselves, for example questioning the accuracy of the different gospel accounts.

This creative edge of play can push us forward to new ways of seeing things. It can just as easily give us comforting access to old ways of seeing things, schemata that used to provide a strong sense of mastery which might be an important way of recharging our confidence to face new learning challenges. The child playing at being a baby, or choosing to do a babyish puzzle, makes use of this function of play. Similarly sometimes it can help to go back to our old, perhaps more simplistic ways of picturing God, as a human parent for example, in order to get to grips with another complicated idea, like the theology of forgiveness.

People can't play very effectively for us. It is something we have to do ourselves; so play is a key factor in active learning. We need chances to take intellectual risks, be maverick, jump ahead and slide back in order to build up *religious* understanding. In a playful mode, it can also be easier to respond positively to cognitive conflict as schemata begin to crumble; to let faith grow rather than evaporate in the light of new evidence. In fact, a playful mode can make a virtue of routinely provoking cognitive conflict as a way of moving learning on.

There can be initial resistance to pairing play with religious learning on the grounds that the stuff of faith is too serious for that. Christians can be unsure how to square a playful approach to learning with a deep-seated respect for orthodoxy and

Box 7.1 An example of learning through 'religious play': the 'Alpha' course

'Alpha' is an introductory course covering some essentials of Christian beliefs. It has proved both popular and successful in deepening knowledge and commitment. It exploits a 'learn as you play' style well in the following ways:

- **Creates a leisure setting** – over a meal, with friends or making friends, often in a social centre, home or pub.
- **Encourages questioning** – the talks or teaching videos are used to prompt questions and debate rather than provide answers. Is designed for enquirers, assumes no existing faith commitment.
- **Safeguards risk-taking** – the authority of group leaders in discussions is carefully played down, and it is made clear that every kind of comment (including critical, disbelief, or incomprehension) is valuable material for working things out.
- **Makes things easy enough to master** – explores a few, basic ideas in ways that directly connect to familiar life issues. The easy, non-academic style (no books or pens, little prior religious knowledge) helps even novices acquire an encouraging sense of mastery. This simplicity-familiarity cocktail has also appealed to existing church members, by offering them a chance to play with the basic building blocks of faith and find exciting new ways of putting them together for themselves.
- **Integrates play and 'serious'** – the topics and issues raised are manifestly profound and all the more engaging (than the evangelism of being invited to a church social) for that.

authority. However, in terms of the cognitive and emotional opportunities for learning described above, play is a serious process that can strengthen the personal foundations of acceptance of religious truth claims. For Christian education to benefit from this, people may need to be given *permission* to play on the grounds of its 'serious' contribution to their learning, as well as opportunities to engage actively and playfully with religious ideas (see Boxes 7.1 and 7.2).

Meta-cognition

Meta-cognition is our awareness of our mind's activities. Educational psychology has discovered that this awareness can significantly enhance our learning power. It is not simply a question of *doing* the things that make learning active (integrating knowledge with personal experience, constructing and demolishing schemata, playing around with ideas and their points of conflict). In addition, education can be about helping people to become *aware* of what they are doing. If they have a better sense of what mental skills they need to use to get the most from religious ideas, they can be *pro*-active about their learning.

Box 7.2 An example of learning through 'religious play': Godly play

'Godly Play' is a method of Christian education originally designed for children, though increasingly used for all ages (Berryman 1991). The approach stimulates learning through play in a number of ways:

- **Hands-on materials** (like nativity sets) are provided to encourage the learners literally to get to grips with the layers of meaning within every religious story and idea as they actively move the pieces of the narrative about.
- **Learning in an environment that provides visible, tangible reminders of what has already been learned**, encourages the learners to make personal connections between materials, stories and their meanings. For example, using the same green underlay to represent the Good Shepherd's 'green pasture' and as an 'altar cloth' for exploring the drama of Holy Communion.
- **Deliberate avoidance of leading questions about the point of each story**. Instead, the teacher joins the group in wondering how that story has spoken to them today – what it opens up rather than what it sews up, encourages playfully moving ideas about rather than thinking in straight lines only.
- **A majority of the 'lesson' time is given to freely chosen individual creative work** in response to a story presentation. They may 'replay' a personally significant aspect of a story, over many weeks if desired, entering into the complex emotions it represents in the safe context of play, drama, art or writing. The teacher's respect for this work helps the child to recognise the serious, transformative value of encountering and discovering living truth within scripture and Christian practice.

For example, when faced with difficult material, people can deliberately look for similarities with models they *do* understand (fitting to an existing schema). Being more aware of this strategy, they should be less thrown if and when the model needs to be scrapped. Meta-cognitive awareness of how schemata are built up, help for a while, and then may need re-thinking means we can explain to ourselves that doubt and conflict are not inevitably crises for faith, but tools we should seize to further Christian learning. Similarly, people can learn that adopting a playful strategy is another way which they should routinely consider to respond to challenging religious ideas.

The psychologist Helmut Reich (1996) found that having meta–cognitive skills was a key component of how people negotiated competing world views, such as learning how to handle both religious and scientific explanations. When faced with more than one kind of explanation, there are several different strategies open to us. One is to compartmentalise the explanations by treating them as completely separate. Another is to reject one of the explanations: for example, rejecting a scientific account of the origins of the world in favour of a religious explanation. It is clear, however, that both of these strategies are restrictive and may impoverish our faith in the long run. Instead of eliminating tension with a quick-fix strategy, we are better off choosing a mental strategy of reconciling and co-ordinating ideas as different perspectives. So, for example, when faced with an apparently conflicting set of ideas about sex before marriage, a deeper understanding could emerge from a dialogue between different views (e.g. secular, religious, ideal and special cases) rather than from restricting oneself to a single cognitive approach (e.g. thinking only along scriptural lines). Deliberately challenging existing frameworks when teaching by playing 'devil's advocate' can also be fruitful.

So, as well as presenting interesting *content* when we teach, and providing chances for people to engage actively with the material, Christian educators also have a role to play in suggesting alternative *ways* of thinking; alternative cognitive strategies with which to think religious thoughts, and to think about religious issues.

SUMMARY OF KEY THEMES

- The downside of conventional didactic learning.
- How active learning provides opportunities to absorb teaching more deeply and personally.
- The need for people to fit new ideas into their existing mental schemata.
- The role of playfulness and creativity in an active learning style.
- Metacognitive awareness as a resource to aid religious learning.

QUESTIONS TO CONSIDER

- Christians are often said to learn their theology from hymns. Why might this be?
- How have art, film, dance, theatre, or poetry provided your faith with opportunities for active learning, schema building, and playful cognitive conflict?

Teaching methods and strategies

What are the key characteristics of good teachers? Psychology provides some helpful concepts to explore this. Two main issues here are a) how teachers set the scene for learning to take place, and b) how teachers can best support the steps in learning itself.

Providing a safe haven for learning

The psychological dynamics of the educational climate can have a great influence over the learning process itself. Teachers are responsible for providing a sense of safety for learners to open up to new ideas, to play, ask questions, take risks, and build up an independent sense of understanding. The emotional state of the learner can be a key factor, determining whether or not they are able to engage their intellect freely and with confidence. So, good teachers attend to the climate just as much as to the content of their teaching.

Often Christian teaching takes place in small groups in which powerful group dynamics may operate. The pressure to conform to other people's opinions (see Chapter 11) can be exacerbated by feelings of ignorance and a desire to hide this from the minister in particular. This can inhibit active involvement. Some people harbour fears about opportunities to examine the understandings behind their faith, anxious that they might lose faith altogether. This too can be a source of emotional resistance to engaging in a way that provokes 'deep learning' (Kolb and Frey 1975).

Previous experiences of Christian education mean that some Christians have acquired a rather restrictive sense of the 'proper' processes for discovering more about the faith (Hull 1985). They may assume an unnecessarily passive role in deference to religious authority, or be particularly reluctant to raise awkward questions, or to leave matters open. (Thinking you have, or should have, closure on a topic, while sometimes appropriate, will put an end to the learning that comes from searching for new perspectives and meanings.)

Teachers can address these predominately emotional issues in various ways. They should set clear ground rules for how individual opinions and honesty are to be valued within the group. 'There's nothing wrong with making mistakes' is a principle that can be modelled in the teacher's own manner, allowing a more vulnerable side to show through in both how she talks about her understanding and in her body language towards others in the group (for example, foregoing the protection of the teacher's special chair or position at the head of the group). Clergy have a special need to exaggerate these ploys, since in other settings, such as preaching, people are well trained to keep quiet about their opinions or their failure to follow what has been said, and may be more used to looking at the minister in the authority of the pulpit than in any other context.

The practice of encouraging people to identify their own learning goals and their anxieties about learning (such as losing faith) can help them to feel more actively committed to the process. It also communicates the value of individual differences and the emotional significance of Christian teaching – it's not just about becoming better informed. Naming a fear is often a helpful way of forming a more rational sense of its threat.

The problem of people coming to Christian education with an overly passive and deferential approach can be addressed in terms of the setting the teacher provides. The associations people have with the church building may not be compatible with a more active, debating or democratic style of learning. The time of day can also be a factor to consider: a group that meets just before or after a formal service may have more difficulty adjusting into a more active, discursive mode. Initial contributions, particularly questions, should be enthusiastically welcomed and where possible the temptation to give definitive answers should be resisted. Making use of a co-leader who debates with the teacher is another way of conveying through the climate the kind of mental skills people need. Also, breaking the group down in the early stages, into pairs for example, can facilitate especially safe ways for people to begin to be more explorative.

Teaching strategies for optimal learning

There is an inevitable dependence built into the teacher/learner relationship, a dependence that can become exaggerated and unwelcome when the teacher is a minister (see Chapter 13). However, the purpose of teaching, especially Christian teaching, should be to liberate people to a new level of personal maturity. Studies of the teaching process led Jerome Bruner (1966) to suggest that the best teachers provide learners with scaffolding: just enough support to get the learner to the next level without providing all the knowledge-building bricks themselves. There is a clear expectation that this scaffolding will soon be surplus to requirements. and so the relationship will not become a dependent one. There is an emphasis on teaching skills (rather than content) here that echoes the points made about meta-cognition above. It is more effective in the long term to teach a child strategies for tackling jigsaws than it is to do half the jigsaw for him. Similarly, an independent prayer life, for example, can be more effectively nurtured by identifying different sorts of prayerful activities and modes of thought, than by telling people exactly what to pray about, where, and when.

Lev Vygotsky provides a similar analysis of the psychological relationship between teacher and learner (Vygotsky 1978). Effective teaching is directed within what he called 'the zone of proximal development'. This zone – the area between what a learner can already do unaided and what they can only do with a teacher's help – is different for each individual and for each task. For some people there may be only a narrow difference between what they understand for themselves about atonement theology, for example, and how far they can follow the explanations of someone more informed. Teaching in these cases needs to take a 'baby steps' approach to stay within the range of their learning zone with lots of opportunities to explore things at more or less the same level. Other people (or other topics) might allow for a more educationally stretching and varied strategy.

The challenge of gauging where these zones of proximal development lie underlines the need for Christian teachers to make careful assessments of individuals, comparing evidence of what they understand alone and the point at which more expert suggestions cease to help. How is an overworked minister going to find the time to do all this? There is some good news and some bad news about this. The bad news first.

Psychologists have observed that experts often find it especially hard to tune into others' zones of proximal development (ZPD). So, as experts in religious knowledge, ministers need to be aware they are liable to make insensitive judgements about how much people can learn. In short, teaching is a challenging and difficult part of Christian ministry. However, the good news is that often people just slightly more able than ourselves are the most sensitive to the boundaries of our ZPD, which lends support to the peer tutoring model of education. In other words, exploiting the diverse teaching or mentoring gifts of members of the laity makes good sense both from the point of view of the limitations of clergy time and from the point of view of educational psychology.

Tailoring teaching to different learning styles

Another way teaching can try to be sensitive to individual learners' needs is to appreciate differences that can exist in preferred learning styles. Kolb and Frey (1975) suggest there are four processes we need to employ to ensure that learning really becomes part of us. These are (not necessarily in this order):

- experiencing
- reflecting
- reviewing and theorising
- taking action / testing out for real.

Peter Honey and Alan Mumford (1992) used this classification in their research into how people handle new ideas. They suggest there are four kinds of learners: pragmatists, reflectors, theorists or activists, each of whom have likes and dislikes as shown in Table 7.1.

In a similar way to personality types (see Chapter 3), particular learning styles can confer strengths in one dimension, but at the expense of the development of other psychological traits and skills. Teachers and learners can find it helpful to recognise this and take appropriate action. Our preferred way of engaging in the learning process has implications for the way we respond to different teaching methods too. For example, by recognising that the reason I can't abide the new minister's penchant for role plays is that I prefer intellectual and theoretical to experiential and playful modes of learning, I might learn to overcome, or at least tolerate, my displeasure.

Our learning style bias also biases the way we like to teach. We tend, egocentrically, to assume that everyone else wants to be taught in the way we most like to learn. Yet it is unlikely that a group will be made up of people just like you (except perhaps by the

Table 7.1 Four kinds of learning style (Craig 1994)

Learning styles	Likes	Dislikes
Pragmatists	The practical 'point' of learning made clear, real life examples and chance to try things out immediately	Learning for its own sake, longwinded theory and rambling discussions
Reflectors	Having a chance to prepare thoughts, to weigh up information, not rushing to form their own opinion	Rushed or superficial coverage, variety at expense of depth, having to speak or act before they've thought
Theorists	Sorting out the pattern of ideas – being logical, critical, exhaustive, reaching 'closure'	'Woolly' explanation based on feelings rather than rational argument, struggle with open-ended learning
Activists	'Having a go' with new ideas, variety, brainstorming, teamwork, 'where could this take us?' excitement	Being told/shown instead of trying for themselves; detail, excessive preparation or *post hoc* reflection exercises.

end of the course when all those who don't share your style have given up and left!). Teachers have to be careful to avoid this by providing a range of learning opportunities that connect to the four different styles. When teaching church groups it could be helpful to justify your various methods as a psychologically valid way to cater for diversity among Christians, so as to avoid some of your techniques being mistaken for 'time fillers' or 'warm up' to the real business of learning. This would also be an ideal opportunity to raise meta-cognitive awareness generally of the processes important to a deep kind of religious learning that really engages with the content.

SUMMARY OF KEY THEMES

- Emotional resistances that plague Christian learning (fear of losing faith, ignorance anxieties, undue deference and passivity).
- The virtues of providing 'scaffolding' rather than prefabricated content.
- Being sensitive to how much help is helpful.
- Four different learning (and teaching) style preferences.

QUESTIONS TO CONSIDER

- What features of 'sound' educational psychology have Alpha (or comparable) courses tried to harness?
- Are there any psychological mistakes in that approach?
- Do you have a recognisable learning style?
- How has this affected your approach to learning and to teaching?

Preaching

Research has found that we can typically recall less than half of the content of a short religious message immediately after hearing it (Pargament and DeRosa 1985). There are some basic factors about a congregation's psychology that affect their reception of sermons. On average, people with higher intelligence, greater religious interest, and who have developed the habit of listening to sermons are better at remembering what the preacher has said (Pargament and DeRosa 1985). These latter characteristics discriminate against seekers' chances of finding the sermon an influence in their call to faith. The same research also found that people are more likely to recall sermon material that is consistent with their attitudes, so ministers are often literally only preaching to the converted. An implication here is that the more controversial the message, the greater the need for clarity and extra efforts to maintain people's attention.

Common-sense psychology about engaging forms of communication are often as far as a psychology of preaching goes. The folklore is that good preachers are careful about their body language, use plenty of humour and illustrations to liven things up, and overcome the one-way nature of communication by posing questions at key junctures along the way. Certainly, without some allowances for people's inattention, incomplete understanding and poor memories the traditional sermon is an unlikely way of making much impact on personal faith and life.

David Buttrick (1987), however, developed a much more closely-observed and psychologically well-informed approach to homiletics. In his view, before you can give a good sermon, you must give careful consideration to the psychological processes that operate in individual listeners hearing a religious message. Sermons can be opportunities to guide faith consciousness in a way that does more than keep people's attention, but rather develops and transforms their faith.

The paramount questions for sermon design in Buttrick's analysis are these: What is likely to be cognitively salient to the passive putty of consciousness? What works for, or against, the underlying movement I'd like to effect in people's hearts and minds? Buttrick offers the following practical suggestions based on this:

- **At the beginning** people's auditory perception needs a few moments to adjust to the preacher's voice. The congregation may not become really conscious of what is being said until about the third sentence. This raises a problem for sermons that hope to arrest listener's attention with an initial key question – unless that question is repeated three times or said very emphatically!
- **Humour or dazzling effects** (e.g. multimedia) can also focus people on the wrong things. These measures are likely to produce an effect, and rate as memorable in their own right. However, it is important to weigh up whether the degree of arousal they might provoke is appropriate to the message itself. This can mean identifying underlying or unconscious motives for preaching in the first place. For example, is the aim to develop the preacher's relationship with her congregation? Are effects designed to impress or invite the congregants to like the minister more? This is likely to distract consciousness away from

aspects of the sermon that might affect a person's faith. We are more easily biased to ruminate about personal relations, given half a chance, than the more challenging and less practised habit of attending to our personal faith.

- **Illustrations and examples** as a rule need to fit the direction of the point being made. They cannot be justified merely in terms of offering wake-up calls to passive consciousness. Illustrations are prime examples of the effects of cognitive salience on our flow of thought. Because illustrations can be processed more easily than arguments, they are a good deal more salient. Illustrations provoke imaginative processing, so they need to be carefully oriented to stir up the right kind of lateral thinking. Otherwise, they distract attention from the subsequent points and the preacher's overall intention to make her sermon a helpful faith experience. Box 7.3 illustrates the potential problems of illustrations.

Buttrick suggests thinking of sermons in terms of 'moves'. Each chunk of information is then seen as contributing to moving the consciousness of the listener forward. The preacher aims to take her listeners' minds on a journey, by providing the fuel, the landscape, and the onward momentum. As in a journey, important features of the landscape have to be seen for long enough to lodge in the mind. Often the main theme of a sermon is too embedded for listeners to recognise its central significance. As they are passively led on this journey of thought and feeling, people need exaggerated signposts and spotlights to focus their attention where it is intended.

Endings can also have a variety of psychological effects on the listener, so there is no single ideal strategy here. A tedious recapitulation of the themes covered can be too lulling. An emphatic final statement can convey absolute closure, effectively switching off the need for further attention and reflection. Ending with an emotional climax is likely to ensure the sermon goes on resounding for some time. However, it may be a relatively short-lived emotional high (or 'downer') rather than contributing to a longer-term, profound conceptual shift. Benjamin Beit-Hallahmi (1986) suggests that sermons may often have powerful effects in less obvious ways. He cites the analogy of visiting an art gallery – people may not recall the details of the paintings they saw, but they may come away challenged and changed nonetheless.

Judged by the standards of effective educational techniques and active learning laid out above, the passive, one-way communication of traditional preaching is a poor vehicle for teaching. However, there is room within a diverse and broadly-conceived Christian ministry for more than one sort of teaching: the active learning favoured by many educational psychologists need not sweep all other methods aside. The traditional sermon, delivered by someone especially and prayerfully prepared to speak on God's word in the context of an act of worship, makes a distinctive contribution to the education of a faith community.

Working within the genre of the traditional sermon, preaching can be a more or less persuasive and engaging form of communication, and a psychological understanding of this can help to optimise its effects. Research undertaken by social psychologists over several decades into effective communication techniques has found that the process of attitude/behaviour change is so complex as to be nearly unpredictable: a disappointing result in some ways, but a relief in others. This complexity

---

Box 7.3 The problems of choosing good illustrations in sermons

In a sermon exploring the meaning of contrition, a visiting preacher shared a personal anecdote about his childhood experience of contrition after he had recklessly cleared a table by pulling its tablecloth.

At first glance this might seem sound psychology – a lively, humorous but gentle example that people can easily imagine. In addition, given the subject, it was perhaps hoped to make clear that the need for contrition wasn't something merely being preached at the congregation, but was a message for the preacher's life too.

On closer analysis, however, this anecdote was more likely to sabotage the faith experience of the listening congregation than to enhance it.

1 The emotional pull of a humorous example drew people's consciousness away from the solemn subject it was intended to amplify. Being so out of context may even have added to the salience and memorability of the anecdote over everything else that was preached.
2 Revealing this personal anecdote drew attention to the person of the speaker, and especially because he was a senior churchman this was likely to provoke people to reflect on the person (indeed, the little boy) behind this religious persona, and lose sight of the topic in hand.
3 As the example of his guilt was necessarily trivial (he could hardly admit to murder from the pulpit) it may have unintentionally trivialised the understanding of sin and guilt, withdrawing the fuel of faith consciousness rather than building it up.

---

preserves human freedom from being tinkered with by well-meaning psychologists, or even well-meaning clergy. We cannot make someone change their attitude or their behaviour.

However, researchers have found that certain factors must be minimally present to enable (although not ensure) persuasive communication. William McGuire (1985) describes a process whereby listeners process and evaluate arguments, and either act accordingly or not as a result of the processing. Below are shown the five stages of the process. It is no wonder that sermons often fail to be effective: they must not only get our attention but also be understandable, persuasive, memorable, and likely to compel action.

- *Attention*
  tuning in, attending, listening.
- *Comprehension*
  learning 'what', generating related cognitions, learning; 'how' (what to do).
- *Yielding*
  agreeing with the communication.

- *Retention*
  storing the attitude change in the memory.
- *Behaviour*
  acting in accordance with decisions made.

First, a sermon must engage the listeners and gain their active attention. For instance, a sermon advocating Christian involvement in initiatives to relieve third-world debt may achieve this objective by pointing out how Christians have in the past been able to influence social and political attitudes. A study by Carrell (2000) on sermons suggests that most preaching is perceived as irrelevant to real life. The conclusion that a sermon will be more effective if it is relevant to a listener's everyday life is reinforced by research undertaken by Petty *et al.* (1981) that shows that personal relevance is indeed a key determinant of whether people are motivated to expend the effort to listen and comprehend a message.

Second, a clearly structured argument, within which information is conveyed in comprehensible segments, is necessary for comprehension. Carrell's sermon survey reported that listeners felt that most sermons rambled and were poorly organised. Many listeners came away not knowing what the sermon was about. They were hoping to learn something from scripture that related to real life, says Carrell, but came away rather muddled.

Third, sermons that seek to make up a person's mind for them will be less effective in terms of yielding decision change because the attitude change (if any) has been passive. Enabling people to weigh up the arguments and to decide for themselves engenders more active participation and therefore better retention. (Retention is also enabled by a clear summary.) Finally, although the relationship between attitude change and behaviour change is a spotty one at best, clearly people cannot change their behaviour if they have no idea how to go about it. A good sermon in this respect will give some practical suggestions, which again relate to real life.

Human beings are not perfectly rational or logically consistent creatures; they process information heuristically as well as systematically. When seeking to persuade through a sermon this should be taken into account. More recent research reveals the conditions under which people will adopt attitudes, not through rationally and systematically weighing up the arguments, but by adopting some other heuristic or short-cut to determine the acceptability of the message. Some examples might be: 'experts (clergy) can be trusted', 'good-looking people are right', 'women cannot present a balanced argument', 'people who are friendly and sincere can be trusted', and so on. A very common heuristic used in religious circles is: 'If the message is spoken in my church's jargon (discourse), then it must be right' (see Chapter 11 on the constraining effects of religious discourse). Clearly this is a less desirable way for people to process sermon material. Both types of processing (systematic and heuristic) can be going on with regard to the same message. If an argument becomes too complex, abstract, or remote then the listener may resort to heuristic processing.

SUMMARY OF KEY THEMES

- Memory, attention and comprehension problems make learning from sermons difficult.
- Aiming for 'cognitive salience' in preaching.
- Stages of processing by listeners: attention, comprehension, yielding, retention, behaviour.
- Skills of persuasive communication.

EXERCISE

Think about devising a research tool – for example, questionnaire, focus group protocol, interview schedule to collect data on the different kinds of effects your sermons have on the congregation. How could you use this to find out about the congregation's profile, about strengths and weakness in your style, about memorability, and about life-changing effects?

QUESTIONS TO CONSIDER

- In a school setting, how might the age of the listeners affect how a minister leads an assembly?
- Think back to a sermon that deeply influenced you.

    1 How was your attention gained?

    2 How was the sermon structured to facilitate comprehension?

    3 What made you agree with the sermon, or 'yield' to its message? Clear explanation of scripture? Illustrations from real life? A feeling of exhilaration? Heuristic processing (e.g. liking the personality of the preacher)?

- Who is the best preacher you have ever heard? Why?
- How would you describe your own aims and style as a preacher?

Further reading

Christian teaching

Berryman, J. (1991) *Godly Play: An Imaginative Approach to Religious Education*, San Francisco: HarperSanFrancisco.

Craig, Y. (1994) *Learning For Life*, London: Mowbray.

Francis, L., Kay, W. and Campbell, W. (1988) *Research in Religious Education*, Leominster: Gracewing.

Active learning/teaching methods and strategies

Brown, G. and Atkins, M. (1988) *Effective Teaching in Higher Education*, London: Routledge.

Egan, K. (1992) *Imagination in Teaching and Learning*, Chicago: University of Chicago Press.

Garvey, C. (1977) *Play*, Glasgow: Fontana.

Hull, J. (1985) *What Prevents Christian Adults from Learning?*, London: SCM Press.

Westerhoff, J. H. (ed.) (1994) *Called to Teach and Learn: A Catechetical Guide for the Episcopal Church*, New York: The Domestic and Foreign Missionary Society PECUSA.

Wood, D. (1988) *How Children Think and Learn*, Oxford: Blackwell.

Preaching

Buttrick, D. (1987) *Homiletic: Moves and Structures*, London: SCM Press.

Part 3

Counselling and pastoral care

8 Ageing, illness, bereavement, and dying

QUESTIONS FOR MINISTRY

- Can a church full of older people still be 'alive'?
- Does faith alter the experience of getting older?
- What special pastoral needs are suggested by older people's psychology?
- How can I help people to cope with illness?
- How can faith be used to promote health and healing; what are the health risks of faith?
- How can I help someone in a major bereavement?
- What do people go through when they are dying?

Introduction

This chapter deals with four significant life issues that are perennial for pastoral ministry – ageing, illness, bereavement, and dying. These experiences have in common a particular potency for drawing out spiritual issues and questions. In order best to help people dealing with these events, and to facilitate the role faith can play in supporting them, it is helpful to be aware of the psychological features of each.

Problems of definition beset psychologists' attempts to study ageing, illness and bereavement. How old is 'old' – is it not a question of being as young as you feel? Where can the line between illness and health be drawn? Bereavement is typically thought of as the process of adjustment following a death, but is it reasonable also to identify bereavement features in responses to divorce, amputations or being made redundant?

Increasingly, ideas arising from the psychologies of ageing, health and bereavement have been appropriated for their wider potential to illuminate experiences of change, dis-ease and loss in many forms. This widened understanding of these experiences, seen from a spiritual perspective, offers a promising opportunity to see these issues in their widest context: ageing beyond merely getting older but as responding to the final challenge to become who God intends us to be, illness as the challenge to discover the true meaning of healing and wholeness, and bereavement as the challenge to realise the ultimate sources of attachment and separation that give meaning to life.

Ageing

> For my soul is full of trouble and my life draws near the grave.
>
> Psalm 88. 3

> They will still bear fruits in old age, they will stay fresh and green.
>
> Psalm 92. 14

Since many churches would be virtually empty without their elderly and ageing members, the psychological and spiritual issues faced by older people must be a major pastoral concern for ministers. In today's world, ageing issues are faced by more people and for longer, since many live on for thirty or forty years beyond their retirement. As people live longer (the number of people aged 80 and over has doubled in the last thirty years), the importance of addressing the heterogeneity of the ageing process increases. While psychologists can speak with confidence about some universals in the pattern of human development in the very young, the longer a person lives and the more different life experiences they have, the more varied the patterns for development become. A key issue for the pastoral ministry of the church is guarding against the unhelpful stereotypes of 'the elderly' that overlook their diversity and treat them as a single homogenous group.

Myths about ageing

It is easy for our impression of older people to be based on biased sources of data, focusing on examples such as the frail old ladies targeted by muggers, the hospitalised elderly, or caricatures from television of physically and mentally infirm and incapable older people. This sort of stereotyping is empirically inaccurate (the majority of those aged 65–80 are in good health, with mental functioning declining only slightly, and then typically only after the age of 75). Stereotyping can cause us to overlook those older people who, though mature in years, are psychologically and physically as healthy and dynamic as younger people, and can prevent us from understanding or forming good relationships with them. Myths and stereotypes can also become self-fulfilling prophecies. If we perceive and treat 'the elderly' as a spent force, beset with illness and intellectually waning, they will be likely to internalise all the bad press about themselves, withdraw from life, and give up on their health and abilities.

Facts about ageing: changes and their consequences

Losing a spouse is a dramatic change that many people face in their ageing years. However, most of the changes associated with ageing are more gradual. There are the familiar physical changes, many of which have psychological consequences. With age, our muscles become weaker, our bones more brittle, our lungs less efficient, our immunity is compromised and our bodies become slower to recover. These changes, together with the simple fact of looking older, can have negative effects on the older person's sexual and social life, their employment prospects and their self-esteem. These negative changes can be offset to some extent by the relatively unchanging picture of cognitive function. Though cortical tissue is lost, there is often little overall change in memory; nor is intelligence affected, especially when people continue to be mentally active. The widespread notion that memory for events in the distant past improves with age, however, is without foundation.

The experiences of change and loss that are part of the ageing process can be difficult in themselves; they are made all the more unsettling by the shadow of death that is cast over them. For Erikson, making peace with this prospect in the light of preceding life experiences is the overriding psychosocial issue at this stage of life (see Chapter 6), though given that these days this stage of life might span more than three decades it is probably unhelpful to assume this issue has equal importance for everyone. However, the experience of minor and gradual changes as we age offers an opportunity to prepare in psychological and spiritual terms for dying itself, when it comes.

Ageing 'well' may depend on seeking out anchoring points of *continuity* that help to put the transformations of getting older into perspective. As certain physical features change, attention is naturally drawn to the deeper characteristics that make up who we are on the inside. Indeed, a sense of the spiritual may be a primary way of identifying what is enduring. Finding this balance between change and continuity, through both psychological and spiritual awareness, may be a key feature of pastoral care with older people.

Retirement

For many, retirement is the life event that heralds the onset of ageing. Adjusting to retirement presents its own set of difficulties, but can also be seen as an occasion for spiritual development. The twin issues of change and loss characterise the psychological challenge of retirement. Research has found that in many cases psychological distress, manifested as agitation and an anxious kind of depression, is actually worse in the period leading up to retirement, and people may benefit from pastoral support in advance of the event.

In addition to the loss of work and a wage, people can experience (or dread) the loss of social status and social role that was bound up with their occupational activity. They can feel emotionally vulnerable and naked without the persona associated with being 'the doctor', 'the teacher' or 'the foreman'. In some cases, it may be appropriate to describe their anxiety in terms of an experience of 'social death' (Grainger 1993). The chance to voice this grief, and to overcome the taboo that surrounds admitting to it, may be important features in a process of adjustment. Retirement may be a more violent break in the pattern of life for some people, and less so for others, but those who deny feeling any sense of loss present the greatest cause for concern. In such cases, difficulties may surface in more florid ways as the unacknowledged hurt is expressed through the irrational communication of the unconscious.

Women tend to outlive men; of those aged 60 or more, one in every two women will be widowed, compared to just one in five men finding themselves alone at this stage of life. Thus, being in a minority might make male church-goers feel marginalised. On the other hand, women may feel uncomfortable with the tendency to normalise the state of sorrow associated with the more common state of widowhood. Another gender difference at this time of life is that women still tend to retire at a younger age than men, which often means retiring before their husbands. When this happens, it means a woman first has to deal with her own retirement, alone, but then also experiences her husband's retirement at close hand – a double dose. On a social level too, husband and wife relations can be specially strained. Sometimes women may dread their husband's retirement and his encroaching on 'her' domestic space. Others may have had high hopes of developing a deeper relationship once the distractions of work were set aside, and feel disappointed and neglected when work is replaced not by wife, but golf or perhaps additional church activities.

A Christian pastoral perspective can help older people to discover a new kind of life beyond the 'death' of work and occupational status. Spiritual language and imagery is ideally suited to taking hold of apparently negative experiences of change, and finding in them hope and deeply reconstructive transformation. People can experience genuine renewal in their latter years, and the increased amount of spare time may be a blessing in this respect. One study found that respondents over 50 years old accounted for more than 40 per cent of religious experiences described as 'life changing' (Koenig 1994) – old dogs perhaps *can* learn new tricks!

When people retire and feel their usefulness is spent, it is tempting to suggest that they can now simply exercise their talents in the service of the church, so the retired bank manager becomes the treasurer, the teacher takes on the Sunday school, and so on; but this may prevent someone from taking time to enter that creative space that retiring makes possible, and from which a new gift or direction could emerge. People's needs for new development should perhaps take precedence over the immediate needs of the church, though in the long run both parties stand to benefit from this enriching process. One potentially fruitful pastoral strategy would be to consider how to encourage people to explore new avenues in which they do not have existing skills.

Facing up to ageing: how faith helps

While there are inaccurate myths about ageing that paint an unduly depressing picture, many older people do face real difficulties that can make ageing a dysfunctional process that spirals out of control. Depleted financial resources can compromise health, illness can be an obstacle to social activities, a lack of human contact can foster a sense of meaninglessness, and a low opinion of self-worth can induce guilt for continuing to live at all – some come to see themselves as a useless burden to others. For many people, faith can help divert and dispel the darker consequences of ageing.

Not surprisingly, one of the biggest problems many older people suffer from is fear of growing older. Proper information can help address some of the unwarranted beliefs contributing to this dread, reassuring them for example that many illnesses can be treated and pain can be controlled, or correcting some of the myths about what normal ageing involves (for a further discussion of cognitive and behavioural counselling, see Chapter 10). However, the quality of *hope* contained in faith offers a more comprehensive way of tackling fear of all kinds. Faith provides a way of seeing beyond even the most appalling, unalterable circumstances such as terminal illness. Koenig make the point that from an Eriksonian perspective the psychological prerequisite for hope is trust, the earliest of building blocks in our psychosocial development (see Chapter 6). As one of the first things 'in', trust is arguably the last thing 'out', so even if our faculties become compromised through dementia or other disease, faith can be an enduring support and antidote to fear.

Faith provides a coherent framework of existential meaning. In obvious ways, such as a belief in life after death, faith can provide a reassuring framework in which to set the meanings and achievements of this life. Research has shown that church attendance is not essential for older people to benefit from the advantage religious beliefs have on their sense of well-being (Koenig 1994); the house-bound and those who prefer not to belong to the church may nonetheless rely on their religious beliefs.

There are a number of ways in which faith and belonging to a Christian community can be a source of social support that keeps isolation at bay. For some the fellowship of church life may be the only regular social contact, for example if family members live at a distance and many close friends have died. Without social contact, social skills can atrophy, which further reinforces the older person's withdrawal and disengagement from others. There is a natural trend for extroversion to decline, and neuroticism to increase with age. However, Christian fellowship can provide a gently counterbalancing social influence to prevent a more introverted and emotional position becoming disabling.

The church itself has to guard against unwittingly contributing to the devalued sense of self-worth of some older people. Congregations are too often judged in terms of how many younger people they can attract. It is important to value and appreciate the contributions make by older members of the church. It is probably no coincidence that older people often take such special care to champion children's interests – both are in danger of being overlooked as being currently 'useless' to the church.

Dementia can affect every area of a person's psychological make-up, disabling memory, attention, language, emotion, to the extent that it seems the core sense of self is eaten away. The appearance of what seems not much more than an empty shell where the 'person' once was is profoundly challenging both in terms of basic and pastoral care. What role can faith have in these cases? Religious practices, rituals, prayers and hymns are often 'over-learned', that is to say they have become deeply ingrained, almost automatic patterns. When, through dementia, the ordinary, intentional access to understanding and memory is barred, these over-learned features may provide alternative routes to a rudimentary kind of knowing and feeling, perhaps the remnant of the self. There is ample anecdotal evidence (e.g. Sacks 1985) of dementia patients who have shown an unexpected quality of response to a religious service or action.

Box 8.1 Counselling needs of older people

- Bereavement, illness, disability, loneliness, marital problems, and problems associated with being a carer (see below) are all common in older people's lives.
- Often depression is not recognised as such; the symptoms of loss of appetite, less interest in social contact, no will to live, sadness and confusion being regarded as 'normal' consequences of ageing and the life events associated with it. Depression can and should be treated at any age.
- Adjusting to the reality of ageing (and mortality) may prompt people to seek spiritual and emotional support. There may be a need to re-examine 'who I am' (regardless of physical changes), or a need to deal with the changes in other's perceptions, for instance finding that people no longer seem to recognise them as a woman or man in a sexual sense.
- According to Erikson (see Chapter 6) old age creates the need to come to a final evaluation of life, weighing up what has been meaningful and positive and what has not. People often find this easier to do by talking, at length, about their life and their interpretation of events. Faith can be an important dimension in this process, providing the biggest kind of perspective through which to view the various ups and downs of their lives.

Christian ministry has a role not only to continue providing for the religious needs of these people, but perhaps also to encourage their carers to recognise the potential of religious stimulation to reach where other means no longer can.

Counselling older people

Reasons why older people might seek pastoral counselling, and approaches that are specially suited to their needs, can be easily inferred from the discussions above. A summary of these is provided in Boxes 8.1 and 8.2.

QUESTIONS TO CONSIDER

- Think about the people you know who you consider to be 'elderly'. What, if anything, do they have in common? In what ways do they differ from each other?
- Do you find yourself stereotyping older people and treating them all the same way?
- What particular ministries are more suited to older people?
- What steps should be taken to prevent older male church members feeling marginalised?
- What are the most effective ways that the church helps people manage the transition from working life to retirement?

Box 8.2 Approaches to counselling older people

- There can be some resistance to psychological language among older people, who can feel affronted by the implication that things are 'all in the mind'. Counselling that adopts ideas and approaches from psychology, but employs more traditionally religious language, may be more appropriate.
- Reminiscence is an important way for older people to make sense of their lives.
- In needing to talk, at length, about themselves the older person may also be trying to connect their isolated life with others. Seeing reminiscence as an attempt to feel more of a social participant guards against our perception that it is merely self-referring, 'going on about themselves'.
- As older people talk and evaluate their lives, they often feel a need to make amends in one way or another. Spiritual counselling lends itself to opportunities for a more confessional expression, especially if the person wants to make peace with someone who is now dead or too far away for an actual reconciliation to happen.

Illness

Among Christians, the idea that sickness is not exclusively a matter of physical symptoms has been established for centuries. However, health psychology provides helpful elaboration of this understanding that body, mind and spirit collaborate in our sense of well-being or dis-ease.

Illness is no longer measured solely in terms of clinical signs, but also in terms of how function is affected (headaches regularly send some people to bed, or make them extremely irritable, others can carry on). The individual's subjective perception of well-being also can be as important as clinical and functional factors in disease (see Figure 8.1). Our psychology plays an important part in how we perceive our own and others' ailments. A headache may be tolerated as normal by one person, an alarming sign of a brain tumour or hint of an impending epileptic seizure for another, or perceived as just desserts following a night on the town. Faith can modulate the experience of illness. For many, faith can enhance their resistance to illness. Others turn to faith when illness strikes, as a way of coping and to seek healing. Caring for the ill can also raise its own emotional and spiritual needs. Sensitive pastoral care that contributes to healing in every sense has much to learn from a *psychological* understanding of the issues faced when we become ill.

The interconnectedness of states of body and mind is most clearly seen in the way the psychological state of stress can lead to physical illness. Stress sets off physiological changes that can reduce our immunity to disease. It is difficult to avoid stress altogether, but reducing it is a key way of protecting health. Faith can help in a

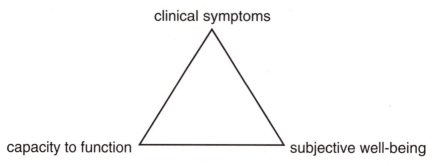

Figure 8.1 Triad of components of illness

number of ways to reduce the build-up of stress in people's lives. This is borne out by evidence that religious people are on average less prone to many diseases, and that some especially religious (often conservative) groups seem particularly to attract this benefit associated with their faith (Ellison 1994).

A religious perspective can alter the way we appraise stressors, for example when the delay of a traffic jam is redefined as a blessing that affords more time to listen to a radio broadcast or to think and reflect. It can also help to regulate our emotions during a stressful encounter. The risk-taking behaviours that stress can encourage (smoking, drinking alcohol, overeating, sexual promiscuity) are often prohibited because of faith, protecting the faithful from many kinds of disease. The fellowship of friends in the faith community is also a factor that is positively correlated with lower stress and higher resistance to disease. Lastly, rituals can have a relaxing effect on physical and mental tensions, combining both emotional arousal and positive cognitive feedback of belonging, and being loved or released from sin.

However, we should not overlook the possibility that in some cases faith can *add* to our stress levels, for example when church demands encroach on time that is needed for relaxation. Religious commitment can divide and weaken marital or family relationships. Beliefs can create stress by nurturing neurotic feelings of guilt and unworthiness. Trying to conform to expectations about sexuality and gender roles can also contribute to stress, especially when these ask people to be very different from the surrounding culture. Stress is often associated with a build-up of negative and hostile emotions, which may be difficult to admit openly among Christian friends, and feeling ostracised from the worshipping community can further increase stress and compromise health. For example, if the church excludes paedophiles this may raise their stress levels and exacerbate the tendency for their condition to be 'expressed'.

When illness strikes: adjustment and coping

When the body goes seriously wrong and the mind is in turmoil, a spiritual perspective can offer a 'third way' through which to find repair and peace. Illness can prompt both religious and non-religious people alike to turn to God, in personal prayer or through the support of religious friends or professionals. However, in the crisis of becoming ill, people can find that they are burdened by as many religious questions as they have questions about their physical condition. Pastoral care needs to balance a sudden desire to question and struggle with a Christian perspective with the need for spiritual assurance and support. Ministers need to avoid simply peddling 'pat' religious solutions and explanations that overlook religious enquiry. Equally, it would be irresponsible in this sensitive period of physical and mental uncertainty to embark on a process of intensive religious education. Of paramount importance, in the short term, must be strategies that minimise stress and assist the body's healing processes.

Facing the need for medical treatment can be an additional source of stress on top of the illness itself. When an illness is first diagnosed, people need to adjust in their minds to their new status. This includes the implications of the illness for the person's sense of self. For example, being diagnosed as HIV positive requires adjusting to the likelihood of suffering from various serious physical problems, and also adjusting to the disease's impact on self-esteem and relationships. This might lead to a (potentially unhelpful) examination of whether untoward aspects of the person's lifestyle may have contributed to their illness, introducing a heightened spiritual awareness of sinfulness.

Developing one's own illness representation model

There are three important stages in the adjustment process through the course of an illness:

1   Developing one's own 'illness representation model'.
2   Action-planning and coping.
3   Appraisal (perhaps identifying the need to revise 1 or 2).

An illness representation model (IRM) is the conceptual picture people form for themselves of what is wrong, usually by answering a series of questions about their plight. It is a vital part of their attempt to make sense of their change from being a 'well' person to being 'ill'. There are at least five components to consider in forming an IRM (see Table 8.1). Sometimes aspects of the model can be underdeveloped or misinformed. For example, a person might harbour illogical ideas about why they contracted the illness (cause component) or wallow in an ill-informed sense of hopelessness regarding the illness's probable course and cure. The support of other people can help in putting together a stable, helpful and realistic mental map of any illness.

While the facts that make up an IRM are a matter for the medical profession, there are a number of ways in which the process of developing this model can be helped by pastoral work. Religious beliefs can modulate the answers a person feels able to accept for each of these components, and pastoral sensitivity is called for concerning how a person's religious perspective contributes to this multifaceted mental representation. For Christians some medical subjects (such as abortion,

Table 8.1 A five-component illness representation model (adapted from Banyard 1996)

Identity	What is this called/like?	The name I can give this illness and what I think the symptoms are.
Consequences	What will happen to me?	My ideas about the short- and long-term effects.
Time line	How long before I get better/worse?	My time frame for this change – accepting long-term illness takes longer.
Causes	How did I get it?	My own doing, external factors, chance?
Cure	What will make me better?	My ideas about cures and healing.

sexually transmitted disease, or mental illness) may be difficult even to speak about directly.

Faith is especially likely to colour the components associated with *cause* and *cure*. Typically, people see God as implicated in personal more than impersonal events, and in positive more than negative events (Spilka *et al.* 1985). Illness is personal, but negative. A cure for illness, however, qualifies as both personal and positive – so God is especially likely to be appealed to as people address this aspect of their IRM. In other words, people are primed by their attributional mindset to regard getting better as spiritually influenced too.

While 'cause' is ostensibly negative, though personal, there can still be a tendency to attribute the cause of medical illness to God – to paraphrase so many of the Psalmist's cries: 'Oh God, why me?' This sense that God is behind the illness can call faith into question. A primitive sense that 'bad things shouldn't happen to good people' can raise the question 'in what respect did I not have enough faith?' or 'what kind of God would let this happen?' If the illness is thought of as caused by God, it may be seen as a punishment or a test, the length of which is contingent on their spiritual record in the past and in this time of trial. People who feel convinced that God has targeted them in their illness may be redefining it as in some sense positive – a specially designed communication and challenge from God just for them. So when God is brought into thoughts about cause, there is scope for faith to feel increased in some cases, while for others faith may be lost or re-examined as insufficient.

Although there are many potential religious dimensions to thinking about illness, lay and ordained people who undertake visits to the sick as part of their Christian ministry will generally find the conversation is much more mundane. Simply providing a listening ear for someone who wants to talk about their illness, symptoms, medication, and prognosis is one of the most valuable and important pastoral tasks. However, identifying what (and how much) is said about each of the different components of the IRM can also help the listener to recognise special issues of concern, or any that are being avoided.

Action-planning and coping

Much of the action-planning required during the course of an illness is negotiated by doctors on the patient's behalf – selecting treatments, operations and tests. However, anxieties and fears about these actions can significantly interfere with their intended contributions to recovery and healing. People need to have, or develop, robust coping strategies to combat the stress involved in facing illness and its treatment.

Coping is how we protect ourselves, psychologically, when a stressful situation such as illness occurs. Psychologists' way of categorising these styles (into 'avoidance' and 'approach' styles) can help ministers to spot a preferred coping style, occasions when this might be unduly one-sided, and how to match spiritual support to this.

Freud noted common ways in which people try to cope with crises through avoidance, using psychological defence mechanisms such as displacement and denial. When a serious diagnosis is made or a difficult operation looms, a person might bury themselves in work to distract their own attention from what is going on in their bodies. Denial obviously prohibits the adjustment afforded in developing an IRM. In general, this kind of coping offers limited protection since the use of defence mechanisms often creates secondary emotional problems, adding to the stress load. Faith can be used defensively too (see below).

Approach styles of coping are more constructive and come in two forms:

- *Problem-focused*
  Looking for ways to sort out the problems, for example by making decisions and taking remedial actions.
- *Emotion-focused*
  Looking for ways to take emotional control; trying to direct thoughts and feelings in a constructive way.

Serious illness, chronic pain or disability, bereavement or irreversible loss in many forms (e.g. hysterectomy, amputation, loss of sight) often present us with situations that can't be 'sorted out' with a problem-solving approach. In these cases, the emotion-focused coping style is especially useful. This is also the level on which faith-based coping seems to operate most naturally.

People often turn to the church for support as they try to deal with their anxieties, not only about their illness, but also about its treatment. Ministers may be asked to 'say one for me on Thursday when I've got my hospital appointment' or find they are frequently regaled with gruesome details of tests and their results. Some spiritual approaches, such as a familiar ritual, can provide reassurance, whereas a conversational approach could explore the role of faith in God. The coping style preferred by some people might lead them to welcome the opportunity to focus on specific issues. For example, operations can raise fears about disfigurement that suggest the relevance of aspects of the spiritual tradition that deal with feeling violated or

Table 8.2   Three sorts of religious control over illness (Rothbaum *et al.* 1982)

Interpretive control	'Things could be worse. This cancer is part of my spiritual journey, not a roadblock.'
Predictive control	'I'm convinced that God will make me well, regardless of medical opinion.'
Vicarious control	'I may not know the future, but God does. I may not know how to be strong, but God does.'

damaged but subsequently transformed and whole. Others may find solace by identifying a specific Biblical role-model who suffered in a similar way.

Keith Pargament *et al.* (1988) suggest we can distinguish three kinds of religious copers among church-goers. Deferential religious copers tend to leave everything to God, perhaps to the extreme of refusing medical treatment. Collaborative religious copers engage in partnership with God in dealing with their medical problems. Self-directed religious copers use religious cognition and activity (such as prayer) much more sparingly with regard to illness. For example, they might refrain from involving God in whether or not their leg ulcer heals, but rely on him to give them strength in the interim. Collaborative copers, and to a lesser extent self-directed copers, make use of their faith in a way that raises their self-esteem and well-being. Ministry with the sick often needs to steer people towards these healthier ways of relying on faith as they cope with being ill.

A constructive, emotion-focused style of religious coping can be effective in lowering the anxiety and depression associated with being ill. Religion seems to help by setting problems (pain, disability, and so on) in a bigger frame of meaning that can transcend the intractability of symptoms faced in the here and now. Religion is also effective because it can offer secondary ways in which the person can try to reclaim some control and sense of meaning. Table 8.2 identifies three ways in which people look to religion for this kind of support.

Participating in religious ritual can also be a valuable way of supporting coping. Ritual can focus and order all kinds of powerful, ambiguous emotions (see Chapter 2). It is also something the person can do at a time when they feel otherwise incapacitated. Prayer can also give this feeling of doing something positive about one's situation.

SUMMARY OF KEY THEMES

- Measuring health and illness by the triad of clinical symptoms, capacity to function, and subjective well-being.
- The connection between stress and illness.
- The risk-taking behaviours that stress can encourage (smoking, drinking, over-eating, sexual promiscuity).
- How Christian fellowship can reduce stress and improve health.

- Developing an Illness Representation Model: thinking about the identity, consequences, time-line, causes, and cure of one's illness.
- Avoidance and approach styles of coping with illness.
- Deferential, collaborative, and self-directed forms of religious coping.
- The need to care for carers.

QUESTIONS TO CONSIDER

- How have you coped with illness in the past?
- What part did your faith play in this?
- How could you stop church-related stress contributing to the stress–disease cycle?

Box 8.3 Pastoral care for carers

- Those who find themselves caring for the sick, especially a family member, can themselves have a number of special psychological needs in which pastoral support can help.
- Becoming a carer usually entails a role adjustment. The relationship between a married couple, when one of them falls ill, can become more like a parent–child relationship, in which the carer loses his or her sexual partner and mutual support.
- Carers can experience an emotional cocktail of love, anger, guilt and exhaustion. The context of faith (e.g. in prayer or through fellowship) may offer opportunities to express this in a safe way, if it is made clear that negative emotions are not necessarily 'unchristian' all of the time.
- Carers can develop too thick a skin as a defence to protect themselves from the reality of their patient's suffering. Learning to be indifferent in this way may prevent the carer experiencing their own vulnerability. Framing suffering in a spiritual perspective may help to overcome this 'defensive' caring style.
- Respite from being a carer is vital but, interestingly, carers often find comfort in opportunities to be supportive to others, such as contributing to self-help groups. This seems to work by providing them with a source of appreciation that is perhaps lacking from their incapacitated spouse, or is of a different order given that care in sickness and health is expected in marriage. Providing help and support to other carers or sufferers maximises the carer's sense of being useful and active rather than feeling passively at the mercy of the home situation.

Bereavement

Death is the one point in our secularised lifestyle where the influence of the church is still sought, through funeral services and attendant pastoral care; indeed, it is estimated that 90–95 per cent of funeral services in the UK are led by a Christian minister (Brierley 1999). Thus, the role of ministers and the wider church in helping the bereaved is crucial.

When a vital relationship has been severed through death, we are faced with the full extent of our vulnerability as humans. The loss of spouse, parent, child, sibling or friend, devastating in itself, also entails changes in the wider network of relationships. There may also be changes to a person's world view; perhaps their faith has been undermined or shattered through this tragedy. As noted above, bereavement can come in many forms. The loss of a limb, physical illness, disability, divorce, miscarriage, job loss, moving house, changing schools, and old age all involve radical change and a sense of diminishment, and so can produce a sense of bereavement. Such experiences of loss also have the potential to revive emotions connected to previous unresolved losses.

Grieving is a process; it is not humanly possible to deal with its devastation all at once. Researchers have observed various stages through which grieving persons need to pass. Elisabeth Kubler-Ross's book *On Death and Dying* (1970) helps us to understand the emotional stages that terminally ill patients experience in their approach to their own death, the ultimate loss. These stages have been found to be broadly relevant to the grieving process as well. In practice, stages may be cyclical, and some might be skipped. Bereavement may progress upwards as a spiral staircase, or zig-zag unpredictably. There is some question about how universal these stages are, as different cultures emphasise different aspects of the grief process. Thus, in caring for the bereaved, the map laid out in Box 8.4 needs to be applied flexibly.

Other aspects of grief described by C. Murray Parkes (1986) are an alarm reaction (anxiety, restlessness and physiological accompaniments of fear), searching (an urge to find the person in some form), feelings of internal loss of self (even of mutilation of the self), and identification (the adoption of traits, mannerisms or symptoms of lost person) (Parkes 1986: 202). These are normal features of the lengthy process of grieving, a process which should not be expected to last less than two years (and may in fact last longer).

Yearning and searching for the deceased can be so real that the person can get glimpses of the dead person, and may even think they are going mad. It is now accepted as normal to feel the presence of the other, a phenomenon which can bring comfort, especially in the early stages of grieving. However, a person can get stuck in seeking comfort through continued contact of some sort with the deceased. Churches can offer a valuable ministry to their communities by offering periodic services of remembrance, where the dead are valued and remembered within a Christian context.

Bereavement raises many important theological issues. Obviously, the fact that many people have a sense of the continued presence of the deceased can be

Box 8.4 Kubler-Ross's six stages of grieving

1 Denial
'It's not true', 'This isn't really a fatal disease', 'Even though she has died, this won't really affect me'.
Denial and isolation. Shock, numbness. Removing oneself from realities that challenge denial. Whether the news of an impending death is sudden or gradual, there can be numbness and denial, a normal feature of shock, which protects the person from being overwhelmed too suddenly.

Pastoral advice
Don't get into arguments or challenge denial strategies directly. On the other hand, don't collude with the denial. Offer plenty of opportunity for the truth to be explored gradually. Provide time to talk, do not leave the bereaved in isolation. Convey the message that there are no taboos, anything can be said. Gently 'steer into the distress'.

2 Bargaining
'If you cure my husband I will be a perfect wife...', 'I promise to go to church if only you will...'.
Bargaining is an attempt to alter the terrible reality.

Pastoral advice
Listen, but do not actively collude with unrealistic hopes or with a view that God can have his arm twisted. It is normal that we try to manipulate God in times of crisis, but eventually we need to acknowledge this. Bargaining takes up a lot of energy, and eventually the person may be glad to give it up.

3 Anger
'Why me? What have I done? It's so unfair, so bloody unfair'.
Anger indicates a fight, an effort to refuse the terrible reality; the person may still be fighting to maintain hope for recovery.

Pastoral advice
Allow the person to express feelings of anger, even anger against the person dying (or who has died) for abandoning the living. Anger at God is often projected onto the clergy or other church members trying to help. Allow the expressions of anger and rage to be expressed. Do not try to defend yourself (or God, or the church), but do find someone outside the situation with whom you can work through your own pain.

4 Guilt
'Is there something I could have done to prevent this? If only I had...'.
Feeling guilt and remorse for the loss, or for what was unresolved in the relationship. Relationships that have been difficult often leave a legacy of guilt.

Pastoral advice

Allow space for the person to talk through regrets and a sense of failure and sin. Do not try to make a person feel better by encouraging them to avoid their sense of guilt. Rather help people gain a realistic picture of what comes from real, objective guilt, and what comes from false, subjective guilt. Children in particular may feel responsible for a death of a sibling or parent, and need help to see that this was not their fault. (See also the section on confession and forgiveness in Chapter 2.)

5 Depression

'There is no purpose in living now...', 'I will never stop grieving...'.

Feeling a profound sense of loss and sadness is the beginning of accepting the loss of the other's life. Depressive and painfully sad feelings are normal, and it is to be expected that despair, hopelessness, or intense grief will surface unbidden and, at times, feel overwhelming.

Pastoral advice

This is part of the vital 'griefwork'. It is hard work, intensely absorbing and energy draining; do not encourage people to be falsely cheerful or to look on the bright side too soon. Anniversaries and birthdays can often kindle intense feelings of loss. Some people seek to avoid their feelings, or feel ashamed of them, and thus need encouragement to express their sorrow. If the person appears to be stuck for some length of time, or the depression is severe, the help of a GP (who can refer onwards to more specialist help if needed) should be sought.

6 Acceptance

As with a person nearing their own death, in grieving, eventually a period of quiescence comes. This acceptance precedes a gradual re-integration with life, and a gradual forming of new ties; a letting go but not a forgetting.

Pastoral advice

People may need to be reassured that it is not disloyal for them to accept the death of the other, and to begin to let go and to say good bye. Reliving memories, going through the photos, talking about and owning what has been good and precious will be helpful. Adjusting to the new reality, hope for the future, and gradual re-entry to social life in time will follow. The social support of a church, involving the bereaved in the normal round of activities, can provide a caring, albeit altered, network of relationships.

interpreted in terms of Christian thinking about immortality and the communion of saints, though these beliefs should not be used in way that obscures the fact that an earthly life has ended. Biblically, the grief of the disciples at Jesus' death is an interesting case study in bereavement. Indeed Jesus' attempt to prepare the disciples for his death (John 14–16) touches many bereavement themes, including loss, glorying, and presence (Harvey 1985).

The loss of the relationship is the primary, major stressor in bereavement: the breaking of the affectional bond. But primary loss is often followed by secondary loss. Secondary loss for a widow could be having to sell the house and living on a reduced income. She may have to face doing taxes for the first time, and to learn to take control of the finances at a time when she is least able to do so. A surviving spouse with children will need to cope with the grief of the children and the grief of in-laws at a time when support is keenly needed. Many families rally at a time of bereavement, but equally, the strain of family members grieving in different ways can exacerbate old wounds.

'No one ever told me that grief was so physical'. The stress of bereavement on the physical body is enormous. The immune system and endocrine functioning are under fire. Eventually the body can become exhausted, and more prone to disease. It is not surprising that many studies show that in the first six months after a major bereavement, especially for men, there is approximately a 40 per cent increased chance of death, either through illness or accident (Stroebe and Stroebe 1993). People with greater social and family ties are more protected from this general increase in the risk of mortality. The importance of the church as a place of re-weaving supportive relationships cannot be overestimated.

Sex differences

Men and women tend to adopt different coping strategies in bereavement. In general, women tend to focus on dealing with their emotions, while men prefer to focus on problem-focused coping strategies such as attending to the practicalities of the changes in their life. In the case of a couple who have both been bereaved (e.g. through the loss of a child) it is easy for partners to feel that the other is not grieving in the right way, and to feel unsupported by their spouse. For parents who have lost a child, the secondary loss may be the strain on the couple's relationship: the woman feels and expresses intense grief; the man bottles it up and, pragmatically, tries to cope. The woman may feel her husband is not really grieving as much as she is. Marital discord could lead to a whole swathe of losses: divorce or separation, loss of the marital home, separation from surviving children, all of which are losses that can be as crippling as the primary loss.

Despite some of the structural inequalities in society that disadvantage women, making for greater secondary losses (smaller pensions, lower incomes, fewer employment prospects especially if juggling child-care), research indicates that, overall, men have a more difficult time than women in coming to terms with spousal bereavement. This has been understood in terms of our culture's taboo on the expression of emotion for men, whereas women are allowed to 'have their cry'. This is certainly one feature. Another, perhaps even more salient feature, is that women tend to be the couple's initiator in terms of other social relationships. Women are more likely to seek out other support networks. Men, when widowed, can withdraw into isolation (a tendency which is exacerbated as men get older). Many women turn to the church after a bereavement and find it a place of spiritual strength and social support. The need for the church to learn to reach out effectively to grieving men, especially older men, is apparent.

Complicated griefs

The shock of a sudden unexpected death can prolong and complicate the grieving process. An unexpected loss can be so much harder to make sense of; bewilderment and protest can endure for years. If the death was traumatic and was witnessed by the survivor, dealing with the traumatic memories of the death may require specialist help. Stigmatised deaths such as suicide, or death through AIDS, add a burden of shame and social isolation for the survivors, as well as continual rumination over guilt. Church practice has historically added to this burden; as recently as the 1950s a suicide was not allowed a Christian burial. The church is now in a position to assuage some of the social stigma of such bereavements.

The termination of a difficult relationship through death tends not to bring a blessed release, as one might wish for, but rather a legacy of unresolved anguish, anger and guilt. Working through the various stages of anger and guilt may require the help of a trained counsellor. At the same time the church has much to offer in helping a person work towards forgiveness of self and other, but this must not be rushed, lest it serve as a bandage over a festering wound (see also the section on confession and forgiveness in Chapter 2).

Death of a child

It is unnatural for a child to die before their parents, at any age. The intense affectional bond between children and parents, and parents' feelings of responsibility for the child make this perhaps the most difficult bereavement. Mothers especially can find it almost impossible to separate themselves from their child, even long after the child's death. At conscious and unconscious levels, parents can feel responsible for the death of their child, as well as suffering from frustration and helplessness that their child could not be saved. To work through the grief of such an intense loss can seem unbearable, and such mourning is often truncated. For instance, sometimes parents turn a sibling into a substitute for the dead child, to both the parents' and surviving child's detriment. Support groups involving other bereaved parents can help a person begin to unravel the chronic grief and irrational guilt that is common among bereaved parents. Certainly, a deceased child is never forgotten; 'the death of a child is forever' (Weiss 1993).

Stillbirth and miscarriage, at any point in the pregnancy, are also bereavements. A child of whatever stage of development is of infinite value to the parents, and the church should not gloss over these early losses. Initial research shows that how parents are treated by hospital staff is an important factor in the grieving process, and hospitals are becoming more sensitive and supportive at this critical time. Parents find it helpful to have the option to spend time with the body of their child, however brief the life, and to say goodbye. Even a procured abortion can be a bereavement, and will also involve guilt, regret and anger. Memorial services which allow parents to remember, love, and grieve for an unborn child may help them come to terms with what is often a silent grief (Smith 1993).

Abnormal grief

Although grieving is a normal, inevitable process, it seems that the process can go awry in several ways. Categories of abnormal grief include:

1   *Chronic grief*
    Grief that is stuck, endless, or inconsolable.
2   *Absent grief*
    Grief that is being denied.
3   *Inhibited grief*
    Grief that is not able to be expressed.

If a person has had good previous attachments and separations (and has an internal model of surviving a loss), it will be easier to survive a major bereavement. If a person has not had the benefit of prior secure attachment, the loss will be much harder to bear (and may require counselling to unravel the earlier problems). In such cases, it may be necessary to get specialist help, either through a professional counsellor or a specialist bereavement counsellor (through organisations such as Cruse). Churches and ministers can provide valuable ongoing spiritual and social support while the complicated, critical issues are being pursued with professional help.

Loss-oriented and restoration-oriented coping

The standard assumption about bereavement, which has been tacit in what has been said here so far, is that healthy grieving involves confronting and coming to term's with one's loss rather than hiding from it and denying one's feelings. However, recent research shows that it is not possible to face the devastation of one's loss and grief head-on and continuously during bereavement. Rather, it is normal and healthy to oscillate between loss-oriented coping (confronting the loss, 'griefwork', and breaking the bond to the deceased) and restoration-oriented coping (seeking distraction from grief, avoiding grief, doing new things, attending to life changes) (Stroebe and Schut 1999; see Figure 8.2). Just as approach and avoidance coping techniques each have their place when dealing with illness, so loss-oriented and restoration-oriented coping styles each have a place in the grieving process. In each case, the avoidance and problem-focused styles more common in men, as well as the expressive and emotion-focused styles more associated with women, have a place in dealing with experiences of loss.

Another assumption of the classic approach to bereavement is that in contemporary Western culture there is no possibility of having any meaningful relationship with the dead. However, a new model suggested by Tony Walter (1996) proposes that one of the purposes of grief is to go on living with the dead, acknowledging that the person is a continuing member of the family and the friendship network, albeit in a changed way. Although we should not deny the reality of their death, there needs to be a recognition that we are who we are, in part, because of who the other person was to us. We

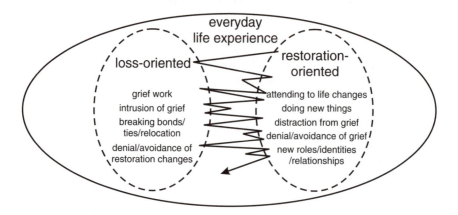

Figure 8.2 Loss-oriented and restoration-oriented coping (Stroebe & Schut 1999)

are denying psychological reality if we try to leave that person entirely behind. In Shona tradition, for example, there is a straightforward and simple burial. There is no attempt to deny that the person has physically died. This is a necessary preliminary to inviting the deceased back into life as one of their ancestors. The dead person is lost and then re-found. It is worth pondering what kinds of church practices might help Christians to maintain a healthy connection with their dead (a need perhaps more pronounced within Protestantism than within Catholicism).

In this new model, the process of grief is not centred so much on working through painful feelings, but leads to an emphasis on talking about the deceased with people who knew them well. In this way the grieving person will be able to develop a more accurate picture of the deceased, and to integrate others' understandings with their own memories and images. This sort of 'reality testing' with others, who may have known different aspects of the deceased, and seen them from a different perspective, can be a very valuable part of the grieving process. The traditional Jewish Shiva, a seven day period when friends and relatives sit in the house to talk about the dead person, seems very suited to this task. Funerals can also contribute to the important task of working out who the deceased really was, drawing from several persons who knew them well. Finding the time to share reminiscences about the person is psychologically very valuable. Within a church, meetings between the bereaved and people who knew the deceased could be encouraged. Rituals and commemoration services can be ways of achieving an ongoing dialogue concerning the deceased, and of honouring the reality of the communion of saints. For Christians, it is the eternal perspective that makes sense of our ongoing relationship with the dead.

SUMMARY OF KEY THEMES

- The stages of a major bereavement:

  1 denial
  2 bargaining
  3 anger
  4 searching
  5 guilt
  6 depression
  7 acceptance

- Pastoral tools for supporting someone through bereavement:

  1 one-to-one bereavement visiting (clergy or lay)
  2 a team of bereavement visitors
  3 initial training in bereavement counselling
  4 remembrance services
  5 providing contacts for professional bereavement counselling
  6 practical advice (e.g. on financial matters) from those in congregation with relevant expertise
  7 including the bereaved in social events
  8 church bereavement self-help groups

- Being aware of how grieving affects every area of life: practical, financial, family relationships, social relationships, and physical health.
- The differences between 'female' (loss-oriented) and 'male' (coping-oriented) forms of grief.
- The importance for the bereaved person of talking to people who knew the deceased person well.
- When it is appropriate to turn to a trained counsellor in addition to Christian pastoral support.

QUESTIONS TO CONSIDER

- What is your own experience of bereavement? Was your church able to offer support to you? What was helpful? Was anything unhelpful?
- What kind of support would you have ideally liked?
- Was support readily offered in the early stages (perhaps when shock was still numbing the reality) but tailed off later when depression was setting in?
- In the light of research mentioned, what might a psychologically helpful funeral (or remembrance) service, sermon or eulogy be like?

Dying

Facing one's own death is the final bereavement, the ultimate goodbye. When working with the dying, we are helping people to come to terms with the loss of self. Fear of death (and of the process of dying) is a natural, biologically based feature of human life. Death involves not only the prospect of physical pain and trauma (often now somewhat assuaged with good palliative care) but a very real and primitive fear, possibly first experienced in infancy, that our own self will be annihilated and will cease to exist. These fears can gain an unhealthy power in our life, holding us in lifelong 'slavery [through the] fear of death' (Hebrews 2. 15). Instinctively we feel that death is a violation and an outrage, a view held also by Jesus, whose eschatological mission is to defeat this final enemy.

Thus death is the ultimate challenge to the meaningfulness of our lives as humans. At the same time, dying is the final stage in our growth in this life. It puts all our relationships in a new perspective and invites us to see ourselves in the context of eternity. Review, repentance and forgiveness are its special tasks. One is also called, if one has time, to put one's affairs in order, so that the living can go on 'living well'.

One of the difficult pastoral issues raised by people who are dying is to what extent they are aware of the fact. Sometimes the person concerned is well aware of this, but maintains the fiction that they are going to get better to avoid upsetting their families. The minister may then be valuable as someone with whom they can be honest. Sometimes they may not be fully aware of it themselves; in which case the minister may play a useful role in helping them to come to terms with it, though on occasion they may be so deeply defended against the idea that they are dying that it would be counterproductive to try to help in this way. The minister needs to tread carefully, being as sensitive as possible to how far people have gone in accepting the fact that they are dying.

The stages of bereavement discussed earlier are based upon Kubler-Ross's (1970) research into the stages of dying. A dying person is being forced to separate from the fullness of this life and human interactions. It is normal for a dying person to respond with vehement feelings, in various stages of: denial, isolation, bargaining, anger, guilt, depression, searching, withdrawal, acceptance, and finally, finding hope.

Pastoral care which enables people to move through the various stages of dying will share similarities with the advice given above regarding the stages of grieving. In each of the stages, in whatever order they arise, the dying person needs the freedom to explore and express their feelings, and to face any issues that need repentance or forgiveness. A person may also need to 'forgive' God, especially if their life is ending well before its time. To live through these stages within the context of family and pastoral care is, in some measure, a victory over death's separating, isolating power. Continued meaningful social interaction demonstrates that death brings radical change, but not an end, to our relatedness to others.

In addition, there can be a restless seeking for the meaning of one's life, a yearning to find that one's life has been appreciated. Perhaps the minister may help the person find a safe place from which to reflect on the ways they did or did not find what they were looking for in life. What is helpful is to gain a realistic picture of one's life, and some sense of how this fits into a larger context of ongoing life, and for Christians, the ongoingness of God's kingdom.

However, our culture tends to disempower people for this final life task. Dying is largely kept hidden from view, as if it were unnatural, something that shouldn't happen. Christians should not collude with this cultural norm by putting on a cheery face that avoids the reality of death, when in fact, the Christian faith provides the resources for this ultimate challenge. Psalms, hymns, poems and scriptures, shared in small doses, (perhaps left at a person's bedside, or shared in a pastoral visit) may enable a dying person to explore creatively, even playfully, the significance of this journey from life, through death, to a continuation of life in eternity (van Gennep 1977). An opportunity for confession to a priest, a final Communion, or last rites, are important ways the church helps people prepare for death. Yet pastoral care is not a one-way street. Ministering to the dying often means allowing them to minister to us. Many who work with the dying in palliative care speak of the gener-osity of the dying, the way they bestow a sense of the sacredness of life upon those around them.

Near the end of their life, a dying person may tend to withdraw from social con-tact. At first this is from more casual relationships, later it may include even close family. It is not necessarily a failure for a person to die just when family members have slipped out for a meal or some much needed rest. The dying need to feel the

security of being loved and cared for up to and beyond the point of death, but within
that, they may need privacy as well. When a person has moved through separating
from this life (with its attendant denial, bargaining, anger, depression, guilt and
fear), and is moving through that liminal, transitional stage in which self is beginning to be dissolved in order to be reformed, what a dying person may most wish for
is the silence that marks the journey towards God.

> We are dying, we are dying, so all we can do
> is now to be willing to die and build the ship
> of death to carry the soul on the longest journey.
> A little ship, with oars and food
> and little dishes, and all accoutrements
> fitting and ready for the departing soul.
> Now launch the small ship, now as the body dies
> and life departs, launch out, the fragile soul
> in the fragile ship of courage, the ark of faith...
> ...upon the flood's black waste
> upon the waters of the end.
>
> D. H. Lawrence

'Trust in God; trust also in me. In my Father's house are many rooms; if it were
not so, I would have told you. I am going there to prepare a place for you.'

John 14. 1b-2

Further reading

Ageing

Grainger, R. (1993) *Change to Life: The Pastoral Care of the Newly Retired*, London: Darton,
Longman and Todd.
Levin, J. (ed.) (1994) *Religion in Aging and Health*, London: Sage.
Twining, C. (1988) *Helping Older People: A Psychological Approach*, Chichester: Wiley.

Illness

Banyard, P. (1996) *Applying Psychology to Health*, London: Hodder and Stoughton.
Hood, R., Spilka, B., Hunsberger, B. and Gorsuch, R. (1996) *The Psychology of Religion: An
Empirical Approach*, 2nd ed., London: Guilford Press, chapter 11.
Levin, J. (ed.) (1994) *Religion in Aging and Health*, London: Sage.
Pargament, K. I. (1997) *The Psychology of Religion and Coping: Theory Research and Practice*,
New York: Guilford Press.

Bereavement

Bowlby, J. (1980) *Attachment and Loss, Vol. 3, Loss, Sadness, and Depression*, London:
Hogarth.
Davies, D. (1997) *Death, Ritual, and Bereavement: The Rhetoric of Funerary Rites*, London:
Cassell.

Grainger, R. (1998) *The Social Symbolism of Grief and Mourning*, London: Jessica Kingsley.
Harvey, N. (1985) *Death's Gift: Chapters on Resurrection and Bereavement*, London: Epworth Press.
Lewis, C. S. (1961) *A Grief Observed*, London: Faber and Faber.
Parkes, C. M. (1986) *Bereavement: Studies of Grief in Adult Life*, London: Penguin.
Raphael, B. (1984) *The Anatomy of Bereavement: A Handbook for the Caring Professions*, New York: Basic Books.
Saunders, C. (1983) *Beyond All Pain: A Companion for the Bereaved and Dying*, London: SPCK.
Stroebe, M., Stroebe, W. and Hansson, R. (eds) (1993) *Handbook of Bereavement*, Cambridge: Cambridge University Press.
Walter, T. (1990) *Funerals and How to Improve Them*, London: Hodder and Stoughton.

Dying

Cook, A. and Oltjenbruns, K. (1998) *Dying and Grieving: Life-span and Family Perspectives*, 2nd ed., London: Harcourt Brace.
Kastenbaum, R. L. and Aisenberg, R. (1974) *The Psychology of Death*, London: Duckworth.
Kubler-Ross, E. (1970) *On Death and Dying*, New York: Macmillan.
Kubler-Ross, E. (1975) *Death, the Final Stage of Growth*, Englewood Cliffs NJ: Prentice Hall.
van Gennep, A. (1977) *The Rites of Passage*, London: Routledge.

Organisations to contact for information (UK)

Cruse (Bereavement care and resources)
Cruse House, 126 Sheen Road, Richmond, Surrey, TW9 1UR
Tel 020 8940 4818 for nearest of 200 local branches.

SANDS (Stillbirth and Neonatal Death Society)
28 Portland Place, London, W1N 4DE
Tel 020 7436 5881
E-mail: support@uk-sands.org
Web: www.uk-sands.org

9 Emotional problems

QUESTIONS FOR MINISTRY

- Many people in the church are hurting. How can we help?
- What are the signs that someone is suffering from a serious emotional problem, such as depression or anxiety?
- When is psychological counselling needed?
- When is a more explicitly religious approach to emotional problems appropriate?
- Are there moral as well as psychological dimensions of emotional distress?
- When should emotional problems be considered as potentially sinful?
- Which emotions are constructive and which destructive of spiritual growth?

Emotional problems such as depression, anger, and anxiety are ubiquitous in our society. Most people experience them at some time, and within any Christian congregation there will be a significant proportion of people experiencing emotional problems. Before considering specific emotional problems in more detail, this chapter will elucidate the general reasons why Christian ministers need to be concerned with them, and briefly consider some basic psychological approaches to emotional reactions and problems.

Christian ministers and emotional problems

There have been historical changes in the ways people handle emotional problems. The cultural norm used to be to suffer in silence. Now it is increasingly common to seek help, though this trend has not gone so far in Northern Europe as it has in America. When Christians experience emotional problems, they may well turn to their minister or pastor for help. This raises the question of where normal emotional reactions become emotional problems.

It is, of course, normal and almost universal to feel sadness, anxiety, or anger from time to time. However, these reactions are sometimes so intense and continuous that they become a severe problem. To respond appropriately to life's circumstances, people need to be able to show some light and shade, and variety, in their emotional reactions. If emotional reactions become jammed in one position, that variety and that appropriateness are lost.

When people are in the grip of emotional problems, they often want to take the opportunity to understand themselves and their situation better. The question 'why am I feeling this?' raises itself insistently. This reflects one of the basic functions of emotional reactions. Psychologists such as Keith Oatley (1992) have proposed that one of the basic functions of emotions is to convey information. For example, anxiety draws our attention to the fact that we are in danger of some kind, and provides the energy to respond appropriately. In a similar way, depression can signal the fact that someone's basic emotional needs are not being met, and provides the impetus for a fundamental change in lifestyle. Given this basic understanding of the function of emotions, it is natural that people experiencing intense and prolonged emotions should ask the question, 'what is wrong? Why am I feeling this?'

This leads on to the question of whether there is any distinctive Christian approach to emotion. Here it is necessary to take notice of the history of the concept. As Thomas Dixon (1999, in press) has pointed out, though the word was an older one, it was only in the nineteenth century that the very broad concept of 'emotions' became an established psychological category. Before that time there had been an older tradition of thinking about what we would now call emotions that was more in harmony with Christian theology and that divided these states into the 'passions' and 'affections' of the soul. The passions of the soul were seen as being signs of and punishments for the original sin of Adam and Eve. The way that lower appetites and desires disobey the will when we are in the grip of passions mirrors the original disobedience of Adam and Eve to God in the garden of Eden. The affections of the soul, on the other hand, were the more refined, spiritual, and aesthetic movements of the soul towards things of truth, beauty, goodness – in short, towards God. The all-encompassing term 'emotions' was introduced as part of a secular psychology that gave much weight to scientific method and much less to the Christian tradition. During the nineteenth century, emotion theorists increasingly stressed the importance of mechanical physical processes at the expense of the will and the mind. So, in asking whether there is a specifically Christian approach to emotions, we are effectively asking whether what was originally a secular concept can be re-integrated into a Christian framework. There is no reason why this should not happen.

SUMMARY OF KEY THEMES

- The trend away from suffering in silence towards seeking help and advice.
- The problem of prolonged or jammed emotional reactions.
- Emotions as sources of information about needs not being met.
- The traditional Christian distinction between passions and affections.

QUESTIONS TO CONSIDER

- How do you let people know that you are available to talk about their emotional problems?
- If you have experienced emotional problems, was there something valuable that you learned as a result?
- What are the relative roles that friends, a minister, or health professionals can play in dealing with different emotional problems?
- How can you help people to learn from their emotional problems?
- Which emotions could be thought of as troubling passions and which as gentler affections?
- What are appropriate reactions to passions? And to affections?

The nature of emotions

Emotions are inherently difficult to define, because they have a number of different aspects, and no one aspect seems to be fundamental. There are three particularly significant aspects of emotions: physical reactions, thought processes, and behaviour. Thus, an anxious person will have a faster heart beat, and other signs of increased activity in the autonomic nervous system, will be thinking anxious thoughts, and will want to run away or in some other fashion avoid the situation. Though there has sometimes been a tendency to claim that one of these reactions is fundamental and that the others are secondary, this has never been convincingly maintained. It seems that emotions are so inherently systemic, that no one response system is fundamental.

In the late nineteenth century, William James tried to argue that the physical aspect of emotions was the fundamental one, but that argument quickly ran into problems. More recently, there has been an attempt to argue that thought processes are fundamental. These have led to cognitive approaches to therapy that have been of great practical value, and these are discussed in Chapter 10. However, it would equally be a mistake to argue that thought processes are the fundamental component in emotional reactions.

As well as these three basic response systems in emotions, there are various broader sets of factors, that shape our emotional reactions. There are three such that need to be briefly considered here: social factors (the influence of our relationships and general social context); cognitive factors (the influence of how we interpret our experience); and developmental factors (the influence of our past history).

Among social background factors, close relationships are particularly likely to produce emotional reactions. For example, people are more likely to get angry with those they are close to than with strangers. The greater the investment in a relationship, the more risk there is of it going wrong in a way that will produce a strong emotional reaction. However, relationships also provide resources that help people to cope with their emotions. For example, as will be seen in more detail later in the chapter, how well people can cope with difficult circumstances largely depends on whether they have a confidant(e) with whom they can share their problems.

However, there is a certain skill involved in eliciting the social support that is potentially available. One of the reasons why normal reactions can turn into prolonged emotional problems is that people are not good at eliciting the social support they need to cope with events. As so often in psychological matters, it is important to avoid the extremes. If people have a low view of themselves, it is hard to bring themselves to seek the social support that is potentially available and would be helpful to them. On the other hand, if people do seek support, they can make such excessive demands that potential helpers 'run a mile'.

The skill that people with emotional problems need to learn is to make prompt use of the emotional support available to them but not to overuse it. Of course, this has implication for carers too. It is good to be sensitive to when people need emotional support to help with potential problems, and an investment of limited time and effort at the right stage can prevent an emotional problem getting out of hand. On the other hand, it is seldom helpful to try to provide excessive emotional support. On the contrary, keeping support within bounds helps a person with emotional problems to contain those problems himself.

Whether or not events produce strong emotional reactions also depends to a large extent on what sense we make of them or, to put it another way, on what cognitive processes are involved. For example, as was mentioned in Chapter 1 in connection with thanksgiving, it makes a great deal of difference how we attribute events. Thus, an experience of failure will produce a more severe emotional reaction if we see it as arising from an inherent lack of ability than if we put it down to fleeting, chance factors. Also, a frustrating event will produce a different, more extreme, emotional reaction if we think it was done on purpose rather than just arising accidentally.

'IT IS SELDOM HELPFUL TO PROVIDE EXCESSIVE EMOTIONAL SUPPORT'

The general background assumption here is that we are all the time making sense of our experiences, and there is considerable variety in how we do this. Emotional reactions arise not from 'pure' events, but from events interpreted in a particular way. Some emotional reactions, such as disgust, seem to arise with more immediacy than others. Some, like guilt, depend on an elaborate set of interpretations of self and society. This is the essence of the distinction between 'primary' and 'secondary' emotions. Particular interpretations of events are also important in turning immediate emotional reactions into prolonged emotional problems. People have a tendency to talk to themselves about upsetting events and this 'self talk' tends to be heavily laden with how the event is interpreted. That can set up a vicious circle that maintains the emotional reaction. Particular modes of interpretation fuel emotions, and emotions in turn fuel maladaptive modes of interpretation.

The third set of background factors are developmental ones. Freudian psychology has been particularly important in elucidating the influence of our earlier personal history on our adult emotional reactions. Though there is currently a lot of psychological research on the development of emotional reactions in children, the important contribution of the Freudian tradition is still that it links childhood experience and adult reactions. However, the basic point is a very simple one, that whether or not events in adulthood produce strong emotional reactions depends very largely on whether they are echoes of painful and difficult events in childhood.

SUMMARY OF KEY THEMES

- The many aspects of emotions: physiological, behavioural, and cognitive.
- The social, cognitive, and developmental factors that shape emotional reactions.
- How to make use of emotional support but not overuse it.
- How problems can be fuelled by patterns of attributions and 'self talk'.
- Childhood experiences and adult emotional reactions.

QUESTIONS TO CONSIDER

- Who (or what) in your life arouses powerful emotions in you?
- What is the appropriate amount of support to offer to someone with emotional problems who seeks your help?
- Do you know people whose interpretations of their lives serve to fuel negative emotions and emotional problems?
- Do you know people whose childhood experiences have made themselves evident in emotional problems in adulthood?

Depression

It is time now to consider some specific forms of emotional problems, beginning with depression. The point was made in the last section that emotional reactions have various different manifestations, and this is especially true of depression. For example, **thoughts** become negative, there are **feelings** of sadness and a loss of interest and pleasure, **behaviour** becomes lethargic, **cognitive functioning** is affected, with problems especially in concentration and memory, and **biological functioning** is also affected with impairment of sleep and appetite. It seems that all of these aspects of depression may affect one another, producing a comprehensive and mutually reinforcing depressive system that is difficult to break out of. Six per cent of the population will go through a major depressive episode at some point in their lives, making it an illness of relevance to every church congregation.

Depression can take a variety of forms. For example, a distinction is sometimes drawn between 'reactive' and 'endogenous' depression. The basic idea is that one form is a response to stressful life events, and the other to some kind of biochemical imbalance, though many authorities have concluded that there is no clear-cut distinction to be made here. The problem is that it is hard to find features of so-called reactive depression that are not also present in endogenous depression. So-called endogenous depression may just be a more severe form of depression in which biological symptoms such as disturbances of sleep and appetite are more prominent. The practical significance of this lies largely in its implications for treatment by medication. Not all forms of depression respond equally well to anti-depressant medication; the best guideline is that where biological symptoms are prominent, treatment by medication is likely to be most appropriate.

A distinction is also made between 'unipolar' and 'bipolar' forms of affective disorders. People with bipolar depression show a slow and fairly predictable oscillation between depressive and manic phases. (This is certainly not to be confused with people who feel bright on some days and down on others.) Bipolar depression is a relatively rare but serious condition, calling for expert treatment, including medication. Unipolar depression, in contrast, has no manic periods.

It is beyond the scope of this chapter to deal fully with all aspects of depression. In what follows, we will focus mainly on the social context and negative thought processes.

Social aspects

There has been much excellent research on the social context of depression over the last thirty years, most notably in the research programme of George Brown (Brown and Harris 1978). First, it has become clear that in the six-to-twelve months before an episode of depression there are often threatening life events. To some extent, what counts as a threatening life event varies from one person to one another, and it is only when you know a certain amount about a person's circumstances and background that you can tell whether a particular event will be sufficiently threatening to be likely to produce an episode of depression. However, there are some recurrent themes, including episodes of **failure**, in which hopes and plans in which the person has invested a good deal come to nought, and episodes of **loss**, in which key relationships and social roles come to an end.

A threatening life event of this kind is not necessarily enough to produce an episode of depression – many people experience failure and loss without becoming clinically depressed. Also relevant are background social circumstances, and in particular having a close confidant(e), though there are other relevant factors such as being in employment and having adequate financial resources. It seems that people can cope with stressful events provided they have good support, and equally that people can manage without good support provided nothing too stressful occurs. It is the combination of stressful events and lack of support that often results in depression.

There is also often a close relationship between depression and marital problems, and once again there can be a vicious circle here. A dysfunctional marriage quite often results in one party becoming depressed, equally when someone is depressed it often puts their marriage under strain. Bereavement is probably the life event that produces depression more commonly than any other (see Chapter 8).

Cognitive aspects

Aaron Beck (Beck *et al.* 1979) has described a triad of negative thoughts in depression; when people are depressed they have negative views about themselves, the world, and the future. They see themselves as relatively worthless, they see the world as a bleak place, and are pessimistic about the future. These negative thoughts often take a stereotyped and repetitive form, so that people are constantly and almost 'automatically' thinking particular negative thoughts.

In addition, Seligman (1975) has elucidated the feelings of 'learned helplessness' that characterise depression. Through a series of failure experiences, people can be reduced to a state of helplessness in which they believe that they cannot change their circumstances for the better. In more recent formulations of this theory of depression, the focus has been on how people attribute events such as failures or losses in their lives. Depression is associated with a tendency to attribute negative events to oneself rather than to external factors, or to stable factors that are unlikely to change, and to see them not as isolated events but as examples of a global and pervasive problem. So, for example, while a non-depressed person who fails a maths test might attribute her failure to not having had her coffee in the morning, not having revised sufficiently, or to the test being too hard, a depressed person is likely to attribute failure to being useless at maths in particular and her stupidity in general.

Not everyone who has this depressive mind-set is necessarily in the grip of a full state of depression. However, such a mind-set is more likely to lead to full depression when circumstances become adverse. Depression is almost always characterised by this negative frame of mind, and it seems that this plays a key role in maintaining the depression. Thus, in a similar manner to the self-pity spiral most people have experienced, depression gives rise to negative thoughts and modes of interpretation, which in turn consolidate the depression.

Depression is also associated with biases in what people attend to and what they remember. Selective memory is often particularly marked in depression, with people selectively recalling the bad times and having difficulty recalling the good times. Similarly, when depressed, people pay more attention to negative experiences, and gloss over the good things that may happen to them.

From what has already been said, it is not surprising that depression is often associated with guilt. Sometimes this takes the form of insistently recalling some bad experiences from the past for which the depressed person feels excessively to blame. The topic of guilt forms a convenient bridgehead between the psychological and religious perspectives on the negative mind-set of depressed people. It has often seemed that there is a clash between the two traditions over guilt. Psychologists have been aware of the harm that excessive guilt can do, and have been concerned to alleviate it. Christians, in contrast, have sometimes highlighted the value of a sense of guilt in leading people to repentance.

In fact, however, there may not be as much of a clash here as at first appears. It is helpful to make a distinction, as Freud among others did, between realistic and neurotic guilt. Neurotic guilt is excessive and pervasive, and it is this that has been the concern of psychologists and counsellors. It is a completely different matter for people to have a bad conscience about genuine wrong-doings. (For a further discussion of the role of guilt, see Chapter 2.)

The fact that depressed people take a more negative view of things does not necessarily mean that they are less realistic. Indeed, they often claim that life really is bleak, but most people go around with a 'rosy glow' ignoring the fact. There is a certain amount of research evidence that supports this claim of 'depressive realism'. For example, depressed people may be more accurately negative in estimating their popularity than are non-depressed people. There is nothing in the Christian tradition that would seek to encourage a facile optimism as a defence against depression.

It is relevant here to consider the nature of Christian hope, and to distinguish it from optimism (Watts 2000). It can be argued that hope, far from denying bleakness, comes into its own when circumstances are too hard to permit mere optimism, and provides the inner resources for continued constructive engagement even in the most dire of circumstances. Psychologists have sometimes said that depression is characterised by a position of 'hopelessness'. However, when you look at the details of this claim, it seems that depression is being equated with a lack of optimism rather than a lack of what the Christian tradition would understand as hope. It may well be that hope, because it is more realistic, would be a more effective antidote to depression than optimism, and that is something that could be an interesting focus of research.

SUMMARY OF KEY THEMES

- The distinction between 'reactive' and 'endogenous' depression.
- 'Unipolar' and 'bipolar' affective disorders.
- The role of threatening life events in triggering bouts of depression.
- Episodes of failure and of loss.
- Marital problems and depression.

- Depressed people's negative thoughts about themselves, the world, and the future.
- Biases of attention and memory in depression.
- The phenomenon of 'depressive realism'.

QUESTIONS TO CONSIDER

- How many people in your congregation have experienced bouts of depression?
- Have they talked to you about them?
- Do you know how to recognise signs of depression?
- Is it wrong for a Christian to seek medical treatment (e.g. drugs) for emotional problems?
- How can depression be exacerbated by negative thought processes?
- How might Christian disciplines (such as confession, thanksgiving, prayer and fellowship) help with depression?

Anxiety

One helpful initial subdivision of anxiety problems is into specific and general anxieties. Whereas depression tends to be an all-pervasive emotional problem that affects almost everything, people can suffer from highly specific anxieties and show no other emotional problems. The most common are phobias of animals such as spiders, though there is considerable variety in the focus of specific phobias. Such highly specific fears are often not unduly incapacitating. However, if they are, they generally respond to 'behavioural' treatment methods in which, in effect, the person gradually practises getting used to whatever they are frightened of.

More serious and incapacitating are anxieties involving other people. These can also take various different forms. For example, there are anxieties about having to perform in public, of which public speaking anxiety is the most common. There are also anxieties about having to meet people in official positions or people with intimidating personalities. Yet again, there can be anxieties about having to make conversation, which largely arise from the person's own lack of social skill, rather than from the personality or position of the other person. Finally, there are anxieties about crowds, which often have an element of 'social claustrophobia' in which the person dreads being trapped in a social situation.

Another specific anxiety that causes considerable problems is agoraphobia. Though etymologically it means a fear of open spaces, the central anxiety is often of not being able to return to a place of safety. It frequently develops in the context of depression, and is associated with acute and unpredictable attacks of panic. Panic attacks are so alarming that they often themselves become a focus of anxiety, and a familiar kind of vicious circle develops. Being anxious about having a panic attack makes it more likely that one will occur, and each attack reinforces the anxiety.

In addition to these various specific anxieties, there is also 'generalised anxiety disorder', which is characterised by worry about almost everything. Pervasive worry can take up a huge amount of mental energy, and because it saps confidence, it makes everything very demanding.

Like depression, anxiety affects people's thought processes, behaviour, and physiological state, as well as their feelings. Once again, the mind-set is one of the most fruitful things to focus on. In pathological anxiety, judgements about what may go wrong become distorted. This has two aspects; there are both exaggerated estimates of the risk of something going wrong, and an excessive catastrophising of the feared eventuality. Once again, people often attend selectively to what is threatening in their circumstances. This, in turn, is exacerbated by the sense that one will not be able to cope and by the fear that other people will be hypercritical or unsupportive.

Just as depression is characterised by a lack of hope, so anxiety is characterised by a lack of trust. Needless to say, it is inappropriate to make things worse by accusing people of a lack of trust. The point is rather that, for whatever reason, they have found trust peculiarly hard to develop. The escape from anxiety often involves the opportunity to 'test reality' and discover that things do not turn out anything like as badly as they had feared. It is also helpful to contain anxious thoughts, so that they are not continually exacerbating an already anxious state. There will be more discussion of these approaches in the following chapter.

SUMMARY OF KEY THEMES

- The distinction between specific and general anxieties.
- Anxiety about public performances and social occasions.
- Generalised anxiety disorder; worrying about everything incessantly.
- Anxiety as lack of trust.

QUESTIONS TO CONSIDER

- Who do you know who is prone to excessive or debilitating anxiety?
- Is their anxiety specific to certain situations or more generalised?
- What thought processes fuel their anxiety?
- Do they form unrealistic appraisals of the likelihood of things going wrong?
- How can you encourage anxious people to be more trusting?
- What Christian disciplines might help to relieve anxiety? Meditation on scripture? Prayer support from others? A confidant(e) or soul friend?

Anger

The final emotional condition that we will consider in this chapter is anger. It is less handicapping than either depression or anxiety, but it is a subject about which Christians have found it difficult to know what to say.

There are specific theological difficulties concerning anger (Campbell 1986), such as the relationship between human anger and the anger of God, a subject that received one of its first explicit treatments by Lactantius in the early fourth century. The Bible, especially the Old Testament, is full of references to God's anger. This has often caused discomfort to theologians, and Campbell distinguishes three main responses that have been proposed: to purge theological thinking of such anthropomorphism, to see anger as part of God's steady purpose, and to emphasise the mysteriousness of God's anger. Lactantius' approach had been to distinguish between different kinds of anger, 'just' and 'unjust' anger. Twentieth-century psychologists such as Eric Fromm and John Bowlby have also distinguished between destructive and constructive forms of anger.

Research shows that anger, at least in contemporary North America and Europe, seems to be a more benign and constructive phenomenon than is often feared. Most anger occurs in the context of close relationships rather than with strangers. It seldom leads on to physical violence and is often followed by reconciliation.

Whether or not we become angry depends critically on our assumptions about whether certain conduct is morally acceptable or not. We only become angry when our standards of conduct are breached. Anger requires not just an unpleasant event, but a reprehensible one. It is important here whether we judge that those who have thwarted us have acted deliberately. The assumption of intentionality seems to be a necessary, albeit not a sufficient, prerequisite of anger.

The moralistic assumptions and attributions that surround anger must be a central focus in pastoral work. In people in whom anger reaches problematic and pathological proportions, this is frequently found, on examination, to be the result of idiosyncratic and intolerant moralism. For example, the excessively angry person cannot allow that someone who has angered them may have defensible standards of conduct, albeit ones that are different in detail from their own. There is also frequently an excessive tendency to assume that people's annoying acts are committed deliberately. Angry people often belabour the faults of others while neglecting to discern their own. Anger can be

a reflection of moral sensibilities that are implicit rather than fully explicit, and can in turn contribute to the development of those sensibilities.

As already noted, a feature of recent theories of the emotions has been a re-focusing on the question of the *function* of emotional reactions. When progress towards a goal is blocked, anger can save people from a state of ineffective helplessness that might otherwise ensue. Frequently, it leads to fresh efforts, either along the same or a modified plan of action. One of the welcome features of anger is the energy and determination it can bring. Anger also conveys useful signals, not only to those who are angry but to those who observe anger in others. However, the combative nature of anger, even when it is useful for the person concerned, can sometimes disguise the fact that an angry person is often feeling wounded. Sensitive pastoral care will involve an imaginative grasp of the situation that has triggered anger, and support for the person in their underlying hurt.

SUMMARY OF KEY THEMES

- The distinction between 'just' and 'unjust' forms of anger.
- The distinction between constructive and destructive anger.
- Anger as a reaction to a perceived *moral* transgression.
- The link between anger and intolerant approaches to morality.
- The combination of excessive anger with failure to criticise oneself.
- Understanding anger rather than condemning it in pastoral care.

QUESTIONS TO CONSIDER

- When and where is anger appropriate and acceptable?
- Can you think of examples of 'just', 'unjust', 'constructive', and 'destructive' anger?
- What makes you angry? What does that reveal about your moral values?
- Who do you know who is particularly prone to anger?
- Are they prone to overlook their own failings?
- How should you deal, pastorally, with someone consumed by anger?

Lack of emotionality

Though excessive depression or anxiety, and even to some extent excessive anger, can be incapacitating, there can also be problems at the other end of the spectrum with people who in a sense have too little emotionality.

Some people respond to stress, not with emotional disorders, but with some form of self-destructive or maladaptive behaviour. This might be abuse of drugs or alcohol, some form of violent, delinquent, or criminal behaviour, attempted suicide, compulsive gambling, or whatever. These forms of maladaptive behaviour are found particularly in the more deprived sections of society and in people in the first half of life. They are also found more commonly in men than in women, though there are a few behavioural problems such as eating disorders that are more common in women than in men. This puts into a different context the apparent fact that women suffer emotional problems more than men. If these various forms of maladaptive behaviour are included with emotional problems then it appears that men suffer as many personal problems as women, but that they often take a different form. Some maladaptive behaviour is closely intertwined with emotional problems such as depression, but sometimes it seems to be a kind of alternative to becoming depressed.

There are also people who seem to be strikingly out of touch with their feelings. This can be simply a reluctance to talk about emotional reactions or admit them publicly, and there are people who are so highly controlled that there is seldom any detectable sign of emotional reaction. Sometimes the lack of emotionality goes so deep that the person concerned is genuinely unaware of their emotional reactions, though other people can observe them in their behaviour and physical state. However, just as with the maladaptive behaviours discussed in the previous paragraph, it seems that personal problems can still 'leak out' in other ways. It has often been noted that a significant proportion of people who have medical complaints for which there is no obvious organic cause are very tightly controlled emotionally and show 'alexithymia' (literally 'no words for feelings'). Though psychosomatic problems often accompany emotional problems, it seems that they can also sometimes be an 'alternative' to them.

Despite the fact that personal stress can take various different forms – emotional, behavioural, or psychosomatic – there is need for caution about the classic assumption that people have a fixed amount of emotional energy seeking some sort of outlet. Freud tended to make this sort of hydraulic assumption about emotional energy, and it has entered the counselling culture. However, it is by no mean always the case that people become less emotional for having expressed emotions. On the contrary, as has been noted several times in this chapter, there are often self-perpetuating vicious circles associated with emotion, such that experiencing one particular emotion in the present makes it more likely to occur in the future.

It is also important to avoid a simplistic 'good' or 'bad' view of emotions. They can be valuable in conveying information about ourselves and our situation, and in helping us to respond appropriately. On the other hand, they can become excessive, all pervasive, and disabling. The wise course is to be sensitive to emotions and to be guided by them without being taken over by them. Therein lies what has been called 'emotional intelligence'. Though the passions can be disabling, there is much wisdom in the affections.

SUMMARY OF KEY THEMES

- Responding to difficulties with self-destructive behaviour rather than through emotional channels.
- Emotional blindness.
- Repressed emotions and physical illness.
- The functions and the dangers of emotions.

QUESTIONS TO CONSIDER

- Do you know people who abuse alcohol or drugs, who gamble compulsively, or who deliberately harm themselves?
- What personal problems might lie behind these behaviours?
- What should the church focus on? The 'presenting' symptoms? The underlying causes? Both?
- Who do you know who represses their emotions?
- How can you encourage them to open up emotionally?
- Can denying emotions (especially negative emotions) appear 'spiritual'?
- Can you think of examples of valuable and enlightening emotions, and of debilitating and excessive emotions?

A religious perspective on emotional problems

In the final section of this chapter, we will look at personal problems from a religious perspective. Though this is important, it needs to be approached in a cautious and circumspect way. It is essential that it should not be seen as the only valid approach to depression and other emotional problems. The religious approach should complement other approaches, not replace them.

This leads to the interesting question of just exactly how the two approaches should be combined (see Benner 1988, Chapter 2). One approach is to try to distinguish between healthy and unhealthy forms of a particular problem. This discriminating approach has a long history within the Christian tradition, and Lactantius' approach to anger is an example. However, it can be misleading to suggest that (a) there are some personal problems which are to be seen wholly in a psychological way and are not spiritual at all, and (b) there are other problems that are to be seen wholly in moral or spiritual terms, and where a psychological approach is irrelevant. Though some problems may be predominantly psychological and others predominantly spiritual, it is good to be attentive to both aspects of every personal problem. There is a helpful analogy with problems that arise in psychosomatic medicine. You cannot divide medical problems into those that are truly medical and others that are psychological. Rather, there are medical and psychological aspects to every problem, even though the psychological aspect varies considerably in its importance.

We also have to be concerned about the impact on people suffering from problems such as depression of talking about them in terms of sinfulness. Depression is, in any case, accompanied by feelings of guilt, and to speak of the sinfulness of depression may exacerbate that guilt in a very unhelpful way. Presenting depression as a kind of sin can also create serious difficulties for members of a church community. What is someone to do if they become depressed, but also belong to a church where depression is condemned as sinful? They may be tempted to cloak themselves with insincerity, and keep smiling, whatever they may feel inside. Alternatively, they may leave the church, either because they see their depression as evidence that they are too sinful to belong, or because in the end they reject the unsympathetic condemnation of their fellow Christians. Seeing a human problem such as depression solely in terms of sinfulness could have very unfortunate consequences. So, in emphasising the moral and spiritual aspects of personal problems, we need to be very careful about the attribution of blame and responsibility. Seeing how our inherent human sinfulness is reflected in our personal problems, or seeing how they become intertwined with our relationship with God, does not mean in any simplistic way that we are to blame for them and should simply 'snap out of them'.

The question is sometimes posed in the stark form of whether someone is 'mad' or 'bad'. It is a discrimination that the courts often have to make when faced with questions of diminished responsibility. If people are 'mad' then they are not responsible for their actions. If they are simply 'bad' then they can be held responsible. Though it is no doubt unavoidable that the courts should approach things in this way, often both things are true. We are all to some extent helpless victims of our circumstances. Nevertheless, most of us are usually sufficiently in control of ourselves to be held accountable for what we do.

It is also important to beware of thinking that because a problem is moral or spiritual, Christians ought to be able to deal with it immediately, whereas if it is psychological it is intractable and excusable. In fact many spiritual problems are insidious and fairly resistant to efforts to overcome them. This is the essence of what is recognised in the doctrine of 'original sin'. Though this is often taken as a slur on humanity, it is in fact a realistic recognition of the intractable and pervasive nature of many spiritual problems. Working to overcome a recalcitrant pattern of sinfulness is much nearer than is usually recognised to working to overcome maladaptive patterns of thinking or behaviour. The cognitive-behavioural methods (see Chapter 10) in which people slowly learn to correct maladaptive thinking and behaviour are probably no easier, and no more difficult, than the correction of sinfulness. In fact, they are rather similar.

Third, it is important to emphasise the constructive value of a religious approach to personal problems. Seeing human problems in terms of sinfulness can all too easily be experienced as a condemnation. However, the point of a spiritual perspective is not to point the finger at people. It is not a matter of saying 'You have got this personal problem, so you must be sinful!' Rather it is a matter of saying: 'If you look at the spiritual aspect of the problem as well as all the others, that will help you to deal with it by giving you access to the additional resources that you need to overcome it.'

It is not difficult to see that there is also a moral dimension to a great many personal problems. They arise from 'sinfulness' and they engender further 'sinfulness'. For example, bullying and abuse have increasingly been recognised as major personal problems, more frequent than used to be supposed. There is surely no doubt that to bully and abuse others is sinful. However, what is particularly sad is that those who have been bullied and abused themselves often pass this on to others in their turn. Another example concerns marital problems, which are also often intertwined with sinfulness.

One interesting example of the moral approach to personal problems is despair (see Bringle 1990). An early approach can be found in the tradition of the seven deadly sins, principally formulated by Pope Gregory the Great, but drawing on earlier lines of thought (for more on psychological and religious perspectives on the seven deadly sins, see Schimmel 1997). It was a tradition that reduced the various passions and propensities of human beings into a list of seven: pride, covetousness, lust, envy, gluttony, anger, and the seventh sin, usually translated as sloth. In fact, Gregory was fusing, in this seventh sin, two sins that had often been distinguished in previous lists. One of these is sadness; the other (almost impossible to translate) is acedia, which is largely defined in terms of a lack of normal interest, pleasure, motivation and energy. Together, they come pretty close to defining what we would now call depression. Many centuries on we can still recognise the realities of what was being described in this tradition of the seven deadly sins. However, though sadness and acedia come very close to modern depression, we are not used to thinking of them as a 'sin'.

Leaping over the centuries we come to Martin Luther. Though he himself suffered from depression to a considerable extent, he was in no doubt that it was sinful. The essence of sin is that it cuts us off from God, and Luther was in no doubt that when he was in the grip of depression he could not love and trust God with all his being. In that sense he felt he was clearly in the grip of sin, and saw depression and melancholy as coming from the devil. Kierkegaard reflected on depression in a somewhat similar way. He was also a notably gloomy character, and part of the richness of his contribution comes in the careful way that he observed and described the depressed mood. Like Luther, he saw depression as being in essence an abandonment of God, and resulting from a sinful failure to love God.

So, what are we to make of this historical Christian tradition that sees depression in essence as sinful? Is it simply a misunderstanding of the past that should be left behind? Or is there anything of value here to be recovered? An approach to personal problems in terms of human sinfulness can appear very negative. Part of the problem here is that the moralistic approach to human difficulties has often been seen as the whole of the spiritual approach, rather than just a part of it. This is certainly a feature, for example, of the historical tradition of thinking about phenomena analogous to modern depression discussed above.

However, a moralistic approach to personal problems needs to be placed in the context of a broader religious approach. A religious approach to personal problems sees them as having a much wider resonance. They are caught up in the whole issue of the relationships between God and humanity, and between good and evil. From a Christian point of view, personal problems, like everything else to do with human beings, arise in the context of God's purpose of salvation for humanity. From this point of view, the key issue is whether the way we handle our personal problems helps or impedes that purpose of salvation. Talking about the sinfulness of human problems can emphasise too exclusively the question of whether and why we have those problems. The more central Christian concern is about how we deal with those problems. It is the central purpose of encouraging a spiritual approach to personal problems to point the way towards the possibilities for redemption. Talking about the sinfulness of human problems, realistic though it is, is only a prelude to that. Whereas psychology is inclined to close down on problems, to pigeon-hole them, to cut them down to size, or to 'therapise' them away (Hillman 1975), the Christian approach emphasises the big picture of which particular personal problems are part.

SUMMARY OF KEY THEMES

- Psychological and spiritual aspects of personal problems.
- The need for caution in thinking about the sinfulness involved in personal problems.
- The overlap between 'mad' and 'bad'.
- The seven 'deadly sins' as emotional problems.
- The bigger picture of God's purposes for the world.

QUESTIONS TO CONSIDER

- Do Christians tend to feel the need to hide their emotional problems?
- Have you ever felt condemned in church for having an emotional problem?
- How can religious resources be used to help people with emotional problems?
- What texts or rituals might be particularly helpful?
- Can you think of examples of personal problems where an emphasis on sin and morality would be particularly appropriate or inappropriate?
- How does a Christian approach to emotional problems differ from a purely psychological one?

Further reading

General

Averill, J. R. and Nunley, E. P. (1992) *Voyages of the Heart*, New York: Free Press.
Collins, G. (1980) *Christian Counselling: A Comprehensive Guide*. Waco: Word Publishing.
Frude, N. (1998) *Understanding Abnormal Psychology*, Oxford: Blackwell.

Depression, anxiety and anger

Averill, J. R. (1982) *Anger and Aggression*, New York: Springer-Verlag.
Campbell, A.V. (1986) *The Gospel of Anger*, London: SPCK.
Dominian, J. (1990) *Depression*, London: Fontana.
Hammen, C. L. (1997) *Depression*, Hove: Psychology Press.
Rachman, S. (1998) *Anxiety*, Hove: Psychology Press.

Marital, psychosomatic and addictional problems

Dominian, J. (1995) *Marriage: The Definitive Guide to What Makes a Marriage Work*, London: Heinemann.
Malony, H. N. (1995) *Win-Win Relationships: Nine Strategies for Settling Personal Conflicts Without War*, Nashville: Broadman and Holman.
Orford, J. (1985) *Excessive Appetites*, Chichester: Wiley.
Totman, R. (1990) *Mind, Stress and Health*, London: Souvenir Press.

10 Counselling and pastoral care

In this chapter we will examine the relationship between Christian pastoral care and psychological counselling. Pastoral care can be defined as 'helping acts, done by representative Christian persons, directed towards the healing, sustaining, guiding, and reconciling of troubled persons whose troubles arise in the context of ultimate meanings and concerns' (Clebsch and Jaekle, 1983). Such a definiton captures the breadth and variety of pastoral care. Counselling, in contrast, is a professional activity for which there are more definite trainings and structures, but which tries to minimise value-laden presuppositions (see Woolfe and Dryden, 1996). It is itself very varied in its methods and orientations but, in this chapter, we will consider three main approaches:

1 Psychoanalytic or (more broadly) psychodynamic counselling.
2 Person-centred or non-directive methods, which are one of the clearest examples of the humanistic approach.
3 A more prescriptive approach to counselling using cognitive-behavioural methods.

Pastoral care is a fundamental feature of church life, and the one where the application of psychology is best established. However, even this well-established application of psychology has been the focus of considerable controversy, and there has been a tendency in the twentieth century for Christian ministers to go to extremes in their attitude to counselling psychology (Pattison 1993). Some saw, at a very early stage, the potential of therapeutic methods to enhance the effectiveness of pastoral care. A striking example was Freud's Lutheran pastor friend, Pfister, who in the 1920s began applying Freud's methods in his pastoral work, and was enthusiastic about the contribution they could make (see Meissner 1984, Chapter 4). In other church circles, counselling continues to be regarded with suspicion, even hostility, and there are understandable reasons for that reaction. Modern counselling sometimes appears to be based on values that sit uneasily with Christian beliefs. In addition, as people turn increasingly to professional counsellors, they turn less than before to their minister, and perhaps less than before to God.

It needs to be emphasised that not all Christian pastoral work consists of counselling. For one thing, Christian pastoral care is structured in a different way. The relationship with the minister is usually well-established before any specific pastoral conversation begins. In Christian pastoral care, people often have a wide range of informal contacts with the minister outside any specific pastoral care that may take place, whereas that hardly ever occurs in psychological counselling. Conversation about personal problems is likely to arise in a broader context and to emerge almost incidentally. It is probably the exception rather than the rule for people to go to a Christian minister seeking help with personal problems. Christian ministers rarely discuss pastoral problems in the neat, scheduled, circumscribed way that obtains with 'sessions' of counselling, though pastoral discussions may continue over a long period of time.

There are also more fundamental differences between Christian pastoral care and counselling. Much pastoral care is not focused around a presenting problem in the way that secular counselling is, but has broader objectives of facilitating Christian growth and development, especially as in spiritual direction or prayer counselling. Pastoral care may also invoke distinctively Christian values and beliefs, and include Christian activities, such as prayer or sacramental confession. So, pastoral ministry cannot be equated with counselling. Nevertheless, there is a place in Christian pastoral ministry for work that is rather similar to secular counselling.

It is also helpful to be reminded that there is a tradition of Christian pastoral care that long antedates the development of psychological counselling in the twentieth century. Many leading Christian thinkers have made contributions to this tradition. One of the early classics was by Pope Gregory the Great. The seventeenth century was one of the later periods in which a number of classic pastoral texts were written, including George Herbert's *The Country Parson* and Richard Baxter's *The Reformed Pastor*. As the new psychological methods made their impact on Christian pastoral care during the twentieth century, there was a tendency to lose touch with this long Christian tradition (Oden 1984). However, there has recently been a wish to return to it, to learn from its richness, and to combine it with secular methods of counselling.

In this chapter, we will take a moderate position in which Christian pastoral care makes circumspect use of modern methods of professional counselling. It is important that this should be done in a way that is not uncritical about counselling, and also in a way that does not lose sight of the distinctively Christian aspects of pastoral care. Though Christian pastoral care is different from psychological counselling in its methods, practice and assumptions, it nevertheless has so much to learn from counselling psychology that it cannot afford to ignore it. After a long period of either excessive enthusiasm or excessive scepticism about counselling psychology there have recently been signs of a more settled consensus being established that counselling psychology and Christian pastoral care are distinct but interrelated.

This has been argued in a particularly rigorous way by Hunsinger (1995). She draws an analogy between (a) the proper relation of psychology and theology in pastoral care and (b) the relation of the three persons of the Trinity to one another, especially as expounded by Barth. She suggests that in both cases, the relationship should be characterised by (i) 'indissoluble differentiation' – psychology and theology should not be simply mixed up as though they were the same thing; (ii) 'inseparable unity' – no attempt should be made to totally divide counselling psychology from theology so that they are in sealed compartments; and (iii) 'indestructible order' – that there should be a strong theory about the nature of their relationship and a clear sense of which has precedence. The first two of these are fairly uncontroversial. However, the third is debatable. Hunsinger seems to want to see theology as taking precedence in dialogue with psychology about pastoral care. However, it is not clear what such precedence amounts to in practice. Moreover, there is a danger that a dialogue in which one discipline takes precedence will amount to one assimilating the other. Theological and psychological perspectives both seem essential to good pastoral care, though their contributions are rather different, and it is not clear that one can be dismissed as subordinate.

SUMMARY OF KEY THEMES

- The tendency to take extreme positions on the use of counselling in pastoral care.
- Pastoral care as more than just counselling.
- The tradition of Christian pastoral care that antedates secular counselling.
- Several different kinds of secular counselling.

QUESTIONS TO CONSIDER

- How much of your pastoral work involves 'counselling'?
- In what ways is pastoral care more than and different from a form of counselling?
- Have you been in pastoral situations that could have been better handled with a knowledge of counselling skills?
- Is it possible to combine a theological outlook with secular counselling techniques?

Psychodynamic counselling

We will look first at the 'psychodynamic' tradition of counselling derived from Freud, to which Michael Jacobs has provided excellent guides (1988, 1991). One of Freud's central assumptions was that material that is too threatening to be admitted into consciousness is 'repressed' into the unconscious. He was almost certainly correct in thinking that such repression can take place, though he may have exaggerated in suggesting that it was the universal basis of psychopathology. Sometimes people, far from repressing what disturbs them, are pathologically preoccupied by it. However, accepting his assumption, it follows that the goal of therapy is to facilitate the re-entry into consciousness of repressed material so that it can be dealt with, and its pathological effects ameliorated. To deal with this, Freud encouraged clients to articulate whatever came into their minds.

It is also a key assumption that repressed material that surfaced in the therapeutic conversation will initially often do so in a disguised form. People sometimes refer to repressed feelings, anger for example, while at the same time denying that they are actually angry. At other times, individual words may leak out into conversation in ways that conceal their true significance; for example someone with a repressed anxiety about death may choose to talk about being 'tickled to death'. This calls for an ability on the part of the counsellor to 'listen between the lines' or, as a psychoanalyst might put it, to listen to the latent content of what is said, not just the manifest content (see Watts 1989). This encouragement to counsellors to listen to things that may not be explicitly expressed is surely helpful in all counselling, and people offering pastoral care in the Christian tradition have much to learn from it. There is, nevertheless, an obvious danger in assuming that the counsellor knows better than the client what they are really feeling. It is important to approach 'listening between the lines' with a proper tentativeness and humility.

Having sensed what is being said 'between the lines', a professional counsellor would help the client to understand this by offering an 'interpretation'. The purpose of an interpretation is to help the client to grasp the full significance of what they are thinking and feeling, and to build up their psychological story. However, it is bad practice for the counsellor to simply blurt out an interpretation as soon as it occurs to them. The depth of an interpretation needs to be well judged. If it is too superficial, it will not lead the client forward; if it is too deep it will be dismissed and do no good. The timing of interpretations is also important; they should be offered when the client is ready for them. The skill is to offer interpretations in a way that is maximally helpful in the counselling process.

David Malan (1979), in an exceptionally clear formulation of psychodynamic principles, has spoken of a 'triangle of conflict' (see Figure 10.1). At one corner of the triangle is (a) the hidden feeling or impulse with which the client is struggling. At the other corners of the triangle are (b) the feelings of unease or anxiety to which this hidden feeling gives rise, and (c) the patterns of thinking and behaving that the client uses to defend themselves against these feelings. Most interpretations in psychodynamic counselling link two (occasionally all three) corners of this triangle

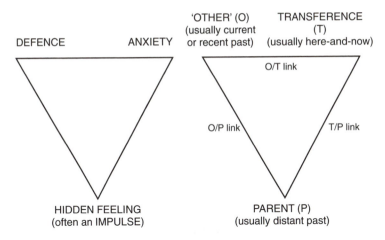

Figure 10.1 Malan's triangles of conflict (Malan 1979)

of conflict. Cumulatively, such interpretations allow the client to explore previously repressed feelings and to understand their significance.

Freud's concern to bring repressed material into consciousness has been widely confused with the rather different idea that suppressed impulses should always be expressed, and acted upon. In fact, people with aggressive impulses are often aware of them and are struggling to control them; the aggression may not be repressed from consciousness at all. The idea that impulses should be expressed comes from a different assumption, that psychic energy that is dammed up will overflow in unhelpful and pathological ways. However, Freud's implicitly hydraulic model of psychic energy has been much criticised, and is too simplistic. There are many cases where impulses are strengthened by being expressed, rather than vice versa. Perhaps the principle that impulses should always be expressed should be replaced by the more modest one, that people should not neglect their basic psychological needs. Doing so often leaves them depressed or embittered. Of course, not everyone has the same needs. For example, celibacy is viable for some people, but not for everyone.

From a theological point of view, it would be hoped that the Christian life would help people to discover and become their 'true selves'; doing so would be seen as part of the will of God. Of course, people can be misled about their true selves and their psychological needs, and there are dangers both of self-indulgence and self-deception. It is also important to recognise that selves can change; our true selves are revealed, as Kierkegaard would say, in 'becoming'. The process of Christian reflection on what we believe to be our needs that takes place, in petitionary prayer for example, can help people come to a deeper understanding of their true needs, and even contribute to the transformation of those needs. This is, of course, psychologically very different from battling against needs and impulses that remain stubbornly untransformed.

Another key idea of Freud's was that the therapist can become a focus for repressed feelings. For example, patients may transfer onto the therapist feelings that really belong to one of their parents. This is indeed a way in which a therapist may become aware of important emotional issues that are not being clearly expressed. It also brings feelings from the past into the 'here and now' in a way that may enable them to be transformed and modified. Indeed, there is reason to think that this transference of emotions onto the therapist may be one of the key requirements of successful psychoanalytic therapy. David Malan (1979) has also helpfully systematised this into a triangle. In this therapeutic triangle the three key people are (a) the client, (b) the significant others in the client's past with whom their personal problems are intertwined, and (c) the therapist or counsellor on to whom feelings may be transferred that really belong to these significant others. Many interpretations are directed towards elucidating the links between two of the three corners of this triangle.

In formal analysis, the therapist maintains a careful anonymity that is designed to facilitate such transference. However, transference may happen to some degree in a wide variety of counselling situations where there is no intention to encourage it or to use it as part of the counselling process. Generally Christian counselling is done in a much more informal way, in which the relationship involved has other features apart from a purely counselling one. That is certainly true of the relationship of a parish priest to his parishioners. Nevertheless, strong feelings that do not really belong may sometimes be projected onto a priest or other Christian counsellor, and it can be confusing and disconcerting. It is helpful to at least be aware that it can happen; when it does, there is a case for consulting an experienced colleague for help in maintaining perspective and objectivity.

Yet another important feature of the psychoanalytic inheritance to counselling is the attempt to weave a coherent narrative about a person's current issues and problems, and how these relate to long-term psychological development. Apparently similar events affect different people in quite different ways, and this cannot be understood without seeing how the people concerned have come to be what they are now. This historical aspect of counselling, based around the development of a narrative, is congenial from a theological point of view (see also Chapter 6 on the role of faith stories in religious development). The Christian story is itself a narrative, and contemporary theologians often espouse what they call 'narrative theology' as a way of making clear the relevance of the Christian narrative for other human narratives. There is indeed a possibility of Christian healing working at this level, as the personal narrative of a person seeking counselling is reworked in the context of the broader Christian narrative. Charles Elliott (1995) has elaborated on this idea in the final chapters of his book, *Memory and Salvation*.

It is always helpful and reassuring for people to feel that they understand their current problems, how they have arisen, and what they signify. Developing such a personal narrative can be liberating and healing. For any one person, there are probably a variety of different narratives that can serve the purpose. A client might go to any one of a series of different counsellors and would come away with different narratives from each of them. Each narrative could be helpful in its own way.

This is not to say that absolutely any narrative can be helpful. Presumably a helpful narrative needs to take the person's actual history seriously enough to have plausibility. Also, narratives may well divide into those that are psychologically helpful and those that are pernicious. One of the reasons why it may be helpful for a person to 'reframe' their problems with a counsellor is that it liberates them from a pernicious and insidiously powerful narrative, such as the one that many abused people seem to carry around with them in terms of their having been abused because they were 'bad'.

The attraction of psychodynamic counselling for Christians is that, more than any other kind of counselling, it is trying to get at the conflicts and frustrations that are at the root of people's problems, and to facilitate people's exploration of these problems. It does this in a way that is rather different from that traditionally adopted by Christians who would often see sinfulness, either that of the individual or the more general fallenness of humanity, as at the root of many problems – though the two approaches are by no means incompatible. As theologians such as Paul Tillich have shown, Freudian thinking can illuminate and flesh out at least part of what Christians would assume to be at the root of people's problems. However, it needs to be remembered that psychodynamic counselling is a demanding business that requires professional training. Though ministers can benefit, in a general way, from being aware of the additional perspective that it opens up, they should be wary of undertaking it without proper training.

SUMMARY OF KEY THEMES

- Readmitting repressed fears and anxieties into consciousness.
- 'Listening between the lines' for concealed feelings.
- Links between hidden fears, anxious feelings, and mental and behavioural defence mechanisms.
- Dangers of expressing suppressed impulses.
- Projection of feelings onto a minister or counsellor through 'transference'.
- Developing personal narratives.

QUESTIONS TO CONSIDER

- How are Freudian ideas about suppressed and unconscious fears useful in pastoral care?
- How far should a minister go in suggesting Freudian interpretations of a person's anxieties?
- How would you deal with being the object of transference feelings?
- Is it enjoyable being idealised? What is it like when transference love turns to transference hate?
- How do you make sense of your life story? What psychological, religious, or other resources might make useful contributions to the construction of personal narratives?

Person-centred counselling

Alongside psychodynamic approaches, a family of humanistic approaches has grown up, of which one of the oldest and most influential is Carl Rogers' 'person-centred approach'. One of the reasons why Rogers developed his person-centred or non-directive approach to counselling was concern at the extent to which the theoretical framework of the counsellor or therapist can dominate the counselling process. He sought instead a way of doing counselling that was centred on the client, and set aside the counsellor's own values and concerns. It is never possible to do counselling in a way that is value-free, and Rogers' own approach to counselling betrays his own liberal-humanistic assumptions. However, the attempt to do counselling in a way that minimises the impact of the counsellor's own preoccupations is a worthy one.

Non-directive counselling is essentially a way of listening, and is the method used by the Samaritans and by student Nightlines. Person-centred counsellors have to learn to be very restrained in what they say, and not to direct the conversation by asking questions, expressing opinions, or giving advice. Instead, each contribution that the counsellor makes to the conversation is simply a reflection of what the client has just said, sometimes just restating it in other words, but aiming particularly to state explicitly the feelings that may have been only implicit in what the client said. The aim is to encourage the client to go further and deeper in exploring their feelings.

Rogers believed that it was important for clients to be offered three key conditions in counselling, warmth (or unconditional positive regard), accurate empathy, and genuineness. They are an interesting trio of interpersonal virtues that are readily compatible with Christian concepts of virtue. Thomas Oden has explored this in his classic book, *Kerygma and Counseling* (1966), in which he states that 'there is an implicit assumption hidden in all effective psychotherapy which is made explicit in the Christian proclamation' (p.9).

The non-directive counselling movement has made explicit what the virtues of the counsellor amount to in practice, and developed reliable ways of assessing them. Indeed, the non-directive approach to counselling was the first to be the focus of rigorous psychological research, notably through the work of Truax and Carkhuff (1967). They developed a procedure for transcribing sessions of counselling, and then rating for the levels of warmth, empathy and genuineness provided. It was possible to define each of these sufficiently precisely that independent raters agreed very closely on the level of warmth, empathy and genuineness provided in a particular session. They also developed a procedure for rating the extent to which the client showed constructive self-exploration, and were able to show that good levels of warmth, empathy and genuineness promoted good levels of constructive self-exploration, and were also related to the overall outcome of counselling.

Those who espouse the person–centred approach to counselling often believe that it should be used unvaryingly with every client. This seems very strange; different people need different kinds of counselling and respond to different approaches. There is something rather paradoxical about a 'person–centred' counselling movement insisting on treating every client in the same way. Some people find the person–centred approach helpful; others can find it artificial and frustrating.

Non-directive methods would not often be used in a pure way in the rather informal context of Christian pastoral care. Nevertheless, it is arguable that the skills of non-directive reflection that Carl Rogers developed should be part of the toolkit of every counsellor. It is salutary to learn the self-effacing restraint of a person–centred counsellor, and once learned, most counsellors will instinctively have the sensitivity to use it when appropriate. For example, there are many counselling situations in which it takes time for it to become clear what the major problems are, and what approach might be helpful. To wade in with a more directive approach at an early stage can be so off-target and unhelpful as to destroy trust and make it difficult to find a way back to a more helpful approach later. It is usually wise to be relatively non-directive at least until it is clear 'how the land lies'. With some people it will be right to remain non-directive. People who have the capacity to explore personal issues in a deep and constructive way will value the opportunity to do so in the presence of a sympathetic ear that minimises intrusions.

Person-centred counselling can also be attractive to the Christian, though not for the same reasons as psychodynamic counselling. In his later years, Rogers sometimes articulated a sense that, when counselling was at its best, his own spirit touched the spirit of the other and became part of something larger, in which a remarkable energy for healing was present (see Thorne, 1998). It is debatable how far this larger energy should be seen as the grace of God. What is clear is that the counsellor's restraint can, in principle, leave room for the grace of God to act. Person-centred counsellors are keenly aware that their own efforts to solve problems will often be futile.

SUMMARY OF KEY THEMES

- Carl Rogers' person-centred approach.
- Rogers' three key conditions: unconditional positive regard, accurate empathy, and genuineness.
- Reflecting and restating in non-directive counselling.
- Adapting non-directive methods to different people's needs.

QUESTIONS TO CONSIDER

- Have you experienced something akin to non-directive counselling? What was helpful about it, and what unhelpful?
- Does humanistic counselling of this sort embody Christian values?
- How does pastoral care differ from humanistic counselling?
- When is it appropriate, and when inappropriate, for a minister to withhold interpretations and judgements?

Cognitive and behavioural counselling

The third approach to counselling to be presented is based on giving advice. In many counselling circles, there is a considerable wariness about this, and for good reason. Where people have major life decisions to make, about the future of an unsatisfactory marriage for example, it is important that they should take responsibility themselves for whatever they decide. Counsellors are right to be wary of absolving people of the need to make up their own minds about such matters, though it is of course possible to help people to clarify the relevant issues without actually advising them what they should do.

There are, however, many cases where there is no doubt what a person wants to do or to achieve, and the question is really just how to go about it. A person who is vulnerable to depression may want ways of warding off their depression; a person who tends to abuse alcohol may want ways of controlling their drinking; or an isolated person may want better ways of trying to establish friendships. It is primarily in such cases, where the objectives are agreed and uncontroversial, that advice may be a legitimate part of counselling. Sometimes, of course, it will be necessary to explore the background reasons for such problems before knowing how best to proceed, though it is sometimes sensible to offer clear advice as a 'first aid', and then to explore the background issues when the immediate problems have receded somewhat. It should also be borne in mind that for some people, especially those who are not particularly psychologically minded, counselling that offers advice may be the preferred form of counselling.

The relationship between client and counsellor is rather different in cognitive-behavioural counselling from the psychodynamic and person-centred approaches considered so far. In many ways, it is a less unusual relationship. Because psychodynamic counsellors are using the 'transference' aspects of the relationship as a tool of counselling, the relationship becomes the focus of close scrutiny and is handled with enormous care. In person-centred counselling, the counsellor behaves with quite unusual restraint, and in a way that can seem rather unnatural. The cognitive-behavioural counsellor, in contrast, is helping people to learn the skill of regulating their thoughts and behaviour in a more constructive way, and they are free to go about this in the same direct, common-sense way as any other teacher of a skill or craft. Perhaps the most important thing is to be careful not to convey implicit disapproval. There should be no hidden message of 'the way you are doing this is stupid' or 'just snap out of it'. The attitude of the counsellor should be patient, sympathetic and helpful.

In recent years, considerable advances have been made in the development of strategies that help people in achieving such objectives, and counsellors are often unnecessarily reticent in drawing on this accumulated knowledge and practice. The available strategies divide up into two main groups, behavioural (what to do) and cognitive (how to think). Either set of strategies can be useful alone, but their value is usually considerably enhanced when they are used together.

The cognitive approach to depression conveniently illustrates the general approach. The evidence suggests it is about as effective as medication in the short term, but more effective in the long term because it equips people with strategies that help them ward off relapse. As explained in the last chapter, depression is seen as being fuelled by a maladaptive cognitive style, such as the tendency to see failure and loss as resulting from stable and global deficiencies of oneself. So, cognitive counselling with depression involves exploring the assumptions the client is making about events in their lives, and helping them to see where these are distorted, maladaptive, or inappropriate. They can then be guided towards adopting a less distorted view of events. In depression, there are also likely to be 'automatic' negative thoughts. Many depressed people are scarcely conscious of such thoughts, but with help they can learn to be more consciously aware of them, to articulate and examine them. Sometimes, it will be helpful to replace them by more constructive thoughts. Normally, these should not be 'mastery' thoughts ('there is no problem') but coping thoughts ('there is a problem but if I tackle it well I should be able to handle it'). There are also times for learning to simply switch off the negative thoughts so that people are left relatively free of rumination and are able to concentrate better.

Behavioural strategies can also make a useful contribution to dealing with depression. For example, most depressed people stop doing things which are potentially satisfying, and to reinstate such activities is a useful step. Depressive patterns of movement, posture and facial expression can also contribute to the state of depression, and it may be helpful to deliberately simulate less depressive postures and expressions. Note that this is not a matter of denying the depressive feelings, just exercising some control over them through the effect of behaviour and posture on mood. Behaviour with other people also forms an important part of depression. The tendency is to behave in ways that other people find off-putting, which eventually leads to them shunning the person concerned, in turn increasing the depression. The depressed person can help themselves considerably by relearning strategies of eliciting appropriate support and encouragement from others.

Such strategies fit quite easily into the Christian tradition. There is nothing alien in the idea that it makes a lot of difference how people think about things. Also implicit in the Christian tradition are ways of reflecting on events and learning to think about them differently. Prayer, for example, probably has as one of its effects that it leads people to think about their lives in a different way (see Chapter 1). St Paul's concept of 'putting on the mind of Christ' can be seen as hinting at the adoption of a different cognitive style. Prayer also often involves a disciplined attentiveness that is parallel to exercises in cognitive therapy. So far, Christian pastoral care has made less use of these recently developed behavioural and cognitive strategies than it might have, and this is one direction in which pastoral care could usefully develop over the coming years. Exceptions to this are Norman Wright (1986), who has provided a helpful introduction to the use of 'self-talk' and imagery in counselling from a Christian point of view, and Neil Anderson (e.g. 1992), whose approach to pastoral counselling, involving knowing and living out one's identity in Christ, is strongly influenced by cognitive therapy.

Many classic books of spiritual direction anticipate the use of cognitive-behavioural strategies and one of the most interesting is Augustine Baker's *Holy Wisdom* (Baker 1972). He seems to have used his long experience as a spiritual director of nuns to make quite exact observations about methods of following the spiritual life. One interesting example of his approach is his advice on avoiding conflict in dealing with 'unquiet passions and distracting images'. He thinks it is unhelpful, for example, to 'call to mind all the circumstances that are apt to kindle indignation and resentment; and as soon as the passion is inflamed, then to suppress it by consideration of the example of our Lord' (p. 178). In contrast, he has some beautiful advice on how to deal with 'hurtful or pernicious' thoughts that are keeping people awake at night. He suggests that 'in case they be simply vain thoughts that then wander unsettled into his mind, let him not wittingly pursue them, but rather neglect them. Whereas if they be sinful imaginations, let him as well as he can, divert quietly his mind from them' (p. 236). It is clear from this that Augustine would have no difficulty with the methods recently developed by cognitive therapists for dealing with maladaptive automatic thoughts.

SUMMARY OF KEY THEMES

- Understanding background reasons before offering directive advice.
- Using cognitive and behavioural strategies together.
- Exploring and replacing automatic negative thoughts in depression.
- Reinstating enjoyable and satisfying activities.
- Prayer as a sort of cognitive therapy.

QUESTIONS TO CONSIDER

- When is it appropriate for a minister to offer direction and advice?
- What are the dangers to be aware of when deciding to give someone advice on a major life decision?
- What cognitive processes lie behind common emotional problems like depression and anxiety?
- How might you encourage someone to engage in more satisfying activities?
- Might the social aspects of church life be helpful here?
- How can prayer be used as therapy?

Systemic counselling

The methods of counselling considered so far envisage a single individual being counselled in isolation. However, there are many circumstances in which it may make sense to involve the spouse, or the whole family, or some other part of the social network. The central reason for doing this is that most people spend a large amount of time in a limited number of close relationships, and how those relationships operate has a decisive influence on their mental well-being. For a counsellor to try to guide someone towards a more constructive frame of mind, when their close relationships are tugging in the opposite direction, is like trying to play King Canute. In contrast, if the decisive close relationships are working in a constructive way, a powerful agent of change is invoked. The counselling movement has perhaps focused too much, for ideological reasons, on the individual in isolation, and been too unwilling to consider the social context. In contrast, it is much more natural in Christian counselling to take the social context into account. The Christian minister will normally be aware of the social context and it is more natural to work with it than to ignore it.

Systemic counselling can take many forms, and each of the three approaches to counselling presented so far can be applied in a systemic way. For example, there can be psychodynamic counselling of a married couple or a family, exploring the hidden conflicts, defences, projections, and so on in the relationship. Equally, it would be possible for a counsellor to take a non–directive approach in working with a couple or a family, reflecting back what was said in an empathic way and facilitating constructive exploration. Another use of the non–directive approach in marital counselling is to train each of the partners to offer to each other a higher level of warmth, empathy, and genuineness.

With a behavioural approach, it also very often makes sense to involve family members or significant others, because much of the behaviour that is being reshaped is interactional behaviour. One promising approach to marital problems is a 'contract' approach in which each partner is asked to set out what behavioural changes they would like to see in the other and then a contract is arranged in which each person undertakes to make specific changes in their own behaviour in exchange for changes they wish to see in their partner's behaviour. At first sight, it may seem that there is a lack of generosity in a contracting appraoch, though it can be a powerful way of helping people to take the first steps towards behaving more considerately towards one another. It is also consistent with a Christian view of marriage as a covenant relationship in which people make undertakings to one another.

There is also sometimes a place for group counselling in which a group of people is assembled for counselling work. One of the principle attractions of group work is, of course, that it is economical of the counsellor's time. Sometimes, the members of a group have no previous acquaintance with one another, though there might also be group counselling with people who already have working relationships with one another. There are clearly important issues about boundaries and confidentiality here that need to be thought through before a group is set up. The important principle is that people should not feel coerced into disclosing personal information in the group context.

Groups can also differ in the similarity of the problems of the group members. Many people who come into counselling have problems in relationships, and it is one of the advantages of a group approach to counselling that these problems become apparent in the course of interaction within the group, and that can provide a focus for counselling. There may also be a place for undertaking group counselling with people who all have some more specific problem in common. For example, it would be possible to offer group cognitive-behavioural counselling to people who all suffered from depression. Whatever the nature of the group, one of the key factors is its cohesiveness, something emphasised by Yalom (1975) in his classic textbook on group psychotherapy. A group that works well together can provide a powerful motivation for change, just as the relationship between the counsellor and the client can provide a vehicle for change in individual counselling.

Yet another mode of counselling is where two 'non-expert' people undertake to counsel one another. First one person has the opportunity to be the client, and the other person listens and counsels; then the roles are reversed. This approach requires a certain amount of sophistication on the part of those concerned, and usually some prior experience of counselling. However, it overcomes the marked inequality that is usually a feature of counselling work, and also has the attraction of being economical on expert counsellor time.

SUMMARY OF KEY THEMES

- Bringing spouse, family, and friends into the counselling process.
- Using a 'contract' approach for marital problems.
- Group counselling.
- 'Non-expert' reciprocal counselling.

QUESTIONS TO CONSIDER

- Are there members of your church who, with some training, could offer some basic counselling in the church?
- Can you envisage setting up a counselling group among members of your church?

- How might the values of humanistic counselling help when dealing with marital problems?
- What kinds of problems in family or church life might benefit from systemic counselling?

Religious approaches

Pastoral counselling is one of a spectrum of pastoral activities that take place in a Christian context. Table 10.1 shows a helpful conceptual framework provided by Roger Hurding in his *Pathways to Wholeness* (1998).

In Chapter 1 we examined how prayer and spiritual direction could be used to deal with personal problems. Just as spiritual guidance can draw one's attention to psychological problems, so secular counselling can raise religious issues. There has been an unfortunate tendency for some counsellors trained in the psychodynamic tradition to regard religion as pathological. On the other hand, there may be an equally inappropriate tendency in some Christian counsellors to welcome religious belief too eagerly. The task of the counsellor is not so much to be 'pro' or 'anti' when religious issues arise, as to help the client to see more clearly how religious and personal issues are intertwined. If people raise religious issues in counselling it is usually because those issues are in some sense a problem to them, and the task of the counsellor is to try to understand the nature of that problem. Some of the most thorough case studies on religious issues in counselling are those presented by Ana-Maria Rizzuto (1979) in which, for example, she draws attention to the very close similarity in the particular client's relationship to their father and to God.

In addition to religious problems that arise explicitly in counselling or in therapy, one can detect that clients are sometimes dealing implicitly with spiritual issues. Just as counsellors in the psychodynamic tradition are used to 'listening between the lines' for the implicit emotional content in what people are saying, it would be equally reasonable to learn to listen for the implicit spiritual content as people deal with issues of trust, hope, belonging, vocation, and so on (see Fleischman 1990).

Though religious issues can arise in counselling, and psychological issues can arise in spiritual counselling, some have gone further and sought an explicit integration of the two. For example, Jung's 'analytical psychology' has a much more explicit place for spiritual issues than most methods of psychotherapy. Jungian approaches to theology will be discussed more fully in Chapter 15. However, it will suffice now to say that the path of 'individuation' is a path to wholeness of personality that is in some ways rather like that of salvation, that Christ functions for Jung as a symbol of the Self, that is, the whole personality, and that the path of individuation requires that the shadow side of the personality be integrated in a way that is in some sense parallel to the Christian concern with the redemption of sinfulness. There is no need to exaggerate these similarities between theological and psychotherapeutic themes to see that the Jungian framework provides a way of touching on spiritual issues in the course of counselling or therapy more than do most approaches.

Another approach that makes explicit provision for spiritual issues in counselling

Table 10.1 Varieties of pastoral activity (Hurding 1998: 175)

	Biblical counselling	Healing ministries	Pastoral counselling	Spiritual direction	Social change
Focus	cognition, behaviour	journey back	relationality, psychological maturity	inner journey, spiritual maturity	community, environment
Doctrinal approach	prepositional	experiential-expressive	esperiential-expressive, cultural-linguistic	two-dimensional (prepositional and experiential-expressive)	cultural-linguistic
Hermeneutics	exegetical	this–is–that	soft-focus, intratextual	spiritual reading (*lectio divina*)	hermeneutics of suspicion
Use of scripture	prescriptive	therapeutic	formative	imaginative	socio-political
Metaphor	teacher, evangelist	healer, deliverer	shepherd	priest (desert-dweller, soul-friend, midwife)	prophet, wise one
Spirituality	evangelical, postevangelical	charismatic, pentecostal	liberal, post liberal	Catholic, Eastern Orthodox, Celtic	liberation, feminist, third-eye
Theology	foundational	experiential	correlational	transcendental	liberational
Key words	Word, cross	Spirit, power	Trinity, covenant	presence, mystery	exodus, freedom

is that of psychosynthesis, developed by Assagioli (Assagioli 1965; Hardy 1987). Central to Assagioli's theoretical position is the 'egg-shaped' Self, shown in Figure 10.2, with lower, middle and higher bands of unconscious, all embedded within the collective unconscious (a concept he shares with Jung).

Within the middle unconscious there is the conscious Self and its associated field of consciousness; at the top of the higher unconscious, there is the higher Self or soul. Like Jung, he emphasises the value of dreams, myths and symbols in counselling work. Also like Jung, Assagioli was interested in esoteric traditions, and his model of personality has links with the Kabbalah and the philosopher's stone. There are also links with humanistic approaches, and, like Maslow, he emphasises the importance of finding meaning in experience.

Yet another integrationist approach is Frank Lake's *Clinical Theology* (Lake 1966, 1981; Christian (ed.) 1991). 'Clinical theology' is difficult to define, and

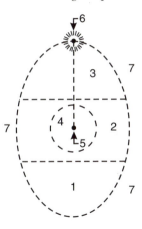

1 The lower unconscious
2 The middle unconscious
3 The higher unconscious or
   superconscious
4 The field of consciousness
5 The conscious self or 'I'
6 The higher Self
7 The collective unconscious

Figure 10.2 Assagioli's egg-shaped Self (Assagioli 1965)

Lake never managed to do so. However, there are central ideas such as the 'dynamic cycle' of what it is to be human, consisting of acceptance, sustenance, status and achievement. This cycle is central both to Lake's understanding of Christ as exemplary man, and also to his clinical formulation of human problems. Though there is much interesting material in Lake's *Clinical Theology*, there are points of concern about it. The basic principles of Lake's approach are never really made clear, and it often degenerates into a sprawling conglomeration of loosely connected insights. Furthermore, he approaches the relationship of psychology and theology in a way that often seems to fuse them, rather than keeping them distinct but exploring the links between them.

Another important issue that arises when counselling is practised in a Christian context is the relationship between counselling and morality (e.g. Browning (ed.) 1983). Most counsellors would seek to be morally neutral, though it is debatable how far neutrality is possible in practice. It is arguable that an explicit neutrality about morals may conceal an implicit moral stance. There are particular contexts of pastoral counselling where moral issues are especially likely to arise. For example, if the question of divorce came up in marital counselling, the counsellor who thought that divorce was morally wrong would be affected by that belief in their counselling. Though there are dangers in importing into counselling moral values that the client does not share, the Christian counselling tradition has at least been more ready than the secular one to acknowledge and explore the role of moral judgements in the counselling process.

This in turn raises the broader question of the relative 'authority' of theology and psychology in pastoral counselling. The basic issue is whether theology and psychology ought to be regarded as two autonomous disciplines that are in dialogue with each other in the context of pastoral studies, or whether one ought to be subordinate to the other. Sometimes psychology has in practice been in a pre-eminent position in pastoral care, though this has seldom been argued for explicitly. On the other hand, a number of writers have argued that psychology ought to

be subordinate to theology, or to scripture, in pastoral care. Such subordination undercuts the autonomy of the subordinate discipline in a way that is ultimately unsatisfactory.

It is more satisfactory to see psychology and theology as two autonomous disciplines in dialogue with one another. It is one of the encouraging features of the present situation that there has been an increasingly rich development of pastoral theology, for example in the handbook of pastoral theology edited by James Woodward and Stephen Pattison (2000). Though the focus of the present chapter is on psychology rather than theology, it is undoubtedly helpful that theology is becoming a stronger partner in the pastoral dialogue; these themes are developed further in Chapter 15.

SUMMARY OF KEY THEMES

- The intertwining of personal and religious issues.
- Listening for implicitly spiritual content.
- The Jungian concept of 'individuation'.
- Counselling and morality.
- Psychology and theology as autonomous disciplines in dialogue.

QUESTIONS TO CONSIDER

- How might distorted religious beliefs lead to personal and emotional problems?
- Do you know people whose God-images are influenced by their relationships with their parents?
- Is Jungian individuation comparable to the Christian idea of salvation?

- Should Christians seek to distance themselves from their sinful shadow side, seek to integrate it, or transform it?
- Is it right for a Christian minister to be more morally engaged and directive than a secular counsellor would want to be?

Combining religious and psychological approaches

The general stance of this chapter has been that Christian pastoral care should learn from modern psychological methods and employ them where appropriate, but that it should combine with the distinctive features of its own tradition. To explore, in a more practical way, how psychological and spiritual approaches can be used alongside one another, it will be interesting to look at how counselling and prayer can be used together in Christian pastoral work. Other examples of distinctively Christian practices might have been chosen, such as Bible study or sacramental confession. However, prayer is perhaps the most widespread and paradigmatic Christian spiritual practice.

Professional counsellors, working in secular settings, have often been very cautious about praying for their clients, feeling that it may be unprofessional! It is of course right, in secular counselling, to respect the values and orientation of the client in the way that counselling is conducted. However, to pray for clients does not necessarily involve deciding what is best for them. The essence of intercession is perhaps to unite oneself with God in loving concern for the person who is the focus of prayer. Thus, for example, in praying for a client who had marital problems, there would be no need to pray either that they should stay together, or that they should separate.

However, the most interesting use of prayer in the context of counselling arises when both pastor and pastored have a strong Christian faith and decide to use prayer as part of the counselling process. It seems that when prayer and counselling are used alongside one another, each can enhance the effectiveness of the other.

There are dangers when Christians use prayer alone, outside the context of counselling, as a way of tackling pastoral problems. It can be used to promote a quick fix for personal problems that avoids the slow, hard work involved in thorough healing and quickly breaks down. When prayer is used in conjunction with pastoral counselling, this is much less likely to arise. It is the job of the counselling to go deep, and to make a superficial 'dash for health' impossible. As the Jungian psychologist, James Hillman (in 'Peaks and Vales', 1976), has pointed out, in pastoral care spirit and soul need to work together. Spirit, left to itself, likes to soar and escape quickly from any difficulties. To prevent this, it needs the countervailing depth that soul can provide. Prayer alone may be too inclined to soar; counselling can ensure the needful depth of soul.

Another advantage of using prayer in the context of counselling is that the counselling clarifies what needs to be prayed for. At the beginning of pastoral work, prayer can often only be general because it is not clear what ought to be prayed for. As counselling promotes greater understanding of the problem, prayer can become increasingly focused and explicit. For example, a depressed person can pray better when they understand what they are depressed about, or an abused person can pray better when they understand why the abuse was so painful.

If prayer benefits from taking place in the context of counselling, the opposite is also true. There are various ways in which prayer can augment the effectiveness of counselling. One of the limitations of counselling is that it may never come to clear focus, or a conclusion. When the problem has been explored in counselling, prayer can be very helpful in focusing that in a commitment to change. In a similar way, when problems of guilt have been explored in counselling, sacramental confession provides a very helpful resolution of the guilt.

Prayer also provides an opportunity for the rethinking of problems in a particular way. Re-construing problems, seeing them in a fresh light, is a fundamental feature of psychological healing. It is one of the distinctive and valuable features of pastoral care in a Christian context that the Christian faith provides a valuable framework within which problems can be rethought. To some extent this can go on in Christian counselling, or in personal reflection. However, it can happen particularly powerfully with the more vivid sense of the presence of God that comes with prayer. Often, people think and say things in the context of prayer that they might not say otherwise, and that can move forward in a valuable way the task of re-construing the problem in hand.

SUMMARY OF KEY THEMES

- Combining secular insights with Christian pastoral care traditions.
- Using prayer in Christian counselling.
- Avoiding praying for someone as a quick fix.
- Prayer as a focus for commitment to change.
- Prayer as a source of creative insights and reconstructions.

QUESTIONS TO CONSIDER

- What are the potential roles of prayer, Bible study, and confession in counselling and pastoral care?
- What sort of prayer would be appropriate to a counselling situation? What sort might be inappropriate or manipulative?
- At what points in a pastoral encounter would it be useful to pray?

Further reading

General surveys of counselling

Hurding, R. (1985) *Roots and Shoots: A Guide to Counselling and Psychotherapy*, London: Hodder and Stoughton.

Woolfe, R. and Dryden, W. (eds) (1996) *Handbook of Counselling Psychology*, London: Sage.

Specific counselling approaches

Blackburn, I. M. (1990) *Cognitive Therapy for Depression and Anxiety: A Practitioners' Guide*, Oxford: Blackwell Scientific.

Corey, G. (1995) *Theory and Practice of Group Counselling*, 4th ed., Pacific Grove: California, Brooks/Cole.

Jacobs, M. (1988) *Psychodynamic Counselling in Action*, London: Sage.

Mearns, D. and Thorne, B. (1988) *Person-centred Counselling in Action*, London: Sage.

Street, E. (1994) *Counselling for Family Problems*, London: Sage.

Religious approaches

Hardy, D. (1987) *A Psychology With a Soul: Psychosynthesis in Evolutionary Context*, London: Routledge and Kegan Paul.

Lake, F. (1991) *In the Spirit of Truth: A Reader in the Spirit of Truth*, ed. C. Christian, London: Darton, Longman and Todd.

Perry, C. (1991) *Listen to the Voice Within: A Jungian Approach to Pastoral Care*, London: SPCK.

Wright, H. N. (1986) *Self-talk, Imagery and Prayer in Counselling*, Waco: Word Publishing.

Relating religious and psychological approaches

Bridger, F. and Atkinson, D. (1998) *Counselling in Context: Developing a Theological Framework*, London: Darton, Longman and Todd.

Hunsinger, D. (1995) *Theology and Pastoral Counselling: A New Interdisciplinary Approach*, Grand Rapids: Eardmans.

Lyall, D. (1995) *Counselling in the Pastoral and Spiritual Context*, Buckingham: Open University Press.

Pattison, S. (1993) *A Critique of Pastoral Care*, 2nd ed., London: SCM Press.

Part 4

Organisation and the church

11   Social processes in church life

Churches are made up of groups of people, and groups behave in ways that are distinct from how individuals behave on their own. Human beings are inherently social, relational beings. We are not immune to the influence of others. It is normal for groups of people to develop a shared identity, and to influence the thoughts and behaviour of their members. Social processes can influence the church towards virtuous ends; they can also move us towards a collective outworking of sin. Social psychology has been studying the social aspect of human life for a number of decades, and many insights are applicable to the church.

Conformity

Conformity is evident when individuals change their own opinion to agree with the opinion of the majority of the group to which they belong, even though no direct request to comply has been made. Churches can be very conforming places, beyond the central matters of faith. This happens simply because of our desire for approval from others, and our reliance upon others to confirm our own uncertain thoughts.

In a famous series of experiments, the social psychologist Solomon Asch asked seven subjects to take part in an experiment ostensibly about visual perception. Each

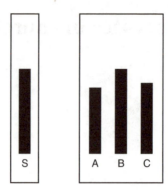

Figure 11.1 Stimulus cards drawn to scale similar to those used in Asch's experiment. S is the sample card; A,B,C are the comparisons (Asch 1956).

participant had to make a series of judgements about which line in a group of three (A, B, C) was identical in size to the initial line they had been shown (Asch 1951, 1956); example stimuli are shown in Figure 11.1.

It was an easy task. A control group of subjects, who made their judgements on this and similar series of lines individually, made virtually no errors (thirty-five of thirty-seven control subjects made no errors at all). The second group of subjects, the experimental group, were asked to sit in a semicircle of seven subjects and to give their judgement out loud in the group. In actuality, six of the subjects were undercover confederates, secretly instructed to give certain answers. Only one subject was a real subject, and that person was placed second to last in the line. The confederate subjects had been instructed to give right answers on six series of lines (the first two series, and four later series). For the rest of the twelve 'critical' series, the confederates were instructed to give wrong answers. This set-up was repeated many times with different groups of subjects. The question of interest was: what does the 'real' subject do when everyone else gives wrong answers?

The results showed that, in the experimental condition, 37 per cent of the judgements made by subjects were erroneous. It appears that these subjects conformed to the incorrect judgements of others. This is in stark contrast to the very few errors made by the control group (0.7 per cent) who made their judgements alone. There were differences between individuals, but the experiment showed that conformity is quite widespread. It is quite normal for people to change their opinions, even distorting their own judgement, when they are at variance with others. Of the 123 real subjects, 28 per cent conformed to others' judgements much of the time, 25 per cent never conformed, and the rest (47 per cent) conformed some of the time.

There are two sorts of social influences that make people conform, the normative and the informational. The reward of group membership or the fear of being rejected by the group are examples of normative influences. Gaining new reliable information about the world through the other members of the group is an informational influence. Both factors influence conformity in different ways, in varying proportions, according to different situations.

Box 11.1 Factors influencing conformity

1 *How large the group is*
   The more people share an opinion, the more that opinion is likely to seem right.
2 *How important the group is to you*
   A group of people who are important to you will have more normative influence; it matters whether they reject or accept you.
3 *The person's own concern with being liked*
   Personality does have an effect; some people are more sensitive to this than others. Women are shown to conform more in face-to-face situations.
4 *How ambiguous the stimulus is*
   The more ambiguous the stimulus, the more people will rely on others to tell them what it's all about.
5 *How expert/authoritative others are perceived to be*
   The opinions of people judged inadequate to the task can more easily be ignored.
6 *Whether or not there is a dissenter in the camp*
   A dissenter who offers you social support is a powerful 'shield' against the pressure of a majority.

In the light of the above factors, churches can be described as having many or all of the factors that lead to a high level of conformity. Churches are made up of a medium to large number of diverse individuals. The opinions of fellow-Christians usually matter to church members. A sense of belonging to the church body is often very important to people, and of course many come to church because they are aware of their own spiritual need, and are hoping to find acceptance. Also, the stimulus (God) is fairly ambiguous, and clergymen or church leaders are considered to be the experts. (Elevated pulpits and church ritual often reinforce the idea that the clergy are 'six feet above contradiction'!) Dissenters in church or Christian groups can be sidelined or demoted; often they eventually leave. It is not surprising that many people feel it is best to conform in churches, not simply in essential matters of faith, but also in non-essential matters such as the way people talk, dress, act and think, at least while in church. Although there are not yet any *experimental* studies of conformity in churches, there are a number of observation studies of churches (where the researcher observes what happens naturally) that attest to this tendency.

What does conformity in church look like? Church cultures display 'group membership badges' (GMBs). These are ways of demonstrating 'I belong', 'I have this type of spirituality'. It is easy to identify the GMBs of some of the more expressive Christian denominations: the 'Amen hallelujah' of the Pentecostals, the 'Are you saved?' of the evangelicals, the genuflectings of Roman Catholics, or the infectious habit of the charismatics of praying using 'just' and 'really' throughout and a member of the Trinity as punctuation (e.g. 'Lord I really just pray that you would just pour out your blessing Father just really fill Dave up to overflowing Lord'). Other churches display their GMBs simply through the absence of these expressions: 'We don't do that sort of thing here'. Not raising one's hands in the air can be just as much a GMB as raising one's hands in the air. These actions become very politically charged. What other people do or don't do in church puts an invisible pressure on church members to do likewise.

Groups of people tend to develop unwritten, yet pervasive, sets of norms. The norms of some churches might be:

- be nice;
- always smile;
- never say 'No';
- pretend everything is OK.

The norms of other churches may be:

- behave with decorum;
- religion is a private affair;
- everything should remain as it is.

While such norms are simply social products, resulting from group behaviour, in church they can take on a religious gloss, and serve as markers of 'our' brand of spirituality.

Conformity brings with it its own rewards. If a person cannot enculturate into a group, they will remain on the fringe. The ideal is a balance between being able to be part of a group, and having the freedom of personal integrity. The negative effect of conformity in churches is that, over time, expressions of faith that were once genuine begin to feel mandatory; they become stale. But people feel the need to demonstrate these GMBs in order to belong. The 'way we do things in this church' takes on a moral imperative: it cannot be challenged because it signifies the existence of the group. In fact, groups, whether they are overtly religious or not, tend to develop their own implicit religion, so powerful is the succour that a group can provide to the individual. The group can function as a deity in its own right (Reed 1978).

Our Christian heritage does provide us with the means to deal with conformity in churches. The Gospels describe Jesus standing against the ground swell of enthusiasm that followed his healings and miracles. With stringent requirements and bewildering, sometimes offensive, statements, Jesus made it difficult for people to follow him except out of a conscienced moral choice. He would 'not allow them to make him king'. Jesus is described as forgoing potential disciples in favour of preserving their integrity. Churches need to find the courage to follow suit.

Box 11.2 Suggestions for affirmative action to curb conformity

- *Talking about it*
  Conformity is so 'normal' it can be invisible. Talking about it blows its cover.
- *Discuss as a church*
  What are our norms of behaviour, our GMBs? Are they the norms we want?
- *Creative changes*
  As habits and traditions ossify, group norms are more fervently adhered to. Making creative changes in church practice can help break up conformity to social norms.
- *Theology of grace*
  Unconditional love strengthens people to know their own worth, and to have the courage to disagree when appropriate.
- *Admitting weakness*
  Clergy can be perceived as authoritative, always right, or not brooking dissent. Admitting fallibility reduces an over-reliance on the leader's opinion.
- *Welcoming dissent*
  Leaders need to reward integrity. One dissenter in a group can be enough to give others the freedom.
- *Caring enough to confront*
  Church leaders can (understandably!) be afraid of defiant or unco-operative behaviour. Being able to confront, in kindness, unhelpful behaviour means that leaders don't have to rely on the pressures of conformity to bring about co-operation.
- *Conscienced choice not conformity*
  Seek to influence people through conscienced choice (minority influence), rather than conformity (majority influence). See below.

Majority vs minority influence

For many centuries, the church has been able to rely on widespread conformity to vaguely Christian norms: going to church, being seen as avoiding the grosser sins, giving to charities. Majority influence can indeed be ubiquitous, but its weakness is that it often results in mere outward actions that can be 'seen by men'. Conformity, the influence of the majority, can change outward behaviour, but not necessarily inward conviction.

The church is no longer in a position to command majority influence. In the words of sociologist Peter Berger (1967), there is no longer a shared Christian world view that provides a plausibility structure which makes sense of the church's claims.

The diminution of the church's majority influence can be perceived as bad news, but it is possible for a minority to exercise influence over a majority. Serge Moscovici and Elisabeth Lage (1976) found that a minority, although few in numbers and lacking the kudos of the majority, can turn the tide of majority influence and 'convert' inward convictions by their own behaviour style. In order to achieve this kind of conscienced conversion, several behaviour attributes need to be in evidence.

Later studies also showed that minorities need to be able to dialogue with their opponents. If minorities are unable to dialogue, their inflexibility may alienate their hearers (Di Giacomo 1980). There are many Christian examples of minority influence bringing about radical change: the early Christians in the Roman Empire, St. Francis of Assisi, Luther, Wilberforce, Desmond Tutu. Jesus Christ himself is our prime example. The kind of change brought about differs in kind from the conforming influence of the majority. Minority influence can cause the majority to analyse and doubt its own unquestioned opinion, and to bring about change to inner convictions.

Box 11.3 Minority influence

To achieve minority influence, groups need to:

- propose a clear position on the issue at hand;
- be unified in their position;
- most importantly, hold that position consistently over time, even in the face of a hostile majority.

SUMMARY OF KEY THEMES

- Conforming as a way to be accepted by the group and to reinforce one's thoughts and perceptions.
- How churches induce conformity.
- Conformity in church as a way of signifying belonging and 'good spiritual standing'.
- Majority 'conformity' and minority 'conversions' within the church.

QUESTIONS TO CONSIDER

- Has someone you know changed their behaviour or thinking radically to conform with his/her Christian group?
- What are the ways in which you tend to conform in your church or group?
- What would happen if you stopped conforming in this way?
- What is valuable in conforming?
- Can conformity be easily distinguished from real 'conversion'?
- Does your church act as an effective minority influence within your town? Why or why not?

Social identity

The phenomenon of conformity is just one of the many examples of how we can be influenced by our social circumstances. In a profound way, what other people reflect back to us becomes an important part of our own personal sense of self. For a child growing up, what her parents reflect back to her is all-important for her developing sense of self. A child's parents are perceived in god-like proportions; their attitudes and pronouncements towards the child are like powerful statements of fact. As we go through life, we are all reflected back in the mirrors of others' feelings and responses. We internalise these attitudes and they become, over time, part of our own identity, although its origins are social in nature. The kind of group we belong to also makes up a part of our social identity. In fact, in response to questionnaires, people answer the question 'who am I?' largely in terms of their affiliations with various social groups (family, church, class, race, employment, college, and so on).

We hammer out our social identity within an incredibly complex social world. To simplify the complexities of the social world, we tend to divide it into neat categories: 'I belong to this group (called the ingroup) and you belong to that group (the outgroup).' Like most of our perceptions, our perceptions of the social world are coloured by our tendencies to simplify and to categorise. We exaggerate the amount of similarity within social groups, and exaggerate the dissimilarity between groups. However, the amount of similarity perceived within groups is even more exaggerated with the outgroup: 'They are all like that (e.g. lazy, stupid, unspiritual).' The perceived similarity of our ingroup is not so exaggerated, rather 'we are a similar, but interesting, bunch of individuals'.

Box 11.4 Evidences of social identity processes in churches

1   Overt and covert criticism of other churches and denominational practices. (This is a difficult area as admittedly there are unresolved theological disputes between churches, and these cannot simply be dismissed out of a desire for 'political correctness'. Inter-group discrimination in this sense is evidenced when the focus is *only* on these areas of dispute, and the areas of commonality are overlooked, or 'poisoned' by association. Indeed, the real difficulty is that theological disputes become intertwined with social identity processes, and the two become indistinguishable.)

2   Dialogue between churches or groups becomes impossible because the markers of group membership (GMBs) are considered as a mandatory 'entrance fee' before dialogue can even begin.

3   Leaving a church or group becomes an evidence of 'backsliding' because of the group's assumed superiority.

4   Ending groups or initiatives becomes difficult because of the investment people have made and the esteem needs the group fulfils. Ending equals 'failure' and loss of self esteem.

5   Dialogue with other Christian groups is handicapped because of the chasm of misunderstanding (partly a result of the oversimplification of the outgroup, and lack of factual information through selective exposure to belief confirming information).

6   The unity of the church seems to be an impossibility, because it is more pleasant to enjoy the distinctiveness of one's own group, and to receive the enhanced positive self-esteem one's group membership confers. To pursue the super-ordinate goal of Christian unity means forgoing some immediate self-esteem benefits.

This perceptual process interacts with our desire to feel good about ourselves, to have positive self-esteem. We have mentioned how identity is comprised of both personal and social aspects. To maintain a positive identity, what kinds of attitudes do we prefer to have about the group we belong to? Studies show a bias towards in-group preference: our group is clearly better than other groups. These two processes, first, a perceptual process by which we simplify the social world through chopping it up into distinctive groups, and second, the desire for positive self-esteem, lead to a comparative process: one's ingroup is *better* than the outgroup.

A striking feature of the theory of social identity is that these processes are exhibited even in the most minimal of group situations. The minimal group experiment (Tajfel *et al.* 1971) goes like this. Volunteers (school boys) were arbitrarily allocated to two different groups. The selection criteria for the two groups is meaningless (preference for paintings by Klee vs paintings by Kandinsky). There is virtually nothing to distinguish the two groups, and the subjects do not even know which groups the others are allocated to. Hence there is nothing that directly links group membership to self-esteem. The two groups are instructed to play a game, and to choose from a selection of pairs of rewards (pennies) to allocate to one's own group, and to the other group.

For instance, on one round, a subject chose to allocate their own group fourteen pennies, while the other group gets twelve. The next time around, the subject chooses to reward their own group nine pennies, and the other group eight. After many rounds, the overall results showed that (while avoiding gross unfairness) each group favoured their own group by most often allocating the greater of the paired rewards to their own group. This held true even if it meant that their own group received fewer pennies in the end than if different allocations of rewards had been chosen; the differential over the other group's reward was chosen ahead of sheer quantity of reward. This finding has proved to be robust across cultures and in different types of experimental and real life situations.

Ingroup preference appears to be endemic in the church. At its worst, it is demonstrated in overt conflict as in Northern Ireland, and religious wars. More often, ingroup preference in the church takes the form of subtle denigration of those who are not 'like us'. As Christians we believe that our church (Reformed, Roman Catholic, charismatic, Orthodox, evangelical, liberal, or whatever) has a better grasp of the truth, a more authentic experience of God, a more genuine faith. Indeed, if we didn't think this already, would we be part of it? We may have originally chosen our church or denomination for prosaic reasons: convenience, tradition, familiarity. Over time, our church's beliefs and practices become to us the marks of its superiority.

SUMMARY OF KEY THEMES

- Personal and social components of individual identity.
- Identity and self-esteem.
- Exaggerating similarities within groups and exaggerating differences between groups.
- Biases towards ingroup and against outgroup.
- Disliking outgroup for no reason.

QUESTIONS TO CONSIDER

Suggestions and discussion points for dealing with inter-group discrimination resulting from social identity processes:

- Begin to talk about ingroup preferences within your own church or group. Without awareness of ingroup preferences we cannot take responsibility for their consequences.
- Examine biblical examples when groups overcame the natural desire for negative outgroup bias. (e.g. the decision to include Gentiles on an equal basis within the early church).

- Change is difficult when we believe that, by it, we have much to lose. What are the benefits to your church/group in maintaining an implicit 'superiority' over other churches/groups? Would membership fall off if your church/group was not 'the best'?
- Give your group a litmus test: how easy is it to leave your church or group? Why is it difficult to leave?
- Efforts at ecumenism may backfire if relying on mere contact to bring about unity. Mere contact can simply intensify perceived differences between groups. Can you think of any instances where this has occurred?
- Discuss the mutually negative perceptions between churches/groups in your area.
- Discuss the relative importance of the major commonalities versus the major differences between Christian groups/churches.

Discourse

Over time, groups of people develop their own way of speaking. In fact, how we use language is a prime indicator of our social identity, and a prime arena in which we exhibit conformity. Our daily use of a particular style of language serves to draw group boundaries and to keep the distinctions between groups alive. Further, the way we use language shapes to some degree the way we experience reality and reflects the categories of thought through which we chop up, and make sense of, social reality.

Any way of speaking and/or writing can be called a 'discourse'. In traditional social psychology, as in everyday thinking, it is assumed that language directly reflects the way things are. Discourse analysis turns this assumption on its head and investigates the ways that language constructs how we experience the way things are. The new field of discourse analysis asserts that the ways in which people use language are the building blocks of social reality, and hence should be analysed in their own right.

This sort of analysis was inaugurated by Michel Foucault's cultural analyses of phenomena such as mental illness, sexuality and crime. Foucault convincingly wrote of the way the social world we inhabit provides boundaries or *contours* to our way of speaking. This in turn, to a large extent, shapes our way of thinking (as once language develops in early childhood, thinking proceeds in largely verbal terms). A discourse uses a limited set of terms in a particular style. Certain grammatical constructions are preferred; these are often organised around specific figures of speech. Phenomena are explained or accounted for in ways that achieve certain (implicit) aims in the users of the discourse.

When we look at spoken or written language in this way, we can ask: what is going on here? Why is this bit of reality being emphasised, and not that bit? How is this discourse persuading me to think? We easily recognise such strategies in the speeches of politicians, but Christian discourse is no exception. Charismatic, liberal, evangelical, fundamentalist, Roman Catholic, and other sorts of Christianity all create their own discourses: ways of using language to depict reality in a certain way. They all have their own particular flavours and emphases. They are each doing something unique.

Religious discourse, like any discourse, makes thinking some thoughts easy and 'self-evident'. At the same time, it makes thinking other thoughts more difficult, either because there are not the words or concepts to describe them, or because those thoughts have been denigrated. When different Christian groups interact with each other, the different styles of discourse serve to reinforce social identities. Discourses create and maintain distinctive social identities; they underscore the valued aspects of group identity.

Christian discourses, like all discourses, reinforce the aims of the social group through presenting a certain version of reality as self-evident. For example, Roman Catholic discourse has a way of presenting the church, the social world, and also the natural world, as unquestionably hierarchically arranged. It is difficult to see other possible social arrangements when hierarchies are presented as natural, God-given and 'self-evident'. Liberal Anglo-Catholic discourse manages to occlude certain internal contradictions. For instance, in some sections of Anglo-Catholicism, while homosexuality is considered acceptable, the ordination of women to the priesthood is not (the latter according to scripture and tradition). This hermeneutic contradiction is evened out through the use of an implicit 'male as norm' metaphor that underlies some of its more polemic discourse. As long as 'male' is considered as the spiritual norm (and the only sex that can represent Christ), these two positions can jostle side by side.

Following are analyses of excerpts from two other Christian discourses, evangelical and charismatic. A weakness of discourse analysis is its subjectivity; the preferences, perceptions and assumptions of the analyst will inevitably colour the analysis. My position thus needs to be stated. I (SS) write as a friendly but critical insider to both

---

Box 11.5 An example of evangelical discourse

An excerpt from a taped public address to a recent gathering of clergy in the UK:

I was just speaking to someone today who has just finished in one of your evangelical theological colleges and awaiting his great ordination for what purpose I'm not sure. At this theological college he assured me that he had had more classroom lessons in liturgical dance than in preaching. That's not to say he had many in liturgical dance, I may say. That is one of the evangelical colleges of your land. That is what you are training! Ballerinas! (*loud laughter*)

Nobody is saved by men who dress up in dresses and flounce around the floor of old buildings. (*laughter*) Nothing about that in the Word of God. You don't think the Apostle Paul was jumping around like that do you? The only one who does it in the Bible is David, and he does it naked. (*laughter*) It's not that these people are saying that we are not to preach, or that Jesus didn't die for our sins, they just teach us other things to do. Other things which of course totally sidetrack us, totally replace the true and living word of God that will transform a man's heart and life and save him out of hell and bring him into eternity with God forever. What an idolatry is liturgical dance! It is an appalling idolatry, lost in this land, which is just full of idols.

God's plan is brought about through the preaching of the word of God, exemplified in the life of the preacher, of course.

---

evangelical and charismatic discourses; I am appreciative of the riches of both traditions, as well as being critical of the 'blindspots'. The examples of discourse analysis cited here provide some illustration concerning how discourses establish and maintain social identity, distinguish the discourse users from others, and accomplish certain aims.

Evangelical discourse

What are the main features of evangelical discourse? Bebbington's (1989) historical survey of evangelicalism in Britain points out four main elements common to evangelicalism: 'conversionism' (the desire for radical and decisive personal transformations), 'biblicism' (the Bible as central and authoritative), 'activism' (an emphasis on action in the world), and 'crucicentrism' (a strong focus on the event and meaning of Christ's crucifixion). The excerpt in the box above displays all four of these characteristics: the preacher here refers to the transformation of a man's heart and life; repeatedly to the Bible; to the importance of preaching; and to the fact that Jesus died for our sins. Those familiar with evangelical discourse, upon hearing these elements of evangelicalism reiterated, will automatically know that 'this is sound teaching'. For newcomers to the discourse, the identity of

Box 11.6 Use of stark contrast followed by three-point list in evangelical discourse

At this theological college he assured me that he had had more classroom lessons in liturgical dance than in preaching.

1   That's not to say he had many in liturgical dance, I may say.
2   That is one of the evangelical colleges of your land.
3   That is what you are training! Ballerinas!

(*loud laughter*).

evangelicalism is established, its boundaries firmly drawn, and its values and norms uncompromisingly asserted.

The rhetorical devices, the grammatical construction, and the narrative flow of any piece of discourse ensure that the discourse is 'doing something'. In this example, several structural features are apparent, especially the tendency to create 'black and white' contrasts, and the use of a three-point list as a rhetorical device to build to a crescendo.

To take an example of the use of stark contrasts, the 'error' of liturgical dance, painted with dramatic words suggesting all that is damnable, is contrasted with the self-evident soundness of preaching: 'What an idolatry is liturgical dance! It is an appalling idolatry, lost in this land, which is just full of idols …. God's plan is brought about through the preaching of the Word of God, exemplified in the life of the preacher, of course.'

Atkinson (1984) has analysed politicians' speeches and found that audience applause could be regularly elicited by the judicious use of a contrast structure ('we are right, they are wrong') followed by three examples to back up the contrast. This rhetorical device cues the audience to respond (in the affirmative) because 'truth' has been upheld and demonstrated. One example is where lessons in liturgical dance are contrasted with a paucity of lessons in preaching, followed by a three-point list.

Later, the speaker creates an increasing tension through contrasting the ridiculous image of liturgical dance (associated through word choice with the threat of gender confusion, cross-dressing, nudity, and the irrelevance of old buildings), which is then resolved by the sensible, biblical affirmation of preaching. The structure ensures that the listener follows the same journey of conversion to right opinion: the listener is required to make a decision. The idea of a crisis – a moment of decision – is central to evangelical discourse. This contrast structure is found in many conversion testimonies within evangelicalism ('I once was lost but now I'm found'). Here, the hearers' participation in the laughter means they have already made those first steps towards the 'altar call' of decision. Through their participation, the speaker already has his 'foot-in-the door', and is very likely to make 'converts'.

Box 11.7 Example of charismatic discourse

Excerpts from a prayer letter following a recent mission to South America:

Well, we're back. And what an amazing trip it was. It had its low points but it had its mountain top experiences as well. And it shows what an incredible God we serve ...

When we arrived at Managua Airport after travelling for 18 hours there was no one there to meet us! There was no working phone at the airport, there were no officials around and we did not know the actual address of the Mission ... We had expected to be met by Brian ... but Roger began by telling us that Brian had gone back to the USA permanently! ... We sat there and thought, 'Lord what is going on? We are here for two weeks and we have no driver, no interpreter, no programme.' We felt terrible. But we said, 'Lord you have spoken to us and to others and you have said that this trip is of enormous significance. So we're holding on to that and we are looking to you to do it.' ... We were there with no programme – just God's call ...

The letter then describes how the team met with the youth group on several occasions.

We spoke, we prayed, and God showed up in power. At the end the young people prayed for Ed and God's power flowed through them. ... All this from nothing. We never preached, just prayed ... 'This is not us, it is God.' Let it continue Lord!

Followed by descriptions of other events and meetings.

On Wednesday we prayed with each of the congregation of 130 and we believe that the church will not be the same again. ... What a trip! How great is our God! ... Thank you for praying. This would not be possible without you. You are part of the battle force that is building God's kingdom in Nicaragua and throughout the world.

Evangelical discourse is not alone is trying to persuade its listeners. This is the goal of any persuasive communication. The present analysis does not aim to suggest that the content of evangelical discourse is invalid, nor that the discourse is untrustworthy. What is clear is that evangelical discourse, like other discourses, achieves the aims of establishing identity, persuading hearers to make a decision, presenting reality in a certain way, and legitimating itself.

Charismatic discourse

There are four main characteristics of charismatic discourse: emphasis on the subjective and experiential; concreteness and anthropomorphism; emotionality and

Table 11.1 Summary of case-studies

Evangelical discourse	Charismatic discourse
conversionism	subjective validation
biblicism	concreteness/anthropomorphism
activism	emotion and warmth
crucicentrism	miracles
stark contrasts	supernatural dualism
(we're right, they're wrong)	
evoking a decision	change through emotional osmosis

warmth; and a focus on the miraculous and supernatural. In contrast to evangelical discourse, which invites listeners to make a decision based on 'rational' criteria, charismatic discourse invites listeners into an experience, an experience of God that is subjectively validated. Statements about the outcome of the mission are experiential rather than empirical, and sound rather vague: for example, 'God showed up in power.' Objective criteria, or any solid proof, are not required.

Charismatic discourse is also characterised by a concreteness and immediacy of expression (not unlike Mark's gospel). For example: 'We spoke, we prayed, and God showed up in power ... God's power flowed through them'; also, God is presented in anthropomorphic terms: 'Lord you have spoken to us and to others and you have said ... '

Emotionality is another feature of charismatic discourse. Things are often described in terms of emotional highs and lows. For example: 'It had its low points but it had its mountain top experiences as well ... we felt terrible ... but You have said this trip is of enormous significance .... What a trip! How great is our God!' The vibrancy and sincerity of the emotional tone should be enough to convince. The warmth of the tone envelops the reader – you are part of it. 'Thank you for praying. This would not be possible without you. You are part of the battle force ....' Conversion happens not so much through concrete choice, but through friendliness and emotional osmosis.

Although not as apparently adversarial as evangelical discourse, charismatic discourse legitimates itself and presents itself as unassailable through its identification with God's activity. Evidences of the miraculous run throughout. What is important is that God is the one seen to be active, not humans. The metaphor of the Genesis creation story is invoked: 'All this from nothing. We never preached, just prayed ... This is not us, it is God.' The idea of a biblical sense of calling is also invoked: 'We were there with no programme – just God's call.'

Nigel Wright (in Smail *et al.* 1995: 75) observed that there are few categories or terms within charismatic discourse to describe natural human processes. As in this excerpt, the world is presented largely in terms of spiritual forces. Complex realities (such as the political and economic situation in Nicaragua) are presented in terms of spiritual dualism: God versus the powers of darkness. 'You are part of the battle force that is building God's kingdom in Nicaragua and throughout the world.' With so few basic categories of thought, it is easy to overlook natural or social causes of events. For example, human realities such as poor planning are occluded as they don't fall neatly into the two extremes of 'God' versus 'not God': 'we did not know the actual address of the Mission … We had expected to be met by Brian … but Roger began by telling us that Brian had gone back to the USA permanently! … We are here for two weeks and we have no driver, no interpreter, no programme.' Instead, the summary of the trip was: 'This is not us, it is God.'

In summary, as these case studies have illustrated, each major Christian grouping has its own discourse in both spoken and written language; each discourse defines and strengthens group identities and social structures as well as conveying information. It is important to recognise the constraining features of our religious discourse, otherwise difficulties arising from differences in religious discourse may be misdiagnosed as having spiritual or theological roots.

SUMMARY OF KEY THEMES

- Discourse as a 'badge' of belonging.
- Screening out other ways of thinking (because there aren't the terms to describe them, or they are denigrated).
- Evaluating the content of one's own discourse (usually positively) and thereby legitimating oneself.
- Evaluating the content of other groups' discourses (usually negatively).
- Presenting one's own version of social reality as 'self-evident'.
- How discourses can unite and divide, enable and constrain.

QUESTIONS TO CONSIDER

- How would you describe the discourse of your church or group?
- What is this discourse trying to achieve? Often the explicit aims are lofty, such as the 'salvation of souls'. What are the implicit aims?
- How does your discourse evaluate itself and others? How does it construct 'we are good and they are bad'?
- How might your discourse be perceived by those outside? Does it exclude them? Can they understand it, or does it sound bizarre?
- Hypothetically, if the speakers of the two excerpts of evangelical and charismatic discourse (above) were in dialogue, what points might they disagree upon? What points might they agree upon?
- Just because discourses have implicit aims (and therefore are not 'neutral') does not mean they are wrong or untrustworthy. It does mean that they exert influence, and we need to be aware of their potentially oppressive nature. What are the ways in which religious discourses can 'oppress'?
- Could we ever be free of the implicit aims of discourse? Is it possible for the way we speak and write to be completely neutral?

Conclusion

Although the group dimension is our emphasis in this chapter, we are not reducing church to a mere nexus of social psychological processes. The spiritual intertwines with the human. Nevertheless, it is to be expected that social processes occur at every level of church life. The present chapter is not exhaustive, and only touches on some of the common social processes that occur in church. Other social processes are discussed in Chapters 2, 4, 8 and 12.

In this chapter we have seen how conformity, ingroup preference, and discourse both enable and constrain church life. In valuing human freedom, it is important for the church to speak openly about the constraining effects of conformity. The minimal group situation shows how easy it is to favour the ingroup, and to bask in its reflected glory. Of course, churches can provide all sorts of religious rationales for such attitudes. It was no different with the first disciples who were incensed at the Samaritans' cold response to their presence (Luke 9. 51–55). The disciples wanted to call down fire on this outgroup. Jesus rebuked them, yet later entrusted them with the task of bringing the gospel to the Samaritans, and to the ends of the earth. Jesus' use of parables, with their multiple layers of meaning, was a masterful bid against the constraining effects of discourse. Jesus used language in order to make people think for themselves, rather than to legitimate his own position. In following Christ, churches need to become self-aware and responsible in their use of language, and to encourage creative modes of thinking that challenge the inevitable effects of our socially shared ways of speaking.

Further reading

Conformity

Brown, R. (1988) *Group Processes*, Oxford: Blackwell.
Hewstone, M., Stroebe, W. and Stephenson, G. (1996) *Introduction to Social Psychology*, 2nd ed., Oxford: Blackwell, especially chapters 15, 16, and 17.
Reed, B. (1978) *The Dynamics of Religion*, London: Darton, Longman & Todd.

Social identity

Abrams, D. and Hogg, M. (eds) (1999) *Social Identity Theory: Constructive and Critical Advances*, Oxford: Blackwell.
Brown, R. (1988) *Group Processes*, Oxford: Blackwell.
Hewstone, M., Stroebe, W. and Stephenson, G. (1996) *Introduction to Social Psychology*, 2nd ed., Oxford: Blackwell, especially chapters 15, 16, and 17.
Turner, J. (1987) *Rediscovering the Social Group: A Self-Categorisation Theory*, Oxford: Blackwell.

Discourse

Potter, J., and Wetherall, M. (1987) *Discourse and Social Psychology*, London: Sage.

12 The church as an organisation

QUESTIONS FOR MINISTRY

- Why are churches often less effective in organisational matters than their business counterparts?
- What makes for good Christian leadership?
- Why does conflict in church often end in disaster? How can church leaders and members learn to resolve conflict?
- How can church members be motivated to become more than just 'bums on pews'?
- What kinds of social undercurrents shape group decisions in churches?

Business and industry have, for many decades, been taking the advice of management consultants. Among the tools of such consultants is organisational psychology, which can be used to promote co-operation, effective leadership, team-building, and successful networks of communication. All of these have been shown to contribute to the maximisation of productivity and profitability. Of course the aims of the church – the Body of Christ – are vastly different from those of a business organisation driven mainly by the desire for ever greater profits. However, especially in view of growing anxieties about dwindling church attendance and ministers' ever increasing administrative workload, it may be time for church leaders to apply to church life some of the insights of organisational psychology, which has been so successfully applied in the worlds of business and commerce.

Leadership

A crucial component of a well-run organisation is an effective leader. In the case of a local church this role is filled by the minister. As yet, there is little specific psychological research on the leadership functions of clergy. There is, however, a substantial body of general leadership theory and research that can be applied to leadership within the church.

Ordained clergy in the church usually go through a lengthy selection process that tests their call, followed by a period of training to equip them to carry out the roles of preacher, priest, counsellor, evangelist, pastor, and so on. Once in post, many find that the role they must exercise most frequently is the role of administrator and manager, a role for which they have received little explicit training. Many churches have shifted from the traditional one-man-show to more diversified team ministries involving both lay and ordained. These provide increased opportunities for collaboration, as well as for conflict. In view of the increasing complexity of Christian ministry, the need for church leaders to draw upon a wide range of leadership skills is evident. (For a further discussion of the multiple roles that clergy need to fill, see Chapter 13.)

Churches are in many ways difficult organisations to lead. Most churches do not have any specific strategic plan, and if there were one, it would be unlikely to command general agreement. Different people within a church often have different objectives, but these are rarely openly acknowledged. One common clash is between those committed to 'maintenance' of church life and those committed to 'mission'. Indeed, this is often a source of conflict between clergy and laity, with clergy more often being committed to mission while most of the laity only want church life to be maintained.

A further problem is that the number of people who have responsibilities within the church is often quite large; indeed, it is desirable that it should be so. However, the vast majority of them are unpaid volunteers, who, to some extent, are bound to discharge their responsibilities on their own terms. Most of these volunteers put in relatively few hours per week to their church work, compared to what would be the case with a team of paid employees. Moreover, much of the work is geographically dispersed and the number of occasions when key members of the congregation meet one another is relatively few. All this can make for serious problems of co-ordination.

These problems are further exacerbated by problems of attitude. Most church people care deeply about what they are doing; otherwise they would not be doing it. This means that they often have strong views about what ought to be done, and how things should be done. They derive emotional satisfaction from things being done in the way they prescribe. Not surprisingly, church issues more readily become matters of high principle than in most organisations. That means that people can be unwilling to modify how they approach things, leading to a degree of inflexibility and conflict.

The search for the 'great leader'

In view of this inherent organisational untidiness, we should not be too surprised that in churches there is a tendency to crave the great man or woman, the 'charismatic' leader who will lead them to the promised land. ('Charismatic' is used here in the technical sense of leadership theory rather than churchmanship!) There also seem to be many clergy who desperately want to be that kind of leader, to be the person whose great gifts and personality inspire others. Certainly there can be real benefits in a charismatic leader who can demonstrate a high level of competence, communicate high expectations of others, inspire confidence that those objectives can be met, and generate agreement to those objectives. Early research into leadership, commissioned by the military and by business and industry in the 1950s, focused on the personality characteristics of this kind of leader. Although there is enormous variety among great leaders, a cross-section of successful chief executives rated the following ten personal attributes (chosen from a list of twenty-five) as the most valuable (Adair 1988: 201):

1   Ability to take decisions.
2   Leadership.
3   Moral integrity.
4   Enthusiasm.
5   Imagination.
6   Willingness to work hard.
7   Analytical ability.
8   Understanding others.
9   Ability to spot opportunities.
10   Ability to meet unpleasant situations.

However, it also needs to be recognised that there can be pathologies associated with this kind of 'great person' leadership. It is tempting for pre-eminent leaders to abuse their position, and a number of stories of grotesque abuse by religious leaders have surfaced in the media (see also Chapter 4). There is also a danger of charismatic leaders of this kind encouraging overdependence, thus disabling those around them. That can be seen in the chaos that ensues when the great leader is not around, and unfortunately some church leaders welcome such evidence of their indispensability. The differences between successful and maladaptive charismatic leadership are quite subtle, and many clergy and congregations would do well to be more alert to the dangers.

Collaborative leadership and team-building

Research has shown that successful leaders can have all sorts of different personality profiles; you do not have to conform to the 'great leader' model to be a successful leader. Indeed, since the 1960s, the focus of psychological work has shifted away from the psychological make-up of the single 'great leader' to a broader investigation of leadership 'functions', which might be fulfilled by more than one member of a group. Research on the emergence of leaders in small groups has shown that often two or more leaders emerge, each performing different leadership functions. For example, one may be task-oriented while the other is more relationship-oriented. Since it is often the case in churches that work is undertaken by quite a diffuse group of people, this way of looking at leadership may be particularly useful for church life.

   Some researchers describe good leadership in terms of enabling followers to obtain their own goals, and to become leaders themselves. Leading by example and then facilitating growth in subordinates in ways that are sensitive to the level of the subordinates' maturity is the real work of leadership, according to theorists such as Fred Dansereau *et al.* (1975). Rather than hugging leadership to ourselves, effective leadership is about raising up other leaders, as Jesus did in preparing and commissioning his disciples (although, as is discussed later in this chapter, this kind of sharing out of leadership tasks can lead to conflicts).

It is a basic fact about church life that there is too much to do. So the establishment of a ministry team, whose members can share out the many jobs and responsibilities, is a key task. In sharing out responsibilities, it must be remembered that many tasks in church are relatively menial, and may not give workers the satisfaction that they are seeking. Leaders must remember that church workers are involved because they really want to belong to a team and to fulfil some of the church's mission directly. The approach recommended by H. Newton Malony and Richard Hunt (1991, Chapter 9) includes 'responsibility with freedom' and 'evaluation with support'. Thus, as far as possible, each member of the staff team (or each volunteer) should be given a discrete area of responsibility, and should be given as much autonomy as possible in pursuing it. For this to work, there obviously needs to be a good match between the aptitudes of the church worker, their approach to the task, and the requirements of the leadership about how it should be tackled. There needs to be both task-related evaluation and personal support; Malony and Hunt make the helpful suggestion that praise should generally be public and criticism private.

Task-oriented and relationship-oriented styles of leadership

A distinction can be made between the 'task-oriented' leader (for whom accomplishing the task is the most important activity of leadership) and 'relationship-oriented', or person-centred, leader (for whom the people being led are the most important aspect of leadership). Fiedler (1967) discovered that a defining characteristic of relationship-oriented leaders was that they had a positive and supportive attitude towards their 'least preferred co-worker' ('You may irritate me, but you're OK, really, and I value your contribution'), while the task-oriented leader had a more negative response.

Fred Fiedler showed in a wide range of studies (e.g. Fiedler, 1967) that the effectiveness of the leader is contingent upon the fit between leadership style (relationship- or task-oriented) and the needs of the situation. In short, when the task is clearly structured and the leader's position is strong (e.g. through having the relevant backing and authority within their organisation), the leader is expected to get on with the job and to be directive (i.e. to be task-oriented). When the task is very complex and unstructured, and the leader is in a weak position (e.g. with little organisational backing), the best strategy is still to be directive and task-oriented, because where there is debate, you need a more directive style to resolve differences. Only moderately complex task situations will favour non-directive, more people-oriented styles (see Figure 12.1). Moderately ambiguous, unstructured tasks favour a permissive, people-oriented leader who encourages the pooling of ideas by all members of the group. In this type of situation, group involvement and co-operation are vital.

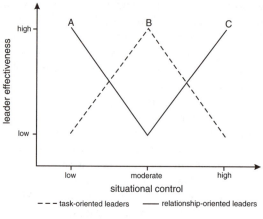

A   Task-oriented leaders (low LPC) are effective
    under low situational control
B   Relationship-oriented leaders (high LPC) are effective
    under conditions of moderate control
C   Task-oriented leaders (low LPC) are effective under
    conditions of high control

Figure 12.1   Fiedler's contingency theory (Baron & Greenberg 1990: 386)

   This research may have some application for the church. First of all, the different situations that leaders of church life find themselves in are likely to range from the highly structured to the highly unstructured. For example, choosing hymns for a service is quite a structured task; deciding by committee would be a waste of time. In contrast, developing a church outreach programme is a more unstructured task; a leader would need the active involvement of participants in both its design and its implementation. However, if too much conflict emerged during this creative process, the leader may have to revert to a more directive style. It seems that church leaders, like all good leaders, need to be flexible: sometimes task-oriented and sometimes more relationship-oriented. Indeed, the evidence suggests that the best leaders are high on both task-orientation and relationship-orientation. Not surprisingly, subjects in a study worked hardest for a leader who was high on concern for the task but also demonstrated personal warmth (Tjosvold and Tjosvold 1995). The principles here are rather similar to those which obtain in bringing up children, where a combination of firmness and nurture provides the most effective approach. This combination may represent the ideal leader; having both task and relationship attributes in abundance may allow for more flexibility in choosing leadership styles according to the needs of the situation.

   Adair (1988) also considers it a mistake to see task needs and people needs as opposed poles. All good leadership, Adair suggests, should involve three interlocking spheres of activity (shown in Figure 12.2).

   An effective church leader needs to be skilled in all three areas. Having the technical knowledge for a task is not enough. An awareness of the group dynamics (how

Figure 12.2 Adair's three spheres of leadership activity (adapted from Adair 1988)

the group develops over time) and of the needs of individuals are equally important. In assessing any course of action, it is important for leaders to consider the consequences for individuals and the team, as well as for the task. Of course, these consequences may vary in the short term and the long term. The leader needs to decide which of these aspects to prioritise at any one time (e.g. is long-term team coherence more important than the achievement of a particular short-term goal?).

Consultation and decision-making

Thus, leaders are frequently called upon to make decisions. Traditionally it has often been assumed that the church minister will take most decisions independently. With more lay participation and shared ministry in the church, however, an autocratic model of leadership is no longer always desired. Church leaders, lay and ordained, need to understand the nature and limits of their authority. A leader who is appointed by a superior body can justly claim to have the final word, whereas a leader who is elected may be expected to put decisions to the vote, and a leader who emerges from within a group, without any formal authority, may be expected to go along with the group if its members disagree with the leader's decision (Adair 1988: 85).

Normative theory (Vroom and Yetton 1973) suggests that, as in leadership, no one style of decision-making is always the most fruitful. In fact, the job of the leader is to select which style of decision-making will be the best in a given situation. Important considerations here will include the potential consequences of the decision (to what degree the right decision will affect important procedures) and who is responsible for its implementation (to what degree is the implementation of the decision dependent upon the commitment and co-operation of subordinates?) Vroom and Yetton suggest that leaders have five basic decision-making styles to choose from (see Table 12.1).

Table 12.1 Potential strategies for leaders' decision-making (Vroom and Yetton 1973)

Decision-making style	Description
A1 Autocratic	Leader solves problem entirely unilaterally using available information.
A2 Autocratic	Leader obtains necessary information from subordinates but then makes decision unilaterally.
C1 Consultative	Leader shares problem with subordinates individually, then makes decision unilaterally.
C2 Consultative	Leader shares problem in group meeting but then makes decision unilaterally.
G2 Group decision	Leader shares problem with subordinates in a group meeting, decision is reached through discussion and consensus.

Most of us in leadership tend to develop a decision style we feel comfortable with, and to use this inflexibly. According to this research, however, good leaders take account of the situation, and select the decision strategy that best accords with it. For example, a minister may determine that on one occasion, following a heated argument within the elders or church PCC, the development of the church's mission statement needs to be a group decision (G2), as it is vital that the church representatives are all committed to the new directives. On another occasion, following a heated argument over baptismal policy, the minister may decide that in this instance, his or her appointment by church superiors means an autocratic decision is appropriate, one for which the minister takes full responsibility: 'the buck stops here'. Choosing decision strategies is a skill that develops with practice, evaluation of previous decisions, and feedback from others.

Moral character

A new direction in leadership studies emphasises not so much personal giftedness or leadership style, but the moral character of the leader. Cognitive psychologist Howard Gardner studied leading minds of the twentieth century. His study revealed that great leaders in the realms of business, politics, and religion had all had stories or messages that struck chords with their followers. Gardner says that the messages (or stories) of these great leaders tended to answer the existential questions of life: who am I? Why am I here? Where are we going? Gardner also states that the truly great leader demonstrates a correspondence between their story and their embodiment of it (Gardner 1997). When in positions of indirect leadership (such as with a brilliant scientist) all that really matters is the message (e.g. the theory of relativity). If their personal life does not live up to their position, so what? But, as we observed in the Clinton and Lewinsky affair, moral character does matter for a direct leader.

Box 12.1 A short course in leadership

- The six most important words: 'I admit I made a mistake'
- The five most important words: 'I am proud of
- The four most important words: 'What is your opinion?'
- The three most important words: 'If you please'
- The two most important words: 'Thank you'
- The one most important word: 'We'
- The least most important word: 'I'

Steven Covey, a current leader in management theory, also emphasises the importance of ethically principled management. Leaders should follow clearly defined moral principles, rather than the exigencies of success. Direct leadership involves being a living example to people. The moral consistency between story and personal life does matter. Leaders such as Jesus, John Wesley, Ghandi, Martin Luther King, Pope John XXIII, and Mother Teresa embodied their story. Who they were was as important as what they did and how well they did it. This emphasis on the message and the moral consistency of the leader finds concurrence with St Paul's defence of his apostleship: ' ... my way of life in Christ Jesus, which agrees with what I teach everywhere in every church' (1 Cor. 4. 17).

Paul led not from an exalted position above his followers, but from 'beneath'. Of the many biblical metaphors that are used to describe Christian leadership (shepherd, pastor, father in Christ, apostle, and so on), perhaps the most telling, and most distinctively Christian, is that of servant. The Christian ideal of servanthood subverts traditional ideas of leadership as a form of dominance or oppression. We all have a natural tendency to 'lord it over' those we direct. However, Christ's life provided a model of how we are to lead for the good of others, for the good of the Kingdom, not just to fulfil our own talents or sense of what is right. As John Adair argues, leadership is as much about meeting individual needs, and the needs of the team, as it is about achieving the task. The key is to develop a way of leading 'which does not humiliate those we lead'.

QUESTIONS TO CONSIDER

- Have you had any experience of strong, gifted leadership in the church? What were the benefits to the church?
- Were there any disadvantages, such as too much control, or dependency?
- Thinking in terms of leadership style, what style of Christian leadership have you experienced? Task-oriented? Relationship-oriented? Both? What is it like being a follower led by a task-oriented leader? A relationship-oriented leader?
- If you are a leader, are you more concerned for the task, or for the individuals, or

for the team as a whole? Is it possible to be concerned for all three in every situation, or only for all three over the long run?

- If you are a leader, would you be able to be flexible if the situation called for a different style of leadership than the one you are accustomed to? What might be difficult for you in adopting a different style? Vulnerability? Loss of control? Unpopularity?
- What method of decision-making do you prefer (as a leader, as a follower)? Autocratic? Consultative? Why?
- If you are a leader, what is your message? Does it meet people's needs? Does it correspond to the way you live your life?
- What does it mean to you to aim not to oppress those whom you lead?

Conflict resolution in churches

It has been stressed above that the diverse and intensely demanding nature of church ministry makes teamwork a necessity. Relationships within teams of employed church staff are particularly important and can provide a model for the wider network of relationships between volunteers. Sometimes there will be quite a large staff team, or there may just be the senior minister and junior minister (a notoriously difficult relationship). Whatever the size, the hope is that teams of church workers will experience and exhibit some level of cohesiveness which reflects Christian teaching on unity. However, the obverse of highly cohesive teams is that church colleagues may feel constrained to be 'nice' to one another when a more open exploration of conflicts would be helpful.

Thus, our first obstacle to resolution of conflict is when conflict itself is considered to be taboo in church circles. It is not uncommon for there to be an expectation that church should always be a perfect, conflict-free environment; everyone should be 'nice'. In practice, however, conflict is normal, and there are numerous sources of conflict extant in churches and church teams:

- Disagreements over values and beliefs (and how to resolve them).
- Clashes of expectations over the pastor's role and responsibilities (for instance, some want the worship and tradition of the church to be maintained, others want more evangelism and visible signs of growth, others want more visiting of the sick and pastoral care).
- Groups within the church have different aims and values (for instance, a preference for different styles of worship).
- The pastor's model of the church may not be shared by all members of the church.
- The church structure may be unclear or may no longer fit the congregation's needs.
- Clergy forgetting the over-committed and busy lives of their congregations when asking for volunteers or scheduling events.
- A new pastor rushing into change, alienating members of the church.
- Blocked communication lines between laity and clergy (people who feel disempowered to speak on an issue often channel this into gossip, resulting in further communication problems).

There have been some interesting case studies of the ethos of particular congregations, and the turbulence than can be caused when clergy arrive with objectives that do not sit easily with the background and orientation of the congregation (see Hopewell 1987, for a model research study of this). Sadly, it is often the case that conflict is handled badly.

Speed Leas (1985: 48) points out that it is common for voluntary organisations to have strong norms that oppose the existence of conflict. Conflict in the church can provoke dread, fear or anger. Perhaps, as unpaid volunteers, people in church have a lower threshold of tolerance for the discomfort of conflict. Churches can add a theological gloss to this: those who disrupt the harmony of the church are morally culpable. To this we bring our own personal experience of conflict, perhaps from our family backgrounds where conflict was either suppressed or handled abusively. Either way, we can grow up ill-equipped to handle conflict. We can easily marshal a religious reason for why we must vehemently defend our own position: the Kingdom of God is at stake! Thus we can use religious beliefs to mask our less worthy motivations (the need to control others, or the need to avoid conflict at all costs).

Rather than being a conflict-free zone, church life seems to exacerbate people's hidden nastiness more than other social organisations. Why is this? First of all, church is a deeply personal matter, intertwined with intense feelings and beliefs about life, God, and holiness. Even small alterations, such as the repositioning of a pew or altar rail, can provoke upset and rage as a whole worldview is felt to be threatened (and indeed may be). Add to this our lower threshold of annoyance regarding conflict in this voluntary organisation, and our higher expectations of its perfection, and it is no wonder church life can act as a poultice, drawing out problems that need transformation.

Factors such as personality, life experience, theological outlook, sex, culture, model of leadership in the church, communication skills, and conflict-resolution style all combine to influence how conflict is handled in churches. Researchers on conflict have noted several styles of conflict resolution. (The following is based on Kilmann and Thomas' (1977) Thomas-Kilmann (T-K) Conflict Mode Instrument.) These styles are fairly regular ways that individuals have of dealing with conflict, depending on past experience, temperament, and how they perceive the current situation. The descriptions of the actions and views of conflict set out in Box 12.2 are based on research in secular contexts; comments have been added here that pertain to possible additional attitudes found in a church context.

These five different conflict-resolution styles can be plotted according to whether they are high on concern for the issue and/or high on concern for the relationship (see Figure 12.3).

Collaboration (high on both the importance of the issue and the relationship) can seem to be the best style for most situations; it certainly reflects dominant norms in our culture. More recent thinking on conflict resolution, however, suggests that each of the styles can be an appropriate way of resolving conflict depending on the situation. For example, towards the end of a PCC meeting, a rather trivial point is brought up and endlessly argued about: should the church barbecue use paper plates or crockery? The minister, in view of the late hour and the need for a decision now,

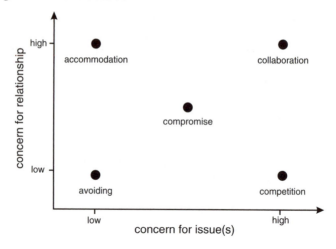

Figure 12.3 Relative concern for issue and relationship in different conflict-resolution styles

takes a unilateral (competing) approach to the conflict, while everyone breathes a sigh of relief. What matters is the appropriateness of the style to the social situation and the issue at hand, as well as a commitment to being constructive. In the above example, it was evident to those present that the minister competed out of a commitment to being constructive. It is possible to use each one of the five conflict resolution styles judiciously with a commitment to being constructive. It may well be right to avoid some conflicts; or accommodate on others, because other battles may be more important.

The emotions in a conflict can easily spiral out of control. It is helpful to be aware that our interpersonal skills and cognitive abilities may undergo some change under

---

Box 12.2 Five views of conflict

1   Competition (win/lose)
Actions
- Control the outcome.
- Discourage disagreement.
- Insist on own view.

View of conflict
- Conflict is an inevitable issue of right and wrong.
- The central issue is who is right.
- Pressure and coercion are necessary.
- The other person is perceived as a problem.
- A high concern to achieve personal goal and a low concern for relationship.

In church context

Some theological stances may encourage this conflict-resolution style when dealing with opponents: 'My viewpoint is God's viewpoint, and must be defended at all costs.'

2 Accommodation

Actions

- Accept the other's view.
- Give in.
- Support.
- Acknowledge error.
- Decide 'it's no big deal'.

View of conflict

- Conflict is usually disastrous.
- Put relationships first, so sacrifice your own interests.
- Fearful that conflict may damage the relationship.
- Keep peace at any price.
- A high concern for relationships and a willingness to give up personal goals.

In church context

In some situations, self-sacrifice is a virtue. At other times, although accommodation can appear as a 'nice' Christian attribute, it can result from co-dependency, a tendency to attribute all goodness to others, and all badness to oneself, so one must please others in order to be accepted. Others are deemed always right.

3 Avoidance

Actions

- Delay or avoid response.
- Withdraw.
- Be inaccessible.
- Divert attention.

View of conflict

- Conflict is hopeless, avoid it.
- Overlook differences, accept disagreement or get out.
- We cannot accomplish personal goals or preserve the relationship in a conflict.

In church context

Avoidance can appear as peace-loving and virtuous, when it may in fact stem from cowardice. At other times, certain church battles are not worth fighting; they simply drain energy and time, and here avoidance may be the wisest option.

continued on next page

4   Compromise
Actions
- Urge moderation.
- Bargain.
- Find a little something for everyone, meet them halfway.

View of conflict:
- Conflict is a mutual difference best resolved by co-operation and compromise; it assumes we cannot get everything we want in a conflict.
- If each goes halfway, progress can be made in a democratic way.
- Push for some of your goals, but not so hard that you sacrifice the relationship.

In church context
Compromise can work well in church situations that allow 'democratic' forms of government where these assumptions are already in place. But in other situations, it may seem to engender a *moral* compromise.

5   Collaboration (win/win)
Actions
- Assert own views while also inviting other's views.
- Welcome differences.
- Identify main concerns and generate options.
- Search for a solution that meets as many concerns as possible.

View of conflict
- Conflict is natural, neutral, normal.
- Differences can be affirmed, individuals' uniqueness prized.
- Recognise tensions in relationship and contrasts in viewpoints.
- Assumes both parties can achieve their goals in the situation and works towards that end.
- Combines high concern for accomplishment of goals with high concern to enhance relationship.

In church context
Church norms that equate conflict with sin may militate against the ability to collaborate. Collaboration means experiencing the pain of conflict, before peace can become a reality.

(Adapted from Kilmann and Thomas 1977 with additions)

Table 12.2 Levels of conflict intensity (adapted from Leas 1985)

Level 1 *A problem shows up*	At this point, there is a desire to resolve the problem without overly personalising it or attaching blame. A win/win solution is possible.
Level 2 *Disagreement*	Real disagreement is apparent between parties, and the problem becomes more personalised. Distrust of others is beginning to emerge, along with face-saving strategies and a desire to come out looking good. There is still a real attempt to solve the problem, with a possibility for consensus.
Level 3 *Contest*	The disagreement moves into a win/lose situation. The focus of the argument is on the representative persons, rather than the issues. Over-generalisations, such as 'you always ...' and 'you never ...', lead into personal attacks. Parties shift from protecting their own interests to winning against the other. (Seek mediation for decision making/conflict resolution at this point.)
Level 4 *Fight or flight*	It is no longer enough to win, it is deemed necessary to get rid of one's opponents. The lines between parties are now clearly drawn, and open communication becomes an impossibility. The focus is on general principles rather than the concrete issue at hand. Disconfirming or contrary evidence to strongly held opinions is rejected. A split in the church, with significant numbers leaving, is likely at this point.
Level 5 *Intractable –* *'Vengeance shall* *be mine!'*	There is no longer any clear understanding of the issues. The opponents are seen as dangerous to society or the church. Word choice implies the destruction or elimination of the other. At this highly destructive stage it may be necessary to remove some members of the church.

the differing conditions of intensifying conflict. Some conflicts can come to the stage where they can only proceed constructively with outside help and mediation. The sad history of church splits and factions reflects the lack of effective, timely mediation. Table 12.2 can help to identify what stage or level of intensity a particular conflict has reached.

Some of us may have experienced the trauma of church conflict escalating out of control. This deeply damaging experience need not occur. If dealt with in the early stages (by Level 3), conflict in church can be an opportunity to achieve great strides forward in the redemption of sin's imprint in our personality and relationships, and can be an occasion for the renewing of church structures. Ideally, church should be a safe place for sin to be exposed and dealt with, and its attendant wounds to be bathed in compassion. If we can allow conflict, in all its ugliness, to be handled responsibly, the church could rediscover itself as a place of authentic change and transformation. To bring in an outside mediator is not a sign of failure; rather it signifies a realistic acceptance that when trust breaks down, and emotional reactions are high, a third party, who is perceived to be neutral by both parties, may be the only way forward to enable two-way communication.

SUMMARY OF KEY THEMES

- Conflict as a normal feature of church life rather than a taboo.
- The five styles of conflict resolution (competition, accommodation, avoidance, compromise, collaboration).
- The balance between concern for the issue and concern for relationships.
- The conditions under which each different style is appropriate.
- How conflict resolution skills may be employed in different ways under 'storm' or 'calm' conditions.
- Deciding when a neutral mediator needs to be called in.

QUESTIONS TO CONSIDER

- What has been your experience of conflict in church?
- Which of the following factors played an important part:

  1 a taboo against conflict in church?
  2 an expectation that church should be conflict-free and perfect?
  3 a leadership style that did not allow confrontation, or any discussion of problems?
  4 my own responses to conflict (flight or fight)?
  5 the chosen conflict resolution style did not match the situation?
  6 the conflict spiralled out of control and no mediator was brought in?
  7 all of the above?

'...WHEN PROBLEMS BEGIN TO OCCUR IN CHURCH LIFE, IT IS OFTEN A GOOD IDEA TO EXAMINE HOW COMMUNICATION IS WORKING....'

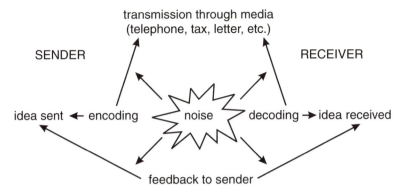

Figure 12.4 A basic model of the communication process (Baron & Greenberg 1990: 335)

Communication

Conflicts within a church are often exacerbated, if not actually caused, by a problem of communication. We all know the power of the 'grapevine': informal, clandestine communiqués that can undermine, or even overturn, formal communications from the pulpit, newsletter, or church meeting. Equally, a 'formal' mode of communication may sometimes be inappropriate or alienating if mistimed or misjudged. So, when problems begin to occur in church life, it is often a good idea to examine how communication is working, and how better communication could help to solve the problem.

The most common problems are simply blocks in communication. People can be somewhat afraid of leaders, or of 'making waves', and thus refrain from speaking openly about issues that matter. As Christians, we can believe it is safer to be 'nice'. Conversely, a leader or group may actively prevent discussion on some topics. Speaking openly becomes an impossibility. In either of these situations, people who feel disempowered to speak on a certain matter will siphon off their opinion and discontent indirectly. Gossip begets gossip, and the grapevine buzzes. Inevitably this filters back, resulting in a further breakdown of trust and communication.

It may be possible to re-establish open communication by gently facing the difficulties in conversation together with the person(s) concerned, encouraging open dialogue. For both leaders and followers, training in the art of communication (including the power of non-verbal cues such as body language) may be of help. Recognising that what a person intends to say is not always what is 'heard' by the other person is a first step. Sometimes it is necessary to seek feedback on what the other person thinks has been said, before proceeding with the next statement. Communication is not a simple process. A basic model consists of the steps illustrated in Figure 12.4.

Accepting that there may be different interpretations of a 'sent idea' can begin to defuse the tensions. If training in communication and fresh attempts at restoring communication do not succeed, the situation may be helped by bringing a neutral

centralised networks   decentralised networks

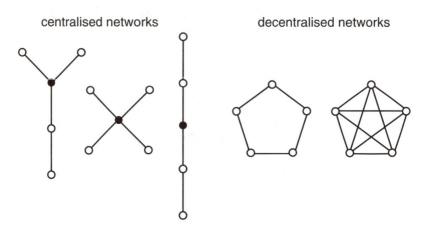

Figure 12.5 Centralised and decentralised communication networks (Baron & Greenberg 1990: 347-348)

third person (preferably with some mediation experience) in to help both parties communicate their concerns. Church consultants and mediators are a growing resource for these common problems (see the suggested contacts at end of the chapter). It is a well-known phenomenon that teams of clergy or church workers often fail to 'get on'. Many vicar–curate relationships are unsatisfactory, yet rarely is action taken to help restore communication. When communication breaks down, wise leaders seek a neutral mediator to enable open dialogue in a safe, controlled environment.

It may also help to examine the formal networks of communication that exist in the church, and to decide whether they are working effectively or not. If, for example, communication to and from the minister always has to pass through a secretary, a bottleneck may occur, restricting the free flow of information, as in centralised networks (see Figure 12.5).

Harold Leavitt (1951) noted the effects of different kinds of communication networks in laboratory experiments (see diagram above). Subjects were seated around a circular table, separated by vertical partitions. Subjects could pass messages through slots to form different kinds of communication networks. The results showed that for simple tasks, the wheel, with a person at the hub, was more efficient. For complex tasks the circle was more efficient at first, later the wheel became more efficient. However, group motivation was always better in decentralised networks, except for the person who before had sat in the centre and had previously enjoyed the power! For example, a minister may wish to be the hub of the wheel, handling the entire flow of information. This may work well for simple, everyday administrative tasks, but may not when the minister wants the group to be motivated to participate. The 'rules' of who communicates with whom need to be made explicit so that the decision strategy a leader adopts corresponds to the formal communication network in place. To attempt a consultative decision style in church for a certain project without a decentralised network of communication is to invite frustration.

SUMMARY OF KEY THEMES

- The importance of effective communication.
- The complexity of the communication process.
- Dealing with gossip and the grapevine.
- Judging when to use formal and when informal modes of communication.
- Centralised and de-centralised networks of communication.

QUESTIONS TO CONSIDER

- Is communication working in your church? Or are there 'grapevines' of gossip compensating?
- How would you rate the communication in a church meeting you have recently attended? Open? Somewhat closed? Closed and hostile?
- How do you react when someone misunderstands what you have communicated? Do you think they *should* have understood you?
- Draw some diagrams of the communication networks in your church (for example, your housegroup, the PCC or elders meetings, the leadership and congregation).
- Are there any situations in your church where communication may benefit from a neutral mediator?

Motivation and group dynamics

Studies in motivation were initially concerned with the productivity of organisations. Psychologists studied the productivity of individuals compared with the productivity of groups. A general trend was observed: individuals work less hard when they are in a group; they tend to 'loaf'. This is a well-known phenomenon in church life: a few people do the most of the work, while the others tend to be 'bums on pews'.

A study by Latané *et al.* (1979) investigated how much noise people could make in a social setting. The amount of noise made per person dropped dramatically as the size of the group increased, even though the overall noise level grew. A shortcoming of this type of experiment, however, is that the groups weren't 'real' groups; rather they were just random collections of individuals. The lack of a meaningful group with real relationships may contribute to social loafing. Another factor that contributes to social loafing is the expectation that 'someone else will do it'. If a person's contribution is not being identified, and the person thinks that others are responsible, social loafing may easily result. When an individual's contribution and responsibilities within a group are clearly *identified*, some studies show that they are much more likely to pull their weight.

There are also times when group effort is in fact better than the sum of the individuals' efforts. The opposite of social loafing, called group facilitation, occurs when the task is complex, and the social interactions between the members of the group are meaningful. In this desirable situation, people try harder in the group and

Box 12.3 The lifespan of a group

1   Forming
Members get to know each other and establish ground rules. People can be a bit confused about how to act in the group and how beneficial it will be to be a member of the group. Once individuals come to think of themselves as a group the forming stage is complete.

2   Storming
Members come to resist control of the group leader(s) and show hostility. A high degree of conflict within the group can be experienced. If not resolved, the group may be disbanded. As conflicts are resolved and the leadership is accepted, the storming stage is complete.

3   Norming
Members work together, developing close relationships and feelings of camaraderie. This is the stage where the group is the most cohesive, and identification as a member of the group becomes strongest. Shared responsibilities for the group's activities are heightened. The norming stage is complete when the members of the group come to accept a common set of expectations that constitute an acceptable way of doing things.

4   Performing
Questions about group membership and leadership have been resolved. Energy may now be devoted to getting the job done. The group's good relations and the acceptance of leadership help the task go well.

5   Adjourning
Groups may disband after meeting their goals, or because members leave. Groups do not last forever. There needs to be official recognition and acceptance of the group's ending; time to grieve and give thanks for what was.

(adapted from Tuckman and Jensen 1977)

perform better. Studies show this is especially the case with complex problems. However, when the social interactions are meaningful, even in a simple task, people worked even harder and exerted more effort than when they were on their own. This principle underlies the logic of 'cell' churches, where small groups replicate in themselves all the functions of church life: teaching, pastoral care, prayer, outreach, and so on, in addition to a regular central church service. People of all ages who are members of a cell group within a church have to pull their weight, as the cell group does not afford the luxury of relying on a few people up front to do the work of the church.

The simple lesson for the church is to facilitate meaningful relationships between group members by fostering open and accepting communication, as well as encouraging people to work together on interesting, complex tasks, for which each person has an identified responsibility. The success of Christian initiatives such as the Alpha course may be partly due to the open communication fostered in the groups, the team-building through shared meals, and shared responsibilities that are woven into the task of reaching others with the Christian message. Here we see the spheres of individual needs, team-building needs, and task needs interlocking to produce a high level of motivation.

Group dynamics

Churches thrive on smaller groups carrying out valued activities: children's work, prayer groups, bible study groups, homegroups, men's meetings, women's meetings, youth groups, mission groups, and so on. Being part of a group meets social needs, and can provide some positive social identity, as well as the opportunity for some valued activity not possible on one's own. Groups are not static entities; every group will have its own developmental lifespan. An effective leader will be aware of these dynamics. These are sometimes experienced in a linear fashion, sometimes cyclically, especially as new members come in and the group has to re-invent itself afresh. Motivation varies during these different stages (see Box 12.3).

Groups in church seem to be at most risk in stages 2 and 5, 'storming' and 'adjourning'. The stage of storming was addressed earlier in this chapter, in the section on conflict resolution. Stage 5, adjourning, also seems to be particularly troublesome for church groups. On the whole, Christians are not good at ending groups. This may reflect in some way our culture's dread of death and finality, or it may be that for Christians to terminate a group activity feels like a spiritual failure: surely anything truly Christian should go on forever. New beginnings, new outreach programs, and burgeoning prayer groups make us feel that we are successful, and that our gospel is successful, but eventually most Christian groups, such as a homegroup, will have served their purpose. Typically, many church groups end in an embarrassed silence. Sometimes people who decide to leave a group or church find they are vilified. Yet, just as we honour the end of a person's life with a funeral, people need a chance to experience this last group stage (or last stage of a member's participation), to honour what was good, and learn from what could have been improved. By celebrating the adjourning of a group, and learning from our experience, we make space for a fresh beginning, rather than harbouring a sense of guilt or failure.

SUMMARY OF KEY THEMES

- The phenomenon of 'social loafing'.
- The importance of meaningful relationships and real group identity.
- How motivation is increased by the complexity of the task and the clear identification of responsibilities.
- Stages of group dynamics: forming, storming, norming, performing, adjourning.

QUESTIONS TO CONSIDER

- What motivates you to work hard in a group activity? What de-motivates you?
- What is enjoyable for you about being part of a group in church? What is dissatisfying?
- Have you ever experienced the conflict of the 'storming' stage? How were things handled?
- What is your experience of either leaving or ending Christian groups?

Decision-making in groups

Polarisation

We tend to consider that the activity of thinking is an essentially private, individual activity. However, empirical studies show that people think and make decisions in groups differently from how they would on their own. Awareness of this was first raised in an experiment carried out by James Stoner (1961). Stoner presented students with 'business decisions' to which they could choose either a risky or a safe alternative. First, the students made their choices individually; afterwards they were asked to come to a common decision in groups. In comparison to the individual decisions, the groups nearly always decided on a significantly more adventurous degree of risk, a phenomenon called 'risky shift'. A number of experiments followed Stoner's, and it was found that the shift wasn't always in the direction of more risk. If the initial, individual choices were towards risk, then the group choice would be even riskier; but conversely, individual cautious choices tended to result in even more cautious group choices, a phenomenon called 'polarisation' (Fraser 1971). The more extreme the individual choices originally were, the more extreme the shift towards either extreme in the group condition. The experiments also showed that the impact of the group's deliberations produced lasting impacts on subsequent individual choices.

There are a number of different explanations for polarisation that are not necessarily mutually exclusive; indeed a multi-causal explanation may be better than any one explanation on its own. One explanation is that group decisions do not tend to be made through an averaging process, but that some individuals within the group (usually with more extreme opinions) are more vocal, and hence more influential.

Box 12.4 Some suggestions to aid decision-making in churches

1 Follow a systematic procedure that starts by identifying objectives and values.
2 A wide range of alternatives should be canvassed, including from sources outside the group.
3 Systematically assess consequences of all viewpoints.
4 The leader should consider remaining impartial during debate, and give an opinion only at the end.
5 Members could take turns playing 'devil's advocate'.
6 The group should consider seeking advice from experts.
7 Avoid isolation of the group.

We have all sat in on group discussions where a dominant minority seem to get more of a hearing.

A second explanation is based on social comparison theory (Brown 1988). When the group shares opinions among its members (even in experiments where discussion of those opinions is prohibited), individuals who made initially cautious choices saw that others were more radical and so now felt able to be more adventurous themselves. People do not like to appear too far away from 'the crowd', so when the group is seen as more extreme than originally thought, it may be that people are then happy to move even further than the group towards their desired pole.

A third, more common-sense explanation, has to do with the gathering of new information. Before group discussion begins, a person may know, for example, two arguments for a particular position. At the end of the discussion, they may now be aware of, say, five; hence they feel justified in a shift to a more extreme opinion.

Finally, a self-categorisation process may be occurring as well. A preferred pole of group opinion may serve as a marker differentiating the ingroup from rival outgroups. The desire to differentiate oneself from an outgroup can result in polarisation of opinion (we are *really* different from them because we think *really* different thoughts). This holds true unless the outgroup has opinions that are even more extreme on the preferred pole. In this case moderation will be preferred as a way of distinguishing between 'us' and 'them' (see Box 12.4).

Groupthink

Groups not only polarise their decisions, they can also make poor decisions by not considering all relevant information or not assessing all the available options. Irving Janis (1972) coined the term 'groupthink' as a result of his analysis of defective decision-making in US foreign policy (1940–1970, most notably the Bay of Pigs disaster). Groupthink is defined as 'a deterioration of mental efficiency, reality testing, and moral judgement that results from ingroup pressures to seek consensus'

(Sabini 1995: 82). Below is a summary of the characteristics of a group that make it liable to suffer from groupthink.

1   High group cohesiveness.
2   The group is isolated from alternative viewpoints and information.
3   The group is dominated by a directive leader.
4   It lacks methodical procedures for search and appraisal.
5   There is clearly a favoured opinion, with strong pressure to attain a goal.

   The unanimity of the group makes everyone feel good; an illusion of invulnerability develops, along with a belief in the inherent morality and rightness of the group. Dissenters are ridiculed, and people begin to censor themselves. A mindset develops that only considers its one favoured option, usually the option of a directive leader, dismissing contrary thoughts.

THE DANGERS OF 'GROUPTHINK'....

   Enquiries into the disastrous consequences of the Nine O'Clock Service (NOS) uncovered some groupthink tendencies. The leader of the service, the Rev. Chris Brain, had an autocratic style of leadership that was legitimated by the outstanding success of his ministry in reaching large numbers of unchurched young people, as well as a tightly knit community dedicated to NOS's goals. With such lofty aims as the NOS group's rationale, it was difficult for dissenting group members and church authorities to listen to alternative viewpoints and to voice their contrary opinions. Even when stories of the leader's abuse of power started to trickle out, these were initially ignored by those within and without the NOS.

The key failing revealed by Janis's study (and in the tragic case of the NOS) was the failure to seek out alternative viewpoints and information. Roland Howard's (1996) analysis of the problems with the Nine O'Clock Service suggest that suspicions were picked up by those in authority early on, but were ignored in favour of continuing to support the faith-inspiring work of NOS among young people. There was one dominant viewpoint and that was that NOS was extremely successful and was pioneering new forms of outreach and worship among young people. The alternative viewpoint (that there were problems of authoritarian leadership and abuse of members) was difficult to embrace. Everyone wanted NOS to succeed.

QUESTIONS TO CONSIDER

- Many of us have sat in on PCC meetings, or meetings of elders, or some other church decision-making group where the group decision was more extreme than individual's prior held opinions. Thinking back to that situation, what was happening under the surface?

    1 Was there a strong voice, such as the minister, or other person(s) with a dominant personality, who eventually held sway?
    2 Were members of the committee anxious about appearing disagreeable? Would people who disagree with the group's more extreme decision seem less spiritual?
    3 Did the new group opinion result from new information? Was this weighed in a balanced manner?
    4 Was there any mention of an undesirable outgroup from whom the committee was distancing themselves? ('We are not like those who shrink back and have not enough faith ... ')

- Have you ever experienced groupthink?

    1 Was the influence of the leader a major factor?
    2 Was it the cosy experience of unanimity that shaped the decision-making?
    3 Was the group isolated?

- When making a decision, how likely is your church to seek outside sources of information?
- Does it seem 'unspiritual' to play 'devil's advocate', to consider systematically the disadvantages (as well as the advantages) of a proposed church decision?
- How far does the Christian norm of being 'nice' affect group decision-making in church?

Conclusion

Churches are often less effective in their organisational dealings than their business counterparts, but this need not be so. The human, organisational side of church life is only one aspect of the overall life of the church, yet it has the power to break (but not make) a church. There are lessons to be gleaned from the study of secular organisations that can be applied, with discernment, to the church. Good organisational practices in terms of leadership, conflict resolution, motivation, group formation, and decision-making can help provide a safe, but elastic, environment in which the church can grow and develop.

Further reading

Psychology of leadership

Adair, J. (1988) *Effective Leadership*, London: Pan Books.
Covey, S. (1990) *Principle Centred Leadership*, New York: Simon & Schuster.
Covey, S. (1992) *The Seven Habits of Highly Effective People*, New York: Simon & Schuster.

Leadership in the church

Beasley-Murray, P. (1990) *Dynamic Leadership: Making it Work for You and Your Church*, Eastbourne: MARC.
Dunn, J. (1995) *The Effective Leader*, Eastbourne: Kingsway.
Greenwood, R. (1995) *Transforming Priesthood*, London: SPCK.
Nelson, J. (1996) *Management and Ministry: Appreciating Contemporary Issues*, Norwich: The Canterbury Press.

Conflict resolution and communication

Avis, P. (1992) *Authority, Leadership and Conflict in the Church*, Mowbray.
Beer, J. with Stief, E. (1997) *The Mediator's Handbook*, 3rd ed., Gabriola Islands, BC, Canada: New Society Publishers.
Cormack, D. (1989) *Peacing Together: From Conflict to Reconciliation*, Eastbourne: MARC.
Stutzman, J. and Schrock-Shenk, C. (eds) (1999) *Mediation and Facilitation Training Manual: Foundations and Skills for Constructive Conflict Transformation*, 3rd ed., Akron, PA.: Mennonite Conciliation Service (PO Box 500, Akron, PA 17501–0500).

Motivation and group dynamics

Adair, J. (1987) *Effective Teambuilding*, London: Pan Books.
Belbin, R. M. (1993) *Team Roles at Work*, Oxford: Butterworth-Heinemann.
Cormack, D. (1987) *Team Spirit*, Bromley: MARC Europe.
Mallison, J. (1989) *Growing Christians in Small Groups*, London: Scripture Union.

Decision-making in groups

Baron, R. S., Kerr, N. L. and Miller, N. (1992) *Group Process, Group Decision, Group Action*, Milton Keynes: Open University Press.
Brown, R. (1988) *Group Processes*, Oxford: Blackwell.
Janis, I. (1972) *Victims of Groupthink: A Psychological Study of Foreign-Policy Decisions and Fiascoes*, Boston, Mass.: Houghton, Mifflin.

Consultancy for churches, mediation and conflict resolution organisations

Psychology and Christianity Project, (for consultancy for churches on a wide range of issues)
 CARTS, Divinity Faculty, University of Cambridge
Contact Sara Savage or Liz Gulliford
Tel. 01223 763002
Email: sbs21@cam.ac.uk
Web: www.divinity.cam.ac.uk/CARTS/christpsych.html

Bridge Builders, London Mennonite Centre, 14 Shepherds Hill, London, N6 5AQ
Contact Alastair McKay
Tel. 020 8340 8775
Fax: 020 8341 6807
Email: bridgebuilders@menno.org.uk
Web: www.menno.org.uk

The Grubb Institute, Cloudesley Street, London, N1 0HU
Contact Jean Hutton
Tel 020 7278 8061
Fax 020 7278 0728
Email: info@grubb.org.uk
Web: www.grubb.org.uk

13 Clergy

QUESTIONS FOR MINISTRY

- Why do clergy burn out?
- What is it that makes being a minister such a demanding job?
- What are the best strategies for coping with the conflicting demands of ministry?
- Do romantic and family relationships need to take a back seat for Christian ministers?
- How can you tell if you're heading towards burnout?

Throughout this book we have stressed the diversity of the discipline of psychology, and the range of areas of psychology that can be applied to the work of the church. In this chapter, we introduce another area of psychology, occupational psychology, focusing on the psychology of the clergy. We will draw partly on general principles of occupational psychology, applying them to the ordained ministry, and partly on the growing body of psychological research, observation, and reflection on the clergy. We will look at clergy personality, burnout and strategies for coping with stress, the relationship between work and home life, sex and sexuality, and lay attitudes towards clergy.

Clergy personality

What kind of people are the clergy? Are they typical of the general population, or different in some way? These are good questions, but difficult to answer because the clergy themselves are diverse. It is rather like the issue we raised in the first chapter, where we saw that religious people differ so much among themselves that it is hard to generalise about them. There may well be differences between the clergy of different countries – for example, there is a suspicion that UK clergy are more introverted than those in the USA – though there are no systematic comparisons. There may also be denominational differences. There are certainly sex differences. All this makes it important not to overgeneralise from studies of limited clergy samples. Another complication is that a variety of different personality tests have been used, making it difficult to compare findings from one study with others.

One contrast that has been investigated quite carefully is the difference between male and female clergy in the UK, and an interesting story has emerged. The personalities of both male and female clergy are both rather atypical of their sexes. Moreover, both can be rather androgynous. Male clergy are sometimes found to be more feminine than most males. This has been reported in a number of studies of American clergy, though the finding has not emerged consistently, and it is not yet clear exactly how far this trend holds up. In contrast, female clergy are sometimes found to be more masculine than most females. One study that illustrates this gender reversal is that of Leslie Francis and David Musson (1999), who studied a sample of Anglican clergy in the UK, using Cattell's questionnaire measuring sixteen personality factors. The fact that both male and female clergy tended to be somewhat atypical of their sexes meant that the usual contrasts between males and females do not hold among the clergy. Francis and Musson found female clergy 'less outgoing, more assertive, less apprehensive, more socially controlled and less tense' than male clergy.

Clergy stress

There is little doubt that many clergy find their work stressful, and there is growing concern about this in the leadership of the church. Two sets of factors contribute to clergy stress. First, there are factors to do with individual clergy, their personalities, their capacity to cope with stress, their religious outlook and orientation, and their personal circumstances, such as their marriage, sexual orientation, and so on. Second, there are factors associated with specific tasks that ordained ministers undertake, both general ones such as leadership of a local church and pastoral care of the congregation, and more specific things such as working in town or country, working alone or in a team, and so on. There is a growing feeling that the stress suffered by clergy may be unnecessarily exacerbated by the structure of their working life.

It is helpful to make the conceptual distinctions between *stress* and *strain*, in which stress is essentially the cause, and strain the effect. Stressful circumstances produce signs of strain in the clergy. Occupational strain shows itself in a variety of ways, such as worry, fatigue, reduced effectiveness, emotional problems, and physical illness. There seem to be particular problems of 'burnout' that affect the caring professions. Christina Maslach and Susan Jackson (1981) have proposed three main facets of burnout: emotional exhaustion, depersonalisation, and lack of personal accomplishment. These findings led to the development of the 'Maslach burnout inventory', which Leslie Francis and his colleagues have adapted for use with Anglican clergy in Britain. The inventory provides a helpful approach to conceptualising and measuring clergy burnout.

Next, there is a distinction between social *positions* and *roles*. Being in an occupational position such as a vicar, sets in motion a complex set of social–psychological processes which are the role the vicar plays. Central to these are expectations of clergy. Problems over role expectations are a major source of occupational stress, and can arise in various ways: when the expectations are *ambiguous*, when there is *conflict* over them, or when they are simply *excessive*. Clergy seem vulnerable to each of these aspects of role stress. Though some aspects of the clergy role, such as taking Sunday services, are very clear, there is much else that is ill-defined. For example, clergy might feel that it was their duty to 'advance the kingdom of God', but it is far from clear how to translate that into a programme of action for work on a Monday morning. Many of the goals laid on clergy are what experts in goal analysis call 'fuzzes' – inherently difficult to make specific and never fully achievable. Role ambiguity also arises through confusion over priorities. The range of things the clergy ought to be doing generally adds up to far more than it is possible to do in the working week, leaving ambiguity about what ought to be prioritised.

Roles that are ambiguous also often give rise to conflict over the role; different people may prioritise different aspects of the role. Equally, there may be a conflict between what the clergy themselves want to do and what is expected of them. Some of these matters were investigated by Leslie Francis and Raymond Rodger (1996) and their study provides an example of the use of questionnaire methods to investigate such matters. First, the clergy role was divided up into seven areas (administrator, celebrant of sacraments, community leader, leader of public worship, pastor and counsellor, preacher and teacher). The clergy were then asked to rate the relative priority attached to these. Being an administrator and community leader were accorded lower priority than the other aspects of the role. Next, clergy were asked about how their priorities had shifted from ordination to the present, and it was noticeable that these two roles (administrator and community leader) were the ones that had increased in priority. (For more on leadership within church life, see Chapter 12.)

Clergy were also asked about what influenced them most in determining their role priorities and these influences were found to be, in decreasing order of priority: the congregation, the church council, the community at large, their family, and the church hierarchy. Finally, the clergy were asked how realistic these various groups were in their expectations, and it was conspicuous that the community at large was regarded as the least realistic. Their own family was regarded as the most realistic, followed by the church hierarchy, the church council, and the congregation. (This study also looked at the relationship between these matters and the personality of the clergy, but most of the correlations were not statistically significant and will not be mentioned here.)

Several broad conclusions are suggested by these somewhat complex findings. First, it seems that most clergy seeking ordination expect to concentrate mainly on their religious duties. However, they find that other things such as administration and community leadership are more pressing than they had expected. Because these were not things to which they attached much priority themselves, they were likely to become a particular focus of role conflict. Second, it is striking that the influences on role priorties that were judged to be most realistic (the family and the church hierarchy) were also regarded as carrying least weight. In contrast, the community at large proved a more significant influence, but was the most unrealistic in its expectations. This also seems likely to be a source of role conflict. Fortunately, the congregation and church council were both regarded as important influences, and fairly realistic in their expectations.

The most thorough empirical study of clergy stress to have been conducted so far is that of Ben Fletcher (1990) on a sample of over two hundred parochial clergy in the Church of England. One of the interesting things to emerge was that the clergy were both satisfied and dissatisfied with their jobs. In fact, occupational psychologists have often found that measures of satisfaction and dissatisfaction are relatively independent of one another. However, the extent to which the two coexist in the clergy remains striking. Though many of the clergy felt negative about some aspects of their jobs, they showed relatively modest levels of depression and anxiety. Feeling that they had the encouragement and help of others improved the satisfaction of clergy with their job, though it did nothing to alleviate their sense of pressure. When asked to tick one of six statements that best represented their degree of satisfaction, 53 per cent of clergy ticked 'I feel it is a worthwhile job and would not dream of doing anything else'; the remaining clergy ticked one or other of the remaining five statements, all of which indicated some degree of dissatisfaction, and the mildest of which was 'I feel it is a worthwhile job, but I wouldn't mind doing something else for a living'.

There was evidence of perceived role ambiguity; for example 38 per cent of clergy found it difficult to distinguish between work and socialising. However, problems of role conflict seemed to be more serious. For example, 60 per cent felt that other people's perceptions of the job were different from their own, and 41 per cent felt that peripheral aspects of the job took over from the primary role. As far as overload was concerned, 77 per cent of clergy found that they were under a lot of pressure, a figure very slightly higher than that found for a comparable sample of teachers. However, the encouraging thing was that only 5 per cent found this pressure a constant source of stress. When individual aspects of work demands were examined, it was notice-able that items focusing on the interpersonal aspects of the job were among those most closely related to anxiety and depression, for example, 'feeling I cannot respond to criticism', 'having to be nice to people', 'having to satisfy the expectations of others', and so on. Lack of tangible results, and a feeling that success or failure was their personal responsibility were also quite highly related to anxiety and depression.

The overall level of work demands proved to be a better predictor of mental health problems (anxiety, depression, and somatic complaints) than either role con-flict or role ambiguity, indicating that feeling overloaded was the main problem the clergy faced. This is consistent with the research of Blackmon (cited by Malony and Hunt 1991: 39) which indicated that the vast majority of ministers were in substan-tial agreement with their laity about the nature of their role; they felt that stress came not from that but from job overload.

In addition to conflicts over what clergy are expected to do, there may be prob-lems over the kind of people clergy *are*. This emerged from a study of ordinands at an English theological college using the Myers-Briggs type indicator (MBTI; see Chapter 3 for detailed discussion), in which the personality profiles of the ordinands were compared with the results of a specially devised questionnaire to discover what personality type lay members of congregations would like to find in their clergy. For example, approximately 90 per cent of the laity showed a preference for extroverted clergy, whereas two-thirds of the ordinands were introverted type.

'... 38% OF CLERGY FIND IT DIFFICULT TO DISTINGUISH BETWEEN WORK AND SOCIALISING'

Though role strain among the clergy is undoubtedly a reality, it is possible to exaggerate it. For example, Carole Rayburn *et al.* (1986), researching a sample of two hundred and fifty American religious leaders in the Roman Catholic church, found that they had significantly *lower* levels of personal strain than the general population. In similar vein, Joseph Fichter (1984) published a paper called, 'The myth of clergy burnout' suggesting that only about 6 per cent of the clergy studied could be regarded as candidates for burnout. While that is not as many as some fear, it is still too high a figure for comfort. Unfortunately, it is hard to know exactly how it compares with figures for other comparable professions.

Coping strategies

The extent to which stressful occupational conditions result in strain depends on how well people cope with their stresses. Though there is no universally agreed taxonomy of coping strategies, various important distinctions have emerged. Questionnaires are now available that assess a broad range of coping strategies (e.g. Carver *et al.* 1989). First, there are *problem-solving* strategies such as planning, devoting increased effort, seeking practical help, and so on. These can be distinguished from more *emotion-focused* strategies, though these are quite varied and need further subdivision.

From the outset, coping theory has emphasised the importance of processes of appraisal and interpretation in coping (e.g. Lazarus 1966). This includes both 'primary appraisal', which is concerned with how the demands or stresses themselves are perceived, and 'secondary appraisal', which concerns the extent to which people feel they have the resources, either in themselves or through others, to cope with the stresses. Not surprisingly, many coping strategies involve a reappraisal of either the stress itself or of coping resources. There is a further important distinction here between positive reappraisals that accept the stress and reconceptualise it as more manageable than was initially thought, even seeing some value in the stress, and other more negative coping attitudes such as denial, avoidance, or resignation.

There are yet other ways of trying to cope with emotional stress, by turning away from the problem altogether, focusing on the emotion itself and trying to find some more effective way of managing it, by relaxation, distracting activities, or whatever. Seeking help and support from others is a coping strategy of central importance, and there is abundant evidence that stresses are much less serious in their effects when people feel supported. However, social support is itself quite varied in its nature, ranging from the problem-focused to the person-focused.

It has become increasingly clear that religion itself can constitute a highly effective coping strategy, and it is included for example in the previously mentioned questionnaire measure of coping strategies developed by Charles Carver and his colleagues (1989). The most important research programme on the role of religion in coping is that of Kenneth Pargament (1997), who has demonstrated the value of religion in coping with a variety of stresses. It seems that religion plays a key role in helping people to find meaning in events. For example, if religious people ask 'how can this be a source of blessing to me?' or 'how is God speaking to me in this?' they are prompted towards a constructive reformulation of the stress they are experiencing. Religion also feeds into the appraisal of coping resources, and the grace of God makes a unique contribution here, in addition to personal resources and the contributions of colleagues. There is a helpful overview of the contribution of religion to coping in Hood *et al.* (1996, Chapter 11).

So far there has been disappointingly little formal research on how clergy cope with their stresses, though one path-breaking study was that of Philip Dewe (1987), studying a sample of two hundred and eighty Protestant clergy in New Zealand. They constructed a questionnaire covering sixty-five different coping strategies and found that respondents tended to cluster into five main groups concerned respectively with social support, postponing action by relaxation and distracting attention, developing a capacity to deal with the problem, rationalising the problem, and support through spiritual commitment. The study provided further information about the extent to which these various strategies were used (though unfortunately it contains no information about their effectiveness.) The extent to which three of these strategies are used was closely associated with the amount of stress the clergy were experiencing (social support, postponing action, and rationalising the problem). The other two strategies (developing capacities, and spiritual commitment) were actually among the most frequently applied by the clergy, though they seem to have been used in a fairly routine way, irrespective of the degree of stress that was being experienced.

Much the best study so far of the value of religious coping strategies in clergy is that of Thomas Rodgerson and Ralph Piedmont (1998) who studied 'burnout' in two hundred and fifty-two American Baptist ministers. They wanted to assess whether a questionnaire measure of religious coping strategies could predict burnout over and above what could be predicted from a more standard personality test. They found some evidence of this, but the additional predictive power of religious coping strategies was not great. They themselves suggest that a different measure of religious coping strategies, more oriented to specific situations, might have had better predictive power. Another problem might have been that the ministers were all too similar in the extent to which they used religious coping strategies, which would make it difficult to demonstrate their value statistically. What religious coping strategies clergy use, how best to measure them, and how helpful they are, are matters that require further research.

A rather different approach to the problem of clergy burnout has been suggested by John Sanford (1982) using a Jungian approach to personality. This was described in Chapter 3 in connection with the Myers-Briggs type indicator, which is based on a Jungian personality typology. The claim is that burnout arises from ego exhaustion, which in turn comes from an over-reliance on a person's dominant personality function, whether that is thinking, feeling, sensing, or intuition. Sanford claims that the only satisfactory response to ego exhaustion is for someone to develop their inferior functions so that the whole of their personality is being effectively employed in their work.

Much work remains to be done on coping strategies in the clergy. It would be a first important step to obtain information about the *perceived* effectiveness of different strategies. It would be even better to look at a sample of clergy before and after a particular stress and to see which coping strategies were most closely related to coping effectively with it. However, a variety of helpful approaches have been developed to enable clergy to identify and remedy the key problems in their ministry (e.g. Miller and Jackson 1995).

SUMMARY OF KEY THEMES

- Three facets of burnout: emotional exhaustion, depersonalisation, lack of personal accomplishment.
- The problem of role ambiguity.
- Prioritising different roles.
- Causes of satisfaction and dissatisfaction among clergy.
- Varieties of coping-strategies: problem-solving or emotion-focused.
- The role of religious coping strategies.

QUESTIONS TO CONSIDER

- What in your life as a minister do you find most stressful?
- Do you feel you might be heading towards burnout?
- Are you aware of occasions when there have been conflicts between the demands of different roles?
- How do you cope with these causes of emotional strain?
- What role do religious strategies play in dealing with these problems?

Personal stresses

In addition to the general stresses associated with nearly all clergy, there are specific areas of stress more closely associated with personal lifestyle such as those that apply to homosexual clergy and those with marital problems.

Clergy marriages and home life

Marital problems are widespread in society at the present time and clergy marriages are not immune from these. In addition, there are various specific problems which make clergy marriages especially vulnerable. David and Vera Mace (1980) found that clergy marriages were characterised by mediocrity, superficiality, and quiet desperation. Janelle Warner and John Carter (1984) compared a sample of ministers and spouses in a small American Presbyterian denomination with a comparable sample of lay church members. They found that the ministers and their wives experienced more loneliness, poorer marital adjustment, and greater emotional exhaustion than the comparable lay marriages. (Even though a lot of newly ordained clergy are women, the research is still mainly concerned with male clergy and their wives.)

One of the most helpful of these studies so far is that of Mary Kirk and Tom Leary (1994). Clergy in the UK are not particularly well paid, though when free housing, contribution-free insurance, and other benefits are considered, the level of remuneration is not as poor as it seems at first sight. There may be particular problems when the minister is significantly less well-off than most parishioners; there may also be problems in the remuneration not being commensurate with the housing. Being in a 'provided' house is often felt to reduce autonomy, making movement out of ministry difficult if it is desired. It is also problematic if parishioners feel they have some ownership of the minister's personal home.

There is another set of problems associated with the expectations of clergy, and their lack of privacy. Clergy are expected to lead exemplary lives, and parishioners' ideas of what constitutes an exemplary life may not be the same as the minister's own. Moreover, ministers live with greater visibility and public scrutiny than most people, and minor aspects of their personal life are open to comment. The irregular working hours, and lack of clear boundaries between work and home life also create family problems. This is exacerbated by the fact that many clergy work from home, with the advantages of freedom and flexibility, though with the disadvantage that work life can intrude on family life, with the telephone and visitors affecting family members far more than would be the case in most jobs.

There are also issues associated with the special nature of the minister's calling and its impact on the marital relationship. There are likely to be ambivalent attitudes here. Most clergy spouses went into the marriage knowing that they were marrying someone who was, or was likely to be, ordained. Indeed, as Kirk and Leary's study indicates, this was often a central part of the attraction. Many clergy seem to have had difficulty in coming to terms with their sexuality, and may have entered the ministry seeking a haven from it. It is consistent with this that sexual attraction seems to be a much less important factor in clergy marriages than in marriages generally. Many clergy marry primarily to find someone to support them in their ministry.

However, the minister's work may take up more time and energy than expected, leaving very little for the spouse. Indeed, many come to resent the pressure placed on them to help in parish work. This 'downside' of being married to a minister may not have been fully anticipated. Moreover, the spouse of a minister may have particular problems in asking for a greater share of the minister's time, as they may feel guilty about taking the minister away from 'God's work'. Equally, some ministers can use the special nature of their calling as a way of shielding themselves from the legitimate demands of their spouse and family.

Malony and Hunt (1991, Chapter 7) distinguish several different models of how clergy spouses can relate to parish work (see Box 13.1).

It would be foolish to try to stipulate which of these models *should* be followed. The important thing is that there should be agreement about which model is being followed, between the minister, the spouse, and the church congregation. Most problems in clergy marriages arise when the spouse disagrees either with the minister or with the congregation about what their role should be in relation to the minister's work. A slow process of education is going on, to the effect that congregations should not have automatic expectations of clergy spouses, and should be willing to adjust to different models with different ministers. That should make a significant contribution to reducing stress in clergy marriages.

Box 13.1 Possible modes of engagement of clergy spouses

1 **Disinterested**
There are some spouses who have no interest in the minister's work, but this is very rare.

2 **Individual**
These are spouses who probably participate in the life of the church, but do so quite independently from the minister to whom they are married. This is quite a common pattern with more educated spouses.

3 **Background supporter**
This is the most common role, and there seems to have been very little change in this over the last twenty years.

4 **Team worker or co-pastor**
These are spouses who are very active with the minister in the leadership of the church and may regard themselves as sharing the ministry on an equal basis. This pattern is particularly associated with a conservative religious outlook.

(Malony and Hunt 1991)

Though the level of problems in clergy marriages seems quite high, there is no good research comparing these with problems in other comparable professions, and it would be premature to conclude that clergy marriages are especially problematic. However, there are two reasons why problems in clergy marriage may make a particular impact. First, there is a widespread expectation, both in ministers themselves and in the wider church, that there ought not to be any problems; this may make difficulties particularly hard to handle. Second, there is an unusually low divorce rate in clergy marriages, even though it has been increasing in recent decades. This is probably largely due to the constraints of the minister's conscience and of the institutional church. The result seems to be that there is a significant proportion of clergy marriages that 'drag on' with chronic unresolved problems.

Though clergy marriages often have their problems, so does enforced celibacy – as is apparent from the series of media reports of sexual abuse by celibate clergy. The dilemma of whether it is best for clergy to be married or not is reminiscent of the issues with which St Paul grappled in 1 Corinthians about Christian marriage in general. There is a case for both marriage and celibacy; each has its advantages and each has its problems. It is probably best not to try to arrive at any uniform expectations or requirements, but to leave each minister the maximum freedom to judge which will be best for them. That is not only a call for greater realism about the costs of enforcing celibacy in the Roman Catholic church, but equally a call for greater care about the hidden pressures in many Protestant churches for ministers to be married and to have model families.

Homosexual clergy

Ben Fletcher (1990) also conducted an interesting survey of the problems felt by homosexual clergy. Working through various support groups, they were able to contact three hundred and ninety such clergy in the Church of England; they hazard a guess that the total number is 1,400. If this is correct, the proportion of clergy that are homosexual is clearly substantial. The normal stresses experienced by homosexuals are, of course, exacerbated by the fact that many Christians, though by no means all, believe that homosexuality is against Christian teaching. The problems are particularly severe for those homosexual clergy who share this view themselves. Most denominations disapprove of clergy living in open homosexual relationships, which leaves homosexual clergy a choice between enforced abstinence or clandestine relationships. Nevertheless, Fletcher found that 25 per cent of the homosexual clergy he was able to survey said they lived with their same-sex partner.

As with Fletcher's more general survey of clergy, quite high levels of job satisfaction were found to coexist with a severe sense of strain in a significant proportion of clergy. Indeed, 26 per cent said they had felt during the previous year that they were going to have a nervous breakdown. It was also clear that homosexual clergy felt significantly more stressed than heterosexual clergy, as was manifested in their levels of anxiety, depression, and so on. Having to put on a public face, and coping with individual parishioners, were among the most common sources of strain.

Fletcher comments that 'the evidence reported here presents a very depressing picture of the health and well-being of homosexual clergy in the Church of England'. One can only speculate on how things might have changed since 1989 when the survey was conducted. For instance, there seems to have been a significant movement towards tolerance of homosexuality in society at large, manifested for example in the increasing number of openly homosexual political representatives. Within the church, it probably continues to be the case that many congregations are more concerned about the quality of ministry they receive from their clergy than their sexual orientation. The attitude of church authorities is quite varied, and perhaps confused. As could be seen in the recent Lambeth conference, on the one hand there continues to be a drive from some quarters to try to eliminate homosexual clergy, but on the other, many members of the church hierarchy reflect the increasingly tolerant and liberal views of society at large. The number of homosexual clergy surely remains high, however, and the official reluctance to admit that openly makes it difficult to help them with the resulting stress.

Sexual misdemeanours

As already noted, sexual attraction seems to have played a much smaller part in the formation of clergy than non-clergy marriages. Indeed, there may be a lack of emotional depth and bonding in many such marriages. While there are undoubtedly problems in secular marriages built on sexual attraction with little underpinning of companionship, there may equally be problems in marriages built only on companionship without any depth of emotional and sexual bonding. Indeed, it seems that an unusually high proportion of married clergy may have been somewhat ambivalent about getting married in the first place. Occasionally, sexual pressures and needs will present themselves in other ways, such as promiscuous relationships or in using pornography, though that is probably true only of a small minority of clergy.

The level of sexual misdemeanours in clergy marriages is a difficult matter on which to get accurate information. Kirk and Leary found that both clergy and their spouses were, with rare exceptions, reluctant to discuss sexuality at all. Nevertheless, they became aware of the occurrence of physical abuse within the marriage, use of prostitutes, use of pornography, and so on. Though the problem of getting accurate data means that any conclusions must be cautious, the suspicion is that sexual problems are more widespread in the clergy than in most comparable professional groups. This may be the 'dark side' of the apparent asexuality of the clergy and their failure to come to terms with their own sexual feelings.

Blackmon (cited by Malony and Hunt 1991: 35f), in a study of American clergy from a variety of denominations, found that 36 per cent admitted to experiencing sexual attraction towards members of their congregation. 37 per cent admitted that they had engaged in inappropriate sexual behaviour, though not necessarily with a member of their congregation. Malony regards these figures as much higher than would be found in other comparable professions. However, there is a trend for estimates of the frequency of sexual problems in all professions to rise as the culture permits more honest reporting. Certainly, clergy are more vulnerable to sexual misdemeanours with parishioners in as far as their role relationships are much less clearly defined than those of most comparable professionals. The clergy are often pastors, priests, neighbours and friends to their parishioners, which makes it much harder to discern where the appropriate boundaries to the relationship fall.

SUMMARY OF KEY THEMES

- Potential problems in clergy marriages: low pay, lack of privacy, ambivalent attitude to sex.
- Need to agree appropriate level of spouse involvement.
- The pressure on clergy marriages caused by high expectations of success.
- Higher levels of stress among homosexual clergy.
- Sexual misdemeanours among clergy: causes and effects.

QUESTIONS TO CONSIDER

- Do you feel that your relationship with your spouse/partner is put under strain by your job?
- Is your spouse happy with the level of his/her involvement in your ministry?
- Are you happy with the level of your spouse's involvement in your ministry?
- How are romantic and sexual relationships different for members of the clergy?

- How widespread among the clergy are sexual misdemeanours and what might be their causes?
- How might you respond to a clergyperson who has committed a sexual misdemeanour (or sexual crime)? What sources of help could you recommend?
- How are your sexual feelings affected by your role as a minister?

Attitudes to clergy

Clergy can find themselves the object of strong attitudes and quite intense emotions. These can be either positive or negative, and most clergy will be familiar with the confusing pattern of some members of their church thinking they are marvellous while others are highly critical of them. There has been surprisingly little formal research on this, but there is some general psychological theory that can be helpful in conceptualising the problem. In part, it is a problem that is common to people in most caring professions, and has been considered particularly carefully in psychoanalysis (e.g. Sandler *et al.* 1973). The implications of this approach for clergy have been discussed by Mary Anne Coate (1989).

Freud introduced the concept of 'transference', though subsequent psychoanalytic theorists have suggested that similar patterns of relationship can arise outside psychoanalysis. Broadly conceived, the concept of transference implies that feelings or attitudes that belong to a significant past relationship are transferred onto the relationship with the analyst or carer. The two key hallmarks are feelings that are a repetition of the past, and inappropriate to the present. The blank screen of anonymity maintained by a psychoanalyst makes them particularly likely to be the subject of such transference. Though Freud initially seemed to have regarded transference phenomena as simply a problem, he came to see that interpreting the transference could be a particularly effective method of psychoanalysis. Because clergy are generally much better known as people than are analysts they are perhaps less vulnerable to transference relationships, though these may still arise.

Though the psychoanalytic tradition assumes that intense emotional reactions to analysts or other carers arise from the transference of feelings from significant problematic relationships in the past, this may not be the only way in which they can do so. There may be more general aspects of how emotionally needy people relate to those that try to care for them that give rise to intense feelings. Strong emotional dependence can give rise to idealisation of the carer, based in part on gratitude for the extent to which emotional needs are met. On the other hand, there can be anger and frustration at emotional needs not being fully met, and perhaps also resentment at being heavily dependent on another person.

In addition, as Coate has suggested, there may be particular aspects of transference that arise with clergy. Laity are often very involved emotionally in what goes on in church, whether the main focus is on the celebration of the sacraments or the preaching of the word. Clergy are easily seen as prophets or as some kind of 'messiah', though they are often naive about the importance that is attached to them. The more the clergy are caught up in being a channel for something that is beyond them, the more they may lay themselves open to being the focus of projections by members of the congregation. The most important element in handling this is for ministers to be as clearly conscious as possible of what is going on, and not to confuse being a channel of God's grace with their own personal qualities. Indeed, many ministers may have a sharp sense of the disparity between the two, as when St Paul spoke of being a mere earthenware vessel containing great treasure (2 Corinthians 4).

Provided that ministers maintain a clear awareness of the projections onto them, they will neither believe them, nor be too disturbed by them. The fact that many clergy are the subject of both positive and negative projections in itself helps to foster a sense of detachment about them. From this starting point, it is then possible to help parishioners to manage their projections onto the clergy. Here, it is important to remember that projections may be serving an important emotional function, and should not be violently or tactlessly disabused. The wise course is to bear them patiently and to take what opportunities arise to introduce elements of reality, and awareness of the nature of the projection.

In caring relationships, projections do not only go in one direction, and in psychoanalytic circles there has been increasing recognition of the importance of 'counter-transference', concerning the projection of the analyst onto the client. In a similar way, clergy can have projections onto their parishioners, and again Coate (1989, Chapter 5) has provided a helpful discussion of the issues.

Like many people in the caring professions, clergy may be meeting their own emotional needs by helping other people. They can project their own neediness onto members of the congregation, and meet their needs vicariously while ostensibly helping other people. This can result in an unfortunate pattern of encouraging excessive dependency in the congregation to help to maintain the minister's own emotional adjustment.

Finally, in most people there is both a nice 'persona' (i.e. mask) and a darker 'shadow' side. People in the caring professions, such as clergy, may be over-identified with their nice side and try to ignore the darker side of their personality. This becomes difficult to maintain, and people can crack under the strain of trying to do so. Equally, the unacknowledged dark side of the personality can be projected onto those being cared for, leading to an unreasonable resentment of them. Once again, the important thing is for ministers to be as clearly conscious as possible of what may be going on in their caring relationships with members of their congregations.

SUMMARY OF KEY THEMES

- Being the object of strong emotional reactions.
- The phenomenon of 'transference'.
- Dealing with emotional dependency.
- Separating projections from realities.
- Acknowledging the shadow side of personality.

QUESTIONS TO CONSIDER

- Are there members of your congregation who have particularly strong feelings towards you?
- Are these positive or negative?
- Can you think of cases you have experienced of transference and/or counter-transference in your role as a minister?
- Are there people who are unhealthily emotionally dependent on you?
- Do you ever encourage emotional dependency to bolster your own self-worth?

Further reading

General

Beit-Hallahmi, B. and Argyle, M. (1997) *The Psychology of Religious Behaviour, Belief and Experience*, London: Routledge, pp. 63–71.
Francis, L. and Jones, S. (eds) (1996) *Psychological Perspectives on Christian Ministry: A Reader*, Leominster: Gracewing.
Malony, H. N. and Hunt, R. (1991) *The Psychology of Clergy*, Harrisburg, PA: Morehouse Publishing.

Stress and coping

Coate, M. (1989) *Clergy Stress: The Hidden Conflicts of Ministry*, London: SPCK.
Davey, J. (1995) *Burnout: Stress in the Ministry*, Leominster: Gracewing.
Fletcher, B. (1990) *Clergy Under Stress: A Study of Homosexual and Heterosexual Clergy*, London: Mowbray.
Irvine, A. (1997) *Between Two Worlds: Understanding and Managing Clergy Stress*, London: Mowbray.

Specific issues

Fletcher, B. (1990) *Clergy Under Stress: A Study of Homosexual and Heterosexual Clergy*, London: Mowbray.
Kirk, M. and Leary, T. (1994) *Holy Matrimony? An Exploration of Ministry and Marriage*, Oxford: Lynx.
Sanford, J. (1982) *Ministry Burnout*, London: Arthur James.

Part 5

Psychology and theology

14   Concepts of human nature

QUESTIONS FOR MINISTRY

- Where do your assumptions about human nature come from? The Bible? Science? Psychology? Popular culture?
- To which sources do you implicitly or explicitly give most authority?
- How do scientific and psychological assumptions fit in with Christian beliefs about the soul?
- What in human nature do you consider fixed and what open to transformation?
- Do you think of human beings as inherently sinful, inherently good, or a mixture of these?

In the preceding three sections of the book we have explored the ways in which psychology can provide valuable insights and practical solutions relevant to the challenges facing the church. However, we have not yet examined the basic assumptions that lie behind these approaches. These final two chapters examine and compare, from a more conceptual standpoint, the fundamental models and assumptions that are used within psychology and within the Christian tradition. This chapter will look at psychological and religious assumptions about human nature; the next one will look more broadly at the general interface between psychology and theology.

Both historically, and in the present, psychological and Christian ways of thinking have provided different models of human nature. However, they have not always been opposed to one another, nor are they mutually exclusive; many people have combined academic psychology with a Christian commitment. In the nineteenth century, when psychology was taking shape as an autonomous academic discipline, there were many Christian thinkers who successfully combined the insights of the new physiological and behavioural psychology with commitments to Christian views about the soul (e.g. James McCosh and G. T. Ladd; see Dixon 1999). This integrated Christian–psychological approach has been lost as a result of the increasing academic separation of theology and psychology in the last hundred years. However, the work of these nineteenth-century thinkers shows that insights about human mental life made from neurological, physiological, behavioural, moral, and spiritual perspectives, can in principle all be combined with a Christian framework.

It is sometimes supposed that psychology and Christianity make conflicting assumptions about what it means to be human. You might think that psychologists always endorse a 'reductionist' model of human nature, and treat human beings as 'nothing but' biological organisms, brains, machines, or computers; whereas Christians might be thought to have emphasised the fact that humans are spiritual beings who differ in crucial ways from animals and machines. However, that would be a simplistic way of contrasting psychological and religious views.

It is important here to emphasise the diversity both of psychological and of religious ideas about human nature. There is no single monolithic view of human nature in psychology that can be pitted against a single religious one. In psychology, for example, Beloff (1973) organised his introductory textbook on *Psychological Sciences* into eight distinguishable sciences that co-exist under the umbrella of psychology: introspective psychology, comparative psychology, differential psychology, behaviouristics, cognitive psychology, social psychology, depth psychology, and parapsychology. This is not an exhaustive or definitive list, and some years later the boundaries between sub-disciplines of psychology might be drawn rather differently. However, it gives some indication of the range of psychologies, differing in their substantive focus, methodologies, and assumptions.

The Christian tradition has also contained quite diverse views about human nature. The most celebrated controversy is that between Pelagius and Augustine, the former taking a more optimistic view of human nature than the latter, and differing about the roles of divine grace and human responsibility. Somewhat similar debates surfaced recently around the 'creation spirituality' advocated by Matthew Fox, which takes a more optimistic view of human nature than many Christian thinkers. Another issue on which Christians have taken a diverse range of views is the extent of human free will. Some have emphasised the importance of human free will, but there are other strands, such as Calvinist theology, that are relatively deterministic.

It is helpful in overcoming a simplistic contrast between psychological and religious views to realise that there is a certain parallelism between the debates among psychologists and the debates among theologians about human nature. Contrasts between optimistic and pessimistic views keep recurring that are rather like those between Augustine and Pelagius. For example, C. G. Jung, though accepting much of Freud's approach, differed from him in taking a less pessimistic view of human nature.

Similarly, within sociobiology and evolutionary psychology there have been debates that are driven more by differences in fundamental assumptions about human nature than by empirical evidence. There have been some, such as Thomas Huxley in the nineteenth century and Richard Dawkins more recently, who have taught that human beings are by nature entirely selfish and that altruism and co-operation can be achieved only by a society that fights against human nature. On the other hand, other sociobiologists such as Edward O. Wilson have claimed that human beings, like many other social animals, are by nature co-operative and altruistic (see Dawkins 1989; Ridley 1997; Wilson 1998).

Even though ideas about human nature in psychology and Christianity seem to be very different, that does not necessarily imply conflict. Much Christian thinking about human nature has been developed within the framework of salvation and concerns moral aspects of human nature and the possibility of change. Much psychology, in contrast, is often morally neutral and concerned with such fine-grained detail as the distinction between different kinds of memory process.

It is also helpful to recognise that within every science there is a distinction between experimental research and broad *a priori* assumptions or world views. The human and social sciences, even more than the mathematical and physical sciences, have always been particularly open to the influence of such assumptions, partly because psychological and sociological theories are never fully determined by the empirical evidence. In the case of psychology, the *a priori* assumptions made about the relationship between mind and body, and the proper method of gaining psychological knowledge, have been particularly influential. Behaviouristic theories and cognitive ones, of emotion for example, differ largely because their fundamental assumptions and methods are different. The same could be said about psychological and religious accounts of the human mind.

It has even been suggested that world view assumptions have influenced some theorists to the extent that their psychological theories are nothing but a particular world view in disguise. This is the allegation made by Richard Webster in *Why Freud Was Wrong* (1995) against certain psychoanalytic psychologists and structuralist anthropologists, especially Freud and Levi-Strauss. He suggests that in adopting, for example, a dualism between reason and emotion, they have perpetuated assumptions imported from Judeo-Christian theology (Webster 1995). However, the relative contributions of Christian, anti-Christian, and unchristian assumptions to the emergence of secular psychologies is more complex than models such as Webster's imply (see Dixon 1999). It is wise to be cautious about simplistic claims that psychology is really theology in disguise, or alternatively that it is implicitly atheistic.

SUMMARY OF KEY THEMES

- Combining Christian, psychological, and scientific views of human nature.
- The diversity of views about human nature within both psychology and Christianity.
- Debates often driven by different assumptions rather than by empirical evidence.
- The issue of whether humans are innately selfish or innately altruistic.
- How 'world views' can shape our assumptions about human nature and psychology.

QUESTIONS TO CONSIDER

- What authority, if any, do you give to theoretical and empirical psychology?
- Have you ever considered psychology to involve assumptions that contradict Christian teachings?
- What are your world view assumptions about human nature, and where do they come from?
- How might your assumptions (e.g. about whether human beings are naturally good or naturally selfish) affect your ministry from day to day?

'Nothing but' views of human nature

One of the major points of conflict between psychological and religious views arises from those areas of psychology that are inclined to take a reductionist view of human nature, that human beings are 'nothing but' this or that. There are at least five such areas. One is the view associated with B. F. Skinner, that human beings are, in effect, nothing more than their external, observable behaviour. However, as a research paradigm in psychology, behaviourism has proved relatively barren and has now run its course. We will not give it detailed attention here. Another long-standing psychological approach that still needs comment is that of Freud, which tends to reduce higher aspects of personality to basic impulses. There are three other approaches, central to current scientific psychology, where 'nothing but' views are still current: evolutionary psychology, neuropsychology, and artificial intelligence. The forms of reductionism involved are related, but subtly different.

It is worth emphasising again that none of these areas of psychology is completely associated with the reductionist view of human nature. Such general views about human nature float along at a different level from psychological research. They are espoused by some people in the field, but not by others, and it is not obvious that it makes a great deal of difference to detailed research whether or not such views are held.

Psychoanalysis

Psychoanalysis has been more influential outside mainstream psychology than within it. Within psychology it remains controversial, and it is necessary to begin with some methodological cautions about it. One problem is its exclusiveness. Psychoanalysis is as guilty of ignoring other traditions of psychology as they are of ignoring psychoanalysis. It is never healthy to pursue a particular branch of the subject in encapsulated isolation. The other problem is methodological. Psychoanalytic theory is too often derived from observation without proper debate about alternatives, and can be deployed in a way that rides roughshod over the facts of a particular case, though this does not always happen.

As so often happens with innovative movements, Freud's followers seem to have been, in many ways, more dogmatic than he was himself. This is captured in a story of a Viennese man who remembered Freud personally. There was a house near to where Freud lived in Vienna where a group of deaf people lived. They had very good pottery facilities, and were noted for the quality of their work; there had recently been an article about it in the local newspaper. Freud wrote and asked whether he could visit. He came, accompanied by a young assistant, and was most courteous and interested in everything he saw. The assistant began to interpret some of the pottery, but Freud rebuked him: 'Be quiet. You don't know the facts; just look.'

Psychoanalytic theory can be, and frequently is, applied with much integrity, sensitivity and caution. These virtues have been extolled, for example, in Patrick Casement's book, *On Learning from the Patient* (1985). Unfortunately, such virtues have been much less in evidence when psychoanalysis has been applied to other disciplines such as history or theology. To some extent this is understandable, as the particular facts which should always guide the development of application of theory are less easily checked than in clinical applications of psychoanalysis.

There are of course a variety of psychoanalytic theories, not just one. This creates the possibility of formulating a variety of different psychoanalytic interpretations about a single individual. They could then be set against each other, and their merits debated. Unfortunately, this has seldom happened; the psychoanalytic task has too often been seen as simply to give a single, coherent account. The comprehensiveness of the account as a total narrative is what is most highly prized; historical truth, in contrast, can tend to be neglected. As Shepherd (1985) has pointed out, there is an interesting similarity between Sherlock Holmes and the Freudian analyst. Both operate as detectives, piecing together a coherent story from the few available clues.

Freudian theory appears to be reductionist in the sense that it sees all aspects of the human psyche as resulting from the 'libido', the primitive, pleasure-seeking, erotic drive that is at the heart of the id. (Freud later proposed a death-wish alongside the libido, but it was a relatively late theoretical development, and one that many Freudian theorists have found unconvincing.) For Freud, all apparently higher aspects of the human psyche are derived from the libido. The super-ego, or punitive sense of conscience, is an introjection of responses to, and constraints upon, the libidinous impulses of the id. Equally, the apparently altruistic ego ideal is a creation of the narcissistic libido, which needs to find something more adequate to love.

Freud's approach has been called by Ricoeur (1970) a 'hermeneutic of suspicion' – an interpretation of human nature that unmasks the apparently higher aspects of human nature and reveals them to be serving primitive needs. However, the 'suspiciousness' of Freudian theorising does not necessarily mean that there is nothing more to human nature than the primitive libido. This is apparent in much subsequent theorising in the Freudian tradition such as that of his former protégé, Jung, who found a way of incorporating the spiritual into an expanded version of Freudian theory. There are other psychoanalytical theorists such as Fromm and Erikson, who are closer to Freud theoretically than Jung, but are less relentlessly reductionist than Freud himself.

Freud's particular contribution is the 'suspicious' perspective that is always ready to unmask high-flown human pretensions. However, that is not necessarily inconsistent with Christianity. There is equally a suspicious strand in the Christian tradition that seeks to expose how human sinfulness lurks beneath the surface of apparent human achievement. Freud has a suspicious view of belief in God, which he wanted to unmask as a reflection of human desire, but equally there is a strand in Christian thinking that is ready to expose how belief in God can be distorted by human limitations.

Evolutionary psychology

We come now to one of the three main 'nothing but' positions about human nature that arise in current scientific psychology. Though there are slight differences between them, the common factor in them all is that they make illegitimate inferences about human beings from explanatory theories of one kind or another. Evolutionary psychology is in danger of committing the 'genetic fallacy' and assuming, that because human beings have evolved from other animals, we are still basically animals. In so far as there was religious resistance in the nineteenth century to accepting that human beings had evolved from other animals it seems to have come largely from the mistaken belief that accepting the theory of evolution for human beings implied that we are still no better than animals.

However, evolutionary theorising does not always commit the genetic fallacy. It can be helpful in understanding a particular aspect of human functioning to see how it has evolved and what has been its evolutionary significance. Recent books on the mind that take an evolutionary perspective have been deservedly popular (e.g. Pinker 1997; Plotkin 1997), and there is no reason why Christians should be in any way iconoclastic about this area of scientific enquiry. It is right for evolutionary thinking to go as far as it can in explaining human nature; that is 'good' reductionism. Problems only come when interesting evolutionary theorising is taken to the point of saying that the evolutionary perspective tells us everything, and that we can infer the nature of something entirely from its evolutionary origin. Evolutionary thinking only manifests what Dan Dennett (1995) has called 'greedy' reductionism when it insists that it is telling the whole truth about human beings, and that there is nothing else.

One of the best known evolutionary books about human nature is Richard Dawkins' *The Selfish Gene* (1989). It is a contribution to the problem, apparent since Darwin himself, of how evolution can explain altruistic behaviour. Dawkins' interesting idea is that natural selection works, not so much on animals, but on genes. Whatever is good for the survival of genes is likely to have an evolutionary advantage, even behaviour that is bad for the survival of individual animals. So far, so good. It all goes wrong when Dawkins succumbs to some loose talk about our genes being 'selfish', and making us do whatever is good for their own survival. One problem with that is that only people can be selfish, not genes; another is that genes only predispose us to do things, they don't control us. However, Dawkins goes further. He moves from saying we have selfish genes to saying that we ourselves are selfish. Thus, an evolutionary explanation of altruistic behaviour ends up saying that we are just products of our selfish genes.

Another important arena of controversy in evolutionary thinking concerns morality. It is certainly an interesting matter how morality has developed in the course of evolution, and there are diverse views about that (e.g. Rottschaefer 1998). For example, morality has sometimes been seen as a agent of evolution, sometimes as antagonistic to it. The problem comes with the view (of which Ruse 1995, is one of the ablest exponents) that ethical systems are nothing but collective illusions put in place by our biology.

Human beings are a mixture of good and evil, as Christians have always taught. Humanity is made in God's image, and called to grow towards God's likeness, but humanity is also 'fallen' and in need of redemption. Placing humanity in the context of evolution raises the question of how the good and evil in human beings relates to other animals. Sometimes there has been a tendency to assume that our sinfulness comes from what we have inherited from other animals, and that goodness is what is distinctively human. Sometimes the argument has been the other way around, with the idea that animals are noble and innocent, and that it is fallen humanity that is distinctively sinful. Both positions seem misconceived. Our animal inheritance is morally ambivalent; there seem to be aspects of it that predispose us to do good and aspects that predispose us to do evil. Equally, what is distinctively human also seems to be morally ambivalent. Our distinctive, reflective consciousness means that we can do both good and evil in a more knowing and deliberate way than is possible for other species. One of the insights of the Christian tradition is that good and evil are interlocked. They are intertwined, both in our animal inheritance, and in what is distinctively human.

Since the controversies surrounding Darwin's theory of evolution in the nineteenth century there has often been a clash between Christian and secular traditions about the relationship of humanity to other animals. The tendency has been for secular thinkers to emphasise the continuity between them, whereas Christian thinkers have generally wanted to emphasise that humanity is special. As with many controversies, the sane position lies in the middle ground. On the one hand, there is probably almost nothing about human beings that does not have its roots in other higher animals – though our reflective self-consciousness and spiritual qualities would be the strongest candidates for distinctively human qualities. On the other hand, there are many functions that are so much more highly developed in human beings than in any other species that it really is justifiable to regard humanity as distinctive. For example, chimpanzees might be deemed to have some of the rudiments out of which language has developed, but it is so primitive compared to that of human beings that it is doubtful whether it can be deemed to be language in the human sense.

It is surprising that Christians have often wanted to argue for the uniqueness of human beings, as this sits uneasily with the biblical tradition, particularly as found in the Old Testament. For example, the writer of Ecclesiastes (3. 18–20) says that there is no fundamental difference between human beings and the animals, because they both return to the dust. Both human beings and the animals have a similar origin in that 'all come from dust'; they both arise within the natural world. The writer also wants to emphasise that we have mortality in common, and he is sceptical about whether there will be a different fate awaiting us after death. As he says, 'Who knows if the spirit of man rises upward and if the spirit of the animal goes down into the earth?' This is not an isolated biblical text. The book of Genesis emphasises that 'the LORD God formed man from the dust of the ground' (Genesis 2.7). Like other animals, human beings are 'flesh'. There is nothing in this biblical tradition to justify Christians denying continuity between human beings and the rest of the animal kingdom.

From a Christian point of view, humanity has a distinctive place within the purposes of God. Some, such as Jacques Monod (1972), have wanted to argue that evolution is a process of pure, blind chance, and therefore incompatible with any notion that God has been at work through evolution, furthering his purposes, but that rests on a misconception about evolution. However, even if we allow that mutations are random, natural selection is clearly not a random process. There seems to be an inherent evolutionary advantage in developing increasingly complex and sophisticated modes of information processing. This is certainly not to suggest that there was anything inevitable about evolution taking exactly the path it did. However, information processing was likely to evolve at some stage and, when it did, it was likely to have a significant evolutionary advantage that it would develop and become increasingly sophisticated. It could well be this capacity for information processing which underlies the distinctively human attributes that could be loosely summarised as the human 'soul'.

By 'soul' we do not mean a 'thing', in the way that the body is a thing. Rather, by soul we mean a cluster of capacities: to reflect, to form relationships, to be moral, to pray, and so on (see Ward, 1992). Above all, saying that human beings have 'soul' means that they have a certain affinity with God and can grow towards his likeness. Many Christians have believed that human souls were specially and directly created by God and somehow joined to the human body, but there is no reason for Christians to maintain that. Rather, soul attributes can be seen as having arisen within the natural world and as being 'emergent properties'. Despite this origin, they have enormous importance, and are no less real for having emerged through evolution. Through our capacity for conscious reflection and moral decision-making, we have a unique capacity to do good or evil deliberately, to turn towards God or away from him. Soul has arisen from the natural world, but enables us to receive God's revelation in Christ and to grow towards God.

Neuropsychology

The basic problem here, and a very old one, is how to understand the relationship between bodily states and states of mind. It may help to start by considering a particular example. Among the most useful states to think about in this context are the emotions, since they so clearly incorporate both bodily and mental features. So, let us consider the example of anger induced by a friend breaking a valued possession. When I become angry at my friend, I go red in the face, my heart rate goes up, I might even start to shake. These are the bodily aspects of the emotion of anger. But there are also mental aspects: I am angry because of a belief I hold about my friend wronging me; my anger is also based on social and moral beliefs about property, responsibility and proper behaviour; I feel subjectively angry; I am inclined to think unkind thoughts about the person who has angered me. So, my anger has both bodily and mental features, but how should I think of their relation, one to the other? Is it my belief that my friend has acted negligently that causes me to become physically upset? Or, on the contrary, does my physical arousal, once triggered, cause me to feel and act in an emotional way? Or, again, are the physical and mental aspects two sides of the same experience?

There has recently been considerable research on the relationship of the brain to psychological functioning that has emphasised how closely brain and mind are intertwined. Advances in neuropsychology have been underpinned by very careful study of patients who have sustained brain damage to see exactly which psychological functions are impaired and which are still intact. Damage to specific areas of the brain has emphasised how tasks that are apparently very closely related seem to be linked to slightly different areas of the brain. For example, recognising faces head-on seems to be linked to a different area of the brain from recognising them sideways. More recently, there have been further advances due to our ability now to 'scan' the brain, to see which parts of their brain people are using when performing particular mental tasks by measuring changes in blood flow.

Even though considerable advances have been made in linking mind and brain, it perhaps needs to be emphasised that this mapping is not exactly the same in each person. People certainly differ in which side of the brain is linked to linguistic capacities; to some extent there are also differences in the mapping of mind on to brain between men and women, and differences due to people's background and experience. There are thus many individual variations around a broadly similar mapping of mental functions on to brain areas.

So far attention has focused mainly on the areas of the brain linked to perception, attention, memory and language; less progress has been made with broader aspects of personality. With emotion, for example, we now have a good idea of which areas of the brain are involved in basic fear (LeDoux 1996), but not yet with more complicated emotions such as guilt. Religious experience will probably be one of the most difficult aspects of personality to map onto specific areas of the brain. The most popular idea has been that the areas of the temporal lobes involved in epilepsy are also involved in religious experience, though the evidence for that is much weaker than is usually supposed (see Jeeves 1997; see also Chapter 1). One problem is that religious experience is so diverse that it is very unlikely that any single area of the brain is associated with all aspects of it. Different aspects of the brain are likely to be involved in different aspects of religious experience. One current theory that points in the right direction here is that of d'Aquili and Newberg (1999) who link different brain systems with perceptions of divine causation and with the mystical experiences of unity.

The central question, then, is how far mind and personality can be explained in terms of brain functioning. Probably a good deal of progress will be made with that over the decades, including the role of the brain in religion. That leads on to the further question of what we can conclude about the nature of experiences from understanding the involvement of the brain. For example, once we have understood which areas of the brain are involved in religious experience, will that show that religious experience is just a spin-off of the physical brain? That is not the only possible interpretation. All that neuropsychology has really established is that there is a close correlation between brain activity and mental functioning; the relationship between them is a matter of interpretation.

One solution to this so-called 'mind–body problem' – the one associated with Plato and neoplatonic Christian thinkers such as Augustine and Descartes – is the doctrine of 'substance dualism'. This is the view of human nature that many people still implicitly hold, that there are two sorts of substance in the world – matter and mind. Dualists adopt various different metaphors to describe the relationship of soul and body: they might say that the soul 'inhabits' the body, or that it uses the body as its 'instrument', or that the body is its 'tabernacle'. All these metaphors emphasise the differentness of soul and body. Sir John Eccles, a twentieth-century Christian dualist and scientist, explores these ideas and others in an unusual debate with philosopher Karl Popper (Popper and Eccles 1977).

Yet another view of human nature that has often been implicitly espoused by psychologists is 'dual aspect monism', of which the most influential and well-known exponent was that heterodox Jewish thinker of the seventeenth century, Baruch Spinoza. The monist denies that there are two sorts of substance, and asserts that reality is fundamentally one. On the monist view, human beings are not dual creatures but unified wholes, and the difference between mind and matter is more one of perspective than of substance. Two of the earliest contributors to scientific psychology in the nineteenth century, Herbert Spencer and Alexander Bain, were keen advocates of dual-aspect monism. They thought that mental feelings – such as the feeling of anger – were the mental 'side' or 'aspect' of neurological and physiological changes, which were the objective or physical 'side' (see Dixon, in press). Note that the monist does not claim that all mental states can be reduced to physical states, or that they are nothing more than physical states, as a materialist would. Rather, the monist simply says that the mental and the physical are two sides of one single (ultimately unknowable) reality. Thus, the dual-aspect monist believes that there is a single sort of substance (rather than two sorts), which has mental and physical properties.

Stronger reductionist interpretations of the evidence see mind (and soul) as nothing but a property of the brain, or even as identical to brain processes. Francis Crick (1992), for example, claimed that we are nothing but a 'bundle of neurones'. There are various different emphases in such reductionist positions. One is that mind and brain are so closely intertwined that they are effectively identical, and that whenever we talk about the mind we could more accurately talk about the corresponding brain state. Another is that conscious experience is, as Thomas Huxley suggested, of no more significance than a steam engine blowing its whistle. On this view, mental states may not be identical with brain states, but all the important work is done in the physical brain. That leads on to the related idea that talk about the mind is a distraction from where the real action is. In their various ways, these views all suggest that the human mind is an unimportant spin-off from the activity of the brain.

A less reductionist version of this 'physicalist' philosophy of mind has been developed by John Searle. He explains his view of mental properties by using an analogy with physical properties. Chemical compounds have properties that do not belong to any of their constituent elements. For example, water has macro-properties of wetness, liquidity, freezing and boiling points that are not possessed by either hydrogen or oxygen. These properties Searle calls 'emergent'. In a similar way he argues that the mind is an emergent property of the brain: beliefs, desires, and emotions are properties of brains but not of individual neurones; they are emergent properties of large networks of neurones (Searle 1997).

There has recently been considerable interest among theologians in such ideas. Nancey Murphy and Warren Brown of the Fuller Seminary in California have argued strongly for the compatibility of Biblical and traditional Christianity with

what they call 'non-reductive physicalism' (W. Brown *et al.* (eds) 1998). This position emphasises those aspects of the Christian tradition mentioned above that value embodiment, and also draws on modern monist philosophy of mind. Their aim is to minimise the dualist aspects of the Christian tradition, and also to minimise the reductive physicalist elements of the scientific tradition in order to effect a reconciliation between Christian and scientific understandings of the person.

Certainly, there are non-dualist strands in Christian thought that emphasise human embodiment. Philosophers and theologians writing under the influence of Aristotle, including especially St Thomas Aquinas, have emphasised that a human being is not just a soul, nor just a body, but is a soul–body unity. The two Christian doctrines that emphasise this most strongly are the Incarnation and the Resurrection. The fact that God chose to become incarnate in the human form of Jesus Christ is an indication of the involvement of God not just in an ethereal spiritual realm but also in the material embodied world. Equally, the fact that he rose again in bodily form reinforces the importance of the bodily Christ. The project of emphasising the convergence between Christian and scientific thought on these points is a very interesting one, though it tends to overstate the compatibility between Christian and scientific models. The mainstream Christian tradition is a long way from what contemporary neuroscience could accept.

There are many complex issues here that are still the subject of active research among scientists and fierce debate among philosophers. However, there are probably a variety of positions that would be consistent with Christian teaching. The central thing for Christians to assert is the reality of human mental and spiritual qualities. Our significance in the purposes of God means that we are much more than a 'bundle of neurones'. However, it is also important to understand that this stance is not threatened in any way by exploring exactly how those mental and spiritual qualities are related to the physical brain. Nevertheless, with the advance of research on the basis of human spirituality in the physical brain, it may become increasingly necessary to challenge those who try to argue that such research shows that the religious life is somehow unreal or unimportant. Properly understood, there is no reason for Christians to feel threatened by advances in neuroscience.

Artificial intelligence

Another approach to mental functioning stems from the analogy between the mind and a computer. Computers manipulate symbols and so process information, and this provides, by analogy, a possible way of talking about the mind. This information-processing approach to mind, which focuses on mental functions, can be distinguished from the introspectionist approach that focuses on the description of mental processes that are accessible to consciousness. Many of those who want to give priority to descriptions of the brain in terms of mental processes are willing to accept the information-processing approach, even if they remain resistant to an introspectionist approach to mind.

The analogy between mind and computer has led to the discipline of Artificial Intelligence (AI), which seeks to simulate the activity of the mind in the form of a computer programme. A good deal of AI is of purely practical interest and, at that level, has been remarkably successful. However, as a theoretical enterprise, it has sought to find ways of capturing the full range of human intellectual functions in computational form. This has proved more difficult than the advocates of AI hoped in the early stages, but real progress has been made. A wide range of intelligent activities, such as playing chess, can now be performed by computers. The key limitation is that, even when computers perform human intellectual functions successfully, they do not always perform them in the same way as people do. For example, computers and humans have different ways of playing chess. It is of little theoretical interest to simulate an outcome unless the strategies of information processing are also simulated.

There are also certain challenges that have continued to pose severe difficulties for AI (see Dreyfus and Dreyfus 1986). Computers can be programmed to operate successfully within a prescribed set of rules, but they are not good at spotting when the rules are no longer applicable. For example, a computer can have an exchange with a person, successfully playing the role of an expert, but it has no way of knowing when the rules of discourse have changed. Computers also lack knowledge about how the symbols they are manipulating relate to the real world. This shows up in translation, for example. In a sentence such as 'the box was in the pen', it is difficult to decide which of the three meanings of 'pen' applies in this context without knowing what in the real world the sentence refers to.

One of the biggest challenges to AI is consciousness. Indeed, it is not even clear what criteria should be used to assess whether or not a computer has consciousness. A computer may store information and manipulate it, but it is hard to make sense of the idea that it knows anything consciously. Equally, a computer may be programmed to have certain aspects of emotion, such as to know when a particular emotion such as anger is appropriate and to show aspects of emotional behaviour, but it is doubtful whether we are justified in saying that it actually feels anger. Despite all the ink that has been spent in discussing whether computers could ever be conscious, there seems a dearth of convincing, principled arguments either way (see Copeland 1993).

The assumption that has underpinned AI has been that it makes little difference whether computer programmes run on the biological stuff of the human brain, or on silicon. However, in recent years, psychologists have become increasingly impressed with how far human cognitive processes *are* affected by the human brain, and have sought to theorise about them in a way that is biologically realistic (e.g. Edelman 1992). A new approach to computer programming has grown up, known as connectionism, that deliberately seeks to model information processing in a biologically plausible way, even though it is debatable how well that is actually achieved. The important point is perhaps that it has now been accepted that it is at least worth trying to write programmes that do things roughly as the brain does them. People have quietly abandoned the old dogma that it made no difference that human beings did their information processing on the grey, biological stuff of the brain.

AI often seems rather dualistic in assuming that human intelligence can be detached from the human brain and replicated in computer form. AI emphasises the separability of mind and body in a way that is reminiscent of substance dualism. One of the oddities here is that many of the same scientists share both the materialistic assumptions of neuropsychology and the dualist assumptions of AI, without noticing what uneasy bed-fellows they are. Some exponents of AI have gone so far as to suggest that, not only intelligence, but even personality or 'soul' can be replicated in disembodied form. This is a key assumption behind Tipler's (1994) strange vision of securing the immortality of each individual human personality by replicating it in computer form. The rather conflicting assumptions of AI and neuroscience have a parallel in the tensions within the Christian tradition. Sometimes, influenced by Plato and Descartes, this has espoused a kind of dualism about the soul that is similar to AI. At other times, influenced by the Hebrew anthropology of an 'ensouled body' and by Aristotle and Aquinas, it has espoused a holistic view of human nature closer to that of neuroscience. Once again, it is not a matter of sciences vs. religion, but of parallel debates breaking out in both science and religion.

The central theological issue raised by AI is the assumed similarity between computer and human intelligence. It is one thing to simulate human intelligence on a computer as far as possible. It is quite another to assume, as do some exponents of AI, that the human mind *is* essentially a computer programme. That involves a confusion between simulation and replication. The partial simulation of human intelligence in computer form that has been achieved so far does not mean that the human mind has been completely replicated on a computer. Nor does it mean that the human mind is 'nothing but' a computer.

There is a fallacy here that is rather like the genetic fallacy that arises in evolutionary psychology. In that case, illegitimate inferences were made from the origin of human beings to their nature, whereas here there is a related attempt to make inferences about the nature of mind from the fact that some partial simulation of it is possible in computer form. The argument often becomes circular. The assumption that the mind is really a computer underpins the belief that it can be completely simulated in computer form; equally, each step towards such simulation is taken as justifying the original assumption that the mind really is a computer.

Whereas evolutionary reductionism focuses on the past, and neuroscientific reductionism arises from the co-existence of mind and brain in the present, the reductionism associated with AI tends to focus on the future. AI tends to be associated with a grand vision of the future in which there will be computers that can do everything that human beings can do now, but without their imperfections and mortality (see Moravec 1988). Christians will recognise this as a secular eschatological vision of future perfection, for which human beings in their present form are only a preparation. There is probably no area of the human sciences that so explicitly offers an alternative eschatology as AI. However, as so often happens, there is a gulf between this grand ideology or world view and actual scientific research in AI. Most practical research in AI proceeds in isolation from big ideological issues, and simply doesn't engage with the Christian view of human nature one way or the other. It is the view of the human mind as essentially a computer, and of the future as being dominated by humanoid computers, that sits uneasily with Christianity.

SUMMARY OF KEY THEMES

- Varieties of 'nothing but' views of human nature.
- The problems with psychoanalysis; reducing everything to primitive impulses.
- How Christianity, like psychoanalysis, is suspicious of human pretensions.
- The usefulness of evolutionary psychology and the reductionism of 'selfish genes'.
- The morally ambivalent status of both human nature and human culture.
- Different ways of interpreting the correlations between mind and brain: substance dualism, dual-aspect monism, physicalism, and non-reductive physicalism.
- What computers can and can't do.
- The secular eschatology of AI.

QUESTIONS TO CONSIDER

- What is wrong with reductionist views of human nature?
- Why do Christian believers often find them unacceptable?
- Is Freudian suspicion a useful tool when trying to understand other people? Or oneself?
- What is it about human beings that makes them more than animals?
- What experiences, emotions, and behaviours most reveal our evolutionary and animal heritage? Are these less within our control than more 'advanced' thoughts and feelings?
- How can Christian doctrines about the soul and an afterlife be interpreted in the light of discoveries of intimate correlations between mental states and brain processes?
- In what ways does body/soul dualism influence the way some Christians think today?

Personality

It would be wholly misleading to suggest that psychology generally takes a 'nothing but' view of human nature. As has already been emphasised, psychology is very broad, and includes non-reductionist elements, of which the most important is 'personality psychology'. There is a good prospect for fruitful dialogue between Christian ideas about human nature and personality psychology, and possibly even a degree of integration between the two (see van Leeuwen 1985; Morea 1997).The breadth of personality psychology can be captured in a number of both/and statements. It both provides generalisations about human nature and also identifies how people differ from one another. It acknowledges a variety of influences on the person, including both the biological and the social; people are seen to be the result of both their nature and their nurture, and the interaction between the two. Though much of personality psychology shares the emphasis of recent psychology on cognition (i.e. ways of understanding), it is also concerned with feelings and emotions, and with the relationship between cognition and emotion. Finally, personality psychology is concerned both with basic theory and research about the nature of personality, but also with applications of that theory in clinical practice; personality psychology has always been characterised by a to-and-fro between theory and application.

The psychology of personality is thus concerned with a broad range of questions, including how people differ from one another in personality and temperament, how they cope with life changes and stresses, what psychological problems they may develop and how they respond to them, people's habitual styles of relating to others and their needs for particular kinds of social support, and patterns of personal growth and development. This is, in large measure, what many non-psychologists think of as 'psychology'. It is also a field of study that has had a central, integrative function within the discipline. One important source has been the clinical work with clients or patients. This provides many psychologists with an unrivalled opportunity to observe and get to know a wide range of people at a level of depth and intimacy that is seldom possible in other contexts.

While keeping contact with its clinical roots, the psychology of personality has generated a substantial body of formal empirical research to try to test its hypotheses. This has never been straightforward, but resourcefulness in personality research has increased with experience, and a fruitful dialogue has been possible between clinical observations and formal research findings. Personality psychology has also maintained links with advances in other areas of general psychology, including cognitive psychology, and has sought to cast its theories in a way that takes account of advances in the discipline of the whole.

It will readily be seen how the contents of this book reflect the breadth of personality psychology. The first section was concerned with religious aspects of personality, taking a psychological view of the spiritual life in general, of how religious life can help or hinder personality development, and of different ways of being religious. Having examined core aspects of religious personality in Part 1, Parts 2 to 4 were concerned with applications, including the range of different applications appropriate across the lifespan; and educational, counselling, social and organisational psychologies. The present book thus reflects the broadly integrative face of psychology seen in the study of personality rather than the restrictive face seen in reductionist movements of psychology.

It is important, once again, to emphasise the diversity both of psychological and of Christian views of human nature. This is one of the merits of Peter Morea's comparison of the two in *In Search of Personality* (1997). For example, Kierkegaard, that great Christian psychologist of the nineteenth century, takes an essentially developmental approach, with three key stages: the aesthetic, the ethical, and the religious. Within this framework, he identifies the obstacles to development, and the requirements of moving from one stage to the next. There are thus many points of contact between Kierkegaard's thinking about human nature and that of a developmental psychological theorist such as Erikson. Of course, that is not to say that they agree over everything, but there is enough common ground for dialogue to be fruitful.

Of twentieth-century Christian thinkers, Thomas Merton has reflected on human nature in a particularly fruitful way. In some ways, he is also a developmental theorist, though with an emphasis on the goal of development rather than on the starting point.

For Merton, in finding God, we find our true selves; in finding holiness we also find wholeness (see Finley 1978). Merton's Christian self-actualisation thus has much in common with the thinking of humanistic psychologists such as Maslow and Rogers. Though humanistic psychology has been much criticised for its assumptions (e.g. by Vitz 1979), Merton's thinking about human nature shows how humanistic assumptions can be turned in a Christian direction. Again, this is not to say that there is complete agreement about self-actualisation between a Christian thinker, such as Merton, and humanistic psychologists, but there is again scope for an interesting comparison.

The dominant paradigm in contemporary psychology is cognitive, with an emphasis on how human beings understand the world. One of the early popularisers of a cognitive approach to personality was George Kelly (1955), who talked about the 'personal constructs' with which particular people make sense of their world. It is a psychological approach, incorporating constructivist assumptions about human perception that are much indebted to Kant's epistemology. There are also theological approaches to human nature that are similarly indebted to Kant, that of Karl Rahner for example, which make good dialogue partners for cognitive personality theorists such as Kelly. Rahner's key move is to suggest that, in addition to the constructs with which we make sense of the material objects that exist within time and space, there are also *a priori* structures that enable us to approach the transcendent.

It would be fair to say that personality psychology has not yet achieved any coherent and generally accepted way of integrating the diverse aspects of personality with which it is concerned. The same could also be said of Christian thinking about human nature. Though there will no doubt be critical points of diversion between the two, it would be fruitful for them to proceed side by side much more than has been the case hitherto in their common quest for an adequate conceptualisation of human nature.

SUMMARY OF KEY THEMES

- The integrative nature of personality psychology.
- Combining understandings of shared human nature and individual difference; nature and nurture; thinking and feeling; theory and practice.
- The possibility of integrating personality psychology and Christian beliefs.
- Finding holiness and finding wholeness.

QUESTIONS TO CONSIDER

- When, in a pastoral context, is it helpful to emphasise to someone the ways in which we are all the same, and when is it best to focus on what makes them a unique individual?
- Is it helpful to think about whether a psychological problem's roots might lie in someone's 'nature' or their 'nurture'?
- What are the pros and cons of cognitive and emotional modes of engaging with the world? And with God?
- In what ways are your psychological ideas and your Christian ones most closely aligned?

Further reading

General

Gregersen, N. H., Drees, W. B. and Gorman, U. (eds) (2000) *The Human Person in Science and Theology*, Edinburgh: T & T Clark.
Holder, R. (1993) *Nothing But Atoms and Molecules? Probing the Limits of Science*, Tunbridge Wells: Monarch.
Ward, K. (1992) *Defending the Soul*, Oxford: Oneworld.

Psychoanalysis

Palmer, M. (1997) *Freud and Jung on Religion*, London: Routledge.
Webster, R. (1995) *Why Freud Was Wrong: Sin, Science, and Psychoanalysis*, London: Harper Collins.

Evolutionary psychology

Dawkins, R. (1989) *The Selfish Gene*, 2nd ed., Oxford: Oxford University Press.
Pinker, S. (1997) *How the Mind Works*, London: Allen Lane.
Ridley, M. (1997) *The Origins of Virtue*, London: Penguin.

Neuroscience

Brown, W., Murphy, N. and Malony, H. (eds) (1998) *Whatever Happened to the Soul? Scientific and Theological Portraits of Human Nature*, Minneapolis: Fortress Press.
Jeeves, M. (1997) *Human Nature at the Millennium: Reflections on the Integration of Psychology and Christianity*, Leicester: Apollos.
Searle, J. (1997) *The Mystery of Consciousness*, London: Granta.

Artificial intelligence

Copeland, J. (1993) *Artificial Intelligence: A Philosophical Introduction*, Oxford: Blackwell.
Puddefoot, J. (1996) *God and the Mind Machine: Computers, Artificial Intelligence, and the Human Soul*, London: SPCK.

Personality

Morea, P. (1997) *In Search of Personality: Christianity and Modern Psychology*, London: SCM Press.
Van Leeuwen, M. S. (1985) *The Person in Psychology: A Contemporary Christian Appraisal*, Leicester: Inter-Varsity Press.

15 Psychology and theology

Relating psychology and theology is a complex business. It will by now have become abundantly clear that psychology is itself a varied discipline encompassing many different approaches: social, cognitive, behavioural, developmental, psychoanalytic, and so on. Throughout this book we have insisted on taking a broad view of psychology, and will continue to do so in relating it to theology.

Theology is also a many-faceted discipline. The previous chapter focused on the area of theology that relates most closely to psychology, that is, how human nature is to be understood. However, there is much more to theology than this. Theology has long embraced several rather different strands, such as the study of the scriptures, the formulation of Christian doctrine, and the history of Christian life and thought. It is also a multi-disciplinary activity that brings a variety of disciplines, such as history, philosophy, and the study of languages and texts, to bear on a common theme. The range of disciplines that can usefully contribute to theology is probably in fact wider than is usually recognised. In recent years, there has been a growing recognition of the contribution of the social sciences and literature. In this chapter, we will suggest that psychology has a significant contribution to make to theology, alongside more accepted disciplines such as history and philosophy.

The next three sections will consider in turn the contribution of psychology to three core areas of theology: biblical studies, church history, and doctrine. We will then look in detail at one particular psychological approach, that associated with C. G. Jung, that interfaces with theology in a particularly rich way.

Psychological biblical criticism

Biblical studies has increasingly espoused a multidisciplinary approach and, in recent years, the sociological and literary approaches have become prominent. Since about 1970 there has also been a remarkable development of psychological contributions to the interpretation of the Bible, and Wayne Rollins (1999) has provided a helpful survey of what has been accomplished so far.

Nevertheless, the merits of psychological exegesis remain controversial. One of the most distinguished examples of the psychological approach to biblical studies so far is Gerd Theissen's *Psychological Aspects of Pauline Theology* (1987), but he felt it necessary to begin by summarising the charges levelled against psychological exegesis.

> Every exegete has learned that psychological exegesis is poor exegesis. It interpolates between the lines things that no–one can know. It inserts modern categories into ancient texts. Because of its interest in personal problems behind the text, it does not let the text come to speech. Above all, however, it relativises the text's theological claim through appeal to factors that are all too human. (1987:1).

Theissen helped to make it clear, by example, that psychological biblical criticism need not have all the weaknesses its critics allege, and he showed how it ought to be approached. First, the psychological approach to the Bible need not be an alternative to other, more traditional approaches to exegesis. For example, for each passage Theissen considered, he provided a careful text analysis and tradition analysis, before going on to the psychological analysis. Though some psychological studies of the Bible have displayed naiveté about the texts on which they are commentating, this is not a necessary feature of the approach.

There has also been a broadening of the range of psychological models used. Both Freud and Jung made contributions to the psychological interpretation of the Bible and for some time most psychological contributions were in one or other of these traditions. However, more recently, a broader range of approaches has been used, including behavioural, cognitive, and humanistic. Some examples of psychological exegesis have explicitly compared and integrated the contribution different psychological traditions can make to the elucidation of a particular text. Again, Theissen set a good example, in that he set out the contributions of learning theory, psychodynamic psychology, and cognitive psychology, for each passage studied. This kind of comparison of the contribution of different psychological approaches helps to prevent the simplistic or uncritical application of any single approach.

The range of psychological exegetical studies is now very broad, as Rollins (1999, Ch. 5) showed in his survey. There have been studies of how images and symbols are used in the Bible; for example the symbolic significance of water (e.g. Henry 1979). There have also been studies that have focused more on the mind of the author or narrator, such as the 'point of view' or unconscious processes of the writers of the Gospels (e.g. Newheart 1995). Many biblical personalities have now been the focus of psychological commentary, with Ezekiel and Paul attracting more attention than most. There have also been studies of religious experience in the Bible such as dreams, visions or conversion (e.g. Johnson and Malony 1982), and studies of how other more ordinary experiences such as anger (Johnes 1990) or temptation (Oates 1991) are handled in the Bible. There have also been studies of the implicit psychology of the Bible, such as concepts of the self, or the role of the heart in the Hebrew understanding of human nature.

Paul's account of his inner struggle in relation to the law in Romans 7 has frequently lent itself to psychological interpretation, and provides a good example of psychological exegesis. Psychological contributions to the interpretation of this chapter include Rubenstein (1972), Scroggs (1977) and Theissen (1987). The chapter is one in which Paul describes his previous relation to the law, and how that has changed in the context of Christ. It is thus a passage that at least seems to be autobiographical, though there has been controversy about that. The most plausible position is that Paul is presenting a general theory of transformation in Christ, but doing so in a way that draws on his own personal background.

One reason why this chapter has aroused particular psychological interest is that it seems to be describing a conflict and ambivalence in relation to the law. Though Paul regards the law as good in principle, he seems to have experienced himself as in bondage to it. This conflict may once have been repressed, but has become conscious. Paul is working here with a three-fold scheme of flesh, law, and Christ that seems somewhat analogous to the Freudian conceptualisation of mind in terms of id (basic instincts), super-ego (over-strict conscience), and ego (the centre of personality). It seems that Christ has enabled Paul to escape from the old conflict between flesh and law. Whereas the law was part of this problem, Christ has proved the solution to it. Looked at from a psychodynamic point of view, it seems that the Spirit of Christ has provided the resources needed to release Paul from his old conflicts. Looking at the passage more cognitively, it seems that Christ has resulted in a major restructuring of Paul's self-perception.

The hermeneutic process, or how the scriptures are read and interpreted, can also be elucidated from a psychological perspective. Again, Rollins (1999, Ch. 6), provides a helpful survey. One of the best-known contributions in this area is Cedric Johnson's 1983 *The Psychology of Biblical Interpretation*. One fruitful way into this area has been via personality types, looking at how different psychological types read and respond to particular biblical texts (e.g. Francis 1997). Though hermeneutics has been a very important aspect of biblical studies in recent years, the psychological contribution to the understanding of processes of reading and understanding has often not been fully appreciated.

Psychological biblical criticism is now a well-established field that can join literary, sociological, and other approaches within the increasingly interdisciplinary domain of biblical studies. By now, a substantial proportion of the Bible has been the subject of psychological study. The field has moved beyond the naiveties of some early examples, and there are now enough exemplary psychological studies of biblical texts for ground-rules to be established and standards set. Two key points are that the psychological contribution should be integrated with other approaches, not used in isolation; also that particular psychological approaches should be used critically, and with awareness of the range of possible psychological approaches to the Bible.

SUMMARY OF KEY THEMES

- How a psychological perspective can complement textual, historical, literary, and sociological perspectives on the Bible.
- The variety of different psychological perspectives that can be taken.
- The psychological interpretation of Paul's view of Christ and the law.

EXERCISE

Either on your own or in a study group, choose a piece of historical narrative, a prophecy, a psalm, a proverb, an allegory, a parable, or a miracle story from the Bible and think about:

- What it reveals about the psychology of the protagonists.
- What it reveals about the author's psychology.
- What psychological issues it raises for you the reader(s).
- What assumptions and values have influenced your reading of the passage.
- What different conclusions would be arrived at by taking Freudian, cognitive, or hermeneutic approaches to these questions.

Christian life and thought

Psychohistory is a relatively well-established area of interdisciplinary work, albeit a controversial one, so the application of psychology to the study of Christian life and thought can be set in a broader context. There are lessons to be learned from psychohistory about how psychology should and should not relate to other disciplines that can be applied to the interface between theology and psychology.

Psychohistory has been dominated by psychoanalytic approaches, stemming from Freud's essay on Leonardo, published in 1910, which was rapidly followed by many similar historical studies by other analysts (see Freud 1963). By the outbreak of the Second World War, psychological studies had been completed on a wide range of historical figures. There followed something of a fallow period, the renaissance of psychohistory being marked by Erik Erikson's study of Luther in 1958. While some have greeted psychohistory as a new dawn in historical studies, others have been strongly critical. Russell Stannard (1980) for example, has accused it of being 'characterised by a cavalier attitude toward fact, a contorted attitude toward logic, an irresponsible attitude toward theory validation, and a myopic attitude toward cultural difference and anachronisms'. Erikson's book on Luther has been a particular focus of controversy and Roger Johnson's (1977) collection of critical essays arising from it is a good reflection of the debate. For a more balanced survey of psychohistory, see Runyon ((ed.) 1988).

Psychoanalytic studies of historical figures such Augustine or Luther are methodologically much more problematic than the analysis of a living client. In the latter case, the refinement of theory is intertwined with the discovery of new facts as the analysis proceeds. Also, clients are involved as collaborators, and their reactions to interpretative hypotheses play an important role in guiding the development of the analysis. None of this is possible with historical figures, and there is a danger that factual claims will simply be 'derived' from the theory, but presented in a way that renders them indistinguishable from historically verifiable facts.

In fact, there is a wide gulf between the best and the worst work in psychohistory. Criticisms that can fairly be made of all too much of it do not necessarily apply to all. There is at least a limited amount of promising work that indicates that psychology is capable of making a careful and defensible contribution to the study of history. Though much psychohistory has used psychoanalytic psychology, other psychological approaches can be applied to historical studies, as to biblical studies. Psychology as a scientific discipline can fairly claim, contrary to Stannard's accusation, to be careful in basing itself on facts, to employ rigorous modes of argument, and to check the validity of hypotheses with care.

St Augustine is perhaps the most interesting example of a Christian subject of psychohistory, and Donald Capps and James Dittes (1990) have edited an excellent and varied series of studies. The *Confessions*, one of the first autobiographies of any kind, is obviously an intriguing document for the psychologist, and gives a remarkably rich indication of the kind of person Augustine was. For Augustine, there was obviously a very close link between his life and his theology, which is what led him to write the *Confessions* in the first place, so we can expect an enriched understanding of Augustine's life to enhance our understanding of his theology as well.

Some psychological work on Augustine has perhaps been over-dogmatic, for example seeing strong evidence of an Oedipal conflict, though the *Confessions* certainly raises the question of whether his strong relationship with his mother was ultimately constraining or liberating. Another interesting issue is the theme of self-reproach that is so pervasive in the *Confessions*, but seems not to be accompanied by a heartfelt sense of guilt. Capps has made sense of that by suggesting that what Augustine experienced was not so much guilt about his actions, but shame about himself (a distinction to which we will return later in this chapter.) It is also worth emphasising the range of psychological approaches that are potentially relevant to the study of the *Confessions*, such as the contribution of cognitive psychology to elucidating the strong emphasis on hearing and speaking that runs through the *Confessions*.

SUMMARY OF KEY THEMES

● The problems of psychoanalysing a figure from a past era.
● The examples of Luther and Augustine.
● The range of different psychological methods that can be applied to historical figures.

EXERCISE

Either on your own or in a study group, read St Augustine's *Confessions*, and then read some of the essays from Capps and Dittes (eds) (1990).

● How would you describe St Augustine psychologically?
● Can you empathise with his inner conflicts and struggles?
● How useful is a psychohistorical approach to a figure like Augustine?
● What different insights do Freudian and cognitive analyses of Augustine reveal?
● Is it anachronistic? Would a 'religious' reading be a better reading?
● Can 'religious' and psychological readings be combined?

Psychological approaches to Christian doctrine

Theology has always accorded a central place to 'systematic theology', the coherent formulation of Christian doctrine. It is intrinsic to the character of systematic theology that it seeks to reformulate Christian doctrine creatively in the context of contemporary thought, and for this reason it is something that every generation has to undertake afresh. For example, there is a strand of twentieth-century systematic theology that has been undertaken in the context of 'existentialist' thought. Feminist theology and liberation theology have also, in different ways, contributed to the reformulation of Christian doctrine in relation to particular lines of contemporary thought. In a similar way, there can be a psychological approach which seeks to reformulate Christian doctrine in relation to psychological thought. It again needs to be emphasised that this is not a matter of 'reducing' Christian belief to psychology.

Sadly, there have so far been relatively few good examples. Perhaps the only major systematic theologian of the twentieth century to have made extensive use of a psychological approach is Paul Tillich, who made use of Freudian psychology, both in his theological understanding of human nature and in his understanding of God. Psychoanalysis helped him to formulate the human predicament of sinfulness (see Tillich 1959) though he did not follow Freud at every point. However, it is in approaching a doctrine of God that Tillich is most fruitfully indebted to Freud (see Homans 1970; Perry 1988).

For Freud, as is well-known, God is a projection of the human mind; the God of religious belief is a 'transference-god'. Tillich, in The *Courage to Be* (1952), is happy to adopt much of Freud's critique of religion and to recognise that the God of traditional theism can often be a transference-god. However, rather than abandoning all

encounter with God, Tillich suggests that the proper human response is to have the courage to encounter the real God beyond this 'transference-god' of theology and religious belief. Freud's critique of religion is thus turned round and becomes an argument in favour of a negative or apophatic theology in which the key task is to unlearn inadequate conceptualisations of God.

Though the psychological contribution to systematics is less developed than it is to biblical criticism, the main lines of the required approach are clear. First, the psychological approach should be integrated with conventional approaches to systematics, rather than replacing them. One of the most explicit examples of this is William Meissner's (1987) approach to the doctrine of grace. He sets out a mainstream theology of grace, following people such as Rahner in emphasising the embeddedness of the grace of God in relationality. He then suggests that alongside the theology of grace there can be a psychological approach that analyses how the effects of grace work themselves out at a human level. His theological focus on relationality leads him to look to the psychology of 'object relations' development for his analysis of the human side of grace.

Second, it is clear that a variety of psychologies can contribute to systematic theology. The Jungian contribution is the best-developed, and will be considered shortly. However, considerable use has also been made of Freudian and Rogerian psychology. The psychology of emotions and attitudes also promises to be fruitful, and Fraser Watts (2000) has approached eschatology from the psychology of hope. Equally, the theology of sin can be approached from the psychology of shame and guilt (Capps 1993). So far, there does not seem to be any work on psychological systematic theology that has brought a variety of different psychological approaches to bear in an integrative way on a single theme in Christian doctrine. However, this is clearly desirable and is likely to be attempted before long.

The doctrine of the atonement is the topic in systematic theology that has lent itself most readily to psychological interpretation, and psychological approaches date back to Robert C. Moberly (1901). One reason for a focus on the atonement is that, though it starts from the divine initiative, it is also explicitly concerned with the transformation of human beings. Throughout Christian history a variety of different interpretations of the atonement have run concurrently. This invites interpretation in terms of the different psychological significance of alternative theories of the atonement. Among psychological approaches to the doctrine of the atonement, Paul Pruyser (1991) has approached it from Freudian psychology, and Don Browning (1966) has approached it from Rogerian psychology. Pruyser takes three classic theories of the atonement, the ransom, satisfaction, and moral example theories, and maps each of them on to a) the human emotions, and b) the components in the Freudian model of mind with which they are correlated.

Pruyser suggests that the ransom theory, that sees the death of Christ as the ransom paid by God to Satan to buy humanity back, has a special resonance for those who feel **anxiety** about uncontrollable, malign impulses. Such people are likely to be those who experience anxiety arising from the primitive impulses of the id. The ransom theory brings them assurance that there is deliverance from dark, near-uncontrollable forces.

Next, Pruyser suggests that the satisfaction theory, that sees the death of Christ as being offered to provide satisfaction to assuage God's righteous anger at humanity's rebellion, and to enable him to be merciful, has a particular resonance for those in whom **guilt** is a powerful emotion. Such people are likely to be those in whom the super-ego is strong and somewhat tyrannical. For them, the satisfaction theory brings the assurance that the price of guilt has been paid, releasing the fullness of God's forgiveness for wrongdoing.

Finally, the moral example theory, that sees Christ on the cross as an example of sacrificial love that transforms humanity by example, has a particular resonance for those whose predominant emotion is **shame**. Such people, will have a strong sense of discrepancy between the ego ideal and the ego. For them, the powerful example of love represented by Christ on the cross will be particularly moving and transforming.

This bald summary of Pruyser's mapping of theories of the atonement on to psychology overlooks some of the subtleties of his paper. It is perhaps a justifiable criticism that, for the purposes of mapping, he distinguishes different theories of the atonement too sharply. There are also specific points at which the mapping exercise seems less than satisfactory. For example, the ransom and satisfaction theories are seen as delivering humanity from anxiety and guilt respectively, whereas the moral example theory is seen as making use of shame to transform humanity rather than delivering humanity from it. Nevertheless, Pruyser has provided us with a path-breaking example of how to map different understandings of Christian doctrine on to psychological understandings of their human impact.

He goes on to raise, in an interesting way, the educational implications of this mapping. Having identified the understanding of the atonement that will speak most powerfully to a particular person, the question arises of whether or not it is best to focus on that theory. To do so may be the best way to enable the doctrine of the atonement to be 'heard' by that person. On the other hand, it may be that there is particular religious and psychological value in people learning to 'hear' understandings of the atonement to which they respond less readily.

Don Browning (1966) has undertaken a somewhat similar exercise, but from the perspective of Rogerian psychology. Like Pruyser, he begins by distinguishing the three classic theories of atonement as defeat of the Devil, the satisfaction of God's honour, and moral influence. Browning also provides a sophisticated advocacy for the analogical approach to theology involved in this kind of psychological mapping exercise, and shows how this does not undercut theological presuppositions. He shows how 'scientific analysis of certain concrete processes of healing which operate between human beings can engender analogies that can constitute a positive clarification of man's interpretation of the *a priori* perfection revealed in Christ' (p. 160).

Drawing on the Rogerian understanding of the core therapeutic conditions (see Chapter 10), Browning argues that the empathic acceptance and unconditional positive regard of the therapist provides a helpful analogy of the love of God shown on the cross. Sin is seen as analogous to 'incongruence' – absolutised values used to validate one's worth but that tend to prevent the full experience of contradictory values. Browning argues that both sin and incongruence involve an over-reliance on finite values for a sense of self-worth, and that absolutising these finite values leads to a sense of estrangement.

This then leads him to conceptualise the atonement in terms of deliverance from these finite values, a view that he believes has most in common with the classic theory, developed by Irenaeus, of atonement as defeat of the Devil. Browning also draws interesting analogies between Irenaeus and Rogerian therapy in how guilt is approached. In both cases, he argues, the problem is not objective guilt as such, but the subjective sense of bondage to it. These are just the key points from Browning's psychological–analogical approach to the doctrine of the atonement, but we hope they will be enough to show its potential fruitfulness.

More work is needed to explore just how many areas of Christian doctrine can be elucidated by this kind of psychological approach. The atonement is clearly one of the most fruitful areas to approach in this way. However, it is clear that the psychological approaches can be integrated with traditional systematics rather than replacing it. It is also clear that alternative psychological approaches can be employed, and that there is scope for critical discussion about which is the most fruitful in any particular context.

SUMMARY OF KEY THEMES

- Psychology as a perspective, like feminism or sociology, that can be applied to systematic theology.
- Combining understandings of human psychology with interpretations of scripture and doctrine.
- The different psychological attractions of different versions of the doctrine of the atonement.

QUESTIONS TO CONSIDER

- How could a psychological understanding of a member of your church help you to tailor doctrines in a way that made them easily accessible? Or in a way that was alien but challenging?
- Can you think of examples other than the atonement where a person's preferred way of understanding a text or doctrine can be partially understood in terms of their particular psychological make-up?

Jungian approaches to Christian doctrine

Though it is already clear that theology has a fruitful interface with various different psychological traditions, Jungian psychology has a particularly rich contribution to make to theology. That stems from several distinctive features of Jungian psychology: the importance that is attached to symbols, the concept of the 'collective' unconscious, which transcends purely individual psychology, and the tradition of interpreting psychological material such as dream symbolism in relation to a variety of cultural traditions.

One of the key questions to be asked about Jung's psychology of religion is how far it is reductionist, seeking simply to reduce religion to psychology. Jung does not seem to do that. Rather, he is engaged in a two-way mapping of clinical material on to a variety of forms of cultural life, including religion but also others such as alchemy. He feels he can understand religion better by relating it to mind, and equally that he can understand mind better by relating it to religious and other symbolic themes. It would be inappropriate to regard this two-way hermeneutic as mere psychological reductionism. Many theological commentators on Jung have argued that he should not have ventured into theology in the way that he did. However, such arguments often end up in the defeatist view that no human understanding of the subject matter of theology is possible at all. It is more fruitful to clarify the nature of the contribution that psychologists such as Jung can make to theology, than to argue that no such contribution should be attempted.

One of the most sustained and interesting theological engagements with Jung has been that of Victor White, seen in his two books, *God and the Unconscious* (1952), and *Soul and Psyche: An Inquiry into the Relationship of Psychotherapy and Religion* (1960). White entered into dialogue with Jung with enormous enthusiasm, and was the only theologian to be accepted as a friend and collaborator by Jung. However, their joint project threw up increasing disagreements. White became unhappy at how Jung handled the relationship between the God image and God himself, and was disturbed by some of the unorthodox movements in Christian thought apparent in Jung's *Answer to Job* (1952). The collaboration between White and Jung has been the subject of a detailed study by Lammers (1994).

Of more recent writers, Christopher Bryant (1983) is one of the most widely-read writers on the interface of Christianity and Jungian thought. Dourley (1995) has provided a careful study of Jung's critique of contemporary Christianity. Brown (1981) has written a careful philosophical study of the hermeneutic principles involved in Jung's approach to Christian doctrine. However, perhaps the most sustained and fruitful work on the interface of Jung and Christianity has come in the numerous books of Edward Edinger such as *Ego and Archetype* (1972). While faithful to Jungian thought, Edinger is, at some key points, less religiously unorthodox than Jung himself.

Most careful students of Jung's psychology of religion (e.g. Heisig 1979) have recognised the extent to which Jung's views evolved over time. His early views advanced little beyond the Freudian concept of God as a projection of the personal unconscious, though there are fragmentary pointers towards his later views. His first major and distinctive statement on religion comes in his Terry Lectures given in 1937; in these lectures Jung makes use of Rudolf Otto's concept of the 'numinous' and largely identifies religion with it. The religious function does not depend on creeds but is seen as the surrender to a superordinate factor or overriding principle. Jung then moves on to a more explicitly theological period in which his major essays on the Trinity and the Mass, both published in 1942, are the key texts. One of the clearest and most systematic statements on religion also comes from this period, 1944, though confusingly it is published under the title, *Introduction to the Religious and Psychological Problems of Alchemy*. Some years later there is his *Answer to Job* (1952), which develops earlier ideas in an increasingly maverick theological direction. There is so much development of views here that one cannot simply speak of Jung's 'psychology of religion'.

It will help in considering the Jungian approach to doctrine to look mainly at one particular aspect of Jungian psychology, namely the life journey that Jung calls 'individuation'. This can be seen as a transition from being centred on the ego, the centre of consciousness, to being centred on the Self, which is the whole personality, conscious and unconscious. The process of individuation also involves an integration of the shadow into the whole personality. Jung contrasts the 'persona' (or mask) and the 'shadow', the dark-concealed part of the personality, and repeatedly emphasises how disastrous it is to try to keep the dark side of our personality hidden. It is perhaps a failing to which religious people are particularly prone.

There is an interesting analogy between Jung's concept of individuation and the Christian concept of salvation, though of course the two are not identical. At the heart of Christian salvation history is the idea of God reaching out to redeem fallen humanity. At several points in the gospels, there is a strong emphasis on recovery of the lost, so that all will be complete. This parallels Jung's emphasis on gathering the shadow part of the personality into the wholeness of the Self. There is thus an analogy between the shadow side of personality and the Christian concept of human sinfulness. Jung's concept of the integration of shadow into wholeness is analogous to the Christian concept of the redemption of sinfulness.

Though this analogy deserves close examination, it might be objected that individuation is a purely psychological process, whereas salvation comes from God. However, on closer examination, there is less of a contrast here than at first appears. For Jung, the Self is as much beyond the ego as God is beyond humanity in Christian theology. Indeed, Jung is as emphatic about the limitations of the ego as any Christian preacher on the limitations of humanity. The ego cannot save itself; it needs to glimpse the Self beyond and to be humble enough to respond to the intimations of the Self.

But still, isn't God *really* beyond us, whereas the Self just *seems* to be beyond us? This raises difficult questions about the status of archetypes such as the Self in Jungian theory. Belonging as they do to the collective unconscious, there is a sense in which they really are beyond each individual person. Also, there is a close relationship between Self and God in Jungian thought. Jung is clear that, as a matter of empirical fact, there is an image of God in the psyche. This psychic image of God both represents the wholeness of personality, which is the Self, and facilitates the process of individuation. What remains ambiguous in Jungian thought is whether or not there is a metaphysical God beyond the image of God in the psyche, though Jung's general line is that that is not a matter for him as an empirical psychologist.

In the journey towards individuation, it is important that there should be a healthy 'axis' between the ego and the Self. The ego needs to be open to the Self, neither so crushed that it cannot raise its sights to the Self, nor so inflated that it falsely presumes to be the Self. This Jungian theme of avoiding the twin pitfalls of a crushed and inflated ego has many parallels in theological thought. The relationship between ego and Self can be seen as, in many ways, analogous to that between humanity and God. Just as the ego needs to avoid being either crushed or inflated, so humanity needs to avoid a concept of God which sees him as wholly transcendent or merely immanent. Maintaining a balance between immanence and transcendence is analogous to maintaining a healthy ego–Self axis.

Similarly, in eschatological thought, it is important to avoid the extremes of an eschatology in which the promised future is so completely realised already that is has no power to inspire hope, or is so distant that it makes no contact with the present (see Watts, 2000) There is a near-consensus that the appropriate way of thinking about the eschatological future is as 'inaugurated', partly here already, but not yet fully here. That involves maintaining a relationship between the present and the eschatological future that is analogous to that which obtains between ego and Self when there is a healthy axis between them.

The question of the shadow, referred to above, raises the related topic of evil. Though Jung seems to assume a close linkage between shadow and evil, it is a point about which he is less than clear. Alongside his emphasis on the integration of the shadow into the whole personality, there is a strong emphasis on the 'reality' of evil. He was repeatedly critical of the '*privatio boni*' doctrine of evil as an absence of goodness, on the grounds that it failed to do justice to the reality of evil. It is intriguing that Jung, a psychologist, has been as emphatic as any twentieth-century figure about the reality of evil, more so than most theologians. Indeed, Jung went so far as to expand the Trinity into a quaternity, including the Devil as a quadrant within the godhead. For this, he had been criticised for making illegitimate metaphysical extrapolations from psychological considerations (e.g. Burrell 1974). Indeed, Jung's concept of God is often highly anthropomorphic, and he is prone to assume that what is true of the human being psychologically is also true metaphysically of God.

This issue is very much to the fore in Jung's treatment of Christ. One can discern three different strands in Jungian thought here. First, and most straightforwardly, Christ is a symbol of the Self, and one that facilitates individuation. In addition, Jung sometimes extends the concept of individuation to humanity as a whole, and sees Christ as playing a central role in the individuation of humanity. Here the analogy with Christian salvation history becomes very close. Edinger (1972) has suggested that the fall corresponds to the birth of the conscious ego out of a previously undifferentiated psychic wholeness. For the first time, the ego realises that it is not the Self. This is consistent with the emphasis in the myth of the fall on Adam and Eve's new sense of the difference between good and evil, and of the difference between themselves and God. There was thus a separation between God and humanity analogous to the separation of the ego from the Self. In individuation, the necessary next stage is that the Self reaches out to the ego and, analogously, in Christian thought, God reaches out to humanity. The incarnation of God in Christ would be seen as the key step in this restoration of relationship between humanity and God, leading on to the possibility of eschatological wholeness.

PSST! YOUR SHADOW-SIDE IS SHOWING!!

There is yet another strand in Jung's thought about Christ which really only comes to prominence in his *Answer to Job*. Here Jung seems to be talking, in effect, about the individuation of God. He seems to see God as initially existing in a kind of undifferentiated wholeness. However, the creation of humanity in his own image marks a step in his 'individuation'. In his dealings with Job, God is seen as still at a fairly early stage of psychological development. On this view, with the birth of Christ, a separate centre of consciousness was established, of which the story of Christ's temptations in the wilderness, and his experience of desolation on the cross, are key markers. The remaining task was the integration of the opposites that had now been fully differentiated, and Jung sees the Spirit as the person of the Trinity in whom that reintegration occurs.

It will be clear that Jung's religious thought is often very heterodox. The question is whether it needed to be so. In fact, Jung's psychological framework could have been applied to theological ideas in a more orthodox way than he himself did, and the theological thought of Jungians such as Edinger is at a number of points more orthodox than Jung's own. It therefore seems justifiable to distinguish between the strangeness of Jung's own theological views and the potential of his psychological framework to elucidate the significance of theological concepts.

In appraising Jung's approach to religion, it is helpful to be aware of the philosophical influences on him (Clarke 1991). The influence of Kant and Hegel is marked, even though Jung is not in any way a systematic philosophical thinker. From Kant, he inherits epistemological assumptions that influence his views on the knowability of the archetypes, and especially on the knowability of God. To put things baldly, Kant assumed that things as we know them are human constructs, but behind them there are 'things in themselves' that we cannot know directly. This is one of the key influences on Jung's view that we can know the image of God in the psyche, but that we cannot know any 'God in himself' that might stand behind the image. From Hegel, he imbibed a number of key ideas including the importance of the reconciliation of opposites. Jung's disparaging remarks about Hegel should not be allowed to obscure the extent of his indebtedness to him.

Jung's view of religion needs to be understood against the background of his sense of the 'spiritual crisis' of contemporary humanity. It concerned him deeply that religious symbols no longer made any effective contact with the unconscious. Divorced from this, they had become void. The result was that people no longer understood what religious symbols were about. It is as though 'we see the cathedral but do not see what is under it, we do not know what a cathedral is, what religion is' (quoted in Dourley 1995: 27). From this came Jung's hostility to conventional religion, but also his concern to rehabilitate it so that it once more connected with the unconscious.

SUMMARY OF KEY THEMES

- Reasons why Jungian psychology is theologically fruitful:
  1 the importance of symbols
  2 the role of the collective unconscious
  3 the way dreams and other symbolic materials are related to religious traditions.
- Jungian individuation and Christian salvation.
- The Jungian shadow and human sinfulness.
- The ego, the Self and God.
- Jung's idea of a 'quaternity'.
- Applying Jung's psychological framework to theology doesn't necessitate agreeing with his heterodox beliefs.

QUESTIONS TO CONSIDER

- How close is the similarity between the salvation of humanity and personal individuation? Make a balance sheet of the similarities and differences.
- Can Jungian psychology enrich the church's understanding of Christ?
- How far are Jungian contributions consistent with more traditional approaches?

Conclusion

Psychology still tends to be regarded with suspicion in many theological circles, and has been welcomed less readily than the social sciences. However, this suspicion of psychology usually arises from misunderstandings about the nature of the discipline. Sometimes, there is a limited understanding of the nature of psychology, and a failure to appreciate its range, scope, and critical rigour. Sometimes there is a view that the gospel is social, whereas psychology is incorrigibly individualistic – but that is to ignore the fact that psychology includes social psychology which is well aware of the social context of psychological processes. Sometimes, there is a fear that if theology engages with psychology it will result in theology somehow disappearing into psychology without remainder – but that is to ignore the scope for there to be a dialogue of mutual respect between two independent disciplines. Sometimes there is the suspicion that psychology, because it is not explicitly religious must be implicitly atheist – but that is to fail to appreciate the extent to which the modern sciences simply bracket out religious questions, without taking a position one way or the other. These suspicions will, in the end, only be overcome by models of good practice. We hope that in this chapter we have given sufficient indication of the fruitful and defensible contribution psychology is beginning to make to theology to encourage more such contributions in the future.

In particular, we hope that this chapter will help ministers who are teaching the Christian faith to do so with a more acute sense of how it will be received at a human level. It is not a matter of 'trimming' the Gospel to fit modern psychology. On the contrary, we suggest that if ministers try to teach the faith in a way that is both doctrinally sound and psychologically helpful, they will find that the two criteria generally lead them in the same direction. Having a more acute ear for how the faith will be 'heard' at a human level can only enhance the effectiveness with which it is communicated.

Further reading

General

Fleck, J. R. and Carter, J. D. (1981) (eds) *Psychology and Christianity: Integrative Readings*, Nashville: Abingdon.

Biblical studies

Rollins, W. G. (1999) *Soul and Psyche: The Bible in Psychological Perspective*, Minneapolis: Fortress Press.
Theissen, G. (1987) *Psychological Aspects of Pauline Theology*, Philadelphia: Fortress Press.

Christian life and thought

Capps, D. and Dittes, J. E. (1990) (eds) *The Hunger of the Heart: Reflections on the Confessions of Augustine*, West Lafayette: Society of the Scientific Study of Religion.
Johnson, R. A. (ed.) (1977) *Psychohistory and Religion: The Case of Young Man Luther*, Philadelphia: Fortress Press.

Doctrine

Malony, H. N. and Spilka, B. (1991) (eds) *Religion in Psychodynamic Perspective: The Contribution of Paul W. Pruyser*, New York: Oxford University Press.
Meissner, W. W. (1987) *Life and Faith*, Georgetown: Georgetown University Press.
Tillich, P. (1952) *The Courage To Be*, London: Nisbett.

Jung

Bryant, C. (1983) *Jung and the Christian Way*, London: Darton, Longman and Todd.
Edinger, E. (1972) *Ego and Archetype: Individuation and the Religious Function of the Psyche*, New York: Putnam's.
Moore, R. L. (1988) *Carl Jung and Christian Spirituality*, New York: Paulist Press.
Palmer, M. (1997) *Freud and Jung on Religion*, London: Routledge.

Afterword

We want this book to be useful to those engaged in ministry. However, we don't intend it to be a 'cookbook', telling them exactly what to do. Neither do we imagine that every Christian minister who reads this book will turn into a psychologist. Rather, we hope it will broaden the horizons of ministers, making them aware of the psychological issues that arise at almost every turn in their work.

Ministry needs to be approached at various different levels, religious and human (including the psychological). Our hope and plea is that ministers will become more aware of the psychological issues and perspectives raised by what they are doing. Whether they are giving personal advice, preaching, devising a special service, or planning a church initiative, there are always human issues about how people will hear, receive, and respond to their ministerial efforts. Psychology can help ministers to be more alert to the human aspects of their work, and suggest ways of working that might be more fruitful.

It is worth reiterating here what we said at the outset, that we have no wish to reduce ministry to a mere matter of psychology. We do not even wish ministers to attend to psychological considerations more than theological ones. Our experience has been that there is simply no conflict here. Forms of ministry that are appropriate and skilled at the psychological level tend to serve God's purposes better and to be preferable theologically too. For example, preaching that uses psychology to enhance awareness of how people are hearing what is said will tend to be better preaching from every point of view. We encourage our readers to test this for themselves. We think that they will find that broader psychological horizons will equip them to be better agents of the Christian gospel.

Bibliography

Abraham, K. (1981) 'The Influence of Cognitive Conflict on Religious Thinking in Fifth and Sixth Grade Children', *Journal of Early Adolescence* 1, 2: 147–154.

Adair, J. (1988) *Effective Leadership: How to Develop Leadership Skills*, London: Pan.

Allport, G. W. (1950) *The Individual and His Religion: A Psychological Interpretation*, New York: Macmillan.

Allport, G. W. and Ross, J. M. (1967) 'Personal Religious Orientation and Prejudice', *Journal of Personality and Social Psychology* 5, 4: 432–443.

Anderson, N. T. (1992) *Victory over the darkness: Realizing the power of your identity in Christ*, Tunbridge Wells: Monarch.

Asch, S. E. (1951) 'Effects of Group Pressure on the Modification and Distortion of Judgments' in H. Guetzkow (ed.) *Groups, Leadership and Men*, Pittsburgh: Carnegie.

Asch, S. E. (1956) 'Studies of Independence and Conformity: A Minority of One Against a Majority', *Psychological Monographs* 70: Whole No. 416.

Assagioli, R. (1965) *Psychosynthesis: A Manual of Principles and Techniques*, New York: Hobbs, Dorman, and Co.

Atkinson, M. (1984) *Our Masters' Voices*, London: Routledge.

Axline, V. (1947) *Play Therapy: The Inner Dynamics of Childhood*, Boston: Houghton Mifflin.

Baker, A. (1972) *Holy Wisdom or Directions for the Prayer of Contemplation*, Wheathampstead: Anthony Clarke Books.

Banyard, P. (1996) *Applying Psychology to Health*, London: Hodder and Stoughton.

Barfield, O. (1957) *Saving the Appearances: A Study in Idolatry*, London: Faber and Faber.

Barker, E. (1989) *New Religious Movements: A Practical Introduction*, London: HMSO.

Baron, R. & Greenberg, J. (1990) *Behaviour in Organizations* 3rd ed., London: Allyn & Bacon

Barr, J. (1981) *Fundamentalism*, 2nd ed., London: SCM Press.

Batson, C. D. and Ventis, W. L. (1982) *The Religious Experience: A Social-Psychological Perspective*, Oxford: Oxford University Press.

Batson, C. D., Schoenrade, P. and Ventis, W. L. (1993) *Religion and the Individual: A Social-Psychological Perspective*, Oxford: Oxford University Press.

Bebbington, D. W. (1989) *Evangelicalism in Modern Britain: A History from the 1730s to the 1980s*, London: Unwin Hyman.

Beck, A. T., Rush, A. J., Shaw, B. F., and Emery, G. (1979) *Cognitive Therapy of Depression*, New York: Guilford Press.

Beit-Hallahmi, B. (1986) 'Religion as Art and Identity', *Religion* 16: 1–17.

Beloff, J. (1973) *Psychological Sciences: A Review of Modern Psychology*, London: Crosby, Lockwood, Staples.

Benner, D. (1988) *Psychotherapy and the Spiritual Quest: Exploring the Links Between Psychological and Spiritual Health*, London: Hodder & Stoughton.

Berger, P (1967) *The Social Reality of Religion*, London: Faber & Faber.

Berryman, J. W. (1991) *Godly Play: An Imaginative Approach to Religious Education*, San Francisco: HarperSanFrancisco.

Bettelheim, B. (1978) *The Uses of Enchantment: The Meaning and Importance of Fairy Tales*, Harmondsworth: Penguin.

Bower, T. (1989) *The Rational Infant: Learning in Infancy*, New York: Freeman.

Brierley, P. (ed.) (1999) *UK Christian Handbook of Religious Trends 2000/2001 No. 2*, London: HarperCollinsReligious.

Briggs Myers, I. (1976) *Introduction to Type*, Oxford: Psychologists Press.

Bringle, M. (1990) *Despair: Sickness or Sin? Hopelessness and Healing in the Christian Life*, Nashville: Abingdon Press.

Brown, C. (1981) *Jung's Hermeneutic of Doctrine: Its Theological Significance*, Chico, CA: Scholars Press.

Brown, G. and Harris, T. (1978) *Social Origins of Depression: A Study of Psychiatric Disorder in Women*, London: Tavistock Publications.

Brown, L. B. (1994) *The Human Side of Prayer: The Psychology of Praying*, Birmingham, Alabama: Religious Education Press.

Brown, R. (1988) *Group Processes: Dynamics Within and Between Groups*, Oxford: Blackwell.

Brown, W., Murphy, N. and Malony, H. (eds) (1998) *Whatever Happened to the Soul? Scientific and Theological Portraits of Human Nature* Minneapolis: Fortress Press.

Browning, D. S. (1966) *Atonement and Psychotherapy*, Philadelphia: Westminster Press.

Browning, D. S. (ed.) (1983) *Religious Ethics and Pastoral Care*, Philadelphia: Fortress Press.

Bruner, J. S. (1966) *Toward a Theory of Instruction*, New York: Norton.

Bryant, C. (1983) *Jung and the Christian Way*, London: Darton, Longman and Todd.

Burns, S. (1996) 'Abuse and Forgiveness – Theological and Psychological Aspects', unpublished M.Litt. Thesis, University of Cambridge.

Burrell, D. (1974) *Exercises in Religious Understanding*, Notre Dame, IN: University of Notre Dame Press.

Buttrick, D. (1987) *Homiletic: Moves and Structures*, London: SCM Press.

Campbell, A. (1986) *The Gospel of Anger*. London: SPCK.

Capps, D. (1982) 'The psychology of petitionary prayer', *Theology Today* 39: 130–141.

Capps, D. (1993) *The Depleted Self: Sin in a Narcissistic Age*, Minneapolis: Fortress Press.

Capps, D. and Browning, D. (eds) (1983) *Life Cycle Theory and Pastoral Care*, Philadelphia: Fortress Press.

Capps, D. and Dittes, J. (eds) (1990) *The Hunger of the Heart: Reflections on the Confessions of Augustine*, West Lafayette, IN: Society for the Scientific Study of Religion.

Carrell, L. (2000) *The Great American Sermon Survey: The Inside Scoop on What Preachers and their Listeners Really Think*, Wheaton, IL: Mainstay Church Resources.

Carver, C., Scheier, M. and Weintraub, J. (1989) 'Assessing Coping Strategies: A Theoretically Based Approach', *Journal of Personality and Social Psychology* 56: 267–283.

Casement, P. (1985) *On Learning From the Patient*, London: Tavistock.

Cavalletti, S. (1983) *The Religious Potential of the Child*, New York: Paulist Press.

Cavalletti, S., Coulter, P., Gobbi, G. and Montanaro, S. (1994) *The Good Shepherd and the Child: A Joyful Journey*, New Rochelle, NY: Don Bosco Multimedia.

Christian, C. (ed.) (1991) *In the Spirit of Truth: A Reader in the Work of Frank Lake*, London: Darton, Longman and Todd.

Church of England (2000) *A Time to Heal: A Contribution to the Ministry of Healing*, London: Church House Publishing.

Clarke, J. (1991) *In Search of Jung: Historical and Philosophical Enquiries*, London: Routledge.

Clebsch, W. and Jaekle, C. (1983) *Pastoral Care in Historical Perspective*, 2nd ed., New York: Aronson.

Coate, M. (1989) *Clergy Stress: The Hidden Conflicts of Ministry*, London: SPCK.

Cochrane, R. (1983) *The Social Creation of Mental Illness*, Harlow: Longman.

Coe, G. A. (1916) *The Psychology of Religion*, Chicago: University of Chicago Press.

Coles, R. (1992) *The Spiritual Life of Children*, London: Harper Collins.

Cook, C. M. and Persinger, M. A. (1997) 'Experimental induction of the "sensed presence" in normal subjects and an exceptional subject', *Perceptual and Motor Skills*, 85: 683–693.

Copeland, J. (1993) *Artificial Intelligence: A Philosophical Introduction* Oxford: Blackwell.

Covey, S. (1992) *Principle-Centred Leadership*, London: Simon and Schuster.

Craig, Y. (1994) *Learning For Life*, London: Mowbray.

Crick, F. (1992) *The Astonishing Hypothesis: The Scientific Search for the Soul*, London: Simon and Schuster.

Dansereau, G., Graen, G. and Haga, B. (1975) 'A Vertical Dyad Linkage Approach to Leadership Within Formal Organizations: A Longitudinal Investigation of the Role Making Process', *Organizational Behaviour and Human Performance* 13: 45–78.

d'Aquili, E. and Newberg, A. (1998) 'The Neuropsychology of Religion', in F. Watts (ed.) *Science Meets Faith*, London: SPCK.

d'Aquili, E. and Newberg, A. (1999) *The Mystical Mind: Probing the Biology of Religious Experience*, Minneapolis: Fortress Press.

Davey, J. (1995) *Burnout: Stress in the Ministry*, Leominster: Gracewing.

Dawkins, R. (1989) *The Selfish Gene*, 2nd ed., Oxford: Oxford University Press.

Deaux, K. and Wrightsman, L. (1988) *Social Psychology*, 5th ed., Pacific Grove, CA: Brooks/Cole.

Dennett, D. (1995) *Darwin's Dangerous Idea: Evolution and the Meanings of Life*, London: Allen Lane.

Dewe, P. (1987) 'New Zealand ministers of religion: identifying sources of stress and coping processes', *Work and Stress* 1: 351–364.

Di Giacomo, J (1980) 'Intergroup Alliances and Rejections Within a Protest Movement: Analysis of the Social Representations', *European Journal of Social Psychology* 10: 329–344.

Dixon, T. (1999) 'Theology, Anti-Theology, and Atheology: From Christian Passions to Secular Emotions', *Modern Theology* 15: 297–330.

Dixon, T. (in press) 'The Psychology of the 'Emotions' in Britain and America in the Nineteenth Century: The Role of Religious and Anti-Religious Commitments', *Osiris*. 16.

Dobson, J. (1986) 'Learning From our Weaknesses', *Fundamentalist Journal* 5, 4: 12.

Donaldson, M. (1992) *Human Minds*, Harmondsworth: Penguin.

Dourley, J. (1995) *Jung and the Religious Alternative: The Rerooting*, Lampeter: Edwin Mellen.

Dreyfus, H. and Dreyfus, S. (1986) *Mind Over Machine*, Oxford: Blackwell.

Edelman, G. (1992) *Bright Air, Brilliant Fire: On the Matter of Mind*, London: Penguin.

Edinger, E. (1972) *Ego and Archetype: Individuation and the Religious Function of the Psyche*, New York: Putnams.

Elliott, C. (1995) *Memory and Salvation*, London: Dartman, Longman and Todd.

Ellison, C. (1994) 'Religion, Life, Stress and Depression', in J. Levin (ed.) *Religion in Aging and Health*, London: Sage, pp. 78–121.

Enright, R. D., Freedman, S. and Rique, J. (1998) 'The Psychology of Interpersonal Forgiveness' in R. D. Enright and J. North (eds) *Exploring Forgiveness*, Madison, Wis.: University of Wisconsin Press.

Erikson, E. (1958) *Young Man Luther: A Study in Psychoanalysis and History*, London: Faber.

Erikson, E. (1959) 'Identity and the life cycle: Selected papers', *Psychological Issues* 1: Whole Issue.

Erikson, E. (1977) *Toys and Reasons: Stages in the Ritualisation of Experience*, New York: Norton.

Faber, H. (1976) *Psychology of Religion*, London: SCM Press.

Festinger, L. (1957) *A Theory of Cognitive Dissonance*, Stanford: Stanford University Press.

Festinger, L., Riecken, L. and Schachter, S. (1956) *When Prophecy Fails*, Minneapolis: Minneapolis University Press.

Fetz, R. and Reich, H. (1989) 'Worldviews and Religious Development', *Journal of Empirical Theology* 2: 46–59.

Fichter, J. (1984) 'The Myth of Clergy Burnout', *Sociological Analysis* 45: 373–382.

Fiedler, F. (1967) *A Theory of Leadership Effectiveness*, New York: McGraw-Hill.

Finley, J. (1978) *Merton's Palace of Nowhere: A Search for God through Awareness of the True Self*, Notre Dame, IN.: Ave Maria Press.

Finney, J. (1992) *Finding Faith Today: How Does it Happen?*, Swindon: Bible Society.

Fleischman, P. (1990) *The Healing Spirit: Case Studies in Religion and Psychotherapy*, London: SPCK.

Fletcher, B. (1990) *Clergy Under Stress: A Study of Homosexual and Heterosexual Clergy*, London: Mowbray.

Forman, R. (1990) *The Problem of Pure Consciousness*, New York: Oxford University Press.

Fowler, J. W. (1981) *Stages of Faith: The Psychology of Human Development and the Quest for Meaning*, San Francisco: Harper and Row.

Francis, L. (1992) 'Christianity Today: The Teenage Experience', in J. Astley and D. Day (eds) *Contours of Christian Education*, Great Wakering: McCrimmons.

Francis, L. (1997) *Personality Type and Scripture: Exploring Mark's Gospel*, London: Mowbray.

Francis, L. and Brown, L. (1991) 'The Influence of Home, Church, and School on Prayer Among Sixteen Year Old Adolescents in England', *Review of Religious Research* 33: 112–122.

Francis, L. and Jones, S. (eds) (1996) *Psychological Perspectives on Christian Ministry: A Reader*, Leominster: Gracewing.

Francis, L. and Musson, D. (1999) 'Male and Female Anglican Clergy: Gender Reversal on the 16 PF?', *Journal of Empirical Theology* 12: 5–16.

Francis, L. and Rodger, R. (1996) 'The Influence of Personality on Clergy Role Prioritisation, Role Influences, Conflict, and Dissatisfaction with Ministry' in L. Francis and S. Jones (eds) *Psychological Perspectives on Christian Ministry: A Reader*, Leominster: Gracewing.

Fraser, C. (1971) 'Group Risk-Taking and Group Polarisation', *European Journal of Social Psychology* 1: 493–510.

Freud, S. (1927/1964) *The Future of an Illusion*, New York: Doubleday.

Freud, S. (1963) *Leonardo da Vinci: A Memory of his Childhood*, trans. A. Tyson, Harmondsworth: Penguin.

Gardner, H. (1997) *Leading Minds: An Anatomy of Leadership*, London: Harper Collins.

Garvey, C. (1977) *Play*, Cambridge, MA: Harvard University Press.

Gibson, H. (1994) 'Adolescents' Images of God', *Panorama* 6, 1: 103–114.

Glock, C.Y. (1962) 'On the study of religious commitment', *Religious Education* 57 (4, Res. Suppl.): 98–110.

Glock, C. and Stark, R. (1965) *Religion and Society in Tension*, Chicago: Rand McNally.

Goldman, R. (1964) *Religious Thinking From Childhood To Adolescence*, London: Routledge and Kegan Paul.

Goldman, R. (1965) *Readiness for Religion: A Basis for Developmental Religious Education*, London: Routledge and Kegan Paul.

Gordon, H. (1997) 'Guilt: Why is it such a burden?', *Baptist Times* 18/25 December 1997.

Grainger, R. (1988a) *The Message of the Rite: The Significance of Christian Rites of Passage*, Cambridge: Lutterworth Press.

Grainger, R. (1988b) *The Unburied*, Worthing: Churchman.

Grainger, R. (1993) *Change to Life: The Pastoral Care of the Newly Retired*, London: Darton, Longman and Todd.

Gulliford, E. (1999) 'Theological and psychological aspects of forgiveness', unpublished M.Phil. Thesis, University of Cambridge.

Hammond, J., Hay, D., Moxon, J., Netto, B., Raban, K., Straugheir, G. and Williams, C. (1990) *New Methods in R. E. Teaching: An Experiential Approach*, London: Oliver and Boyd/ Longmans.

Hardy, J. (1987) *A Psychology with a Soul: Psychosynthesis in Evolutionary Context*, London: Routledge and Kegan Paul.

Harvey, N. (1985) *Death's Gift: Chapters on Resurrection and Bereavement*, London: Epworth Press.

Hay, D. (1990) *Religious Experience Today: Studying the Facts*, London: Mowbray.

Hay, D. and Nye, R. (1998) *The Spirit of the Child*, London: Fount.

Heisig, J. (1979) *Imago Dei: A Study of C. G. Jung's Psychology of Religion*, Lewisburg, PA: Bucknell University Press.

Heller, D. (1986) *The Children's God*, Chicago: University of Chicago Press.

Henry, P. (1979) *New Directions in New Testament Study*, Philadelphia: Westminster Press.

Herbert, M. (1988) *Working With Children and Their Families*, London: British Psychological Society and Routledge.

Hillman, J. (1975) *Re-visioning Psychology*, New York: Harper and Row.

Hillman, J. (1976) 'Peaks and Vales: The Soul/Spirit Distinction as Basis for the Differences between Psychotherapy and Spiritual Discipline', in J. Needleman and D. Lewis (eds) *On the Way to Self-Knowledge*, New York: Knopf.

Hinkel, S., and Brown, R. (1990) 'Intergroup Comparisons and Social Identity: Some Links and Lacunae', in D. Abrams and M. Hogg (eds) *Social Identity Theory: Constructive and Critical Advances*, Hemel Hempstead: Harvester Wheatsheaf.

Homans, G. (1950) *The Human Group*, New York: Harcourt Brace.

Homans, G. (1974) *Social Behaviour: Its Elementary Forms*, rev. ed., New York: Harcourt Brace.

Homans, P. (1970) *Theology After Freud: An Interpretive Inquiry*, Indianapolis: Bobbs-Merrill.

Honey, P. and Mumford, A. (1992) *The Manual of Learning Styles*, 3rd ed., Maidenhead: Peter Honey.

Hood, R., Spilka, B., Hunsberger, B. and Gorsuch, R. (1996) *The Psychology of Religion: An Empirical Approach*, London: Guilford Press.

Hopewell, J. (1987) *Congregation: Stories and Structures*, Philadelphia: Fortress Press.

Howard, R. (1996) *The Rise and Fall of the Nine O'Clock Service: A Cult Within the Church?*, London: Mowbray.

Howard, R. (1997) *Charismania: When Christian Fundamentalism Goes Wrong*, London: Mowbray.

Hughes, A. (1999) 'Research exercise on applications of the psychological study of religion', unpublished MPhil Thesis, University of Cambridge.

Hull, J. (1985) *What prevents Christian Adults from Learning?*, London: SCM Press.

Hull, J. (1990) *God-Talk With Young Children: Notes for Parents and Teachers*, Birmingham: University of Birmingham; Derby: Christian Education Movement.

Hunsberger, B., Alisat, S., Pancer, M. S. and Pratt, M. (1996) 'Religious fundamentalism and religious doubts: Content, connections, and complexity of thinking', *International Journal for the Psychology of Religion* 6, 3: 201–220.

Hunsberger, B. and Brown, L. (1984) 'Religious socialization, apostasy, and the impact of family background', *Journal for the Scientific Study of Religion* 23: 239–251.

Hunsinger, D. (1995) *Theology and Pastoral Counselling*, Grand Rapids: Eerdmans.

Hurding, R. F. (1998) *Pathways to Wholeness: Pastoral Care in a Postmodern Age*, London: Hodder and Stoughton.

Innes, R. (1996) *Personality Indicators and the Spiritual Life*, Cambridge: Grove.

Irvine, A. (1997) *Between Two Worlds: Understanding and Managing Clergy Stress*, London: Mowbray.

Jacobs, M. (1988) *Psychodynamic Counselling in Action*, London: Sage.

Jacobs, M. (1991) *Insight and Experience: A Manual of Training in the Technique and Theory of Psychodynamic Counselling and Therapy*, Milton Keynes: Open University Press.

Jacobs, M. (1993) *Living Illusions: A Psychology of Belief*, London: SPCK.

Janis, I. (1972) *Victims of Groupthink: A Psychological Study of Foreign-Policy Decisions and Fiascoes*, Boston, MA: Houghton Mifflin.

Jeeves, M. (1997) *Human Nature at the Millennium: Reflections on the Integration of Psychology and Christianity*, Leicester: Apollos.

Johnes, B. H. (1990) 'Anger: Psychological and Biblical Perspectives', unpublished thesis, Colorado State University.

Johnson, C. (1983) *The Psychology of Biblical Interpretation*, Grand Rapids, MI: Zondervan.

Johnson, C. and Malony, H. N. (1982) *Christian Conversion: Biblical and Psychological Perspectives*, Grand Rapids, MI: Zondervan.

Johnson, R. A. (ed.) (1977) *Psychohistory and Religion: The Case of Young Man Luther*, Philadelphia: Fortress Press.

Jones, C., Wainright, G. and Yarnold, E. (1986) *The Study of Spirituality*, London: SPCK.

Jung, C. G. (1944/1953) *Psychology and Alchemy* in H. Read, M. Fordham, and G. Adler (eds) *Collected Works of C. G. Jung* vol. 12, London: Routledge and Kegan Paul.

Jung, C. G. (1952/1964) *Answer to Job*, trans. R.F.C. Hull. London: Hodder & Stoughton.

Jung, C. G. (1958) 'Transformation Symbolism in the Mass', in *Collected Works* vol. 11 *Psychology and Religion: West and East*, trans. R.F.C. Hull, London: Routledge and Kegan Paul.

Kegan, R. (1982) *The Evolving Self: Problem and Process in Human Development*, Cambridge, MA: Harvard University Press.

Keirsey, D. and Bates, M. (1978) *Please Understand Me: Character and Temperament Types*, 3rd ed., Del Mar, CA: Prometheus Nemesis.

Kelley, H. H. and Thibaut, J. W. (1978) *Interpersonal Relations: A Theory of Interdependence*. Chichester, Wiley.

Kelly, G. (1955) *The Psychology of Personal Constructs*, New York: Norton.

Kilmann, R. H. and Thomas, K. W. (1977) 'Developing a forced-choice measure of conflict-handling behavior: The "MODE" instrument', *Educational and Psychological Measurement*, 37: 309–325.

Kirk, M. and Leary, T. (1994) *Holy Matrimony? An Exploration of Ministry and Marriage*, Oxford: Lynx.

Kirkpatrick, L. A. and Shaver, P. R. (1990) 'Attachment theory and religion: Childhood attachments, religious beliefs, and conversion', *Journal for the Scientific Study of Religion* 29, 3: 315–334.

Koenig, H. (1994) 'Religion and Hope for the Disabled Elder', in J. Levin (ed.) *Religion in Aging and Health*, London: Sage, pp. 18–51.

Kolb, D. A. and Frey, R. (1975) 'Towards an applied theory of experiential learning', in C. L. Cooper (ed.), *Theories of Group Processes*, New York: Wiley.

Kubler-Ross, E (1970) *On Death and Dying*, New York: Macmillan.

Kubler-Ross, E. (1975) *Death, the Final Stage of Growth*, Englewood Cliffs, NJ: Prentice Hall.

Kuhn, M. H. and McPartland, T. (1954) 'An Empirical Investigation of Self-Attitudes', *American Sociological Review* 19: 68–76.

Lake, F. (1966) *Clinical Theology*, London: Darton, Longman and Todd.

Lake, F. (1981) *Tight Corners in Pastoral Counselling*, London: Darton, Longman and Todd.

Lammers, A. (1994) *In God's Shadow: The Collaboration of Victor White and C. G. Jung*, New York: Paulist Press.

Lash (1988) *Easter in Ordinary: Reflections on Human Experience and the Knowledge of God*, Notre Dame: Notre Dame University Press.

Latané, B., Williams, K. and Harkins, S. (1979) 'Many Hands Make Light the Work: The Causes and Consequences of Social Loafing', *Journal of Personality and Social Psychology* 37: 822–832.

Lawrence, D. H. (1972) *Selected Poems*, ed. K. Sagar, London: Penguin.

Lazarus, R. (1966) *Psychological Stress and the Coping Process*, New York: McGraw-Hill.

Leas, S. (1985) *Moving Your Church Through Conflict*, Washington, DC: Alban Institute.

Leavitt, H. J. (1951) 'Some Effects of Certain Communication Patterns on Group Performance', *Journal of Abnormal and Social Psychology* 46: 38–50.

LeDoux, J. (1996) *The Emotional Brain: The Mysterious Underpinnings of Emotional Life*, New York: Simon and Schuster.

Lee, R. S. (1955) *Psychology and Worship*, London: SCM Press.

Leech, K. (1994) *Soul Friend: Spiritual Direction in the Modern World*, rev. ed., London: Darton, Longman and Todd.

Levin, J. (ed.) (1994) *Religion in Aging and Health*, London: Sage.

Levine, S. (1999) 'Children's Cognition as the Foundation of Spirituality', *International Journal of Children's Spirituality* 4: 121–140.

Loewenthal, K. (1995) *Mental Health and Religion*, London: Chapman and Hall.

Lofland, J. and Skonovd, N. (1979) 'Conversion motifs', *Journal for the Scientific Study of Religion* 18: 419–423.

Lonergan, B. (1958) *Insight: A Study of Human Understanding*, London: Longmans.

Lyall, D. (1995) *Counselling in the Pastoral and Spiritual Context*, Milton Keynes: Open University Press.

Mace, D. and Mace, V. (1980) *What's Happening to Clergy Marriages?*, Nashville: Abingdon.

Mader, S. T. (1986) 'Depression as loneliness in post-generative women: A crisis of faith development', unpublished PhD Dissertation, University of Boston.

Malan, D. (1979) *Individual Psychotherapy and the Science of Psychodynamics*, London: Butterworth.

Malony, H. N. (1995) *The Psychology of Religion for Ministry*, New Jersey: Paulist Press.

Malony, H. N. and Hunt, R. (1991) *The Psychology of Clergy*, Harrisburg, PA: Morehouse Publishing.

Malony, H. N. and Lovekin, A. A. (1985) *Glossolalia: Behavioral Science Perspectives on Speaking in Tongues*, Oxford: Oxford University Press.

Maslach, C. and Jackson, S. E. (1981) 'The measurement of experienced burnout', *Journal of Occupational Behaviour* 2, 2: 99–113.

May, R. (1982) *Physicians of the Soul: The Psychologies of the World's Great Spiritual Teachers*, New York: Crossroad.

McGuire, W. J. (1985) 'Attitudes and attitude change', in G. Lyndzey and E. Aronson (eds) *Handbook of Social Psychology*, 3rd ed., vol. 2, New York: Random House.

Meissner, W. W. (1984) *Psychoanalysis and Religious Experience*, New Haven: Yale University Press.

Meissner, W. W. (1987) *Life and Faith*, Washington: Georgetown University Press.

Miller, W. R. and Jackson, K. A. (1995) *Practical Psychology for Pastors*, 2nd ed., Englewood Cliffs, NJ: Prentice Hall.

Moberly, R. C. (1901) *Atonement and Personality*, London: John Murray.

Monod, J. (1972) *Chance and Necessity: An Essay on the Natural Philosophy of Modern Biology*, London: Collins.

Moravec, H. (1988) *Mind Children: The Future of Robot and Human Intelligence*, Cambridge, MA: Harvard University Press.

Morea, P. (1997) *In Search of Personality: Christianity and Modern Psychology*, London: SCM Press.

Moscovici, S. and Lage, E. (1976) 'Studies in Social Influence, III: Majority vs. Minority Influence in a Group', *European Journal of Social Psychology* 6: 149–174.

Murphy, G. R. (1979) 'A Ceremonial Ritual: The Mass', in E. G. d'Aquili, C. D. Laughlin, and J. McManus (eds) *The Spectrum of Ritual: A Biogenetic Structural Analysis*, New York: Columbia University Press.

Murphy, R. (1978) *The Development of Religious Thinking in Children*, Leicester: UCCF.

Nelson, J. S. (1997) 'Faith Among Adolescents: Joining, Drifting, Searching, Owning', *The Way Supplement* 90: 60–76.

Ness, R. C. and Wintrob, R. M. (1980) 'The Emotional Impact of Fundamentalist Religious Participation: An Empirical Study of Intra-Group Variation', *American Journal of Orthopsychiatry* 50: 302–315.

Newberger, C. M. (1980) 'The Cognitive Structure of Parenthood: Designing a Descriptive Measure', *New Directions in Child Development* 7: 45–67.

Newheart, M. W. (1995) 'Johanine Symbolism', in D. Miller (ed.) *Jung and the Interpretation of the Bible*, New York: Continuum.

Nye, R. (1998) *The Spirit of the Child: The Child's Voice in Education*, London: Church House Publishing.

Nye, R. and Hay, D. (1996) 'Identifying Children's Spirituality: How Do You Start Without a Starting Point?', *British Journal of Religious Education* 18, 3: 144–154.

Oates, W. E. (1991) *Temptation: A Biblical and Psychological Approach*, Louisville: Westminster/Knox.

Oatley, K. (1992) *Best Laid Schemes: The Psychology of Emotions*, Cambridge: Cambridge University Press.

Oden, T. C. (1966) *Kerygma and Counseling: Toward a Covenant Ontology for Secular Psychotherapy*, Philadelphia: Westminster Press.

Oden, T. C. (1984) *Care of Souls in the Classic Tradition*, Philadelphia: Fortress Press.

Osborn, L. and Walker, A. (1997) *Harmful Religion: An Exploration of Religious Abuse*, London: SPCK.

Pargament, K. I. (1997) *The Psychology of Religion and Coping: Theory, Practice and Research*, New York: Guilford.

Pargament, K. I. and DeRosa, D. V. (1985) 'What was that sermon about? Predicting memory for religious messages from cognitive psychology theory', *Journal for the Scientific Study of Religion* 24: 180–193.

Pargament, K., Kennell, J., Hathaway, W., Grevengoed, N., Newman, J. and Jones, W. (1988) 'Religion and the Problem-Solving Process: Three Styles of Religious Coping', *Journal for the Scientific Study of Religion* 27: 90–104.

Parker, R. (1993) *Forgiveness is Healing*, London: Daybreak.

Parker, R. and Lawrence, R. (1996) *Healing and Evangelism*, London: Triangle.

Parkes, C. M. (1986) *Bereavement: Studies of Grief in Adult Life*, London: Penguin.

Parks, S. (1990) 'Faith Development in a Changing World', *The Drew Gateway* 60: 4–21.

Pattison, E. M. (1968) 'Behavioral Science Research on the Nature of Glossolalia', *Journal of American Scientific Affiliation* 20: 73–86.

Pattison, E. M., Lapine, N. A. and Doerr, H. A. (1973) 'Faith Healing: A Study of Personality and Function', *Journal of Nervous and Mental Disease* 157: 397–409.

Pattison, S. (1993) *A Critique of Pastoral Care*, 2nd ed., London: SCM Press.

Peatling, J. (1981) *Religious Education in a Psychological Key* Birmingham, AL: Religious Education Press.

Peatling, J. H. (1973) 'The Incidence of Concrete and Abstract Religious Thinking in the Interpretation of Three Bible Stories by Pupils Enrolled in the Episcopal Church in the USA', unpublished Ph.D. dissertation, University of New York.

Percy, M. (1996) *The Toronto Blessing*, Oxford: Latimer House.

Percy, M. (1998) *Power and the Church: Ecclesiology in an Age of Transition*, London: Cassell.

Perry, J. (1988) *Tillich's Response to Freud: A Christian Answer to Freud's Critique of Religion*, Lanham: University Press of America.

Persinger, M. (1987) *Neuropsychological Bases of God Beliefs*, New York: Praeger.

Petrovich, O. (1988) 'An Examination of Piaget's Theory of Childhood Artificialism', unpublished D.Phil. thesis, University of Oxford.

Petty, R.E. Cacioppo, J. T., and Goldman, R. (1981) 'Personal involvement as a determinant of argument-based persuasion. *Journal of Personality and Social Psychology* 41: 847–855.

Phillips, D. Z. (1965) *The Concept of Prayer*, London: Routledge and Kegan Paul.

Piaget, J. (1926) *The Language and Thought of the Child*, New York: Harcourt.

Piaget, J. (1951) *Play, Dreams and Imitation in Childhood*, trans. C. Gattegno and F. M. Hodgson, London: William Heinemann.

Piaget, J. (1953) *The Origins of Intelligence in the Child*, New York: International Universities Press.

Pinker, S. (1997) *How the Mind Works*, London: Allen Lane.

Plotkin, H. (1997) *Evolution in Mind: An Introduction to Evolutionary Psychology*, London: Allen Lane.

Polkinghorne, J. (2001) 'Prayer and the Scientist', in F. Watts (ed.) *Perspectives on Prayer*, London: SPCK.

Popper, K. R. and Eccles, J. C. (1977) *The Self and Its Brain*, New York: Springer International.

Pottenbaum, G. (1992) *The Rites of the People*, Washington DC: The Pastoral Press.

Proudfoot, W. (1985) *Religious Experience*, Berkeley: University of California Press.

Pruyser, P. W. (1991) 'Anxiety, Guilt, and Shame in the Atonement', reprinted in H. N. Malony and B. Spilka (eds) *Religion in Psychodynamic Perspective: The Contributions of Paul W. Pruyser*, Oxford: Oxford University Press.

Pruyser, P. W. (1976) *The Minister as Diagnostician*, Philadelphia: The Westminster Press.

Rayburn, C., Richmond, L. and Rogers, L. (1986) 'Men, Women, and Religion: Stress Within Leadership Roles', *Journal of Clinical Psychology* 42: 540–546.

Reed, B. (1978) *The Dynamics of Religion: Process and Movement in Christian Churches*, London: Darton, Longman and Todd.

Reich, H. (1996) 'Relational and Contextual Reasoning in Religious Education: A Theory-Based Empirical Study', in L. J. Francis, W. K. Kay and W. S. Campbell (eds) *Research In Religious Education*, Leominister: Gracewing.

Repicky, R. A. (1988) 'Jungian Typology and Christian Spirituality', in R. L. Moore (ed.) *Carl Jung and Christian Spirituality*, New York: Paulist Press.

Ricoeur, P. (1970) *Freud and Philosophy: An Essay on Interpretation*, New Haven: Yale University Press.

Ridley, M. (1997) *The Origins of Virtue*, London: Penguin.

Rizzuto, A-M. (1979) *The Birth of the Living God: A Psychoanalytic Study*, Chicago: University of Chicago Press.

Rodgerson, T. and Piedmont, R. (1998) 'Assessing the Incremental Validity of the Religious Problem-Solving Scale in the Prediction of Clergy Burnout', *Journal for the Scientific Study of Religion* 37: 517–527.

Roehlkepartain, E. (1998) *Building Assets in Congregations: A Practical Guide for Helping Youth Grow Up Healthy*, Minneapolis: Search Institute.

Rokeach, M. (1960) *The Open and Closed Mind: Investigations into the Nature of Belief Systems and Personality Systems*, New York: Basic Books.

Rollins, W. G. (1999) *Soul and Psyche: The Bible in Psychological Perspective*, Minneapolis: Fortress Press.

Rothbaum, F., Weisz, J. R. and Snyder, S. S. (1982) 'Changing the World and Changing the Self: A Two Process Model of Perceived Control', *Journal of Personality and Social Psychology* 42: 5–37.

Rottschaefer, W. (1998) *The Biology and Psychology of Moral Agency*, Cambridge: Cambridge University Press.

Rowe, D. (1987) *Beyond Fear*, London: Fontana.

Rubenstein, R. (1972) *My Brother Paul*, New York: Harper and Row.

Runyon, W. M. (ed.) (1988) *Psychology and Historical Interpretation*, Oxford: Oxford University Press.

Ruse, M. (1995) *Evolutionary Naturalism: Selected Essays*, London: Routledge.

Sabini, J. (1995) *Social Psychology*, 2nd ed., New York: Norton.

Sacks, O. (1985) *The Man Who Mistook His Wife for a Hat*, London: Duckworth.

Sandler, J., Dare, C. and Holder, A. (1973) *The Patient and the Analyst: The Basis of the Psychoanalytic Process*, London: Maresfield Reprints.

Sanford, J. (1982) *Ministry Burnout*, London: Arthur James.

Savage, S. (1998) 'Fundamentalism and moral reasoning: Rules for a perfect world', unpublished PhD thesis, University of Cambridge.

Savage, S. (in press) 'A psychology of fundamentalism: The search for inner failings', in M. Percy (ed.) *Fundamentalism, Church, and Society*, London: SPCK.

Schimmel, S. (1997) *The Seven Deadly Sins: Jewish, Christian, and Classical Reflections on Human Psychology*, Oxford: Oxford University Press.

Schneiders, S. (1986) *New Wineskins: Re-imagining Religious Life Today*, New York: Paulist Press.

Schuller, D. (ed.) (1993) *Rethinking Christian Education*, St. Louis: Chalice Press.

Scroggs, R. (1977) *Paul for a New Day*, Philadelphia: Fortress Press.

Searle, J. (1997) *The Mystery of Consciousness*, London: Granta.

Seligman, E. (1975) *Helplessness: On Depression, Development and Death*, San Francisco: W. H. Freeman.

Shepherd, M. (1985) *Sherlock Holmes and the Case of Dr Freud*, London: Tavistock.

Shorter, B. (1996) *Susceptible to the Sacred: The Psychological Experience of Ritual*, London: Routledge.

Slee, N. (1996) 'Further on from Fowler: Post-Fowler Faith Development Research', in L. Francis, W. Kay and W. Campbell *Research in Religious Education*, Leominster: Gracewing.

Smail, T., Walker, A. and Wright, N. (1995) *Charismatic Renewal*, London: SPCK.

Smedes, L. (1988) *Forgive and Forget: Healing the Hurts We Don't Deserve*, London: Triangle.

Smith, N. (1993) *Miscarriage, Stillbirth and Neonatal Death: Guidelines in Pastoral Care for Clergy and Hospital Chaplains*, 2nd ed., London: Churches Committee for Hospital Chaplaincies.

Spilka, B., Shaver, P. and Kirkpatrick, L. (1985) 'A General Attribution Theory for the Psychology of Religion', *Journal for the Scientific Study of Religion* 24: 1–20.

St. Clair, M. (1994) *Human Relationships and the Experience of God: Object Relations and Religion*, New York: Paulist Press.

Stannard, D. E. (1980) *Shrinking History*, Oxford: Oxford University Press.

Stokes, K. (1989) *Faith is a Verb: Dynamics of Adult Faith Development*, Mystic, CT: Twenty-Third Publications.

Stoner, J. (1961) 'A comparison of individual and group decisions involving risk', unpublished Masters Thesis, Massachusetts Institute of Technology.

Stroebe, M. and Schut, H. (1999) 'The dual process model of coping with bereavement: rationale and description', *Death Studies* 23: 197–224.

Stroebe, M. and Stroebe, W. (1993) 'The mortality of bereavement: A review', in M. Stroebe, W. Stroebe and R. Hansson (eds) *Handbook of Bereavement*, Cambridge: Cambridge University Press.

Stroebe, M., Stroebe, W. and Hansson, R. (eds) (1993) *Handbook of Bereavement*, Cambridge: Cambridge University Press.

Szasz, T. (1961) *The Myth of Mental Illness*, New York: Harper and Row.

Tajfel, H., Flament, C., Billig, M. G. and Bundy R. P. (1971) 'Social Categorisation and Intergroup Behaviour', *European Journal of Social Psychology* 1: 149–178.

Tamminen, K. (1991) *Religious Development in Childhood and Youth: An Empirical Study*, Helsinki: Suomalainen Tiedeakatemia.

Taylor, J. (1989) *Innocent Wisdom: Children as Spiritual Guides*, New York: Pilgrim.

Theissen, G. (1987) *Psychological Aspects of Pauline Theology*, Philadelphia: Fortress Press.

Thibaut, J. and Kelley, H. (1959) *The Social Psychology of Groups*, New York: Wiley.

Thorne, B. (1998) *Person-centred Counselling and Christian Spirituality: The Secular and the Holy*, London: Whurr Publishers.

Tillich, P. (1952) *The Courage To Be*, London: Nisbett.

Tillich, P. (1957) *Dynamics of Faith*, New York: Harper.

Tillich, P. (1959) *Theology of Culture*, New York: Oxford University Press.

Tipler, F. J. (1994) *The Physics of Immortality: Modern Cosmology, God and the Resurrection of the Dead*, Basingstoke: Macmillan.

Tjosvold, D. and Tjosvold, M. (1995) *Psychology for Leaders: Using Motivation, Conflict, and Power to Manage More Effectively*, Chichester: Wiley.

Truax, C. B. and Carkhuff, R. R. (1967) *Toward Effective Counselling and Psychotherapy*, Chicago: Aldine.

Tuckman, B. W. and Jensen, M. A. (1977) 'Stages of small group development revisited', in *Group and Organization Studies* 2: 419–427.

Turner, D. (1995) *The Darkness of God: Negativity in Western Christian Mysticism*, Cambridge: Cambridge University Press.

Ulanov, A. and Ulanov, B. (1982) *Primary Speech: A Psychology of Prayer*, Atlanta: John Knox.

van Gennep, A. (1909/1977) *The Rites of Passage*, London: Routledge

van Leeuwen, M. S. (1985) *The Person in Psychology: A Contemporary Christian Appraisal*, Leicester: Inter-Varsity Press.

Vitz, P. (1979) *Psychology as Religion: The Cult of Self-Worship*, Tring: Lion.

Vroom, V. and Yetton, P. (1973) *Leadership and Decision Making*, Pittsburgh: University of Pittsburgh Press.

Vygotsky, L. (1978) *Mind in Society: The Development of Higher Psychological Processes*, Cambridge, MA: Harvard University Press.

Walter, T. (1996) 'A new model of grief', *Mortality* 1, 1: 7–25.

Ward, K. (1992) *Defending the Soul*, Oxford: Oneworld.

Warner, J. and Carter, J. (1984) 'Loneliness, Marital Adjustment and Burnout in Pastoral and Lay Persons', *Journal of Psychology and Theology* 12: 125–131.

Watts, F. (1989) 'Listening Processes in Psychotherapy', in F. Flach (ed.) *Psychotherapy*, New York: Norton.

Watts, F. (1999) 'Cognitive Neuroscience and Religious Consciousness', in R. Russell, N. Murphy, T. Meyering and M. Arbib (eds) *Neuroscience and the Person: Scientific Perspectives on Divine Action*, Vatican City State: Vatican Observatory Publications.

Watts, F. (2000) 'Subjective and Objective Hope: Propositional and Attitudinal Aspects of Eschatology', in J. Polkinghorne and M. Welker (eds) *The End of the World and the Ends of God: Science and Theology on Eschatology*, Harrisburg, PA: Trinity Press International.

Watts, F. and Williams, M. (1988) *The Psychology of Religious Knowing*, Cambridge: Cambridge University Press.

Webster, R. (1995) *Why Freud Was Wrong: Sin, Science, and Psychoanalysis*, London: Harper Collins.

Weiss, R. (1993) 'The death of a child is forever: the life course impact of child loss' in M. Stroebe, W. Stroebe and R. Hansson (eds) *Handbook of Bereavement*, Cambridge: Cambridge University Press.

Westerhoff, J. H. (ed.) (1994) *Called to Teach and Learn: A Catechetical Guide for the Episcopal Church*, New York: The Domestic and Foreign Missionary Society PECUSA.

White, V. (1952) *God and the Unconscious*, London: Harvill Press.

White, V. (1960) *Soul and Psyche: An Enquiry into the Relationship of Psychotherapy and Religion*, London: Collins and Harvill.

Wilson, E. O. (1998) *Consilience: The Unity of Knowledge*, London: Little Brown.

Wolff Pritchard, G. (1992) *Offering the Gospel to Children*, Boston: Cowley.

Woodward, J. and Pattison, S. (2000) *The Blackwell Reader in Pastoral and Practical Theology*, Oxford: Blackwell.

Woolfe, R. and Dryden, W. (1996) *Handbook of Counselling Psychology*, London: Sage.

Wright, H. N. (1986) *Self-talk, Imagery and Prayer in Counselling*, Waco: Word Publishing.

Wulff, D. (1997) *Psychology of Religion*, 2nd ed., New York: Wiley.

Yalom, I. D. (1975) *The Theory and Practice of Group Psychotherapy*, 2nd ed., New York: Basic Books.

Index

Page numbers in italics refer to illustrations: page numbers in bold refer to tables.

Leavitt, Harold 240
'levels of parental awareness' 89, **91**
libido 271–2
liturgy 25–6; *see also* worship
Loewenthal, K. 64
Luther, Martin 181

Malan, David 186–7, 188
Malony, H.N. 117, 254; on clergy marriage
    258, 259; on dual role relations 69; on
    sexual behaviour 261; on speaking in
    tongues 32, 34, 35; on teams 227
manipulative techniques 65
'Maslach burnout inventory' 251
Maslach, Christina 251
'master story' 97, 98
maturity 116–18
May, Robert 15–16
meditation 21
Meissner, W.W. 108, 291
mental health 63–4
Merton, Thomas 16, 282–3
metacognition 126–8
mind-body problem 275–7
ministry *see* pastoral care
minority influence 211–12
miscarriage 158–9
monism 276–7
Monod, Jacques 274
morality 73–4, 230–1, 273
Morea, Peter 281; *In Search of Personality*
    282
Moscovici, Serge 212
motivation 42–7, 241–3; extrinsic and
    intrinsic 43–4, **43**; and group dynamics
    241; and imprisoning features 45–6, **46**;
    and liberating features 45–6, **46**; quest
    45, 62
Mumford, Alan 131, **132**
music 25–6, 35–6
Musson, David 251
Myers–Briggs Type Indicator (MBTI) 49–52,
    51; cautions in use of 54–5; and clergy
    254; value of 55
mystical experience *see* spiritual experience

'narrative theology' 188
Nelson, J.S. 95
neuropsychology 275–8
New Religious Movements (NRMs) 65–6
Newberg, A. 7, 21, 276
Newberger, Carol 89, **91**
Nine O'Clock Service (NOS) 246–7
non-directive counselling 190–2

normative theory 229
'nothing but' view *see* reductionist view
Nye, R. 92

Oatley, Keith 167
Oden, Thomas, *Kerygma and Counseling*
    191
ordination of women 217
'original sin' 180

paedophiles 71, 148
panic attacks 174
parents 27–8, 81, 89
Pargament, K.I. 133, 152, 255
Parkes, C.M. 154
Parks, Sharon 114
pastoral care 183–203; and adolescents 96;
    and anger 176; and applied psychology
    184; and balance 46–7, 105; and
    bereavement 154, 155–6; combines
    religion and psychology 201–2; and
    converts 119; and counselling 184, 185,
    197–200; defined 183; and dying 162–3;
    and emotional problems 107–8, 166–7;
    and illness 149, 150; and intrinsic/
    extrinsic distinction 44; and neurotic
    religion 61; and older people 142, 143,
    144, 146, 147; and personality functions
    52; and religious development 100, 120;
    and stages of faith **110–11**, 112–14; and
    theology 185, 200
patriarchy 63
Pattison, E.M. 34, 37
Pattison, Stephen 200
Paul, St 194, 231, 259, 263, 287
Pelagius 268
Pentecostal church 31, 32, 33, 36
Persinger, Michael 6–7
person-centred counselling 190–2
'persona' 49, 295
'personal constructs' 283
personality; development 105; functions
    50–4, **51**, **53–4**; and motivation 44;
    profiling 47–9; and religion 1–76;
    transformation of 54; types 49–52, 58
Personality Inventory (EPI or EPQ) 48
personality psychology 281–3
petition 12–14
Petrovich, O. 87–8
phenomenology 7
Phillips, D.Z. 10
phobias 174
Piaget, Jean 84–5, 102, 124
Piedmont, Ralph 256